RENDEZVOUS WITH DEATH

Anzac Stories of the Great War
1914-1918

Published by Brolga Publishing Pty Ltd
ABN 46 063 962 443

PO Box 452
Torquay Victoria 3228
Australia

email: markzocchi@brolgapublishing.com.au

National Library of Australia
Cataloguing-in-Publication data
John Ramsland, author.
ISBN 9780909608996 (paperback)

NATIONAL LIBRARY OF AUSTRALIA
A catalogue record for this book is available from the National Library of Australia

Printed in Australia
Cover design by WorkingType Studio
Cover photo by Capt Frank Hurley, 1st AIF
Typesetting by Elly Cridland
aeledapublishingservices

RENDEZVOUS WITH DEATH

Anzac Stories of the Great War
1914-1918

John Ramsland

The Sydney Mail 3D.
Wednesday, Mar. 24, 1915.
THE LAST CARTRIDGE
WAR ISSUE=No. XXXIV.

Rendezvous

I had a rendezvous with Death
At some disputed barricade,
When Spring comes back with rustling shade
And apple-blossoms fill the air —
I have a rendezvous with Death
When Spring brings back blue days and fair.

It may be he shall take my hand
And lead me into his dark land
And close my eyes and quench my breath —
It may be I shall pass him still.
I have a rendezvous with Death
On some scarred slope of battered hill,
When Spring comes round again this year
And the first meadow-flowers appear.

God knows 'twere better to be deep
Pillowed in silk and scented down,
Where love throbs out in blissful sleep,
Pulse nigh to pulse, and breath to breath,
Where hushed awakenings are dear …
But I've a rendezvous with Death
At midnight in some flaming town,
When Spring trips north again this year
And I to my pledged word am true,
I shall not fail that rendezvous.

Alan Seeger
Killed in Action, 1916

Contents

1

A Cosmic Fellowship of Suffering

A rendezvous with death is an evocative phrase when applied to the Great War of 1914–1918:

> And I looked, and behold a pale horse: and his name that sate on him was Death, and Hell followed with him.
>
> *Revelations, 6:8*

It becomes more specific, personalised and individual with Alan Seeger's war poem:

I had a rendezvous with Death
At some disputed barricade.

Technically, a *rendezvous* was a place appointed for the assembling of troops or ships and was adapted from the French language. It was a meeting place agreed upon and 1914–1918 could be considered as a dramatic series of appointed places or rendezvous where both sides in the

Anzacs of the 2nd Australian Infantry Division on the march to a "rendezvous" at Pozières after a dreary time in Armentières (AWM)

conflict were compelled to meet and where they beheld 'a pale horse' that meant metaphorically 'Death'.

At large, the Great War could be conceived as a collective suicide madness that had the capacity to almost destroy European civilisation in its nationalistic sense of European Empires together with their world-wide colonies and territories and bring misery to millions for the rest of the century as a major, but not exclusive centrepiece of its history – thus, the metaphorical Fall of Eagles.

The War Graves Commission

The idea of mass graves of soldiers pertains especially to the early twentieth century. While there are 2,500 British war cemeteries in France and Belgium, and that figure is not counting Germany and other European nations, a sophisticated observer of the neatly uniform rows of headstones will, without a doubt, suspect that the bodies below are, in reality, buried in mass graves – as put clairvoyantly by the early twentieth-century English novelist Thomas Hardy – 'like sprats in a tin'.

After the war, the provision of over 500,000 headstones was the greatest challenge faced by the Graves Registration Commission which became the (British) Commonwealth War Graves Commission. Apart from finding enough high quality stone, engraving British regimental and national badges (in the case of Dominions like Australia, Canada, South Africa, New Zealand and so on) and inscriptions, some of which were required or requested by families of the fallen, was a particularly time-consuming affair.

Millions of plants were grown in an effort to transform

cemeteries into living memorials of perpetual beauty and to soften the seemingly endless rows of headstones. For this the Commission established its own nurseries. Started in 1919, the Commission's program was not complete until 1938.[1]

Edmund Blunden, the English war poet, recalled with gentle irony and sympathy, a wrecked French village churchyard near the frontline which had an odd appeal to the 'morbid curiosity' of troops crowded together to stare at the open vaults and graves:

> Greenish water stood in some of these pits; bones and skulls and decayed cerements there attracted frequent soldiers past the "No Loitering" notice-board.[2]

Why should this sight lure men who were trying to forget their own mortality? Weren't they soon to have a rendezvous with death themselves?

Royal Assassination at Sarajevo, 28 June 1914

The Great War was far worse than had been expected: eight million people at least were destroyed. The irony of the situation was they were to have a rendezvous with death because of two persons – on 28 June 1914 – the Archduke Franz Ferdinand, heir to the Hapsburg monarchy of the Austria-Hungary Empire, and his consort, the Countess Sophie Chotek. They had been shot in an open car by Gavrilo Princip, a Balkan nationalist fanatic and member of the Black Hand terrorist organisation. This occurred when they were on an official visit to Bosnia, a territory annexed in 1908 by Austria-Hungary. They were attempting to

1 'A History of the Commonwealth Graves Commission', www.cwgc.org.

2 Cited in Paul Fussell, *The Great War and Modern Memory*, Folio Society, London, 2014, 6-7.

consolidate their empire's power and popularity through a state visit with grand ceremonies for the Bosnian people in the capital Sarajevo.

Instead, they had a rendezvous with a violent and sudden death which was understood to be yet another symptom of the wider problem: the tottering, decaying and collapsing multinational empire of Austria-Hungary. It seems that all that held this central European empire together was its monarchy. The ageing Emperor Franz Joseph, at 84 years of age, had been on its throne since 1848. And now it's heir was dead.

The details of the rendezvous with death for the fifty-year-old Franz Ferdinand and his wife were the following: just before the assassination, the chauffeur who did not know the streets of Sarajevo well took a wrong turn and was called to stop. He braked and then backed up.

A thin, pale youth, Gavrilo Princep, standing in the waving crowd two metres away, stepped forward, levelled his revolver and fired two shots into the back of the car. One bullet struck Franz Ferdinand in the neck. The second hit his wife in the abdomen. Both died within fifteen minutes of being shot. It has been argued that security for the Royals in Sarajevo was lax.

The assassin attempted then to commit suicide, but one of the onlookers who took hold of him knocked the revolver from his hand in the mêlée of police and civilians. He then attempted to swallow a cyanide capsule that had been issued by the Black Hand terrorist organisation, but he puked it up as he was hauled away. Ironically, he was not to die in an Austrian prison until 1918 of tuberculosis. Some of his co-conspirators were caught and hanged in the state prison; others were murdered by lynch mobs.[3] The death toll had already started before any declaration of war, but two shots eventually became 15 million dead as a result of the Great War in Europe alone.

Political chaos ensued that, step-by-step, was to lead into the war of 1914-1918.[4]

The assassination as illustrated in the Italian newspaper *Domenica del Corriere*, 12 July 1914 (by Achille Belrame)

The crude intention of the assassin was to free Bosnia from the Austria-Hungary Empire and integrate it with Serbia. The deadly shots triggered a chain of events of political and military manoeuvring.

There was frenetic letter writing at the beginning between blood-related monarchies. In a failed attempt to prevent war, George V of Great Britain, who was married to the Princess of Teck in Germany, wrote to Emperor Wilhelm II of the German Empire who responded cautiously. They were unsuccessful, however, in an attempt to have a peace-keeping conference of Royals.

It was clear that the power of monarchs was in decline. Nothing could stop the political and military fission that took

3 Neil Faulkner, 'Assassination Sarajevo, 28 June 1914', *Military History Monthly*, issue 41, February 2014, 14-20.

4 Joan Beaumont, *Broken Nation. Australians in the Great War*, Allen & Unwin, Crows Nest, 2013, 6-7.

only thirty-seven days after the assassinations in Sarajevo to engulf Europe in war.

Under their treaty, Russia and France aligned against the German Empire; Austria-Hungary and Turkey aligned with the German Empire. The United Kingdom and its Dominions and colonial territories were dragged into this mix as allies of France and declared war on Germany on 4 August 1914[5].

The Time Bomb Ultimatum

The trigger that forced the European war was not only the assassinations of the Royals at Sarajevo, but the ultimatum from the Austrian government in Vienna that followed. It was the ultimate diplomatic time-bomb at the height of the European vacation period for the elites when most of the royalty, aristocracy and political leaders were away in pleasure resorts or at sea in luxury cruise ships in the Mediterranean and elsewhere.

In the ultimatum, the Austrians demanded a full and immediate enquiry into Serbian involvement in the assassinations in Sarajevo and insisted that Austrian investigative officials took a major part in such an investigation. They gave the Serbian government only 48 hours to respond.

As Winston Churchill, then the First Lord of the Admiralty, recalled: 'it was an ultimatum such as had never been penned in modern times'. He believed that no national state in the world could accept it. He was right!

Mobilisation for War

The Serbian government found themselves with little

5 Roland Perry, *Monash. The Outsider who won a War*, Random House, Sydney, 2007, 147.

diplomatic room for manoeuvre, because of both the hawkish belligerence of the Vienna government and the red-hot nationalism of the Serbian newspapers. They hoped their allies, Russia and the Tsar, would come to their aid, but they only offered verbose moral aid at first.

It hardly mattered. The Austrian ambassador immediately left Belgrade, the Serbian capital, by train. Vienna had already made its decision: on 28 July 1914 the Austria-Hungary Empire ordered the partial mobilisation of its armed forces and declared war on the kingdom of Serbia. They opened fire on Belgrade across the Danube River. What was, at first, styled as the Third Balkan War had begun.

The face of Hapsburg Austria was transformed in an instant. The streets of Vienna were filled with shouting citizens, patriotic flags and ribbons. The bands played martial music to stir the crowds that formed in the main streets of the city. Columns of Austrian soldiers in blue-grey uniforms marched from barracks through the streets of the city and the crowds shouted: 'Death to the Serbian dogs'.

A new-found patriotism in Austria was engendered by propaganda and crowd behaviour. There was a new-found enthusiasm by ordinary people for the Habsburg monarchy and cause. A strong warlike nationalism had engulfed the Austrian Empire[6].

The whole thing related to the Sarajevo assassinations had a strangely domino effect: Russia came to support Serbia; Germany supported Austria; France supported Russia and England supported France. Declarations of war followed in an inexorable sequence: Germany, Russia, France, Great

6 Faulkner, 'Assassination', 14-20.

Britain, Belgium, Austria-Hungary, Serbia and others, including the Ottoman Empire. All the pieces were in place for the sinister deadly game, but it was confidently expected to end by Christmas. But international treaties can have deadly, but slower consequences.

★ ★ ★

What effect did this have on the Commonwealth of Australia, isolated far away in the South Pacific, nevertheless an important Dominion of the British Empire, the Anglo-Saxon defenders of the so-called British race in an Asian world?

War as Adventure

While some in Australia, especially among the young, were unmoved by and remote from any martial or Imperial enthusiasm, the majority overwhelmingly hailed England's declaration of war on Germany on 4 August 1914 with great enthusiasm. It sounded to many like an adventure that would be over in a few months.

It was, most probably, the most complete enthusiastic harmony of emotion in Australia's history up until that time. And yet the harmony of emotion was undercut by a sense of caution about the very size of the war. In the cities, crowds gathered to celebrate the declaration in much the same way as Austrians in Vienna did when they gathered to celebrate the declaration of war against Serbia.

In the Australian celebrations, crowds surged at first with great strength, joy and confidence. Men in the countryside and cities sang with vigour, "Rule Britannia" and "God Save the King", after work in the pubs. Strangers embraced as brothers, cheers were given on the slightest of pretext, Union Jacks were waved frantically; 'tumult and merriment ruled everywhere'.[7] The emotional pressures on men to enlist were enormous.

Recruiting

Males, some as young as thirteen or as old as seventy-one, tried to enlist among the many that were in fact eligible. Outside makeshift recruiting offices in the city suburbs and country towns, lines of volunteers seemed endlessly long with the earliest news of the beginnings of the European war in late 1914.

A pride of race, nation and empire, in terms of being British subjects in early post-colonial Australia, was a powerful influence on all those swayed into taking practical steps in attempting to enlist. Recruiting for the Australian 'Expeditionary Force' to head for German New Guinea commenced on 11 August 1914, seven days after the declaration of war against Germany by the English and, therefore, the British Empire as was communicated across the world on that day. As Gammage points out, on that day, an 'orderless mass jostled' and fought before the recruiting tables associated with the Victoria Barracks, Paddington, a major centre for enlistment in Sydney as well as elsewhere.

By night, the exhausted enlisting officers had already chosen 3,600 of them[8].

At the same time, there were unpleasant racist scenes where German Australians were spat upon, sacked from

7 Bill Gammage, *The Broken Years. Australian Soldiers in the Great War*, Melbourne University Press (MUP), Carlton, 2010, 3-6.
8 Gammage, *The Broken Years*, 8.

their jobs for no reason than having German origins, expelled from masonic lodge associations, abused at Protestant and Catholic churches, refused service in grocery, hardware and other stores as well as theatres. Their homes were stoned and windows broken. Some were beaten up brutally at night by street gangs, not necessarily made up of adolescents. They were even discriminated against at universities, where they were refused enrolment, and in trade unions. German-born university academics were dismissed. Some people changed their names and left districts they had lived in for many years.

To enlist, men headed into the capital cities from the countryside by railway and then from the remote outback by other forms of transport, or simply by walking or marching in groups on dusty roads. The army were looking for men at least five foot six inches in height, with a chest expansion of at least 34 inches and their stomach measurement less. They had to be between nineteen and thirty-eight years of age. Those under twenty-one had to seek written permission from parents.

They would be rejected because of flat feet, infected teeth or bad corns and bunions on their feet. Many were rejected and disappointed – they were in reality the fortunate ones as it turned out by Armistice Day 1918, at the eleventh hour on eleventh November.

★ ★ ★

While remembering that World War I statistics have to be considered variable, 330,770 men, or 331,781 or

331,814 – depending on how they were counted – embarked from Australia for active service abroad in various successive theatres of war, for example, Gallipoli and then the Western Front.

In his account of landing at Gallipoli, Captain Hugh Knyvett referred to two songs that roused the Anzac spirit as troopships neared the Cove on 25 April 1915. On board, the men gathered round their padre and – with some premonition of facing death – sang "God Be With You Till We Meet Again", all swept away by the sentiment of the imperial refrain. Then they launched more lustily into Australia's battle-song, "Australia Will Be There":

Rally round the banner of your country,
Take the field with brothers o'er the foam;
On land or sea, where ever you be,
Keep your eye on Germany.
But England, Home and beauty have no cause to fear.
Should Auld acquaintance be forgot?
No! No!! No! No!! No!!!
Australia will be there.
Australia will be there.[9]

Even Sydney University men who enlisted had their own song, "The Company March".

Don't you hear the tramping of our feet?
Can't you hear us coming down the street?
We have chucked up books and learning,
For with martial fire we're burning,
And we're off to help our country from defeat.

9 Cited in Robert Holden, *And the Band Played On*, Hardie Grant Books, Melbourne, 2014, 86.

Chorus:
Then roll up, men of the 'Varsity,
Fall in lads double quick,
When we meet the Turk or Hun
We will make the beggars run,
And we'll fight for the honour of the 'Varsity.[10]

Gallipoli (1915) had a death toll, at the end, of 8,700 and over 19,400 wounded. The total Allied dead, including the French, came to over 44,000 and 97,000 wounded.[11]

The majority of Australians – about 295,000 – served on the Western Front in France and Belgian Flanders. About 63,163 Australians, or possibly a little fewer, had a tragic rendezvous with Death. This was about one man in five serving on the battlefronts. As well, 152,422 were otherwise made casualties of their encounter; 4,084 Australian soldiers became prisoners-of-war; 3,848 had been captured on the Western Front in France and Flanders.

About 2,000 soldiers who returned to Australia were permanently hospitalised as a result of the war. By 1926, however, 22,742 war veterans were in hospital with that number rising in 1939 to 49,157. In sum, two of every three Australians in uniform were killed or wounded and the proportion of casualties – dead or wounded – of those who embarked was 68.5 per cent.[12]

The twenty percent who did not return to Australian

10 *Hermes*, XXIV, 3, November 1918.

11 Figures cited in Richard Reid, *Gallipoli* 1915, ABC Books, Sydney, 2002, 134.

12 Gammage, *The Broken Years*, Appendix 2, 289; KS Inglis, *Sacred Places. War Memorials in the Australian Landscape*, Miegunyah Press, Carlton, 1999, 92.

shores lie in the soil of foreign lands: the Western Front of France and Belgium, the Middle East, Gallipoli and Great Britain, and other places. Some were buried at sea. While the majority were identified before burial and headstones were erected over their graves, many were not. In some cases their bodies were never recovered or found. These were commemorated in large memorials at Lone Pine, Menin Gate, Pozières, VC corner Fromelles and Villers-Bretonneux.

Some survived the battles only to die in the 1919 influenza pandemic. Some succumbed years later to war injuries, both physical and mental.

The Dardanelles and Publicising Australian Casualties

On 19 May 1916, the illustrated *Sydney Mail* – a Fairfax weekly – as well as other well-distributed urban and country newspapers published a two-page spread of a consolidated list of the names of casualties, both the dead and the wounded, who had been engaged in the Dardanelles campaign. They were organised under each state and territory of Australia and in the following categories: Killed in Action; Died of Wounds; Reported Missing; Dangerously Wounded and Wounded – the last category being the largest in each state. Photographic portraits, only of the Wounded, lined the top and bottom of the pages. It would, apparently, have been distressing at this stage to produce portraits of other categories.[13] All the images were studio ones frequently submitted to the newspaper by family or friends. Most were in uniform. Some bare-headed, others in three varieties of caps. Each portrait was named, their rank and battalion given, and the state of the Commonwealth

13 *Sydney Mail*, 19 May 1915, 19, 37.

they belonged to listed together with the word 'Wounded'.

The published list came as a severe shock to the Australian population and families and friends became worried and very fearful, despite press reassurances and positive propaganda. The war had lost its sense of adventure. This had evaporated into thin air, but newspapers continued to sell well as the anxious civilians remained intensely interested in the so-called progress of the war.

For the general Australian public, Captain Charles Bean, at the time the Commonwealth Official Press Representative who was on Gallipoli, was the main interpreter or filter of what was going on there. Sometimes romantically described as the Anzac spirit personified, he was ever conscious of what he believed to be his role in moulding public perception of what he argued to be Australia's new idea of nation, as expressed symbolically in war. Soon after the war, he was to lead the effort to establish the Australian War Memorial in Canberra and to become its first director.

Witnessing the landing with Brigadier General Sir William Thorsby Bridges on his ship the *Minnewaska*, Bean was to portray it, with verbal dramatic intensity, as Australia's baptism of fire as a nation. Seeing the deck of the ship awash with blood from the wounded brought aboard unnerved him.[14]

Bean's war reporting always aimed to pursue a polemic purpose and was not always particularly objective.

---

14 *Sydney Mail.* Bridges, the Australian commander was soon to meet his death after he was badly wounded on the beaches at Gallipoli. He died aboard the *Minnewaska*. Bridges, who was in charge of training Australia's national army, argued that it should not be absorbed into the British Army; so it was named the Australian Imperial Army (AIF) of which Bridges is considered the founder.

Captain Charles EW Bean, Australia's official war correspondent at Mena Camp, March 1915 (AWM A05381)

An early example of his reported commentary accompanies the casualty lists in the *Sydney Mail* of 19 May 1915. He described the landing of Australian troops at Gaba Tepe: the place of landing consisted of 'a small bay about half a mile from point to point' with two larger bays north and south. The countryside resembled 'the Hawkesbury River of New South Wales the hills rising immediately from the sea to a height of 600 feet'. As he described it, to the north of these ridges was 'a cluster' nearly a thousand feet high. Further on in the same direction, the range became even higher. Later, he described the deep gullies 'very much like the hills and gullies about North Sydney'. They were covered with low scrub 'very similar to dwarfed gumtrees'. There were 'many precipices and sheer slopes of gravel'. He was attempting to enable the reader to visualise the terrain using landscape familiar to them in and around Sydney.

After this fairly objective, detailed geographic description compared with the Hawkesbury and North Sydney terrains for his readers, he sets out to portray the landing itself, in which the first gunfire came from the Turks who were on the two knolls a hundred feet or so above:

> The 3rd Brigade (comprising Queenslanders, South Australians, Western Australians and Tasmanians) went over the hills with such dash that within three-quarters

> of an hour of landing, some had charged over three successive ridges. Each ridge was higher than the last and each party that reached the top went over it with a wild cheer. Since that day the Turks never attempted to face our bayonets. The [Australian] officers led magnificently, but, of course, nothing like accurate control of attack was possible.

He saw that the 3rd Brigade had made its name in history that would never die. 'They all fought fiercely and suffered heavily.'

In the case of Western Australia, the *Sydney Mail*'s consolidated list had: two **Killed in Action** (both officers, a captain and a lieutenant of the 15th Battalion); one, a sergeant, had **Died of Wounds** and two were **Reported Missing** (believed dead – both lieutenants, 16th Battalion) and three privates, 16th Battalion were **Dangerously Wounded** and most probably would soon die. There followed a long list of the **Wounded**, some listed as slightly wounded, but most badly wounded; their lives were not threatened at this stage, only later.

They were a heterogenous list of different ranks from a social-class viewpoint, but mainly privates from a variety of battalions, mainly the 11th and the 16th. There were a few from the 12th. This list comprised ninety-six human beings, some who would never fight again. The list of encounters with death shocked the home front to its core. The Western Australian community's anxiety was heightened. Captains and Lieutenants are seen in this sample to be generally in a most dangerous position of frontline leadership. The casualty lists of all Australian states reflected the same pattern.

The Intensity of Gallipoli Battles

The intensity of the battles on Gallipoli can be illustrated on Quinn's Post or Chessboard in the attack of 19 May 1915 in which 3,000 Turkish frontline troops and approximately 160 Australians were killed. Around one million rounds of ammunition was fired on that one day. The short distance of No Man's Land – only 10 or 15 yards apart – between the two opposing forces was heavily littered with the dead after that day. The stench had become so unbearable that Turkish leaders successfully negotiated a nine-hour ceasefire with the Anzacs, so that both sides could recover and bury their dead.[15]

Alan Moorehead described the tension at Quinn's Post, because of the closeness of the two opposing forces, as 'a palpable thing in the air, an inflammable essence that might explode at any moment'. He went on to describe the temporary ceasefire in terms of the recovery of the wounded and the dead who were then buried in mass graves:

> And the bomb shower stops dead – for the moment; but, all the time, from that fiery crest line which is Quinn's there comes a slow constant trickle of wounded – some dragging themselves painfully along; others being carried along on stretchers. Bomb wounds all; a ceaseless silent stream of bandages and blood. Yet three out of four of 'the boys' have grit left for a gay smile or cheerful little nod to their comrades, waiting for their turn as they pass, pass, pass, down on their way to the sea.[16]

Named after Major Hugh Quinn, 15th Battalion, Quinn's

15 Australian War Memorial, P02649.025 (photo taken by Surgeon General Captain Charles Ryan, 24 May 1915).

16 Alan Moorehead, *Gallipoli*, Macmillan, Melbourne, 1975, 127, 132.

Post was the closest point to the Turkish trenches in the Anzac sector – only a matter of metres away. It became the centre of ferocious bomb throwing and tunnelling on both sides for the vast majority of the campaign. It was hilly, gully-ridden terrain.

Quinn's Post changed hands on several occasions throughout most of the campaign of 1915. A big Turkish attack of 29 May pushed the Allies back. Major Quinn, commander of C Company, at the age of 27, took a bullet in his brain during that day's defence. He was a boxing champion from Charters Towers Queensland where he practised professionally as an accountant and auditor. Fifty-four troopers of the 2nd Light Horse attacked the enemy trenches at Quinn's Post and all but one were shot.[17]

When they first reached the area of Quinn's Post in their original charge, Ellis Silas reported with horror:

> Up we rushed – God, it was frightful – the screams of the wounded, bursting of the shells, and the ear-splitting rackling of the rifles. In a very few minutes the gully at the foot of the hill was filled with dead and wounded – thee [*sic*] poor lumps of clay had once been my comrades, men I had worked and smoked and laughed and joked with – oh God, the pity of it.[18]

'To the last man and the last shilling'

This was how Andrew Fisher, the Leader of the Australian Labor Party – who, within a few weeks after the war

17 Harvey Broadbent, *Gallipoli the fatal shore*, Viking, Camberwell, 2005, 101, 67-69, 199.

18 Beaumont, *Broken Nation*, 88. (Silas, Ellis, Diary, 2 May 1915, MLMSS 1840, NSW State Library, 54).

began, became Prime Minister of the Commonwealth of Australia for the third time – characterised the Dominion's commitment to England as the so-called Mother Country. His words reflected the official feelings of patriotism, particularly by politicians, in response to their Country's call.

Men from every walk of life, social background and class had rushed to set-up recruitment centres. After the disaster of Gallipoli, when the Australian Division arrived in France in 1916, the Western Front was already literally bogged down in stalemate.

The 1st Division AIF was to join the Somme Offensive and was ordered to take Pozières with the 2nd and 4th Divisions in reserve. The 5th Division was to take Fromelles and the Messines sector as a diversionary move.

The Western Front's mud-churned battlefields were much different to the Gallipoli campaign of steep hills and gullies. As deadly chemical warfare had been introduced, gas masks were issued as well as steel helmets ('tin hats') for protection against shrapnel. Australian troops had bulky khaki four-pocketed tunics and matching breeches, with long wrapped-around putties and were armed with Lithgow-manufactured short magazine Lee Enfield .303 rifles. Pozières was taken at disastrous cost in life by the Australians, one of the very few gains in the disastrous Allied offensive.

In the stalemate war of attrition, particularly in 1917, Australian troops were frequently used as shock troops in the battles of Albert, Bapaume, Bullecourt, Messines, Ypres, Passchendaele, Amiens, Warfusée-Abancourt and, in1918, at

Mont St Quentin and Péronne.[19] Collectively, the casualty rate on Gallipoli was soon dwarfed by Anzac deaths on the Western Front.

After the War

After the war, Australian survivors made their way back, on several occasions individually, or in groups on tour, to parts of the Western Front. One of the many was Alec Horne who visited the battlefields and cemeteries of Belgium and France. From the town of Courtrai in Belgium, he travelled by car after World War II as an elderly man to Ypres, Passchendaele, Zonnebeke, Broodseinde, Ploughstreet, and so on…

Passchendaele was only a pile of rubble when Horne had last seen it in 1917. By the time of his visit, the town had been completely rebuilt and he found it unrecognisable. He found the mighty well-kept cemetery of Tyne Cot in which lay the remains and headstones of 35,000 British and Dominion solders – 75 percent of them unknown. Tyne Cot Cemetery is the largest Commonwealth War Graves Cemetery in the world.

> On each such grave stands an oblong headstone stating that the body of an unknown soldier lies there, and each stone bears the badge of the soldier's country. There are thousands of 'Rising Suns' on the various stones throughout this large cemetery.[20]

Two Australian Victoria Cross winners are buried at Tyne Cot.

---

19 Monty Wedd, *Australian Military Uniforms 1800-1982*, Kangaroo Press, Kenthurst, 1982, 98-99.

20 Alec Horne, 'Flashback to France', *Reveille*, 1 January 1948, 27.

Two VC Heroes from Australia buried at Tyne Cot

They were Captain Clarence Smith Jeffries, 34th Battalion, 9th Brigade, 3rd Division, and Sergeant Lewis McGee, 40th Battalion, 10th Brigade. Both were Australian born – Jeffries in Wallsend NSW and McGee in Campbell Town, Tasmania.

McGee, a married man with a daughter, worked as an engineer driver for Tasmanian Railways. Jeffries, unmarried, was a mining surveyor at Abermain Collieries NSW. On 23 May 1916, McGee became a lance corporal. He was promoted to corporal at Armentières on 4 December of the same year and to sergeant on 12 January 1917. He took part in the successful battle of Messines.

Jeffries had embarked for the Western Front as a second lieutenant.[21] In the division's training period, he was gazetted as a full lieutenant as from 1 August 1916. Like McGee, he fought in the battle of Messines, but was severely wounded in the thigh on 9 June 1917. He recovered and rejoined his unit at the Front in September. He was promoted to captain and company commander on 26 June 1917.

It was during the step-by-step Battle of the Third Ypres, the attack on Broodseinde Ridge, that Lewis McGee performed the acts for which he was awarded the Victoria Cross. McGee's unit approached Broodseinde Ridge in Belgium and encountered withering fire from the German trenches and thickly garrisoned pillboxes. The Germans were the 212th Regiment. Ten machine guns were firing into McGee's battalion from the front and the left with a thick hail of deadly bullets. The situation was critical. The

21 Michael Grealy, 'Trail links war stories', Road to Remembrance series, *Star*, 24 January 2018, 8.

Australians with the New Zealanders commenced an attack on the pillboxes to put the machine guns out of commission.

In this engagement, McGee's platoon which he was leading was severely suffering. His unit was halted by extremely heavy machine-gun fire from the closest pillbox completely blocking their advance. Suddenly, McGee rushed it alone armed only with a revolver. He was successful in silencing the pillbox by shooting some if its crew and capturing the rest of its occupants. Thus, he enabled the advance to proceed. He re-organised the remnant of his platoon and continued to lead them intelligently through the rest of the advance. He led several more pillbox attacks before the objective was taken.

Nearly all the pillboxes were overcome by acts of individual daring. By 9.12am, the 40th Battalion was in complete occupation of its objective – the village of Broodseinde and its German defensive structure. The Battle of Broodseinde fought on 4 October 1917 was a stunning victory, but when it began to rain heavily that afternoon any chance of exploiting the success vanished. The Battle of Broodseinde was the first operation launched by the British Second Army as part of the Third Battle of Ypres after Polygon Wood. It involved the I and II Anzac Corps fighting together for the first time.[22]

The Battle of Passchendaele that Captain Clarence Jeffries was involved in happened soon after. In the assault on Passchendaele Commander Jeffries was faced with

22 Lionel Wigmore with Bruce Harding, *They Dared Mightily*, 2nd edition revised by Jeff Williams, Australian War Memorial, Canberra, 1986, 76-77,91-92; Chris Coulthard-Clark, *The Encyclopaedia of Australia's Battles*, Allen & Unwin, Crows Nest, 2001, 132-33.

winding duckboard trails floating on a sea of mud and then plank-roads stretching across the shell-blighted landscape of more mud – a measureless bog of military rubble, shattered houses and tree stumps – huge pools of water and occasional clumps of charred tree stumps where once a forest grew. The Anzac infantrymen took up to five hours to cross a mile of ground. The terrain had become a great slough. Soldiers did not dare venture off the duckboards as they would sink into quicksand-like slime and drown.

Assault troops found it difficult to keep up with the creeping artillery barrage of the British guns. Mules, horses and men laboriously trudged painfully across the bleak landscape of Flanders fields carting guns, ammunition and supplies to the frontline. Some collapsed and sank into the mud-filled craters. Many drowned or totally disappeared into the morass before they could be rescued. Every twenty paces or so revealed a soldier's mutilated body. Nevertheless, Jeffries and his men pressed on. He provided his company with every comfort and support in the most difficult of circumstances.

In the 34th Battalion's attack, the first point of strong resistance they encountered east of Augustus Wood (now only a one-time forest of gaunt black remnants of trees) was two strongly-built and well-designed German fortresses called by the troops simply as 'pillboxes'; they were studded with deadly machine guns and their skilled detachments.

Machine guns in 'pillboxes' like these were the most potent weapon on the muddy battlefields. They were responsible for untold deaths; they could fire between 400 and 600 rounds a minute. One machine gun not taken out by the Allied troops could effectively fulfil the tasks of over 80 rifle-armed foot infantrymen.

Thus Captain Jeffries and his men were confronted with a most powerful and dangerous obstacle to their advance. He had to come up with a solution quickly!

And he did not hesitate, organising a twelve-man party armed with grenades and .303s. He led them in a surprise attack across the hellish No Man's Land to the first pillbox fortress. They captured two machine guns and took twenty prisoners in a brilliant manoeuvre. He then led his company successfully to their objective under heavy artillery and machine-gun fire.

As the 34th Battalion prepared for the next stage in their advance, they were harassed by more lethal machine-gun fire. Captain Jeffries organised and led another twelve-man party to take out dangerous machine-gun placements. While he was instantly killed in the attack by machine-gun bullets – a heroic rendezvous with death – his group successfully captured two more machine-gun nests and took thirty prisoners-of-war.

The unit's advance continued to a second planned objective, but every officer became a casualty, either dead or wounded, before it was successfully completed. The 9th Brigade of the 34th that Jeffries belonged to prior to his death took the second objective, but unfortunately did not have enough men and supplies to hold it for very long and were ordered to withdraw.

It took ten men about fourteen hours to bring Jeffries' shattered body back from the frontline in heavy mud and ceaseless rain. He was only twenty-three years of age. For his service on 12 October 1917, Clarence Smith

Jeffries ("Jeff") was posthumously awarded the Victoria Cross for conspicuous bravery in attack. He was buried near Passchendaele in the vast Tyne Cot Cemetery. His headstone is inscribed:

On Fame's eternal camping ground
Their Silent tents are spread.[23]

★ ★ ★

Lewis McGee was awarded his VC for his bravery on 4 October and Clarence Jeffries on 12 October, the day he was killed in action. Ironically, McGee was killed eight days after his award while trying to take out another German machine-gun post. He was shot in the head and died instantly. It was exactly the same day that Jeffries died in Passchendaele.

It seems most fitting that they were both buried at Tyne Cot Cemetery.

Sergeant McGee's VC is on display at Queen Victoria Museum and Art Gallery in Launceston, Tasmania. Captain Jeffries' VC medal is held in the Warriors' Chapel in Christchurch Cathedral in Newcastle, NSW.

In 1929, McGee's wife Eileen Rose remarried, but remained living in Avoca where she and McGee first settled when they married. His medal was auctioned in 1984 and became the possession of the Queen Victoria Museum. When Jeffries' mother Barbara Jeffries died in 1954, a

23 John Ramsland, 'Clarence Smith Jeffries VC. War Hero, local hero, school hero', in John Beach *et al*, *To Climb the Hill. A People's History of Newcastle East Public School*, Newcastle East Public School, 2016, 64-67; 'Passchendaele' – World War's "Worst Front"', *Reveille*, 28 February 1929, 11-12.

ceremonial chair in his honour was donated to the Abermain Holy Trinity Church by his uncle and aunt.

McGee and Jeffries' graves are amongst 1,368 other Australians – 578 are named and 790 are nameless.[24]

At one end of Tyne Cot's huge cemetery is a large stone wall. Carved in stone tablets on the wall are the names of those buried there whose identity was officially known. The whole cemetery is beautifully kept, as are all the cemeteries in Belgium, numbering 115 altogether.[25]

Passchendaele in 1917

Passchendaele is the name of a ruined Belgian village and its ridge, but it is also a name that evokes images of suffering, mutilation, horrific conditions, torrential rain and the muddy clay whiteness of the death in a quagmire, sometimes by drowning in water-swamped craters, or lungs destroyed by mustard gas.[26]

The very word 'Passchendaele', with its suggestion of human passion and fatal endeavour, was subtlety appropriate. It was as if such sacrifice could not have come to flower at any other place but Passchendaele, a pre-ordained point on a trench map.

Intuitively, trench soldiers knew what was going to happen. The English pronunciation sounded like 'Passion - dale', (dale = a valley especially in the wintery bleak

---

24 Ramsland, 'Clarence Smith Jeffries', 76-77; Wigmore, *They Dared Mightily*, 76-77, 91-92; Robert Hamilton, *Victoria Cross Heroes of World War I*, Atlantic Publishing, Hertfordshire, 2015, 252, 256.

25 Horne, 'Flashback', 27.

26 John Ramsland, 'The Road to Passchendaele', *Digger*, no 61, December 2017, 55-58.

north of England), thus it was associated with the notion of the Valley of Death, even though it was on a ridge.

The Battle of Passchendaele, or the Third Battle of Ypres (Third Ypres) – between 31 July and 10 November, lasting 103 days, in the autumn of 1917 – took place over 100 years ago. It comprised several assaults or associated battles, like the Battle of Polygon Wood on the German front and was planned in the expectation of crashing through the German defences to reach the German submarine bases on the Belgian coast. But it soon degenerated into the most horrific battle of the entire war, mainly due to awful weather conditions coupled with high command mismanagement under Field Marshal Douglas Haig, commander of the British Expeditionary Forces.[27]

The British veteran war poet and scholar Sir Herbert Read captured the physical conditions in the Battle of Polygon Wood of Third Ypres even though it was a singular victory for elements of the Fourth and the Fifth Australian Divisions under Major General J Talbot Hobbs of I ANZAC:

There are a few left who will find it hard to forget
Polygonveld.
The earth was scarr'd and broken
By torrents of plunging shells;

27 Ian Westwell, 'The Battle of Passchendaele', *The Ultimate Illustrated History of World War I*, Hermes House, Leicestershire, 2009, 178-9.

Then wash'd and sodden with autumnal rains.
And Polygonbeke
...
Spread itself like a fatal quicksand, —
A sucking, clutching death.[28]

The Australians had attacked through the ruins of the bombarded wood across 1,500 metres at first light after a huge bombardment of the German stronghold.The German dugouts and trenches were badly hit by the barrage, forcing them to withdraw hurriedly to a back position from which they were forced to withdraw even further. Australian casualties, however, amounted to 5,770.The Battle lasted a week and was a notable success.[29]

Major General Hobbs was moved to write:

> We have fought the Boche to a finish, defeated him, inflicting on him very heavy losses.
>
> To good discipline, thorough preparation and training, and, above all, the whole-hearted co-ordination [achieved by the frontline signallers] and co-operation of all arms and branches of the [5th Australian] Division our success is due ...[30]

Passchendaele village was eventually captured by the Canadian 2nd Division in a bloody battle, but before that happened, at least half a million soldiers – British, French, Canadian, Australian, New Zealanders and Germans with

28 Sir Herbert Read, *Collected Poems*, Faber and Faber, London, 1946, 41; (veld = wood; beke = watery swamp).
29 John Ramsland, *The Other Side of No Man's Land. Arthur Wheen World War I Hero*, Brolga, Melbourne, 2015, 202.
30 Cited in Ramsland, *The Other Side of No Man's Land*, 202-3.

many others – had become casualties.[31]

For some time, Haig had intended to launch a major attack east of Ypres. The start was the prelude made with General Sir Herbert Plumer's carefully prepared, highly successful seizure of Messines-Wytschaete Ridge, from where the Germans had been able to overlook and spy on the Ypres salient.

The success was achieved by patient tunnellers over a two-year period digging nineteen mines under the German-held ridge, including one at Hill 60 which was prepared by an Australian company of soldiers. The mines, simultaneously detonated, caused the destruction of German forces – around 10,000 casualties and 7,500 German POWs taken – in and around the enemy-occupied villages of Messines and Wytschaete south of the British-held salient of Ypres. Two huge craters suddenly appeared. At the time, it was by far history's largest war explosion and was heard across the Channel in southern England. It then led to 80,000 British forces advancing to what became Third Ypres.[32]

The main Third Ypres offensive was not so well conceived and easily revealed beforehand to the German observers. Troops were sent to the attack across the low-lying clay plain which a preliminary bombardment of 4 million, 250 thousand shells combined with two weeks of heavy rain had transformed into a sea of mud.[33] The Germans had the

31 Philip Warner, *Passchendaele*, Wordsworth Editions, Hertfordshire, 1999, 1.
32 John Ramsland, 'Commemorating James ("Big Jim") Hartley Antcliff No 2029, 36th Battalion AIF', *Digger*, no 61, December 2017, 20-25.
33 Leon Wolff, *In Flanders Fields*, Longmans, Green & Co, London, 1960, 193. Of the estimated 61,720 Australians who died on active service in World War I, 46,319 were lost on the Western Front in Belgium and France. Approximately 18,000 of those have no known grave. The number wounded totaled 152,171. About 5,750 more were gassed. Many survivors died young.

advantage of higher ground and the British and Imperial troops suffered many losses. The offensive culminated at Passchendaele village after a continued struggle in the mud from July to November that finally convinced Haig – and the whole world – that his tactics were fatally flawed.

Haig appointed General Hubert Gough to lead the offensive with the British Fifth Army instead of the brilliant Herbert Plumer. In the first phase of Third Ypres, Gough's attack failed badly with the assault down the Menin Road to the south-east of Ypres blocked. There was a huge loss of life. Haig dismissed Gough.

Haig then, belatedly, gave Plumer command of the floundering offensive in late August. Plumer devised new tactics. He took into account the awful weather conditions and launched a series of limited offensives with limited objectives that were more successful than those of Gough. He made sure of consolidation before the troops moved forward again.

Plumer transformed Haig's dream of the all-out, war-winning offensive into a battle of steady attrition. He launched several attacks between 20 September and 10 November, beginning with the Battle of Menin Road (20–25 September) in the south east, culminating in what became generally known as the First and Second Battles of Passchendaele in the north east between 12 October and 10 November when Third Ypres ended. The British had extended the Ypres salient by 8 kilometres (5 miles). The British and Empire troops suffered around 300,000 casualties while the Germans recorded 260,000.[34]

Ironically, the attack had begun with some success on 31 July. Within a day, however, unseasonably heavy rain began turning the region into a vast bog. It rained solidly for a fortnight.

Haig had used, mercilessly, many of his best formations, including all five Australian divisions. The 1st and 2nd Divisions attacked east ofYpres on 20 September as part of the Battle of the Menin Road. Later in the month, men from the 4th and 5th Divisions successfully continued the piecemeal advance under Plumer by driving the Germans from Polygon Wood in the battle of that name. On 4 October, the 1st and 2nd Divisions were joined by the 3rd Division and the New Zealand Division and forced their way in a brilliant set-piece operation on the commanding Broodseinde Ridge.

Haig then tried to push the advance further using the 2nd, 3rd and 4th Australian Divisions, but the weather again broke and he was forced to limit his ambition.[35]

Anzacs were involved in Third Ypres in the assaults on Menin Road, Polygon Wood, Broodseinde, Poelcappelle and Passchendaele and had many casualties.[36] While they were all sequences in Third Ypres or Passchendaele, some Australian historians view them as separate battles without looking at the broader context of British strategy.

---

34 Donald Summerville (ed.), 'The Battle of Passchendaele', *The Complete Illustrated History of World War I*, Centenary Special Edition, Media Factory, Sydney, 2014, 178-9.

35 Ian Grant, 'Ypres, Third Battle of', *A Dictionary of Australian Military History*, Random House, Milsons Point, 1992, 413-4.

36 Robert Likeman, *Australian Doctors on the Western Front*, vol 3, Rosenberg, Dural, 2014, 24-5.

Images of Passchendaele abound

A popular 1917 postcard and poster depicts the Battle of Polygon Wood and the planting of an Australian flag on the so-called Anzac Redoubt.[37]

A participant in this attack, Joseph Maxwell, who was to receive a Victoria Cross in 1918, wrote about this image in his chapter 'Pill-boxes and Carnage' in his memoir:

> Some days later the incident was featured in illustrated papers ... and long after I returned to Australia I saw postcards that depicted a lone Digger holding aloft an outsize in Australian flags and gallantly charging a formidable pill-box. The fact was that Lieutenant Hull, who was killed a few days later, had ... received a parcel from home. In it was a small Australian flag of paper about three inches by four inches. He stuck this in a tin of bully-beef and placed it on the corner of Anzac House where it was blown to pieces by a shell later in the day.[38]

In the towering ANZAC Memorial of New South Wales in Hyde Park, Sydney, the bas-relief sculpture of the Western Front by Rayner Hoff captures the catastrophe of Passchendaele graphically, precisely and realistically, incorporating aspects of modern industrial warfare: an aeroplane pilot and machine gun, signallers laying telephone wire, infantry in an attack against gas accompanied by a tank. The style is matter-of-fact and neither pathos nor heroics are portrayed in a chaotic scene when wounded, gassed and

37 The postcard for sale had all profits directed to the Australian Comforts Fund: AWMH00563.

38 Joseph Maxwell, *Hell's Bells and Mademoiselles*, Angus & Robertson, Sydney, 1936, 121-2.

dying men fall.[39] Hoff had fought in the Great War in the 18th (Service) Battalion of the King's Liverpool Regiment. He crossed the Channel on 11 December 1916.[40] Hoff was born on the Isle of Man in 1894. He moved to Australia after the war and soon became Sydney's leading sculptor, working on various war memorials.

Maxwell powerfully captures a similar image:

> The first flush of dawn revealed the sorry spectacle of smashed trenches, tangled wire, and remnants of the garrison huddled in pits and hollows. Everyone had lost the power to think. That terrible racket and the avalanches of mud and clods had paralysed brains. On the parapet, slashed and torn by the gunfire, lay blood-stained bundles, all that remained of many who had been our cheerful joking comrades the night before. They had been pushed out of the trench to make room for the living to stand erect. Among these pitiful bundles lay the broken body of a dark-haired young officer with a revolver still clutched in his lifeless grey fingers in the iron grip of death. I broke the grip and flung his revolver into an adjacent shell-hole. A sergeant with his ashen face towards the dawn-flushed sky and with his arms stretched out lay near by. It was but a few days earlier that he had returned from Blighty leave.[41]

Passchendaele was a 'long, drawn-out horror', a 'classic ironic narrative' of protracted mud-sodden attacks on

---

39 Deborah Edwards, *'This vital flesh'. The Sculpture of Rayner Hoff and His School*, Art Gallery NSW, Sydney, 1999, 57.

40 See Deborah Beck, *Rayner Hoff. The Life of a Sculptor*, NewSouth, Sydney, 2017, 42-3.

41 Maxwell, *Hell's Bells*, 127.

Passchendaele that, finally and literally, bogged down in early November 1917. One staff general on a visit to the Front muttered: '"Good God, did we really send men to fight in that?" A man beside him replied tonelessly "It's worse further up"'.[42]

If Messines showed what imagination and surprise could do, the attacks toward Passchendaele indicated once more the old folly. More than four million shells were fired. The bombardment churned the ground, rain fell and turned the dirt into mud. The shelling destroyed the delicate water-management system of the Flanders flatlands.

Thus the battlefield, or the 'battle–bog' of Passchendaele ended.

Just before Third Ypres, David Lloyd George, British Prime Minister from December 1916, uttered the words he never forgave himself for: 'Give us a victory'. Later, he felt he should have stopped the Passchendaele Offensive in its tracks.

Many experts see the whole battle, which had pushed the line forward a few miles at the cost of huge casualties, as a monument to military stupidity and an unforgivable failure of civilian politicians to protect the lives of civilian soldiers placed at the disposal of arrogant military commanders.[43]

The silent witness of the famous photograph of five Australian soldiers crossing on a fragile duckboard in the waterlogged Passchendaele battlefield by Australia's brilliant official photographer, Captain Frank Hurley, says it all. In the background are the black stumps of what was once Polygon Wood; in the foreground is a sea of shiny water and mud.

---

42 Fussell, *The Great War*, 17, 34, 93

43 Neil Faulkner, 'Passchendaele', *Military History Monthly*, issue 83, 2017, 24, 26-38.

The five men have been relieved from the Front. They silently gaze at the camera. They would appear to be the living remnants of a whole platoon that had become its own miniature army in the bite-and-hold tactic of General Plumer, the master tactician.

Another Hurley photograph shows six stretcher-bearers carrying a wounded soldier as they struggle through the thick mud. The bearers are up in mud from one's ankles to another's thighs.

All day, the walking wounded in their bandages drift back, punctured and lacerated, their heavy boots resembling huge blobs of mud. Some got lost at night and ended back at the wire. At the aid posts a few hundred feet rearwards, doctors worked swiftly applying routine first aid or undertaking amputations.[44]

★ ★ ★

In the Well of Contemplation within the ANZAC Memorial in Sydney, NSW, while thinking about Passchendaele, we can ponder on Rayner Hoff's brilliantly-conceived sculpture *Sacrifice*. It is a cathartic cleansing experience: a simple visual image of the futility of war as dramatically demonstrated by the tragic events along the road to Passchendaele.[45]

We are invited by Hoff in a solemn response to look over the balustrade down at the gleaming central bronze man, almost a youth, a soldier, naked and vulnerably stretched over

---

44 Wolff, *In Flanders Fields*, 185.

45 See Christopher Mooney & John Ramsland, 'Apollo must contemplate a world of which he had never dreamed', Gretchen Poiner (ed.), The *National Estate – Civic Heritage*, Proceedings of 2008 Conference, Independent Scholars Association of Australia, Canberra, 165-91.

his shield and sword in a Christ-like position of sacrifice.

Below, three column-like women – one carrying a baby – sustain their prostrate burden.[46] They symbolise both the bravery of the stretcher-bearers of war and the continuing grief of the homefront mothers, sisters, wives and children.

Set in the floor below them is a jagged shiny golden circle of the devouring flame of war.

Rayner Hoff's bronze enlivens, beautifies and humanises a circular public space that also can be witnessed from below through an opening, or from above. It is the only war memorial in this country that works both as a sculpture in its own right and as symbolic remembrance.[47]

The highlight is the wife who, in an intimate grieving gesture, holds, in one hand, the head of the soldier and, in the other hand, their child – a symbol of the future generation she must now guide and nurture alone.[48] Hoff wrote of *Sacrifice*:

> Thousands of women ... lost all that was dearest to them – sons they had borne and reared, husbands, fathers of their children, friends and lovers ... They endured all man's sacrifice quietly. In this spirit I have shown them carrying their load, the sacrifice of their menfolk.[49]

Hoff's work is an emotional one. The balustrade is carved to represent a wreath. We bow our heads from above in reverence to view the figures below. The dome above is filled with stars representing all the men and women from

46 Inglis, *Sacred Places*, 311.
47 See Graeme Sturgeon, 'Public Sculpture: the pleasure and the pain', *Art and Australia Quarterly*, vol 25, no 2, 1987, 222-7.
48 Deborah Edwards, 'Race, Death and Gender in the ANZAC MEMORIAL', *Art and Australia Quarterly*, vol 28, no 4, 1991, 476-81.
49 Rayner Hoff, *The Home*, 1 May 1932.

New South Wales who fell in the Great War. Winged torches hover over the doors. Amber light filters through the grand arched windows etched with the rising sun.[50]

A wounded patient at the No 4 Australian Military Hospital in Randwick, Sydney, who had been repatriated after the Battle of Third Ypres (Passchendaele), wrote feelingly about a fallen mate:

> There's a lonely field in Flanders, where the snows of winter fall,
> And the chilly winds blow ever, through the trees so bare and tall;
> 'Tis there, the pride of a mother's heart, and a father's hope and joy
> Is laid to rest, 'neath a snowy crust – their well-loved soldier boy.
> But a crude little cross, to mark their loss, and tell of a comrade's fall
> Alone on the field, no fence to shield, the bravest of men all.
> Just a twisted broken rifle, with a bayonet tied across
> And a helmet for a headstone, left to mark a nation's loss.[51]

At the cemetery of Polygon Wood, Zonnebeke, Alec Horne noticed on his journey through Flanders and France a large monument erected to the memory of the fallen soldiers of the 5th Australian Division. In Belgium, there are no exclusively Australian cemeteries, but one at Toronto Avenue cemetery. All are British and are the last resting places of all British and Dominion soldiers. All

50 Mark Ferson & Mary Nilsson (eds), *Art Deco in Australia Sunrise over the Pacific*, Craftsman House, St Leonards, 2001, 184.

51 GTG, "A Grave in Flanders", *Remnants from Randwick*, no 1, 1918, 14.

are distinguished, however, by the badge carved on the headstone of each soldier.

In his car, Horne approached Passchendaele from the city of Ypres which 'has been rebuilt into a beautiful and flourishing place'. He then passed Mousetrap Farm which was the British Army's first objective in the Third Battle of Ypres, October 1917, commonly known as Passchendaele. Mousetrap Farm in Horne's time still had the remains of well-built German gun emplacements, then being used by local farmers as cowshed and equipment outhouses, partly because they were built of solid concrete – most difficult to remove. Nevertheless, they were stern reminders of war, or rather the remains of war. Some farms had piles of shell cases and other war implements collected from the fields.

At Vancouver Cross Roads, Horne stood at the entrance of a large memorial to Canadian soldiers who had lost their lives there. They were mainly the victims of the first German gas attacks in the war. This attack took the Canadians completely by surprise – they had no gas masks. Over 1,000 men were killed by gas at Vancouver Cross Roads at the time the Anzacs were still fighting on Gallipoli.

At S'Graventafel, a large memorial was erected to New Zealanders who fell there. Quite near had been the huge crater at Messines Ridge in which the British and Dominion miners had totally destroyed two German-held villages by well-laid explosives. The story goes that David Lloyd George, then the British Prime Minister, stood on a cliff at Dover at the appointed time for the Ridge to go up and he claimed to have heard very distinctly the terrific explosion, the biggest explosion at that time.[52] Another story has the Prime Minister hearing the explosion from the study in his residence at 10 Downing Street, London.

* * *

Henry Lawson, Australia's so-declared national poet, too 'old and too deaf to be sent to the Front', as he claimed on several occasions, put the whole rendezvous with death in a horrific bitter way that, nevertsheless, conveyed truth:

War because of one poor blunder made in panic far away,
While a thousand men were lying on the battlefield to-day;
Dead heaped on the helpless dying, blinded eyes and brains that swim,
Parched or choked with their own life-blood, battered head and broken limb.
Wounds too ghastly to be pictured. Things to seem like men no more,
Crying out to Christ for water, and oblivion – that is war.[53]

The Trail to commemorate Death ...

Recently, through an Australian Government initiative, a two-hundred kilometre trail was established with the cooperation of the Belgian and French Governments. The trail has an educational purpose to cover the ground where 295,000 Australians served and 46,000 were killed with 132,000 wounded. It starts in Belgium's rebuilt city of Leper/Ypres at the trail's northern end, the place where

52 Horne, 'Flashback'.

53 Henry Lawson, "Nemesis" (1904), *A Fantasy of Man. Henry Lawson. Complete Works 1901-1922* (compiled & edited by Leonard Cronin), Lansdowne, Sydney, 1984, 227.

the troops marched past the ruined medieval towers of the Cloth Hall and out through the Menin Gate to the seemingly endless battles.

Frank Hurley, the famous photographer, said on observing and photographing the Cloth Hall that it was a 'pitiful apology of a brick dump, scarred and riddled with shell holes'. Its beautiful carved facades were 'smallpoxed' with shell splinters.

Today, the rebuilt Cloth Hall houses the Flanders Field Museum as one sort of memorial to the fallen. At the Menin Gate, the famous "Last Post" Ceremony is held every evening on the covered cobblestones. On the Menin Gate memorial the names of 6,000 missing Australian soldiers are carved.

At Zonnebeke on the Australian trail is the Memorial Museum Passchendaele 1917 with re-created trenches and dugouts that highlight the terrible Australian losses in 1917. Nearby is the Tyne Cot Cemetery.

The Plugstreet Museum in Belgium tells the story of the Battle of Messines in June 1917. Not too far away is the Toronto Avenue Cemetery, a small wooded exclusively Australian burial ground of great atmosphere.

The Australian Remembrance Trail then heads south into northern France past Fromelles and Arras to reach Bullecourt where is found Peter Corlett's "Cobbers" sculpture at the Australian War Memorial.

The Jean and Denise Letaille Museum illustrates and memorialises the two 1917 Battles of Bullecourt in which Australians suffered 10,000 casualties. It is named after the local school principal and his wife who were devoted to Anzac history.

Further on at Pozières is the 1st Division AIF Memorial

commemorating the Division's first significant action on the Western Front near the town at the Windmill site where Australia suffered 23,000 casualties in a little more than six weeks from July 1916.

At the southern point of the trail is the new Sir John Monash Centre opened on 24 April 2018 outside Villers-Bretonneux at the Australian National Memorial which carries the names of more than 10,700 Australians with no known grave.

The Trail runs past several other memorials relevant to Australia heading east near Péronne where the Second Division's memorial recalls its biggest victory, the capture of Mont St-Quentin.

As well, there is the Fourth Division's memorial on the heights above Bellenglise, that marks its successful advance just before the war ended.[54] Even in successful encounters many on both sides were to die.

In his brilliant translation of Erich Maria Remarque's *All Quiet on the Western Front*, Lieutenant Arthur Wesley Wheen, a brave signalman in the 1st AIF and an outstanding scholar, captures the essence of a relentless rendezvous with death across an early morning battlefield:

> Mist and the smoke of guns lie breast-high over the fields. The moon is shining. Along the road troops file. Their helmets gleam softly in the moonlight. The heads and the rifles stand out above the white mist, nodding heads, rocking carriers of guns.
>
> Farther on the mist ends. Here the heads become figures; coats, trousers, and boots appear out of the mist as from a milky pool. They become a column. The column

54 Grealy, 'Trail links'.

> marches on, straight ahead, the figures resolve themselves into a block, individuals are no longer recognizable, the dark wedge presses onward, fantastically topped by the heads and weapons floating off on the milky pool. A column – not men at all.[55]

Wheen captures the inevitability of death approaching while Frederic Manning, another Australian scholar who served in a British regiment, confronts death itself as he saw it on the Western Front:

> After all, the dead are quiet. Nothing in the world is more still than a dead man. One sees men living, living, as it were, desperately, and then suddenly emptied of life. A man dies and stiffens into something like a wooden dummy, at which one glances for a second with a furtive curiosity. Suddenly he remembered the dead in Trones Wood, the unburied dead with whom one lived, he might say, cheek by jowl, Briton and Hun impartially confounded, festering, fly-blown corruption, the pasture of rats, blackening in the heat, swollen with distended bellies, or shrivelling away within their mouldering rags; and even when night covered them, one vented in the wind the stench of death. Out of one bloody misery into another, until we break. One must not break. He took in his breath suddenly in a shaken sob, and the mind relinquished its hopeless business.[56]

By falling asleep, but then to dream …

---

55 Erich Maria Remarque, *All Quiet on the Western Front*, translated from the German by WH Wheen, GP Putnam's Sons, London, 1929, 66-67.

56 Frederic Manning, *The Middle Parts of Fortune*, Text Publishing, Melbourne, 2000, (first published 1929, Peter Davies), 13.

The Mate, Will Dyson, war artist (AWM ART 02231)

2

The Assault on German New Guinea

Prelude

On 27 June 1914, an election in the form of a double dissolution of the Federal Parliament was announced to take place in September of the same year. On 30 July, the Australian Governor-General dissolved both Houses of Parliament. In the interim, the outgoing Prime Minister, Sir Joseph Cook, took charge of a caretaker government.

The following day in the Bosnian capital Sarajevo, the Austrian Archduke Ferdinand and his wife were assassinated by a Serbian student belonging to the 'Black Hand' extremist organisation. This triggered a rapid train of events which led to a declaration of war on the German Empire by the British Government on 4 August 1914.

In the course of the previous month, urgent telegrams flowed to and fro between London and Melbourne where the Australian Federal Government was temporally sitting. They warned of imminent war – Sarajevo was merely the trigger. In reality, there were already requests for Australian troops and offers of support to help Australia deal militarily with the threat of the German Empire in the Pacific.

The Labor and the opposing conservative parties in Australia were united on foreign policy toward such a possibility of war, so the accession of Labor's Andrew Fisher to the office of Prime Minister in the new Labor government made no difference to the then military preparation that had been well in hand since 1910 and Lord Kitchener's vital Australian visit. Australia had already become part of the arms race and preparation for war with the probable clash of empires.

On 31 July, Cook opined in Parliament: 'Whatever happens Australia is a part of the Empire and is in the Empire to the full; when the Empire is at war, Australia is at war'. Equalling his rival Cook, Fisher was emphatically patriotic for the benefit of both the Australian public and the British government: 'Should the worst happen after everything is done that honour would permit, we Australians will help and defend the mother country to our last man and our last shilling'.

Historian John Laffin reacted ironically to such Empire patriotism: 'Before the war was over Australia had nearly spent her last man and shilling'.[1] Thus, when the people went to the compulsory electoral polls on 5 September 1914, they knew both parties stood hand-in-hand in foreign policy. Fisher became Prime Minister (for the third time) on 14 September and was sworn in by the Governor-General. He immediately got busy to implement in practical terms the bi-partisan foreign policy.

On 8 August, London had cabled an urgent request that Australia should take immediate military action against German colonies in the South-Western Pacific, particularly to silence the radio stations on Nauru and at Bitapaka in East New Britain, that part of German New Guinea described as

1 John Laffin, *Digger. The Story of the Australian Soldier*, Cassell, London, 1959, 33.

Kaiser Wilhelm's Land on all German maps of the Pacific.

Five days after the declaration of war, a public announcement was made that a military task force – the Australian Navy and Military Expeditionary Force (AN&MEF)[2] – would be made up of six companies of naval reservists and an infantry battalion, with the support of the Australian Army Medical Corps (AAMC):

> ... for operations in the Pacific region. Established on August 19th 1914, and serving until February 19th 1915[3], the objectives entrusted to the force were the capture of German wireless stations and the occupation and administration of Government for the colony in German New Guinea.[4]

During the Great War, Australia fought on three continents and became known to the peoples of almost every nation. They fought in the snow. They fought in the tropics – in the jungle of German New Guinea. They fought in every element – air, land and sea, and under the sea. The total number of volunteers raised in Australia was 416,809, of whom at least 330,000 were sent overseas.[5]

The men of the AN&MEF were the first Australians to be recruited and sent overseas in the 1914–1918 war. They

---

2 Colonel Robert Likeman, CSM, *From the Tropics to the Desert. German New Guinea, Egypt & Palestine, 1914–1918*, The Australian Doctors at War Series, vol 2, Slouch Hat Publications, Macrae, 2012, 13.

3 The AN&MEF continued to serve in the former German New Guinea until the end of the war.

4 Juan Mahony, *From the Home Front to the Front Line. Images of the Great War*, self-published, 2001, 156.

5 FMC (Frederic Morley) Cutlack, 'Australian Imperial Force', Arthur Wilberforce Jose & Herbert James (eds), *The Illustrated Australian Encyclopaedia*, Angus and Robertson, Sydney, 1925, 99.

consisted of 3,100 men of Australian origin, fifty-six of them were to die in Kaiser Wilhelm's Land by the war's end. Some were lost in battle, but most died of tropical illness, accidents or suicide.[6]

The German colonial presence in the south-western Pacific in 1914 was a strong aggressive one and could even be considered as a direct military threat to Australia and its sovereignty.

German trading companies first arrived in the Pacific in the 1850s. By 1870 and the unification of the German states in Europe into one powerful imperial nation under Prussia's control, most of the commercial trade in Samoa, Tonga and the islands of Micronesia north of the Equator was by German enterprises. They also established trading stations on the islands of the Bismarck Archipelago, near Eastern New Guinea.

In 1883, the Queensland Premier feared that this commercial presence might lead the Imperial German Government to claim all of Eastern New Guinea. In order to pre-empt that event, he ordered the nearest Queensland Government officer, the Thursday Island police magistrate, Henry Chester, to sail to Port Moresby where he was to claim all of Eastern New Guinea for Queen Victoria; that is, to become part of the British Empire and to be closely connected commercially with Queensland. The move did not succeed. The British Government disavowed the Queensland Premier's action and then negotiated an imperial compromise with the German Government with

6 Michael Piggott, 'Stonewalling in German New Guinea', *Journal of the Australian War Memorial*, no 12, April 1988, 3.

no consultation with Queensland.

In November 1884, Britain and Germany partitioned Eastern New Guinea: a German protectorate was to be established in the Bismarck Archipelago and the adjacent north-east portion of mainland New Guinea, which soon became known as Kaiser Wilhelmsland in honour of the German Emperor, Kaiser Wilhelm II.

A British protectorate was established in the south-east of New Guinea. On 1 September 1906, British New Guinea, which was renamed Papua and transferred to the Australian Federal Government's administrative control – not to Queensland. German New Guinea became a central part of the colonial empire that Berlin was establishing progressively between 1884 and 1899 in the Pacific. Germany was late in establishing a colonial empire which was much smaller than those of Great Britain and France.

In essence, in the Pacific the German Empire consisted of three island groups: in the North Pacific, German New Guinea and Nauru and Samoa in the south. Rabaul was considered its overall capital. While overshadowed by mountains and volcanoes, Rabaul had an outstanding harbour, Simpsonshafen, where a large fleet of warships could safely assemble posing a threat to Australia. By the beginning of 1914, Rabaul had a mixed population of 3,271 people: 266 mainly German Europeans, 452 Chinese, 79 Malays, 27 Micronesians and 2,447 Melanesians.

The Germans had divided the town along racial grounds into three districts: White Rabaul with well-built tropical bungalows and tree-line avenues; a Chinese town of huts and small businesses; and the Native Compound on the edge of town to supply a labour force. Thus a place where native workers lived and could come and go. The total population of Kaiser Wilhelmsland was unknown and never accurately counted, but roughly estimated at 115,000 people outside those living in Rabaul. Papua, the Australian administrative territory, had roughly the same number of European inhabitants, but was poorly provided militarily by the time war broke out.

It was believed in the Australian Parliament that German New Guinea posed serious military threats to Australia at the eve of the Great War. The German naval East Asiatic Squadron, with a powerful base in Tsingtao in China, consisted of armed heavy cruisers *Scharnhorst* and *Gneisenau* and light fast cruisers, the *Emden*, *Leipzig* and *Nürnberg*, which could use Rabaul's harbour as a forward operation base in the possible attack on the Australian coastline. There were also five functioning German radio stations in the Pacific by August 1914 – Yap and Angaur in the Caroline Islands and, principally, Nauru, Apia in Samoa, and, most importantly, at Bitapaka near Rabaul in German New Guinea. In addition, there were some commercial German radio companies active in Australia that needed closing down. These radio stations had the capacity to direct the German Pacific fleet in time of war – dangerous even before war was declared. The Australian government considered it important to capture Kaiser Wilhelmsland in the event of an international war involving the European Empires.[7]

Australia's first Pacific military operation overseas in the Great War was almost a total success and certainly stunning,

7 John Connor, 'The capture of German New Guinea', in Craig Stockings & John Connor, *Before the Anzac Dawn*, NewSouth, Sydney, 2013, 283-303.

as John Laffin colourfully described:

> Meanwhile, Australians had already been in action. Within about a month after the declaration of war Australian and New Zealand ships had lowered the German flag in every one of the German possessions in the Pacific. This was a surprise to the Germans, for her military and political writers had said many times if a great war occurred Australia would declare her independence and set up a republic. On August 31, Samoa was surrendered to HMAS *Australia*. Early in September the Union Jack was hoisted at Rabaul, the capital of German New Guinea (Kaiser Wilhelm's Land) and at Herbertshohe, the administrative centre of the Bismarck Archipelago.
>
> It is wrongly supposed that the first casualties of the AIF occurred during the brief New Guinea-New Britain campaigns. But in fact these men were not part of the AIF but the ANMEF [AN&MEF]. Nevertheless it was here that the Germans first realized that Australians were men to be reckoned with. Among their other exploits was the destruction of the great German wireless mast at Bitapaka. The German commander of the post later reported to his Governor that the defenders had underestimated the skill of the Australians in jungle fighting; it had been expected that they would be confined to the roads. This was not the first time the enemy found that Australians were never confined to the beaten track, nor the first time they were underestimated.[8]

Colonel William Holmes, who had been 'a prominent

8 Laffin, *Digger*, 35.

citizen soldier' in the militia in NSW before the war, was given command of the AN&MEF. Holmes and the AN&MEF left Sydney on the troopship *Berrima* with about 1,500 men, two machine-gun sections and signalling and medical detachments. Eleven days were spent on Palm Island off the Queensland coast in training activities. The *Berrima* was embarked again and reached Blanche Bay in New Britain on 11 September, by then escorted by HMAS *Australia* and three destroyers.

The medical element of the Expedition consisted of another prominent and famous figure as the Principal Medical Officer, the iconic Lieutenant Colonel Neville Howse VC, the Boer War hero. He had under his command three Medical officers and 36 other ranks (Orderlies). All of the Australian Medical Corps were recruited in New South Wales.[9] Howse hurriedly left his medical practice in Orange with some fanfare to get to Sydney by train before the ship departed.

Neville Reginald Howse (26 October 1863-19 September 1930) was Australia's first Victoria Cross winner. His courageous saving of a soldier's life in the South African War was an iconic event for the Australian public. It made him an Australian celebrity for the rest of his life. Born in Stogursey village in Somerset, he migrated to Australia after completing medical training in London and was registered in New South Wales as a doctor in Newcastle on 11 December 1889.

At twenty-six, he set up practice in Taree on the Manning River and after postgraduate training, once again in London, he returned to Australia and settled in Orange in the Central West of New South Wales. He was acclaimed as the first man

9 Likeman, *From the Tropics*, 13; Cutlack, 'Australian Imperial Force', 99-100.

to enlist in Orange when World War I broke out, setting a very public example to others.

After his appointment as principal medical officer of the Naval and Military Expeditionary Force, on his own initiative, he obtained drugs and medical equipment suitable for a tropical campaign before the *Berrima* left. Returning to Sydney soon after the successful assault in German New Guinea, he joined the Australian Medical Corps, at first as an extra-numeracy medical officer. He travelled with Major-General William Throsby Bridges.[10]

Colonel William Holmes Commander AN&MEF at Rabaul, 1914 (l to r standing): Lieut FG Cresswell, Captain RJ Travers; (sitting) Colonel Holmes & Major FB Heritage (AWM J03102A)

Major-General Holmes

The commanding officer of the Naval and Military Expeditionary Force, Major-General William Holmes (1862-1917), was born in Sydney into a dedicated military family and grew up within Victoria Barracks, Paddington which was, at the time, the epicentre of military affairs in Australia. He was educated at Paddington Public School. On leaving school, he joined the NSW Public Service while pursuing a

10 John Ramsland, 'Australia's first Victoria Cross Winner. Sir Neville Howse, Rural and Military Doctor, 1863-1930', *Medal News*, vol 55, no 6, June/July 2017, 24-27.

parallel career on weekends in the militia as a part-time citizen soldier. He fought in the South African War like Neville Howse. He was Captain of the 1st NSW Mounted Rifles. He was awarded the DSO and mentioned in despatches as a distinguished officer. He was wounded at Diamond Hill. Returning to Sydney, he was promoted to lieutenant-colonel and appointed Commander of the 1st Infantry Regiment from 1910 to 1911. In 1912, he was promoted to colonel and appointed Commander of the 6th Infantry Brigade.

Thus, he was the most experienced and obvious choice for the command of the AN&MEF in 1914. Like Howse, after the surrender of the German colonies, he returned to Australia in February 1915 and immediately joined the AIF. He was promoted to brigadier-general. He commanded the 5th Brigade at Gallipoli and the Western Front on the Somme, including the Battle of Pozières. In January 1917, he was again promoted to major general in charge of the 5th Division through the Battles of Messines and Bullecourt. He was tragically killed by a shell while showing William Holman, the NSW Labor Premier, around the Messines battlefield.

Holmes is buried at Trois Arbres cemetery. His son Major Basil Holmes DSO served with the AN&MEF with his father as a lieutenant. He too fought in Gallipoli and in France. In December 1917, he transferred to the Indian Army where he rose through the ranks.[11] Both father and son were distinguished Empire men of the elite senior officer class.

Even as a child of ten, William Holmes was a bugler in the 1st Infantry Regiment of the New South Wales colonial forces. He was highly regarded as the epitome of the

11 Likeman, *From the Tropics*, 15.

successful citizen soldier and the official historian Charles Bean, among others, cited his example when arguing merits of the citizen soldier over the regular professional officers for senior command in war.[12]

First Australian Blood Sacrifices of the Great War

> The Kabakaul party, after advancing about two miles, came under rifle fire from a small entrenched position across the Bitapaka road: reinforcements were quickly landed from the destroyers and the *Berrima*, and the enemy surrendered. The wireless station was captured that evening. Two Australian officers and three seamen were killed, and four seamen wounded [one fatally] – the first Australian casualties in the war.
>
> (F.M.C.) F.M. Cutlack, 'Australian Imperial Force'[13]

Ironically, Captain Brian Colden Antill Pockley, a young medical graduate of the Faculty of Medicine at Sydney University, killed in this military offensive on 11 September 1914, gained three dubious distinctions: he was the first Australian soldier to die in action in the Great War; he was the first Medical Officer to be killed in action; and he was the first University of Sydney man to die in battle in the same war. Moreover, he was killed while carrying out a series of gallant humane acts under heavy fire from the enemy.

Five sailors – Able Seaman Billy Williams, John Walker (alias John Courtney), Harry Street, Signaller Robert Moffat and Lieutenant Commander Charles Elwell of the Royal

---

12 Peter Dennis *et al* (eds), *The Oxford Companion to Australian Military History*, Oxford University Press, Melbourne, 1997, 295 (entry on 'Holmes, Major-General William').

13 In Jose & Carter (eds), *The Illustrated Australian Encyclopaedia*, 100.

Captain Brian Pockley, the first medical officer and soldier killed in the Australian forces during WWI, 11 September 1914 (AWM H19316)

Australian Navy – and one soldier, Captain Brian Pockley, were killed in action or died of wounds in the fight in the jungle to capture the German radio station at Bitapaka in German New Guinea. Pockley was shot at close range through the abdomen and spine shattering several vertebrae on the morning of 11 September 1914. In the same encounter, one German soldier and about thirty New Guinean policemen of the German colony were killed and several others wounded. Both Brian Pockley and Able Seaman WGV Williams died aboard HMAT *Berrima* during the afternoon after being mortally wounded in the fierce encounter. Pockley died about 2pm and Williams minutes later.

★ ★ ★

Brian Pockley was born on 4 June 1890 in North Sydney, the son of the prominent Sydney ophthalmic surgeon Dr Francis Antill Pockley whose surgery and official address was at 227 Macquarie Street.[14] He grew up in Wahroonga

14 In 1853 Brian's grandfather, Robert Francis Pockley, a former sea captain and harbour master, built "Pictonville" located on the corner of Bay Road and Edward Street, North Sydney. He developed the Pockley Estate, mainly acquired from Alexander Berry, which covered five acres extending from the intersection of Berry Street and Lane Cove Road (now Pacific Highway). He sold the house to Francis Adams in April 1881 who renamed it "Doohat". It was later demolished in the late 1930s/ early 1940s.

and attended Sunday School at St Andrews Church of England. He was educated locally at North Sydney Church of England Grammar School (Shore) where he gained an open scholarship and, three years later, achieved a Senior Scholarship. In his final year, Pockley captained the First Rugby team and the Greater Public Schools Combined Fifteen (GPS). Shore won the GPS Premiership in Rugby in 1908 and 1909 under Pockley's captaincy.

Brian was an all-round sportsman who distinguished himself in rugby, cricket and athletics. He represented his school at the Amateur Athletics Association carnivals of the Greater Public Schools sport events. A fine sprinter and broad jumper, he won the running broad jump with 20ft in-distance – a record held for many years – and the 440yards in 55.4-5 sec. in 1908.

Pockley was also a fine all-round scholar. He won school prizes in Science, for Merit in public examinations and for General Merit in the Headmaster's weekly reports. He always showed promise. He achieved the Junior Certificate and the Matriculation in the Senior Certificate that led to his entry into the Faculty of Medicine at the university.

As well as sport and academic scholarship, Brian Pockley stood out in the School's cadet unit in which he was commissioned as a lieutenant when two companies were formed in his final years at the school. He attended the December camps at La Perouse, which provided training in rifle shooting and other drill, and took part in battalion parades at Centennial Park before a large audience of proud parents from his school. At Sydney University, his training in the militia continued in the so-called University Scouts as a commissioned officer. The period of military training for boys and youths had been made compulsory by the Federal Government in 1910.

At the University of Sydney, as a residential student at the prestigious St Paul's Church of England College, Brian Pockley won a Blue for athletics and Rugby in his final year of medicine while representing New South Wales in Rugby. In the New South Wales representative games against Queensland in 1914, New South Wales won 20-16, 13-0 and 20-11. Had the Great War not intervened, Pockley had the potential to have played Rugby for Australia. He was credited with being one of the fastest and most elusive three-quarter backs in the senior district competition, playing for Sydney University.

The day war was declared, Pockley, who was a resident medical officer at Sydney Hospital at the time, volunteered for active service. His application for a commission on 14 August 1914 was also successful since he was a highly fit rugby man with strong athletic ability and proven leadership qualities. He was appointed captain and assigned as an army medical officer in the Australian Military Corps. He was twenty-four years three months, single, five foot nine inches tall and weighed eleven and a half stone.

A Military Expedition to the Tropics

On being informed of the British declaration of war on 4 August 1914, Australia and New Zealand governments implemented their plans to create expeditionary forces. The next day, the British government requested the two enthusiastic dominions to raise separated forces to take

German New Guinea and German Samoa.

The New Zealand force of 1,374 personnel, including six nurses, left Wellington on 15 August. They were escorted by HMAS *Australia* and other warships and landed in Apia on 29 August. They occupied the German colony without any armed resistance. Not a shot was fired.

New Guinea was to be a sterner situation for Australia. The creation of the Australian Naval and Military Expeditionary Force was delayed by three days because of the absence of Colonel Gordon Legge, the new Chief of General Staff, who was still on a passenger ship returning from a secondment with the War Office in London under Lord Kitchener. Then, the AN&MEF was announced by the Defence Minister as a small mixed naval and military force for service within or without Australia and separate to the Australian Imperial Force (AIF) which was being raised at the same time.

On 18 August, Brian Pockley was appointed captain in the Naval and Military Expeditionary Force. He sailed from Sydney with the first Australian Expeditionary Force for New Guinea on 19 August 1914.

Australia's immediate anxiety was to discover the whereabouts of the German Pacific naval squadron whose warships had not been located since mid-June 1914. Since their nearest base was at Simpsonshafen in New Britain, the Australian naval squadron was sent to look for them. On 7 August, the federal government had received an official message from London saying that the seizure of the German wireless stations at Rabaul, Yap and Nauru would be 'a great and urgent Imperial service'.

A motley volunteer force of Royal Australian Naval Reservists, infantry and machine-gun sections was raised under the command of Colonel Holmes. The force included Pockley as a medical officer under Neville Howse. It was despatched from Sydney Harbour on the troopship HMAT *Berrima* with about 1,500 men – as already described, six companies of naval reserves, a battalion of infantry, two machine-gun sections and signalling and medical detachments. This force had a mere eleven-days training on Palm Island, the Aboriginal settlement off the Queensland coast. They then reached Blanche Bay in New Britain on 11 September, escorted by HMAS *Australia* and three destroyers that had already done the same service for the New Zealanders.

Before dawn the same day, at 6am, two parties under the command of Lieutenant-Commander Rowland Bowen landed at Kaba Kaul (Kabakaul) and Herbertshöhe (now Kokopo), Rabaul. They had orders to discover and capture a wireless station somewhere inland in the dense jungle in an elevated spot and in constant contact with the German naval squadron. In other words, it was the nerve-centre of the German naval war machine in the area and had to be taken out.

Captain Pockley and one orderly accompanied the Kaba Kaul force. No stretcher orderlies were provided. They advanced slowly inland with great difficulty for two miles through dense thorny jungle infested with mosquitoes. Then they came under heavy fire from an unseen enemy entrenchment positioned across the Bitapaka road that led to the Bitapaka radio station. Some opened fire in the ambush from hidden trenches and others, mainly German New Guinea native police, from trees.

Bowen stopped the advance under heavy fire and desperately sent back for the reinforcements. One of the first to be hit in this assault was a German Sergeant of Police who Captain Pockley attended, providing first aid strapping. The German's wrist was shattered almost completely and the hand had to be amputated as quickly as possible. The wounded prisoner-of-war was then sent without delay to the rear with a naval reserve guard. The German policeman, whose surname was Mauderer, had extended his arm to Pockley and bit down on his cigar as Pockley performed the field amputation of his shattered hand. Witnesses later recalled that the German's 'face did not betray for one second the pain he endured'.[15]

Meanwhile, as Able Seaman Williams started to move down the road on the battlefield, a shot rang out from the trees. The round entered the right side of his chest and exited the left side. His companion Stoker William Kember picked the wounded man up and carried him nearly a mile towards the beach. Hearing of Williams' wound, Pockley set off to find him. When he found him with Kember, he examined his wound and realised it was mortal. He instructed Kember with another assistant to carry him to the beach and the ship. In an act of selflessness, Pockley removed his Red Cross brassard and tied it to Kember's hat in an attempt to give safe passage since enemy fire had increased. The small party got the wounded sailor back to the staging area.

Later, Pockley had to attend to another wounded man

15 Michael Kelly, 'First to Fight', *Wartime*, issue 67, Winter 2014, 44.

some distance back in the jungle and, after attending to him, reached Lieutenant Brown, also wounded and lying behind a fallen log. Another urgent call was made for the doctor and Captain Pockley, despite warnings that, in the absence of his distinguishing Red Cross mark, he would be a target, wormed through the bush, reached the badly wounded man and, while he was stooping over him, was fatally wounded through the abdomen and spine at point blank range. Thus Captain Brian Colden Antill Pockley was the first Australian soldier to fall in the Great War: Killed in action, New Guinea, September 1914.

The German prisoner-of-war, whose hand Pockley had to amputate, was later described in the *Sydney Morning Herald* on 22 September 1914 as a well-set up man of about thirty-five with a soldierly bearing and a moustache of the type that the German Emperor had made popular. He did not speak English and the newspaper reporter communicated with him through an interpreter in the Liverpool prisoner-of-war camp back in Sydney. He gave a colourful eye-witness account of the first instance of war for the Australians. His wound was healing well and he held the rank equivalent to 'our sergeant of police'. He claimed that the German forces in the engagement consisted of 210 native troopers and about 38 German police officers and others.

The German, when asked, considered that the Australian advance was conducted 'skilfully enough' in scrub that was so dense. He pointed out that the regular service rifle, either of the German or English pattern, could drive a bullet through any ordinary tree in the jungle they fought in. He remembered that Dr Pockley was right up with the first party of Australians in the thick of the fight and that there were no stretcher bearers in sight. He noticed that, when he saw Pockley treating another wounded man, he was not in a trench, but a hole in the ground a few feet deep made by a big tree having been blown out by the roots.

When the German sergeant was being treated by Pockley, he spoke a little broken German. The German advised Dr Pockley to get back out of the firing line or put up a big Red Cross flag (which he did not have) as the native police would not have any respect for the brassard on his arm, but might respect a big flag. Pockley calmly went on with the operation, saying he had no big flag with him.

The sergeant described Pockley to the journalist as a brave, cool and 'very humane man'. He took his hand off without chloroform, as none was available, while the tough German smoked using his other hand. The German then recalled that the Australians made a sort of stretcher with two rifles and carried him back some hundreds of yards. Then he felt strong enough to walk the rest of the way to the beach where, he said, he was taken aboard the ship and treated well.

He recalled that Pockley too was later taken on board in the afternoon after he was shot. The prisoner showed that he regretted the death of Dr Pockley very keenly.

Back to the action itself. Reinforcements had been quickly landed from the destroyers and HMAT *Berrima* and the enemy was forced to surrender. A German officer, Lieutenant Kempf, raised a white flag. The wireless station was captured that evening and destroyed. The Herbertshöhe party had penetrated five miles inland without opposition and had then returned to the coast.

On the 12th, Rabaul was occupied without opposition by an AN&MEF attachment. The next day, the military occupation of the island was formally proclaimed. On the 21st, the enemy troops, German and native, laid down their arms and surrendered.

A Sydney newspaper editorial on 12 November 1914 as well as others at the time promised that the soldier Captain Pockley and the five sailors, including Lieutenant Commander Charles Elwell, would always be remembered. The scale of the carnage that followed in the Great War, as historian John Connor emphasises, meant, instead, that these six men were forgotten. The centenary of the 1914-1918 war provided an opportunity to remember their sacrifice and to re-examine the importance of this short, fierce, but successful campaign in Australia's immediate neighbourhood – the closest the war got geographically.

At the University of Sydney, however, Captain Brian Pockley was indeed remembered. In August 1915, *Hermes*, the Magazine of Sydney University, set up a highly decorated memorial page commemorating those killed in action who were Sydney University men. It read:

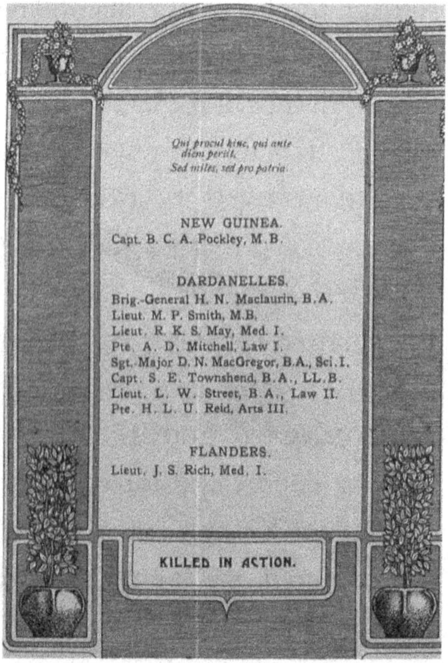
Qui procul hinc, qui ante diem periit,
Sed miles, sed pro patria.

NEW GUINEA.
Capt. B. C. A. Pockley, M.B.

DARDANELLES.
Brig.-General H. N. Maclaurin, B.A.
Lieut. M. P. Smith, M.B.
Lieut. R. K. S. May, Med. I.
Pte. A. D. Mitchell, Law I.
Sgt.-Major D. N. MacGregor, B.A., Sci. I.
Capt. S. E. Townshend, B.A., LL.B.
Lieut. L. W. Street, B.A., Law II.
Pte. H. L. U. Reid, Arts III.

FLANDERS.
Lieut. J. S. Rich, Med. I.

KILLED IN ACTION.

Hermes memorial

In the several various Honours Lists that *Hermes* published in the period between 1915 and 1919, Captain Pockley was always faithfully remembered.

In 'The War Records of the University of Sydney' that appeared in their magazine in May 1917 compiled by John Le Gay Brereton BA, a full-length studio portrait of Captain Brian Pockley appeared, accompanied by a short account of his life story, including some of his school and university records and achievements leading to the tragic account of the military expedition and his gallant death. On the 'Roll of Honour' in the same issue was quoted a stanza from John Milton's "Samson Agonistes":

Nothing is here for tears, nothing to wail
Or knock the breast, no weakness, no contempt,
Dispraise, or blame, nothing but well and fair
And what may quiet us in a death so noble.

Captain Brian C A Pockley, who was originally buried close to where he fell at Kabakauland Kokopo with others killed in the action, was disinterred and re-buried with Lieutenant Commander Charles B Elwell of the Royal Australia Navy and three naval ratings – W Williams, H W Street and J Courtney (alias John Walker) – in Rabaul Cemetery, Rabaul Island, New Guinea, in separate plots with headstones in the same ceremony with full Naval and Military Honours.

Under the wide and starry sky,
  Dig the grave and let me lie.
Glad did I live and gladly die,
  And I laid me down with a will.
These be the words you grave for me:
  'Here he lies where he longed to be;

Home is the sailor, home from the sea
And the hunter home from the hill.'

Robert Louis Stevenson, "Requiem"

Dr Frank Pockley, Brian's father, wrote to the officer-in-charge of the Victoria Barracks on 26 September 1919:

> I went to New Guinea four years ago with some idea of having the remains [of my son] brought back to Sydney, but, on finding the burial had been made with full military honours, close to where my son fell, and a very handsome headstone and railing erected, and that the grave was being carefully tended by the garrison at Kokopo, I decided to leave things as they were. Had I known, however, that the body was to be exhumed, I should have had it brought to Sydney and re-interred in the family burial ground.[16]

Although he was Brian's next-of-kin, Dr Pockley had not been informed by military authorities at the time of the re-burial service for his son with full military honours.[17]

Despite the validity of John Connor's remark about the huge death rate in the subsequent war causing forgetfulness of the initial deaths in action, Dr Brian Pockley was given substantial recognition. He was mentioned in despatches. The High Commissioner for Australia in London reported

16 The iron railing around the grave of Captain Pockley was provided by his uncle, Dr Guy Pockley, also a medical practitioner and the brother of his father Dr Frank Pockley. The railing made the grave stand out from the others.

17 Dr Frank Pockley's son John was also killed in action in World War I. Lieut John Pockley, aged 26, was shot in an assault near Hangard Wood on 30 March 1918. He died later unconscious in the Dressing Station. His remains were buried in Hangard Wood. He was in charge of B Company, 33rd Battalion AIF.

to Pockley's father:

> The King has read with the greatest interest and pride the account of the noble manner in which your son gave his life for Empire. Their Majesties desired me to convey their true sympathy with you and deep regret for his loss. Letter follows.

A memorial tablet for the 'Late Captain Pockley', who fell while on active service with the first Australian military expedition, was erected at the Sydney Hospital in Macquarie Street, Sydney. It carried his college motto: *Deo, patriae, tibi* – God first, country next, self last of all.[18]

Present at the unveiling ceremony on 22 December 1915 were Brian Pockley's proud parents, his uncle Dr Guy Pockley and several other relatives as well as a collection of well-known Sydney doctors. The brass tablet was formally unveiled by Dr Ralph Worrall, the senior honorary gynaecologist surgeon of Sydney Hospital. The final part of the tablet read: 'He died through giving to a wounded comrade the badge protecting his own life'.[19]

For six months before his voluntary enlistment, Dr Brian Pockley served as one of the resident medical officers of the Sydney Hospital and during that time he won the esteem of his medical colleagues. It had been anticipated that he would have had a bright future, but these high hopes had been blotted out by his death in action. He was amongst the first to answer his country's call.

By the time the tablet was unveiled in December 1915, other Sydney Hospital medicos were known to have died

18 The motto of St Paul's College, The University of Sydney.

19 'Medical Heroes. Memorial Tablet. Late Captain Pockley.', *Sydney Morning Herald*, 23 December 1915, 8.

on the battlefields: Drs Muir Smith, Eric Giblin and Arthur Verge, but Brian Colden Antill Pockley, MB, ChM was the very first. They were all fine types of Australian manhood.

After the war, Dr Francis Pockley was moved to fund and establish a memorial for his two sons, Brian Colden Antill and John Graham Antill, at their school. The Shore Church of England Grammar School (SCEGS) War Memorial Playing Fields are found at Sailors Bay Road, Northbridge NSW. As well as playing fields, the sandstone memorial, set in a garden with plaques dedicated to Brian and John, was once a drinking fountain for the benefit of the boys playing sport.

★ ★ ★

Pockley Brothers memorial SCEGS
(NSW State Library memorial inscription)

Rear Admiral Sir George Patey, first Flag Officer Commander of the Australian Fleet, led the naval actions against the small, but active and potentially dangerous German Pacific Squadron aboard the flagship HMAS *Australia* while the hastily formed, but effective land force was under the command of the experienced citizen militia officer Colonel William Holmes. Holmes claimed his successful occupation of German New Guinea on 17 September 1914. The German authorities and their one hundred native troops formally laid down their arms four days later.

This brisk, brilliant and, in some places, bloodless campaign by the AN&MEF was darkened by disaster at sea on 14 September. The Australian submarine AE 1 had disappeared from the waters of Rabaul. All thirty-five officers and men aboard perished. Her hull was never found and the circumstances remain a mystery.[20] The men had died in the vast silence underneath the surface of the sea.

AE 1 was one of two 'E' class submarines laid down in 1911-1912 and launched in 1913. They had six inches of armament, were 181 feet in length and a beam of 22 feet 6 inches. They had 4x18inch torpedo tubes and a speed of 15 knots submerged. They were identical to the British 'E' Class. They had arrived in Sydney's Garden Island Dockyard a few weeks before the outbreak of the Great War. Both served in New Guinea waters, aiding the capture of German New Guinea underwater.

AE 1 was then lost in these operations, presumed sunk by an uncharted reef – a tragic accident.

AE 2 went to assist in the Gallipoli Peninsula and became the first submarine to penetrate the Dardanelles, torpedoing a Turkish cruiser on the way, after negotiating Turkish minefields and avoiding destroyers and fire from

---

20 AK Macdougall, *Australians at War. The Illustrated History*, Five Mile Press, Scoresby, 2012, 44.

land-based guns. After reaching the Sea of Marmara, the AE 2 spent five days disrupting Turkish shipping, but failed to sink any more vessels. On 30 April, with all its torpedoes used up, AE 2 was attacked by Turkish gunboats. Lieutenant Commander Stoker was forced to scuttle the ship and the crew were captured and remained in a Turkish prisoner-of-war camp until 1919.[21]

Meanwhile back in the Pacific, Rear-Admiral Patey saw the destruction of the German cruisers as his first priority and HMAS *Australia* with her massive 12-inch guns was potentially capable of the task.

Japan's entry into the war against Germany on 23 August 1915 strengthened the Allies hand in the Pacific Ocean and the remaining German possessions – New Ireland, the Admiralties, Bougainville, the German Solomons – were occupied by small forces of AN&MEF soldiers sent by Colonel Holmes. Meanwhile, Japan just as bloodlessly seized the German Island groups to the north of the Pacific.

It was hard to locate the German cruisers in the Pacific. Vice-Admiral Count Graf von Spee's East Asian Squadron of two heavy cruisers and three light cruisers was a doomed command. His only feasible plan was to escape around Cape Horn and link up with the German Caribbean squadron and then make for home.

Captain von Müller of the *Emden* got permission from von Spee to detach from the East Asian squadron to raid Indian Ocean shipping. Disguised with a false funnel, the *Emden* slipped through Sumatran waters. By 14 September,

21 Dennis *et al* (eds), *The Oxford Companion*, 221.

the *Emden* had played havoc capturing or sinking nine merchant ships. On 21 September, she shelled Madras Harbour and captured ten more ships off Ceylon. Later, she steamed confidently into Penang Harbour and sunk a French and a Russian war ship. Then she disappeared and sank Allied merchant ships off the coast of east Africa. The inability to locate the *Emden* in the Indian Ocean and von Spee's squadron in the vast Pacific caused the Australian and New Zealand governments to delay the expeditionary AIF forces going to Egypt by a convoy of troopships. The government feared the Australian troopships would be attacked and sunk with a huge loss of life without ever reaching the battlefront.

By 5 October, the Australian Admiralty was aware that von Spee's squadron were heading for the South American coastline. A hastily dispatched British fleet caught von Spee near the Falkland Islands and sank all his ships except the *Dresden* which was destroyed four months later. Admiral von Spee went down in his flagship *Scharnhorst*.

The Capture of the *Emden*

Officers & sailors of the German light crusader SMS *Emden* while their ship was undergoing repairs in dry dock. The *Emden* was sunk on a reef by HMAS *Sydney*. 134 died & 65 wounded

On 1 November 1914, the 26 troopships of the 1st AIF and 10 others from the New Zealand Expeditionary Force left for Egypt in a huge convoy of 38 ships – two more transports were added – in three long lines a mile apart. The convoy was passing the Cocos Islands in the dawn of 8 November when its wireless operator heard the island operator reporting: 'Strange warship approaching' and then 'SOS'. It could only mean one thing – the *Emden* was at the Cocos Islands.

Eventually, HMAS *Sydney* was ordered to steam there. Racing west at 25 knots, the *Sydney* sighted the *Emden* eight miles away. She closed to five miles distant and opened fire. In the ensuing battle, the *Sydney* suffered 15 hits from the 38-pound German shells before its powerful 100-pound shells swept away two of the *Emden*'s funnels in direct hits and destroyed her steering gear as well as killing many of the crew.

Realising he was defeated, Captain Karl von Müller ran the wreck of his cruiser onto a coral reef on Keeling (Cocos) Island. After a gunfight lasting about 25 minutes, Captain John Glossop RN of the *Sydney* wired what was soon to become a famous message: **'*Emden* beached and done for'.**

He immediately went after the enemy coal supply ship *Buresk* and put it out of action as well. Returning to Keeling Island, the *Sydney* fired two more salvoes at the burning *Emden*, but those who remained alive on board the wreck managed to hoist a white flag of surrender. A total of 134 German sailors had died in the savage encounter. The *Sydney* had lost only four men. It then took on board the 190 *Emden* survivors as prisoners-of-war. The German ship had on board crews captured from the merchant ships they had previously sunk.

The *Sydney*'s captain wired the request that there be no cheering when they entered Sydney Harbour in honour of the German dead. The carnage, in Captain Glossop's mind – as a gentleman of the old school – had been terrible. The wounded German sailors needed consideration for what they were going through.[22]

While most of the *Sydney*'s crew were British-born, the news of this victory – the Royal Australian navy's first in its history – was received with great jubilation on Australia's home front where it was widely interpreted as a confirmation of Australia's fighting spirit. The *Sydney*'s superior size, speed and firepower had given it the advantage in the fight.[23]

Even a packet of flour was given the name "Sydney" : 'We use it every day …' – went the promotional jingle created by Jack Lumsdale. The flour packet carried an illustration of HMAS *Sydney*.

There was cheering at home; the victory made the *Sydney* an overnight sensation. 'What about our Tin Pot Navy now!' shouted in triumph one member of the Federal Parliament. The defeat of the *Emden* symbolically marked the end of the German Imperial Empire in the Pacific, both at sea and on the land.

---

22 Macdougall, *Australians at War*, 44-48.

23 Dennis *et al*, *The Oxford Companion*, 225-6.

What happened to the German POWs from the Pacific?

Three large camps in New South Wales were eventually established to house German prisoners-of-war who were the crews of captured German battleships, like the *Emden*, or soldiers or police from German territories in the Pacific, like New Guinea. They were Holsworthy camp near Liverpool and two abandoned colonial prisons still in reasonable or repairable condition: Berrima Gaol in the New South Wales countryside and the Public Works Gaol at Trial Bay on the northern coast. Others detained in the same three concentration camps were German residents of British territories in South-East Asia and from those captured in German Asian territories and colonies.

Among the interred were 4,500 German persons who lived in Australia, but who were considered by the Federal Government as 'enemy aliens'. Some were temporary representatives of foreign, usually German firms or companies; others were permanent residents in Australia of German birth, including 700 nationalised British subjects.

'*Emden* beached and done for', painting by Arthur Burgess in the AWM. After her destruction by HMAS *Sydney*, her commander Capt Karl von Müller ran the *Emden* onto a coral reef. The crew were then captured – those who were not dead. (Macdougall, *Australians at War*, 47)

In all, there were 6,890 detainees in these three prisons: Holsworthy, Berrima and Trial Bay. The naval and army officers tended to be placed at Trial Bay Gaol, whereas other ranks were place at either Holsworthy or Berrima.[24]

★ ★ ★

The AN&MEF was notable for the fact that it was the first to leave Australia under the direct control and command of Australian officers, without Imperial supervision, as in the past in the South African War and earlier in other British colonial wars. Though the objective was most successfully obtained and men gave their lives, were wounded or suffered fatal tropical sicknesses as surely as their comrades did in Gallipoli, Palestine and the Western Front in France and Belgium, no war record of honour was ever bestowed on them – not even a campaign medal. This remained 'a sad bone of contention' with most members of the AN&MEF after the war ended.[25]

It says much for the patriotic spirit of the men of the AN&MEF that, within a few months, 80% of them re-enlisted in the AIF and served on the Gallipoli peninsula, in Egypt and France.

The occupation of German New Guinea and elsewhere in the Pacific islands, which had been colonised by the Germans, continued for the whole of the Great War.

---

24 Ernest Scott, *Australia During the War. Official History of Australia in the War of 1914-1918*, vol 11, Angus and Robertson, Sydney, 1936, 114-26; Nadine Helmi and Gerhardt Fischer, *The Enemy at Home. German Internees in World War I Australia*, UNSW Press, Sydney, 2011, 29-30.

25 Lance Corporal John William Martin, 'The First Away', *Reveille*, August 1955, cited in John Gatfield with Richard Landels, *The RSL Book of World War I*, Harper Collins, Sydney, 2015, 11.

In October 1914, the *Sydney Morning Herald* commented that the capture of New Guinea meant that Australia would have to think of extending more permanent responsibilities of the islands in the Pacific – a wider sphere of influence, perhaps as a new colonial power of a British Dominion – Australia.

By 1918, the British government decided that the former German colonial empire of the Pacific should be retained by the victors. Initially, President Woodrow Wilson opposed such imperialist ambitions. Australia's Prime Minister William Morris Hughes began an international political campaign against Wilson's opinion to ensure Australia kept New Guinea to develop and exploit its resources and to provide a defence against possible Japanese interference and aggression.

At the Paris Peace Conference in January 1919, he argued: 'as Mexico is to the United States … so is New Guinea to Australia'. In May 1919, Hughes got his way – the conference allocated the former German colonies of New Guinea and Nauru to Australian control. New Guinea and Papua remained Australian territories until independence in 1975.[26]

Hughes had been in London when the Armistice was signed and was ambitious to ensure Australia would be represented by their own leadership at the peace conference that would follow. At Paris, he had taken a strong line on the issue of reparations, the annexation of German New Guinea and the racial equality clause of the proposed covenant of the League of Nations.

His clash with President Woodrow Wilson on a number of issues became famous, at least in Australia. He succeeded

26 Connor, 'The capture of German New Guinea', 301.

in getting his way on matters of importance to Australia, but it was more probably that the Great Powers had little interest in the future of the South Pacific at the time.

Hughes returned to Australia to some popularity, but by 1922 he was forced from office as Prime Minister when the Country Party, holding the balance of power, refused to work with him. As a politician, he was highly controversial and regarded by many in the Labor Party as a 'rat' for creating one of the first splits in that party. His legacy was mixed, although he was an energetic war leader.

New Zealand soldiers in Samoa 1914
with a captured German Imperial flag

3

Neville Howse VC and the 1st AIF

Neville Howse's medical career neatly fits into four chronological periods: his time as a rural doctor in the Manning Valley of the mid-northern coast of NSW in the 1890s; his involvement in the Boer War as a medical officer for the British Empire and, especially, his award of Australia's first Victoria Cross for gallantry; his brilliant leadership in setting up the Australian medical services in World War I and their efficient management; and his significant contributions as the first Minister of Repatriation after the war, together with other aspects of his colourful professional life and significance in military history.

Major-General Sir Neville R Howse, Director of Medical Services Australian Imperial Force 1915-1919 (AWM A01189)

Loving the creak of the pack and saddle leather,
Howse worked tirelessly on the Manning
Even when the blue-forked lightning smashed skies.
But what did it matter if the creeks were up?
Then the lone horseman, drained out, trotting slowly home
Until the lights of Taree faintly flickered
And the road in the first light gleamed curving down.
Thankfully home, at a gallop came the tired medical man.

John Ramsland, "The Man on the Silver-Grey Stallion"

Even in the early stages of his distinguished medical career while working in the small rural town of Taree, Dr Neville Reginald Howse displayed a great deal of dash as a daring horseman in carrying out his duties in the town and its vast bush district with physical courage and innovation that was to characterise his military career. His work as a country doctor on the Manning and then at Orange in the Central West was in itself significant in nature and ran beside his military career.

One local Taree historian was to note: 'No man has ever won such popularity nor was so widely or intimately known as Dr Howse.'[1]

To find such acceptance in a small politically-divided town, which was difficult for the newcomer, was no mean feat. But he was indeed a dashing, personable young man already of brilliant surgical ability – a field of medicine unusual in rural Australia.

He was of robust character, good humour, great courage and ability and of bold, but worthy ambition. Decisive in nature, he lived out his life after migrating from the north of England into the very centre of medical, military and political affairs in Australia, whether in peace or wartime. It would not be possible to encapsulate fully, in a mere nutshell, his contributions to Australia in a lifetime of achievement.

Beginnings

Neville Howse was born in the small village of Stogursey in rural Somerset on 26 October 1863. Similar to Taree in

1 Cited in John Ramsland, 'Dedication of the Neville Howse VC Rest Area', *Digger*, no 51, June 2015, 40.

New South Wales. Stogursey was in a river valley close to the Irish Sea with steep hills as a backdrop. The landscape of the Manning Valley may have attracted Howse, reminding him of his birthplace and childhood in the shadow of the Quantock hills. It was probably one of the reasons Howse was to take up a demanding rural practice.

After his secondary education in 1880 at Fullard's House School, a small grammar school in the county market town of Taunton, he began to study medicine at the age of seventeen at the Royal London Hospital in the depressed East End on the Mile End Road. London Hospital with 790 beds at the time was the largest hospital in Britain and offered medical students a broad and exacting range of experiences. Howse was on a scholarship. In 1886, he completed his studies and was awarded Membership of the Royal College of Surgeons (MRCS) and the Licentiate of the Royal College of Physicians (LRCP). Howse became employed as a demonstrator in anatomy at the University of Durham in the cold north-east of England some 22 kilometres (14 miles) south of Newcastle-upon-Tyne. Durham University, founded in 1832, was England's third seat of learning after Oxford and Cambridge. Howse was accommodated at University College while employed as a demonstrator in the Faculty of Medicine. University College was housed in the former Durham Castle.[2]

Declining health in the cold, windy climate – an unspecified respiratory problem – forced the young doctor to migrate to the then British Colony of New South Wales

2 John Ayto & Ian Crofton, *Brewer's Britain & Ireland*, Weidenfeld & Nicolson, London, 2005, 360-1 (entry on Durham).

on the coast and to a more temperate climate than in the north of England. In industrial Newcastle, he was registered as a doctor on 11 December 1889 soon after his arrival. He set up a small practice in the Lodge of the Mutual Society for workers in industry. Due to the relative shortage of trained medicos in New South Wales, opportunities for a young, energetic doctor were good. Howse was well-aware of such opportunities in rural New South Wales – places where a young medico could make a start.

In Howse's mind, such countryside opportunities were most suitable. His major ambition was to become a well-recognised rural doctor, like his father in Somerset, in a position that was challenging and varied.

Neville was the second of four sons to Dr Alfred Howse, country doctor and a prominent army surgeon in the Crimean War, and his wife Lucy. He had six sisters as well. As an elementary schoolboy at the Free School in Stogursy, Neville was slightly built. He suffered from respiratory ailments growing up. These had recurred at Durham University after he turned twenty-one. A persistent chest condition finally decided him to migrate, despite the career possibilities available at Durham University in Anatomy, a field he was an expert in.

The Making of a Rural Doctor, 1890-1895

Setting up a practice in industrial Newcastle appeared to be a mistaken decision. His respiratory problem had flared up and he decided to move north up the coast to the Manning River. He considered this a paradisal location beside a healthy free-flowing river with a warm semi-tropical climate.

While the region was highly favoured, it was remote and suffered economically from the tyranny of distance from the metropolis. A person suffering a serious farm injury or illness had to be transported on a pitching coastal steamer route or by an unreliable, lengthy land route to Sydney for treatment in hospitals there. The delay in receiving treatment and hospitalisation proved, all too frequently, fatal and was a serious local concern.

The river was another source of danger, especially in flood time. Accidents with farming equipment were frequent. Infectious diseases requiring urgent treatment was another difficulty in the bush.

Faced with such health concerns, the Manning communities united its resources to obtain its own district hospital. But it had been a hard struggle to raise sufficient funds before the Manning River District Hospital could be officially opened on 2 February 1889. The hospital was a potent symbol of progress in the late nineteenth century, especially as a promised railway link by government had not come to fruition. They still had to rely on a small coastal steamer to get to Newcastle and Sydney and this was the mode of travel Howse used.

Dr Herbert Curtayne, a Tasmanian, was the first resident medical officer of the District Hospital. He arrived in 1880 on the Manning after training in England and soon developed a good reputation in the community. There were frequent work accidents and injuries in the mixed farming and timber-getting industries. The District Hospital became a busy place of necessity. The position of the resident doctor was vital to the whole process.

Curtayne was replaced by the young Dr Neville Howse. He acted for a brief period as Curtayne's locum tenens before taking over his position when Curtayne took up a private practice. Howse had arrived with a trunk on the *Rosedale* and had been deposited on the Wingham Wharf at the end of the navigable river at the town of Wingham in 1886. Howse was ill and had to be carried off the steamer.[3]

While convalescing, he stayed with his uncle, Mr John Conroy, the Government Surveyor in Wingham west of Taree. He remained there for about twelve months, even when he started work at the District Hospital. He rode to and fro each day to Taree.

Nevertheless, Howse was soon to establish himself in the District Hospital as a medical man of 'exceptional skill' and even of daring. He gained a reputation for giving praiseworthy attention to his patients. He learnt a lot in the process that would aid his success in his military career.

★ ★ ★

Neville studied medicine at London Hospital, learnt how to amputate a leg or two,
Then ventured north to Durham University as assistant anatomy demonstrator.
Where the sword of Damocles dangled over him
As he coughed flecks of blood from coal-dust-laden lungs.
So he migrated to Australia seeking sunshine, in a lowly-paid Lodge practice in Newcastle.

---

3 John Ramsland, *The Struggle Against Isolation. A History of the Manning River*, Library of Australian History, North Sydney, 1987, 108-12.

He soon realised the Big Smoke was not for him so he
moved up the coast.
A small place like Stogursey he found at Taree beside
the mighty Manning River.
He made his first appearance as locum there and became
the hospital's sole medical officer.
Soon he became a familiar tall horseman on a big
snorting, silver-grey stallion,
In town and country, and up the steep road to the
Comboyne Plateau
To the new dairy farms there in the burning noon.

Ramsland, "The Man on the Silver-Grey Stallion"

The *Rosedale* on which Neville Howse first travelled to Taree (*Australian Town & Country*, 17 April 1886)

Taree was the ideal place for Howse to regain his health. He became physically fit by swimming in the river regularly in the early morning; he did an extensive amount of horseback riding to and from his patients in the countryside and he even played rugby and soccer in local fixtures.

The *Sydney Mail* on 4 August 1894 reported that his brother Dr Oswald Howse arrived on the scene. After migrating, Oswald set up practice in Wingham. He also played with his brother in rugby and soccer fixtures.

Neville's work as a medico was varied. He was required to show versatility – and he did! He was skilled in stitching nasty gashes and flesh wounds, mending broken bones in arms and legs and dealing promptly with serious and remote emergencies.[4]

One case Howse dealt with soon after his arrival was that of the ship's mate on the *Rosedale* who was badly injured on crossing the sand bar at the mouth of the Manning. He fractured his skull on the roof of the cabin. Howse inserted a silver plate in a difficult operation.

Soon after Howse's arrival, he added to his fame by more brilliant surgery. A worker on the breakwater at Harrington at the northern mouth of the river was badly crushed under a large rock. He was brought by horse and cart to the hospital in a serious condition, but still conscious. On examining him, Howse, at first, thought his leg needed amputating military-style, but the patient pleaded saying he would rather have his throat cut than lose a leg. So the doctor promised to do the best he could with a risky treatment as an alternative. The man needed prolonged attention. After twelve months, he left the hospital on both legs unaided, but with a limp.[5] He was able to return to his occupation.

Fame is the Spur

When Howse's brother Oswald set up practice in the government town of Wingham and some other doctors departed for fresh fields, this made the two brothers virtually

---

4 John Ramsland, 'Dedication of the Neville Howse VC Rest Area', *Digger*, no 51, June 2015, 38-42; John Ramsland, 'Neville Howse: Surgeon and War Hero', in Maurie Garland (ed.), *At the Going Down of the Sun. A Manning Valley Remembrance*, vol 1: 1885-1918, Manning Valley Historical Society, 2014, 16-21.

5 Garland (ed.), 'Dr Neville Howse on the Manning', 16.

in control medically of the whole Manning River district from the towns of Nowendoc to Laurieton. They serviced the towns of Wingham and Taree, but also the small villages of Coopernock, Croki, Cundeltown, the Wallamba, Mambo districts and the islands of Mitchell, Oxley and Dumaresq.

★ ★ ★

This required extensive travel on horseback, by sulky as well as using rowboats to the islands of the Manning River. While Howse was not a trained horseman when he first arrived, he soon became a first-class one, an expert in rough and dangerous bush tracks:

> He rode out with his trusty leather bag to the ailing, the injured and the dying.
> The creeks and fords were often fetlock deep as he splashed across on the silver-grey.
> He rode the tracks tough and stony, long and hard.
> Sometimes clouds of squawking galahs barred the way and, then, relentlessly on.
> And thus a shining reputation was made in the timber towns and farms.
> Even when the dark shadows thunder hurtled through the air
> He would ride like the wind and match it
> To every frightened expectant mother or sobbing child.
>
> Ramsland, "The Man on the Silver-Grey Stallion"

During his time in Taree, Howse was to save many lives and was well appreciated for it in the whole community.

There were many examples. On 9 June 1891 in the District Hospital on 'Hospital Hill', Howse performed a dangerous tracheotomy upon a little girl who had got some corn caught in her windpipe which set up an inflammation stopping her breathing and endangering her life. This rendered an urgent operation. After he performed the procedure to allow her to breathe freely, the girl was able to cough up the corn and made a complete recovery. Howse was reported in the press of having saved the little girl's life.[6]

Tommy, an Aboriginal man in the employ of Mr HW Flett, a prominent settler, was felling a tree in early November 1891 in the bush when it fell on his left leg and broke it badly at the ankle. Howse raced to the scene and set the fractured limb.[7] Tommy recovered. Howse was then appointed by the New South Wales Government as the official doctor for the local Aboriginal communities. He was able to develop a special trust with them.

In September 1891, Howse was riding to Landsdowne along a rough bush track to come to the aid of a six-year-old boy who had badly broken his right thigh when his horse put its foot in a hole and suddenly rolled over. On his way there, the doctor fell from his horse, bruising his leg and head and was unconscious for a time. Eventually, he remounted and rode on. He set the infant's limb and put the little sufferer on his horse and took him to the hospital.[8] Howse's fame spread up and down the New South Wales coast as he was reported in newspapers like the *Sydney Mail*, *Maitland Mercury*, *Macleay Argus*, even the *Armidale Express*.

---

6 *Macleay Argus*, 9 June 1891.

7 *Maitland Mercury*, 12 November 1891.

8 *Maitland Mercury*, 8 September 1891.

In 1894, a third Howse brother Percy arrived on the Manning as a temporary locum. Together, they performed a difficult, important operation on a well-known woman resident. With difficulty, they removed a large stone the size of a pigeon's egg from one of her kidneys. She progressed favourably. The *Richmond River Herald* of Lismore on the far north coast claimed: 'There appears to be no limit to the surgical achievements of the Hospital's skilful medical officer whose fame has now become a household word on the North Coast'.[9]

Things were to come to an end for Neville Howse in Taree in June 1895. The *Maitland Mercury* reported:

> A public testimonial will be awarded to Dr NR Howse, who is leaving the Manning for England. The testimonial is to take the form of an address and a purse of sovereigns. During his stay on the Manning he has been considered as a good Samaritan travelling in many instances for long distances in all kinds of weather, at day or night, to the call of sick patients even though he would get nothing for his trouble. His departure is looked upon with great regret by residents of the Manning River.[10]

Such was a newsman's insightful rating of Dr Howse's achievement on the Manning that put him on the most wanted list in affluent regions, like the Central West. The *Maitland Mercury* and the *Sydney Mail* had spread his fame to Newcastle.

Moreover, his rugged experiences in the most difficult of

9 *Richmond River Herald*, 14 December 1894.
10 *Maitland Mercury*, 15 June 1895.

circumstances in fire, floods and storms made him ideal for appointment as a medical officer in a war zone.

His later return to London to pursue postgraduate qualifications and to bring his surgical skills up-to-the-moment proved successful. Three years in its making made him a Fellow of the Royal College of Surgeons (FRCS) which he could place after his name on any plaque – in private or in public practice. In London, he topped the examinations and was first on the list.[11] He intended to return to Australia. He now regarded countryside Australia as his spiritual home. His postgraduate studies in London made him one of the best-qualified surgeons in Australia.

Although he returned to the Manning briefly, he was attracted to the more affluent town of Orange in the Central West where he would be able to set up a financially successful practice that would pay better than the poorer mixed farming and timber industry on the Manning.

A First Victoria Cross Winner in the Boer War?

As Neville Howse was building his private practice in Orange, it was widely reported on Monday, 30 October 1899 which he must have read in the press, that on the previous Saturday patriotic fervour had reached fever pitch in the Sydney population. The NSW contingent of soldiers who were bound for the Transvaal marched gaily through the streets of the city.

It was intended that volunteers from the premier British colony of New South Wales would join troops in South Africa from other Australian colonies as well as a contingent from

11 *Manning River Times*, 8 January 1898.

New Zealand and Canada. Volunteers had been committed by each colony to assist Britain fight the Boer War that had broken out two weeks previously. It was planned that they would fight 'shoulder to shoulder with the mother country' to defend the so-called rights of the British Empire.

The *Sydney Morning Herald* described the huge patriotic crowd which had cheered the soldiers. It was argued that such support demonstrated the eternal mother-country's unbroken links. This motivated Australian men and women to support Britain fight its battle against the rebellious Boers: 'The rain fell in torrents, but it in no way modified the desire of the spectators to participate in the demonstration of loyalty to the Empire that was to be so remarkable a feature of the passing of the troops.' – the *Herald* dutifully reported.

The people in the streets, on every available balcony and in all the windows along the route of the march, waved patriotic support. There was, however, a minority that opposed the military involvement.

When the imperial war broke out in October 1899, Neville Howse had just purchased a practice in Orange, a fine Central West town some 200 kms west of Sydney. On 30 October 1900, the NSW Premier Sir William Lyne and a large parliamentary party visited the town looking at the site as a possibility for the capital of the Australian Commonwealth. A large number of townspeople cheered as the Premier and his colleagues alighted from the train at 7am to the sound of a brass band. Even though it was not to be, Howse thought it an excellent place to put down his roots permanently. He arrived in Orange on 8 November 1899. Eight weeks later, he enlisted into the NSW Army Medical

Corps and was commissioned at the rank of lieutenant. He sailed for South Africa on 17 January 1900 with the Second New South Wales Contingent to leave Sydney.

Before he departed, Howse had been energetic professionally in Orange after taking over the practice of Dr GA Van Somersen, who then promptly proposed the newcomer as medical officer of the hospital. His first innovation was to give a series of lectures for hospital nursing staff who had only some training, or none at all. Other doctors were canvassed to assist him in their fields of expertise. He insisted that end-on examinations always be conducted for each subject that caused some resentment with some doctors who could not be bothered. But in the end, they conformed – he usually got his way with the medicos.

He improved the health environment of the hospital by insisting the windows be opened to let in the fresh country air of the uplands. General cleaning of the hospital was vastly improved.

During November 1899, Howse carried a huge workload at the hospital. This can be measured: the hospital had admitted 19 males and 6 females had been eventually discharged; the total of hospital patients he treated was 48, as well as a further number outside or in day care. The average bed stay at the hospital was eighteen days. Howse saw each patient at least once a day. Nineteen were suffering from typhoid. Diphtheria accounted tragically for some child mortality.

So Dr Neville Howse, from his arrival in Orange, settled into a busy, varied schedule as a surgeon, while continuing a hectic social life as he had done in Taree. He became respected by all except for a few jealous doctors who resented his popularity with patients. He was not afraid to speak out firmly and directly on any controversial issue he felt strongly about – there was a growing public robustness about his personality as he got into his thirties.

He was soon to experience a dangerous and exhausting military campaign over the rugged landscapes of South Africa. In his youth, he had read so avidly about such adventurous things in the Empire.[12] He had had many conversations when he was growing up with his beloved father Albert, who had been involved in the Crimean War and the rigours and challenges that campaign provided.

The two campaign medals Lieutenant (then Captain) Neville Reginald Howse was awarded from the Boer War reveal a nutshell summary of the battles he was involved in. They are the Queen's South African Medal and the King's South African Medal. These symbolise the divide between Queen Victoria and her death and the ascension of King Edward VII to the throne of the imperial power, as well as two chronological phases in the Boer War and the endgame of Lord Kitchener's savage victories over the desperate and poorly treated Boers.

Howse's Queen's South African Medal proudly bears four ornate clasps symbolising the particular campaigns he was present in as a medical officer: 'Cape Colony'; 'Johannesburg'; 'Diamond Hill', and 'Witteberger'. His King's medal holds two generic rather than campaign clasps: 'South Africa 1901' and 'South Africa 1902'.[13]

12 Michael B Tyquin, *Neville Howse. Australia's First Victoria Cross Winner*, Oxford University Press, Melbourne, 1999, 1-8.

13 Nine miniature medals, Maj Gen Sir Neville Howse, VC, RELAWM 16321.

When, on 17 January 1900, Howse was appointed to the NSW Army Medical Corps as a lieutenant, he was thirty-five years of age with two major experiences as a rural surgeon and country doctor under his belt. Attached to a unit of engineers, he sailed with them from Sydney and arrived in Cape Town just before the British defeated and captured Cronje's Army in Paardeberg.[14]

On arrival in Cape Town on 18 February. Howse was ill with typhoid and hospitalised for eight weeks, thus missing the first action in which NSW medical officers were engaged. After recovering, he was posted to General Hamilton's unit for the advance to Pretoria during May and June 1900.[15]
The Second Contingent to which Howse belonged was made up of nine military and medical officers and 85 other ranks, mainly troopers with 52 horses, 5 ambulance wagons and 12 carts – all of which came across on the *Moravian.* The mounted stretcher-bearers unit came across on the *Southern Cross* – two officers, 23 other ranks, with 33 horses and 6 carts. Of these, 2 men eventually died and 11 officers and 106 others soon returned, apparently as surplus to requirements or unfit for frontline action.

Even at this stage, the Medical Corps was a complex organisation within the army with much transport to move as quickly as possible from place to place in a rapidly-changing

14 Sir Kingsley Norris, *Annual Post-Graduate Oration. Major-General Sir Neville Howse VC*, reprinted from the *Bulletin* of the Post-Graduate Committee in Medicine, University of Sydney, vol 22, no 11, February 1967, 214-36.

15 Eric Richardson, 'The Manning's Victoria Cross Connection 24th July 1900 at Vredefort, Orange Free State', Typed MS, Manning Valley Historical Society, Wingham.

Officers of the NSW Army Medical Corps; on right Lieutenant Neville Reginald Howse before the frontline incident that won him the first Australian Victoria Cross. (NLA Tyquin 68-9)

war. Two other medical contingents were to follow as the war progressed.

The whole of the Military and Medical Corps in the Second Contingent were 30 officers, some of them doctors like Howse, 338 other ranks, some of them orderlies and stretcher-bearers, including those on horseback, cart and carriage drivers and horse wranglers, 16 ambulance wagons and 46 carts (that is, transport wagons) that had to move with the troops or follow in their tracks. They virtually included a fully-equipped mobile hospital managed by officers – doctors like Howse. The other essential was a section of women nurses strictly trained under the Nightingale Scheme made up of a Lady Superintendent and 13 volunteer nurses. The doctor officers supervised their crucial work in saving lives. Among the officers, eight were eventually promoted, one being Neville Howse, from lieutenant to Captain of the Australian Army Medical Corps (AAMC) after he had won the Victoria Cross.[16]

16 Lieutenant-Colonel PL Murray, *Official Records of the Australian Military Contingents to the War in South Africa*, Govt Printer, Melbourne, 1911.

The Second Contingent took part in operations: Transvaal and Orange River to 31 May 1902; action at Vet River, Zand River Johannesburg, Pretoria, Diamond Hill and Belfast. As related, Howse won the Queen's Medal with six clasps, more than any other officer, military or medical in the Second Contingent. He returned to South Africa with the AAMC after Federation until 1902,[17] with an extraordinary level of keenness, responsibility and patriotism. He was, indeed, the absolute Empire man.

With Howse all the way from Taree to Orange to South Africa and back to Orange was Alfred Henderson Polson, Howse's faithful horse handler or wrangler and carriage driver.

Alfred was the only son of William Angus and Annie Polson who held land on Oxley Island on the Manning. They were a well-known family with Aboriginal connections. When Alfred was eight years of age, the family moved to Taree where they ran a boarding house for workers.

After leaving school, young Alfred went to work for Dr Neville Howse. A very deep personal friendship developed between the doctor and his personal horse handler and batman over the years. After the Boer War, Alfred became employed as a dispensary assistant in Howse's practice in Orange – a position he held for thirteen years before he came back to the Manning and lived in retirement on a farm at Pampoolah with his wife Christina Cameron.

January 1900 and February 1901 show Dr Howse's engagement in the South African War. Some records show that Alfred was with him on an unofficial personal basis

17 Murray, *Official Records.*

caring for his horses.[18] It has been reasonably claimed that Alfred was there when Howse committed the act of gallantry saving the life of the young wounded trumpeter, Sidney Berkeley.

Later, Alfred Henderson Polson (No 1351) stretcher-bearer was registered in the nominal roll of the Commonwealth Contingent in official papers, which at least proved his presence in South Africa.

The Act of Gallantry: Australian First VC Winner

During the conflict at the village of Vrefort, the Australian Mounted Infantry Brigade, under Brigadier-General CP Ridley to which Howse was attached, received information from spies on 24 July 1900 that the wily General Christian De Wet and his elusive commando had passed through during the previous evening. They had commandeered men, food supplies and horses from the village. Australian mounted troops sped after the enemy and captured grain wagons lagging behind De Wet's fast-moving commando.

On hearing gunfire, De Wet quickly mustered a force to return and met the allied troops near the large Stinkhoutboom farm house. A sharp clash ensued. Boer pom-pom artillery was added to the heavy exchange of gunfire. Ridley's mounted infantry engaged the Boer commandoes. They included the NSW Mounted Rifles working with men from other British and Commonwealth units. The Army Medical Corps set themselves up in the Stinkhoutboom farm house where the British had captured exhausted Boers who were asleep in bed still fully clothed. They were made prisoners-of-war.

18 Dr Phil, <phil_rutherford@ozemail.com.au>, 26/6/19.

De Wet had sent back a party of Danie Theron's Scouts to carry out the counter-attack supported by the two pom-pom guns that opened fire from concealed positions on higher ground to the right. As a leader, Theron was daring and resourceful and had 400 men picked for their skill in horsemanship and marksmanship. They were up against a combined British force of about 600. The battle was fought on an open plain. The Boers 'charged magnificently' and some got to within two-hundred paces of the enemy. They then dismounted and, lying on the ground, 'opened a fierce fire'. Their horses had been placed in a hollow behind them. [19]

Howse was observing the action that took place in about an hour's duration. Several hundred men from both sides were engaged near the farm less than 200 metres away from him. At first, Ridley's mounted troops found it impossible to hold the ground due to the concealed heavy guns and were forced to retreat in an orderly fashion with one of the captured grain wagons as some protection from the guns.

The climax of the battle came when Ridley's two pom-pom guns belatedly arrived and began firing at the Boer position, thus forcing them to withdraw leaving behind seventeen casualties, including two dead men. The British and Commonwealth Force suffered 39 casualties, including three South Australians killed and several wounded. The engagement as a whole, however, was principally notable for the heroic act of Lieutenant Neville Howse at the height of the battle.[20]

---

19 ·Stuart Braga, *Anzac Doctor, The Life of Sir Neville Howse Australia's First VC*, Hale & Iremonger, Sydney, 2000, 64-66.

20 Chris Coulthard-Clark, *The Encyclopaedia of Australia's Battles*, Allen and Unwin, Crows Nest 1998, 83-84.

As he watched, Howse noticed a young trumpeter fall about 200 metres away in the foremost line of a cavalry charge at the enemy. At the time, the crossfire between the two opposing forces was extreme; bullets were flying everywhere with gay abandon.

Despite the dangers, Howse did not hesitate, but immediately mounted his silver-grey stallion that was already saddled up by Alfred Polson, his faithful retainer. Howse galloped flamboyantly onto the exposed battlefield to rescue young Sidney Berkeley. Halfway to him, Howse's prized stallion was shot from under him despite the fact he was wearing the Red Cross armband.

Howse ran on, doggedly, weaving as best he could to the stricken soldier. He reached him and coolly dressed the young man's wound caused by a stray bullet through his bladder. Howse, a powerful man, lifted the small young bugler onto his shoulders and, in short bursts, reached safety behind the grain wagon.

William Dargie's painting. The incident for which Neville Howse was awarded his VC at Vredefort, July 1900 (AWM ART29246)

As Sidney's wound was serious, Howse carried him to the old farmhouse where he examined the injury more carefully on the kitchen table. He then operated on the perforated bladder. He knew what to do in such an emergency from his Manning River experiences in the bush.

His spectacular actions soon attracted a recommendation for the Victoria Cross from his superiors.

The *London Gazette* citation of 4 June 1901 several months later read more boldly and succinctly that Howse went out under heavy fire and picked up a wounded man and carried him to a place of shelter. The military investigation Howse received in written form revealed much more detail:

> At the height of the fighting, Lieutenant Neville House saw a trumpeter fall wounded in the foremost line and galloped out under extremely heavy fire to rescue the man. Howse dismounted, treated the man's wound, and carried him out of the action. According to some accounts, Howse's horse was shot from under him before he reached the trumpeter, while other accounts say the horse was shot after Howse dismounted. The Victoria Cross was the first awarded to an Australian soldier and remains the only one received by a qualified medical member of the Australian forces. Although his citation gives his rank as 'captain', Howse was a lieutenant at the time.[21]

This statement clarifies the event as far as the facts are known. The VC Committee did not hesitate to award the supreme decoration of gallantry in battle to Dr Neville Reginald Howse.

Of the Victoria Crosses awarded to men in the Australian military forces, Howse's VC had been, as related, the sole one awarded to a qualified medical officer and the first occasion the VC was awarded to a member of the Australian (then

21 Cited in Anthony Staunton, *Victoria Cross. Australia's Finest & the Battles they fought*, Hardie Grant Books, Prahran, 2006, 3.

the NSW) Military Forces in action during a declared war.[22]

The 'old fox' De Wet escaped this fierce encounter, but several were seriously wounded on both sides and were all cared for by Neville Howse and his team within the old homestead Stinkhoutboom near Vredefort. Enemies lay side by side in the makeshift hospital.

Within a few weeks, Howse was promoted to the rank of captain and continued with his mounted unit. Later, during a fairly similar type of encounter near Rustenburg, having operated under heavy fire on a badly wounded officer in a kopie, Howse gallantly volunteered to remain behind in the small temporary field hospital as the enemy came forward and the division had to retreat.

Howse was taken prisoner where his health rapidly deteriorated under the appalling conditions. He fell ill with typhoid symptoms and was invalided from Cape Town aboard the *Orotava*, which docked at Southampton on 28 November 1901. He returned to Australia when he recovered. Then, he went back to the South African War as part, this time, of the Australian Medical Corps, as an honorary major in February 1902.[23] In the London *Times* of 9 July 1902, he was listed as 'Major RN Howse Aust. AMC'.

In the South African War, the Australian soldiers were well regarded for an ability to shoot straight while riding on horseback even though the majority of Australian troopers had received no training. They were sent almost straightaway into battle on their arrival. The fighting conditions, as

---

22 John Ramsland, 'Australia's first Victoria Cross Winner. Sir Neville Howse, Rural and Military Doctor, 1863-1930', *Medal News*, vol 55, no 6, June/July 2017, 24-27.

23 Ramsland, 'Australia's first Victoria Cross', 26.

Howse was later to reveal, were very harsh for both riders and their horses. Many British and Colonial soldiers died of disease, exhaustion and starvation on long treks of 3,000 kilometres, or more. In a harsh war, Australian troopers were used in sweeping the countryside, preventing Boer commandoes from returning to their farms and families in the countryside.

The Boer farms, homes and livestock were ruthlessly destroyed and the inhabitants – women, children and old folk – were imprisoned in unsanitary concentration camps where thousands died.

'I pitied the women and children who knelt before us and begged and prayed that their houses and food might not be destroyed, but it was an order, and my finer and humanitarian instincts had to be sacrificed …', wrote Captain DJ Ham, the Commander of the Victorian Bushmen Regiment, in such a situation where Kitchener wanted to end the war by the most ruthless means possible.[24]

Around 16,000 Australians fought in the Boer War. Of this, more Australian soldiers died of disease (286) than those killed in combat (282).[25]

* * *

Neville Howse was one of six Australian Victoria Cross winners in the South African War.

---

24 RL Wallace, *The Australians at the Boer War*, Australian War Memorial, Canberra, 1976, 303.

25 Peter O'Meara and Scott Deverish, 'Sir Neville Howse (VC) Private John Simpson Kilpatrick and Private Martin O'Meara (VC) and their contribution to Australian military medicine', *Australian Journal of Paramedicine*, vol 8, issue 1, 3.

But he was to become the most honoured. At the war's end, he was 37 and was to live another thirty eventful years, becoming Mayor of Orange and leaving that public office to hastily enlist in 1914 to seize German New Guinea (Kaiser Wilhelm's Land). Joining the AIF at the last moment, he landed at Gallipoli on the first day to set up the first field hospital beside the beach. As the war progressed, he became Surgeon-General and Director of independent Medical Services for the AIF.

After the war, he turned to Federal politics as the member for Calare in the National Party, serving in the Cabinet three times. In addition to his VC, Howse was created a Knight Commander of the Bath, Knight Commander of St Michael and St George and a Knight of the Grace of the Order of St John of Jerusalem.

★ ★ ★

While he became the most honoured of the six Australian VCs of the Boer War, the others showed they were not men for whom a single act of bravery was enough. They were: Lieutenant Frederick William Bell of the 6th Mounted Infantry; Trooper John Hutton Bisdee of the 1st Tasmanian Imperial Bushmen; Lieutenant Leslie Maygar of the Victorian Mounted Rifles; Sergeant James Rogers of the South African Constabulary and Lieutenant Guy Wylly, another of the 1st Tasmanian Imperial Bushmen.

Both Trooper Bisdee and Lieutenant Wylly were awarded the Victoria Cross for their part in an action on 1 September at Warmbad in the Transvaal. They were awarded the VC before Howse as they were gazetted in November 1900, whereas Howse's award was not gazetted until 4 June 1901, more than ten months later. Despite the delay, Howse, in terms of the actual gallant event – 24 July 1900 – was still the first VC award, chronologically, to a man serving in an Australian unit. He had been recommended by General William Birdwood and Brigadier-General CP Ridley, his commanding officer. To receive endorsements by two generals was a rare event, indeed, and not possible to fail.[26]

All six winners of the VC shared similar or related experiences on their way to the Victoria Cross. Each one rode into heavy enemy fire, sometimes to go to the rescue of their comrades. Like Howse, both Bisbee and Wylly went to the rescue of wounded comrades. Each of the six either lost his horse to gunfire or took a wounded man's horse. Each one acted with cool courage and each lived to have some significant success in civilian life or as a professional soldier.

Maygar, who was born in Kilmore, Victoria, volunteered in the AIF in 1914 and served on Gallipoli, like Howse. He rose through the ranks to command the 8th Light Horse and as colonel was a temporary commander of the 3rd Light Horse Brigade in South Africa. He died of his wounds in 1917 from an attack by an enemy plane at Beersheba.

Bell, who was born in 1875 in Perth, joined the British Colonial Service in Somaliland and became a notable big-game hunter. He enlisted again in 1914 with the Royal Irish Dragoon Guards. By 1918, he was a lieutenant-colonel commanding an embarkation camp. He returned to Kenya

26 Braga, *Anzac Doctor*, 67.

in Africa after the 1914–1918 War and served in the Colonial Service until retirement. He died in Bristol in 1954.

Bisdee, born in Tasmania in 1869, remained in the regular Australian Army. In 1915 he volunteered for overseas on 25 July and was given the command of the 12th Light Horse as a major, was wounded in the leg, then served as assistant provost marshal in Egypt. He had a spell back in the 12th and was promoted to lieutenant-colonel and was second in command of the Anzac Provost Corps. His VC in the Boer War was followed by an OBE in World War I. He retired from military life to his family farm in Tasmania until his death in 1930.

Rogers, who was born in 1873 on the Murray River in NSW, was commissioned as a lieutenant in the regular Australian Army in 1902. He fought at Gallipoli and was wounded there. Like Bisdee, he served in the Anzac Provost Corps until he was invalided in 1916 with the honorary rank of captain. He stayed with the reserve officers until 1922 and then ran a grazing property until his death in 1961 in Concord Repatriation Hospital, Sydney.

Wylly, who was born in Hobart in 1880, transferred to the Indian Army in 1902. In 1909, he was appointed as aide-de-camp to Lord Kitchener. He served as a staff captain and then a brigade major in the Great War with the Indian Cavalry Division in France. He was badly wounded in the face, but posted as a staff officer with the Australian troops from mid-1916. He was awarded a DSO in January 1918 and went back after the war to the Indian Army on the North-West Frontier until retirement from active service as an honorary colonel in 1933. He died in Camberley, aged

82 in 1962. Like Howse, he was created Companion of the Order of the Bath.[27]

Howse's Award at the Victoria Barracks

On 5 December 1901, the *Sydney Telegraph* reported a ceremony at the Victoria Barracks, Paddington:

> Yesterday was a red-letter day in the military annals of New South Wales. In the midst of a brilliant assemblage, Captain Howse of the New South Wales Medical Corps, had pinned upon him by the Lieutenant-Governor, Sir Frederick Darley, the coveted bronze Cross.[28]

Neville Howse had already received his campaign medals. Queen Victoria had authorised a silver campaign medal for the war in South Africa – "The Queen's Medal" with a ribbon of red, white, blue and orange to bear clasps embossed with the names of each major battle in which he served. King Edward VIII authorised a similar medal with a ribbon of green, white and yellow – "The King's Medal". Howse received both, with six clasps on his "Queen's" and two on his "King's".

After the ceremony at the Sydney Barracks, Howse returned in triumph by train to Orange, on 22 February, still in uniform and wearing his medals. Almost the whole population and a brass band were at the station to meet him. The thudding drums were almost drowned by the cheering crowd. His life was never to be the same; they were welcoming a thirty-seven-year-old conquering hero at the prime of his life. The *Bulletin* in June 1901 proclaimed:

27 Kit Denton, *For Queen and Commonwealth*, Time-Life Books, Australia, 1987, 135; Staunton, *Victoria Cross*, 7.

28 Norris, *Annual Post-Graduate Oration*, 217.

> Surgeon-Captain Howse, of NSW military medical staff, who has just been gazetted VC (for recovering a wounded man, under heavy fire, at Vredfort S'Africa is an Englishman who has been for a dozen years resident in NSW. Dr Howse, after been invalided to England, has now resumed practice at Orange, NSW.[29]

Fame and prestige were to remain with him for the rest of his life. Such was the lasting achievement of the award of the Victoria Cross in capable and responsible ambitious hands.

The award of the VC not only acknowledges 'extraordinary deeds of great bravery', but also provides leadership and example to all. The entire nation drew pride and inspiration from such as Neville Reginald Howse. The VC was quite simply the 'highest form of recognition' available to all ranks of society for unselfish courage in the face of the enemy.

The prominent Australian artist William Dargie captured in oils the exciting incident showing Howse carrying the wounded Sidney to safety. It hangs in the Australian War Memorial in Canberra and maintains Howse's fame well after his death.[30] His photographic portrait even appeared on an Australian postage stamp in 2000.

"There's no place like home", Orange 1902-1914

Neville Howse, as a renowned war champion of the British Empire, returned to Orange. For the great majority of district denizens, his return was as the all-conquering hero, even before the news of the award of the Victoria Cross had filtered through in the media.

---

29 *Bulletin*, 15 June 1901, 13.

30 Peter Burness, 'The Victoria Cross in Australia', *Conflict*, issue 46, July 2009, 16; also William Dargie's oil painting, AWM ART 29246.

Howse remained dedicated to Empire. After all, he had been politically educated at the height of the Victorian Age and its colonial triumphs in war.

Nevertheless, he viewed Orange and the surrounding fertile countryside as his permanent safe haven; a place he could lay down his roots, where he could achieve much and continue to receive fame as a dedicated rural doctor and surgeon during peacetime. He realised and feared that the world would soon be split asunder by the militarism and the Arms Race of rival European Empires of Russia, Germany and Austria-Hungary all of which, ironically, had eagles as warlike symbols on their flags.

As well as keeping up-to-date reading medical texts ordered through Angus and Robertson books store in Sydney, he maintained an eye on international political affairs, particularly those concerning Great Britain. He was also enjoying immersing himself in the local social life – what his youngest daughter much later called becoming an 'Authentic Australian'.[31] He was a public figure and leader in the district.

In a speech to a crowd on his first return from South Africa, Howse claimed with patriotic enthusiasm for what he had witnessed about the military exploits of the Australian Contingent in South Africa and was able to give them much praise as soldiers, particularly as fighting horsemen and riflemen. He gave a public commitment in the Orange Town Hall, at the age of forty, that 'if ever another war broke out, he hoped he would be one of the accepted men'. This is a clear statement of future intention.

31 Alison Neville Starr, *Neville Howse VC. Biography of an Authentic Australian*, self-published, Sydney, 1991.

He went on to tell his audience that he felt even prouder of his adopted country than his country of birth, but he added they coalesced. Significantly, the meeting concluded with a roaring three cheers for King Edward VII who had only just come to the throne after Queen Victoria's death. [32]

For the sixty-four-year-old monarch – yet to be tried – they sang "God Save the King" for the first time since mid-nineteenth century. The Victorian Age had ended, but many of its values remained in the Edwardian Age that followed.

The 'genial' doctor settled well into civilian life again. He had gained the 'good opinion of men' by his brave acts in South Africa.[33] He successfully applied for one of two surgical positions at the Orange Hospital where he had worked before going to imperial glory. Several local doctors had also applied, so a ballot was required. The committee voted 11 for Howse, 6 for Bray and four others got minor scores. It was competitive, but decisive for Howse. He relished the success.

While in civilian life both professionally and socially in Orange, Howse managed to maintain his interests in military affairs, especially as he began to have prolonged legal battles with the British colonial authorities.

His difficult dealings with the imperial paymaster began in late 1902. He pointed out that, while on his second tour-of-duty, he had been entitled to pay at 25/- a day plus his VC annual grant; he had actually been paid a captain's pay of 12/-. He was entitled to daily pay for his time in London while convalescing as an army officer in hospital.

To his annoyance, the wheels of 'the War Office' turned

32 Braga, *Anzac Doctor*, 79-80.

33 *Orange Leader*, 9 Feb 1901, cited in Tyquin, *Neville Howse*, 23.

slowly'. On 23 June 1903, Howse was obliged to write to the Military Pay Department stating that he did not receive one penny he was owed while on service in South Africa, or while in London with the exception of the VC gratuity allowance. He had received £374, leaving £318 14s 4d outstanding. This was a fairly large sum owing him at that time. He continued to battle this issue until 19 September 1905 when it was resolved.[34] It had given him some fairly important hardship in return for his loyalty to the Crown and his outstanding wartime record. He was not a man to be trifled with and always stood his ground firmly.

During the early 1900s, regular reports in the *Orange Leader* of Howse's achievements in operating on local folk consolidated his fame as a local hero. Some operations had to be carried out on kitchen tables in remote homesteads in emergencies which reminded him of his South African exploits. He charmed many patients, colleagues and, especially, local ladies of all ages.

Evelyn Gertrude Northcote Pilcher found him so attractive as a mature forty-one-year-old local hero that she decided to accept his marriage proposal. They had 'kept company' almost since his first settling in Orange. Evelyn was the reserved twenty-seven-year-old daughter of George de Vial Pilcher, a well-regarded Orange solicitor. The couple were married at 8pm on 31 January 1905 in the drawing room at 'Orton Park' in Bathurst, the residence of Evelyn's grandfather, Charles Macphillamy. On their marriage certificate, Neville Reginald Howse was described as a 'Surgeon' of Orange, a bachelor of 41 years and Evelyn Gertrude Northcote Pilcher

34 Tyquin, *Neville Howse*, 27.

was described as a 'Gentlewoman' and 'Spinster' of 29 years, the daughter of George de Vial Pilcher, 'Solicitor', and Emily Smith Macphillamy. The couple were married according to the rites of the Presbyterian Church. Neville declared his place of birth as 'Stogursy, Somersetshire'. Neville's cousin on his mother's side from Wingham, JM Conroy, signed the Certificate with Charles Macphillamy and G de V Pilcher.

By 1911, Neville Howse decided to move his family, which then included four children: Everil ("Eril") born 1906; Neville Charles ("Cha") born 1909; Evelyn ("Garda") and John born in 1913 – a little out of Orange on a 3,000 acre property, "Suma Park".[35]

Howse had become active in local politics. As a decorated major of middle-age prosperity, he remained an ambitious and patriotic Empire man who enjoyed the challenges of life. He was mayor of Orange on three occasions. He was conscious of current international affairs while practising medicine. He was well-aware of the 15 January 1900 Bubonic plague in Adelaide and, a few days later, in the Miller's Point/ "Rocks" and lower George Street in Sydney and the government efforts to contain it while he was soldiering in South Africa.

On 1 March 1904, Howse noted that the Commonwealth Defence Act came into being setting up a volunteer reserve army and empowering the government to conscript men between the ages of 18 and 60 for military duty in time of war. Such service was limited to within the Commonwealth territory – Howse realised he could play a role in the military.

35 Braga, *Anzac Doctor*, 81-83; Tyquin, *Neville Howse*, 28-29. A fifth child, Alison Neville, was born in 1915 when her father was on active service in Gallipoli.

He understood the significance of the 31 August agreement that was reached to align Russia, France and Britain against the triple Alliance between Germany, Austria-Hungary and Italy. While Italy turned to the Allied side and was replaced on the Central Powers of Germany and Austria-Hungary side by the Ottoman Empire of Turkey. He could see the great fault-line with potential for a European war on the evidence of the developing armaments race in all these European countries that might engulf the British Colonial Empire with the Mother-home.

The rapid flow of international events continued to fill Howse's thinking as his worked as a surgeon. Within 1907 alone, Lenin was exiled from Russia, but Britain granted New Zealand the status of a Dominion which carried with it military responsibilities and Baden Powell, another heroic figure in South Africa, founded the Boy Scout Movement that provided a form of military training for the very young. The movement spread rapidly across the British Empire.

On 8 April ship-to-ship wireless telegraphing was first used in Australian waters when the German mail steamer *Bremen* notified HMS *Encounter* on her arrival time in Sydney Harbour. This was for peaceful means, but could revolutionise wartime in the watery world of the oceans.

In 1909, Howse noticed that the Fisher Labor Government ordered three British-built destroyers in an attempt to create an Australian naval squadron for military purposes. By 28 June, the Imperial Conference in London agreed to the establishment of an independent Australian naval fleet. On 8 December, Prime Minister Alfred Deakin consolidated this decision by ordering the construction of the battle cruiser HMAS *Australia*.[36]

Towards the year's end, military training for men and boys was made universal and compulsory introduced by the Deakin government under the Defence Act. The trainees were divided into cadets – junior cadets, boys between 12 and 14, and senior cadets from 14 to 18 years of age – as well as citizen forces (18-20). They were paid on days spent in official training camps along with reserve forces up to the age of 26. There was some political opposition, but enlarging compulsory military training was considered important by the majority of the community.

With a great deal of fanfare, Field Marshal Lord Kitchener of Khartoum arrived on 23 December. Howse would have remembered that Kitchener ground down the resistance of the Boers by interning civilians in concentration camps, burning their farms and building 8,000 blockhouses to prevent the Boer troops from moving freely across the countryside. The end of the Boer War in May 1902 was a victory largely because of Kitchener's ruthless methodological perseverance.[37]

Kitchener was in Australia to advise on the nature of the new Australian military forces under invitation of the Deakin Government. He came to observe and evaluate the reserves of Australian personnel and their armaments. He swiftly released his report by 18 February 1910 that claimed Australia needed a force of 80,000 troops to ensure its national security. One half was to defend the capital cities; the other to be a mobile strike force. He pointed out that

36 *Morton Bay Courier* to the *Courier Mail*, 1846-1992, Portside Edition, Fishermen's Bend, Vicotria, 1992, 91-94.

37 Braga, *Anzac Doctor*, 48.

the present force of 29,000 was quite inadequate in number, organisation and munitions of war to defend Australia. Nevertheless, he praised the fighting spirit of Australians in the field during the South African War as he recalled it.[38]

★ ★ ★

While being aware of the military events and the build-up of Australian militarism, Neville Howse structured his great success in Orange on the basis of being an eminent surgeon and supportive rural doctor. He invited his younger brother Cyril Beresford Howse, who was always known as "Jack", to join his rapidly growing practice. Just like Neville, Jack had gained his postgraduate Fellowship of the Royal College of Surgeons (FRCS) in London. He had served in the Boer War in a British unit, the Royal Army Medical Corps. He accepted Neville's invitation to immigrate and arrived in Australia in 1909. Like Neville, Jack became a reservist in the Australian Army Medical Corps.

When Jack arrived in Orange for a while, he became Neville's third partner in his practice. Dr Arthur Colvin joined at about the same time and was well qualified as a medical practitioner. Like his senior partner, Colvin was to have a distinguished record of service in World War I as well as being the Mayor of Orange. The three doctors gained the respect of the community at large with distinguished careers, but Neville Howse was, without question, the leader of the pack.

Living in the first decade of the twentieth century,

38 *Australia Through Time. 126 Years of Australia's History*, Random House, Sydney, 1994, 181-2; Bill Gammage, *The Broken Years. Australia's Soldiers in the Great War*, Melbourne University Press, 2010, 32.

these medicos saw the decline of the horse and buggy era which gave way to the introduction of the motor vehicle. Neville and Jack fell in love with fast motor cars and were often noticed speeding around the township and on the connecting roads in the rich sheep and wheat countryside – sometimes, but not always, racing to medical emergencies. Neville drove an imported 191 L Darracq, a touring car suitable for rough country roads, and Jack a Benz. As there were few motor vehicles on the road in the district, they demonstrated a good level of prosperity in their practice.[39]

Cyril (Jack) Howse would spend thirty-nine years in practice in Orange, marrying Marjorie Bowman of Bathurst in 1915. Unlike Oswald and Neville, he did not go to the 1914-1918 European War. He was a government medical officer from 1927 to his death in September 1947. Like Neville, he was a deft and skilled surgeon who was an early exponent, like Neville, of modern abdominal surgery. In South Africa in 1900, he served in the colours as Regimental Medical Officer of the 11th Battalion, Middlesex and Kent Imperial Yeomanry and was mentioned in despatches. He wrote several articles on his war experiences in the *London Hospital Gazette*.[40]

The Drums of War

During 1914, the war clouds were fast gathering in Europe and Howse was closely following events taking place on the other side of the world. One of his biographers claimed extravagantly: 'His feet were itching, pawing the ground

39 Braga, *Anzac Doctor*, 84-85.
40 Tyquin, *Neville Howse*, 28-29.

like those of an old war horse at the trumpet. On the day war was declared, Howse left by train to offer his services to Major-General Williams, the Director of Army Medical Service.'[41] This was not exactly so, but perhaps the spirit of the situation was neatly captured.

At the start of the war, Howse was into his second term of office as mayor. A surgeon of his abilities attracted paying middle-class patients from a wide area and he was involved in honorary work in Orange Hospital. He was looked upon by his medico colleagues as a leader. There were, however, a few pockets of professional jealousy, even about his popularity with ordinary people of the rural population. His wife and her family were distinguished locals and Howse had a wide circle of influential friends among Central West graziers and wheat growers. He was always in attendance at stockyard sales, agricultural shows and important social events in the town. At the age of fifty in 1914, he was still gregarious and a great charmer, whereas his wife remained reserved and content with quiet home life.

Early on 10 August 1914, an urgent telephone call from Sydney was made to Howse's residence. He was not there as he was performing an urgent abdominal operation on a remote property. On his return, rather tired, he found the message from Colonel Ernest Townshend Wallack Commander of the 2nd military district (ie the NSW division) requesting him to contact Victoria Barracks urgently. He returned the call. He was asked whether he would like to be the medical officer for an urgent overseas expedition to German New Guinea being raised: 'If you want to go, and are prepared to get off

41 Norris, *Annual Post-Graduate*, 218.

promptly, come down and see me tomorrow morning'.

Howse decided immediately and then discussed it with his pregnant wife Evelyn. She showed concern about his being involved in what could be a dangerous circumstance at his age, but acquiesced, no doubt understanding his driven nature.

His war service in the South African War, his seniority and rank in the Australian Army Medical Corps reserve and his Victoria Cross meant he was an obvious person on any list for urgent recall to the colours.

Howse hastily reassigned his operating schedule to his partners, packed a bag, said "goodbye" to his family and managed to board the Sydney overnight train with a minute to spare. Arriving in Sydney the next morning at 9.30, he headed straight for the Barracks. In the office of Colonel Fiachi, he was offered the post of Assistant Director of Medical Services (ADMS) to accompany a small expeditionary force to tropical New Guinea. Howse would have preferred to accompany the AIF to Europe, but Colonel Charles Ryan had already been appointed to that position.[42]

Fiaschi managed to win Howse over to the tropical expedition by upgrading his appointment to Principal Medical Officer with the rank of lieutenant-colonel. Howse accepted and signed up, aged 50 years and nine months. It was a full-time commission. He was recorded as being 5ft 10 inches (178cm) and weighing 12 stone (70kg). His wife was given as next-of-kin, his address as Suma [Station] Orange and his occupation as 'Surgeon at Orange NSW'. In answer to the question of military experience, he referred to the

42 Tyquin, *Neville Howse*, 30-31; Braga, *Anzac Doctor*, 93-94; Howse Papers, AWM 2DRL331, Item 44.

South African war and his rank of major in the Australian Army Medical Corps (AAMC), but not to the award of the Victoria Cross.[43]

Under Howse's direct command in the Australian Naval and Military Expeditionary Force (AN&MEF) were three young medical officers: Captain (later Colonel) FA Maguire, who had given Howse his medical examination on his enlistment, and two recent graduates from Sydney University: Captains Brian CA Pockley[44] and JE Donaldson, both having recently received commissions in the AAMC (Military). There were thirty-five other ranks of the AAMC in the proposed tropical expedition: stretcher-bearers, hospital orderlies, and the like. Most of these men were chosen because of their St John Ambulance first aid qualifications or nursing experience. Howse was quickly able to unite the medical officers in effective team work. He provided thorough training and focus under the circumstances for the other ranks of the AAMC. He made his presence felt with powerful, but supportive leadership and decisiveness of action throughout his energetic involvement in the New Guinea Campaign. He soon realised it would become a garrison sideshow to the war in Europe. Howse had six days to make his AAMC ready for action.

Volunteers of the entire AN&MEF were attested at the Royal Sydney Showground and underwent thorough medical examinations by the medical officers. In two busy days, 1,106 men were sworn in and inoculated against

43 Application for a Commission in the AIF, Neville Reginald Howse, 14 August 1914.

44 See Chapter 2 for details concerning Pockley's death-in-action as the first Australian to fall in the Great War.

typhoid,[45] a procedure far from standard in that period.

From his arrival at the Victoria Barracks, Howse lost no time in organising his corps for the tropical expedition. He aimed to protect the lives of about a thousand military and five hundred naval fighting personnel presently camped at the showground. He took direct personal charge of medical arrangements with vigour and initiative as he was to do in the next four years of the Great War,

Together with his three medical officers working as a harmonious team, he examined and inoculated the men. Two anti-inoculations were given: the first in the Showground camp and the second on board the transport *Berrima* on its way north. Howse also had the fighting men inoculated aboard ship for smallpox. These were lessons well-learned the hard way by Howse in South Africa.

Maguire and Howse prepared other medical concerns before departure as there had been little forward planning in terms of medical support for the operation, because of the urgent and insistent call of the motherland to the rescue of the Empire in the Pacific. Howse was later to report stoutly:

> We were given very little information of the medical conditions that we would probably experience, nor were we told the number of stations we should have to form, the facilities for medical treatment e.g. if there were hospitals at Herbertshöhe, etc. The Defence Department should have prepared and supplied me with all such information, so that I could have made my arrangements.

Howse sent his number "Two", Maguire, scouting Sydney

45 Tyquin, *Neville Howse*, 31.

stores to find and procure supplies of quinine to prevent malaria as well as mosquito nets and other tropical medical supplies. He succeeded as best he could.

No provision had been made for a dentist, so Neville Howse obtained a university student in his final year in dentistry, JK Henderson, who had to bring his own equipment with him. He came highly recommended by the Faculty's Dean. Howse deliberately bypassed military procedure. He was delighted with such challenges. His aim was to make sure Australia's first fighting force were as fit as he could personally make them. He had a good eye for detail for what was required.

When the force sailed for Townsville on 19 August 1914 on the P&O liner *Berrima*, he had the vessel thoroughly cleaned and fumigated beforehand, knowing that it would be crowded. 'There was little disease on the voyage apart from a few mild colds and flu and one case of pneumonia. There were no others and no infectious diseases… Before landing five grams of quinine was given to every man.'[46]

Howse had no experience of tropical medicine *in situ*, but he had read the latest medical texts on the subject. He prepared printed lectures on malaria, heat stroke and dysentery and distributed copies among the men to read, understand and pass on.

On 11 September 1914, Brian Pockley was shot through the spine early in the day of the first battle while working with the troops at the Front. He later died that day aboard the *Berrima*. Howse held him in high regard as a courageous young man of marked ability and ensured he was properly

46 Braga, *Anzac Doctor*, 95-98.

buried in the military manner.[47] Pockley and Maguire were first in a long line of youthful medical officers who drew inspiration from their commander in the 1914–1918 war.

★ ★ ★

Within a few days, all armed resistance of German New Guinea and associated German colonies had ended, but Howse's task remained – the maintenance of the health of the AN&MEF in the form of a defensive garrison in an isolated tropical malaria-ridden region of the world. He issued stern orders about hygiene and made sure they were carried out. He improvised to make hospital accommodation adequate for a garrison in Rabaul. Then he exponentially handed over his command to Major Maguire.

He hurried back to Sydney in an endeavour to join the first convoy of the Australian Imperial Force about to depart to join in the European War. He succeeded as they had been held back because of the dangers of the powerful German Pacific Squadron under Admiral von Spee.

In Sydney, the ambitious Howse immediately met Surgeon-General WCD Williams of the AAMC, requesting the command of a Sanitary Section – a small medical unit as part of the first convoy. Williams refused. Instead, he appointed him as a supernumerary officer for the voyage as his staff officer. Howse was happy to go in any capacity.

They sailed three days later. AG Butler clarified the events in his usual balanced manner:

> The force [first convoy] was to sail for Europe towards the middle of September [1914], but the departure was

47 Braga, *Anzac Doctor*, 99-100.

postponed because of the presence of German warships in the Pacific. The delay gave an opportunity to press on with training. It permitted also, as a last-minute appointment, the attachment to the staff of the DMS of the officer in medical charge of the troops in New Guinea, Lieutenant-Colonel NR Howse, VC, who, when the object of that expedition was achieved, had obtained permission to return to join the AIF. On the recommendation of Surgeon-General Williams, he was attached to headquarters as a 'supernumerary medical officer', and detailed to assist the DMS for the voyage, acting as his staff officer.[48]

Howse had gone through the correct military channels to achieve his purpose.

Thus, on November 1, in the clear sunlight of the early Sunday morning, the vast convoy of thirty-eight ships carrying 30,000 men and 10,000 horses steamed slowly out of Albany Harbour. For Howse it was an unforgettable majestic sight as the ships formed into three long lines, half a mile apart with a similar interval between each transport. It was the greatest sea transportation of troops to a distant seat of war that the world has ever seen.

Howse, excited about the whole venture, had been placed aboard the flagship *Orvieto*. On board was Major General WT Bridges who developed a close friendship with Howse during the long voyage. Bridges held the anomalous dual command of the AIF and of the First Division.

48 Colonel AG Butler, DSO, VD, BA, MB, Ch B (Camb), 'The Gallipoli Campaign', *The Australian Army Medical Services in the War of 1914-1918*, vol 1, AWM, Melbourne, 1938, 33.

Surgeon-General Sir WCD Williams was appointed Director of Medical Services (DMS) responsible to Bridges as the Force Commander. Colonel Charles ("Charlie") Ryan, Assistant Director of Medical Services (ADMS), was Divisional Commander to Bridges. Williams was the only permanent, rather than citizen soldier. He was elderly, immersed in the past dating back to the Suakin expedition of 1885 and was highly decorated. He didn't mix well with the military staff and kept to himself on the long voyage using Howse to represent him on many committee occasions, thus providing him with a significant role in decision-making.

Ryan was a most active and colourful surgeon from Melbourne, who had once served in the Russo-Turkish War on the Ottoman side and had a valuable understanding of his new enemy. Williams took little part in the important staff discussions that Howse appeared to take over, but diplomatically in front of Bridges. Howse emphasised the urgent need for careful medical planning to meet the many problems he believed they were about to face, but timed the right moment to raise such issues. In discussions, he would seem outspoken and yet he was listened to – at least to some extent. He was tactful as well and used his considerable charm. He well understood the military mind and avoided alienating authoritarian individuals. His many qualifications, including his battle experiences in South Africa as well as his common sense and imagination, stood him in a strong position:

> … with his insight, his tact, his pleasant approach and his convincing address, Howse was accepted as the medical authority. His effective personal relations with the

combatant staff were an outstanding feature of his long military career and enabled him to exercise an important influence on events outside the medical service.[49]

This was one estimation of his ability to function and handle the chain of command of the professional military world. During the voyage, it is certain that Neville Howse had won the confidence of William Bridges and a deep and lasting friendship with Colonel (Sir) Cyril Brudenell White, chief of staff who survived the whole war.

As the Australian convoy sailed through the Suez Canal, General Bridges received the disturbing news that Turkey had entered the war on the side of the Central Powers. Turkey presented great problems for the Allies in the Middle East and another warfront with which to deal. While still in the Red Sea, Bridges received a secret signal from the British War Office that, instead of the vast convoy proceeding to its destination in England, the Australian troops were to disembark in Egypt and to train there until further notice. It was to be a major change in deployment of a large number of fresh and untried Dominion troops.[50]

As a 'supernumerary' medical officer, when Howse came off the ship in Alexandria where the Australian troops were disembarking, he was yet to be given a specific role in the new situation. He was left up in the air with no duties. The AIF had been merely designed as a field force and no medical units other than field ambulance had been included. Confusion reigned.

Surgeon-General Williams, Director of Medical Services

49 Cited by Norris, *Annual Post-Graduate*, 221.

50 Norris, *Annual Post-Graduate*, 221-3.

for the AIF, went almost immediately on to London for discussion with the War Office, leaving behind the confusion about who was to provide medical aid for the 30,000 troops in training: for example, a general hospital, stationary hospitals in various locations, the casual clearing stations, the depots of medical stores and the convalescent depots. Only after Bridges' force had been organised and bivouacked on land in Egypt was it discovered that Australia was also required to supply its own facilities rather than the British Army and ultimately the British government. And yet there were 30,000 men from Australia and New Zealand in training around Cairo where a significant medical situation would soon develop.

On arrival in Egypt, the 1st Division set up a tented camp at Mena, a village at the foot of the pyramids, after travelling by train from Alexandria.

Bridges appointed Howse as Disembarkation Medical Officer in the middle of the organisational chaos to meet immediate demands, including the provision for a number of serious and contagious sick discharging from the transports alongside the docks at Alexandria. Under the circumstances, he did a good job cutting red tape. He went straight to Sir John Maxwell, supreme officer commanding the British Forces in Egypt, who at once made available the things Howse needed in the immediate situation. This was typical of Howse's approach – to decide quickly and go straight to the top.

When all the troops were tented, medical personnel from the field ambulance took over the existing Mena Hospital and Howse was put in charge, although he had no confirmed appointment as yet in writing.

Aboard the *Orvieto*, which as a flagship carried all the

key staff officers of the AIF, Neville Howse had been highly effective in laying the foundations of his future brilliant medical career through his personal people-skills derived, in part, from his diverse experiences in both rural Australia and South Africa. He was not a Victoria Cross recipient for nothing. His relationship with the general staff on board had been impressive. He was, as Butler described: 'Possessed of great tact, insight, charm of manner, incisive … [and with] an ambitious resolve to make his presence felt'.[51]

Colonel Charles Ryan was moved to the position of Consultant Surgeon and was replaced as ADMS 1 Division by Colonel Neville Howse, an appointment directly made by General Bridges without reference to the DMS AIF General Williams, who was in London anyway, or to the DGMS in Melbourne. When Williams returned to Egypt in February, these changes were a *fait accompli.* There now remained no clear role for Williams to perform[52] other than approve Howse's various initiatives. He seemed relieved and content to do so.

When General William Birdwood took command in Egypt of the Australian and New Zealand troops, which was then named the Anzac Corps, there was no provision on his establishment for a senior staff medical officer. This anomaly was pointed out by Howse, but to no avail. He knew they would soon be on their way to the Dardanelles and the clear dangers of a difficult warfront once their training was completed.

It was merely announced that the Anzac Corps would

51 Butler, 'Gallipoli Campaign', 42.

52 Likeman CSM, *From the Tropics to the Desert. German New Guinea, Egypt & Palestine 1914-1918*, Slouch Hat Publications, McCrae, 2012, 39.

be administered medically from Cairo – to Howse it was an impossible, crazy situation. He was proved to be right, given the casualty toll on Gallipoli in the first days.

Howse landed on Gallipoli with Divisional Headquarters on the first day of the landing and was faced with a tremendous medical problem. The rapidly mounting casualties wandering or being carried down by comrades to the overcrowded beach – also cluttered with animals, men, munitions and stores for the 20,000 troops – was overwhelming. Because of the high ground rising suddenly from the edge of the beach, there was no other suitable place for casualties to be placed on a temporary basis. This was the chaotic situation Howse found on his arrival.

Sir Brudenell White, Birdwood's Chief of Staff, later recalled:

> ... at the landing at Gallipoli, Howse was invaluable and indispensable. Human power of seeing into the future is at very best limited and the medical provision for the great landing displayed much of human frailty. The medical orders were not in Howse's possession long before the event, but with characteristic vigour he represented the palpable defects and insufficiencies. That some remedy was applied was entirely due to him. But, alas, for a time the beach at Anzac looked like a holocaust. Then it was that Howse became a giant. He took the whole matter into his own hands, giving and disregarding orders in a manner quite shocking but strangely and rapidly productive of results. Shells and bullets he completely disregarded. To the wounded, he was gentleness itself; his capable hands eased many a patient while his cheery voice and bearing brought comfort and consideration. April

25, 1915, was a black day on the beach but it produced many heroes. Could they now be asked to name the greatest, the palm would go to Neville Howse.[53]

Without orders, Howse organised the evacuation of about 1,700 casualties to the ships offshore, especially to the hospital ship *Gascon*, on any small craft he could muster through the night of the first day. The following morning, he had cleared the beach of the dying and the wounded.

★ ★ ★

When Major-General Featherstone, the acting GDM, arrived in Egypt some months later, he realised at once that the Australian medical arrangements should be directly under Australian control and Australia should be represented at the War Office where arrangements were controlled covering Australian casualties arriving in England.

This recommendation was accepted by the Australian government. Featherstone further recommended that Neville Howse be promoted to Surgeon-General, Director of Medical Services to the AIF.[54] Who else was there?

★ ★ ★

The observant Gallipoli correspondent Charles EW Bean, close to the action, had already noticed that, when he arrived on the beach at Gallipoli, Howse was already busy there, along with 'White, Glasford, Blamey … and Foot', all members of the General Staff.

53 Cited in Norris, *Annual Post-Graduate*, 223-4.
54 Norris, *Annual Post-Graduate*, 224-5.

When Major-General William Bridges, the Commander of the AIF, was fatally wounded, Howse went with him to the ship. Staff Captain Richard Casey and Brudenell White went to visit him on the ship and they later reported to Bean that the General could hardly talk, but he was still conscious and probably aware he was dying as Howse tenderly cared for him. The wound on his thigh had turned gangrenous through the failure of blood supply. There was no way Howse could see that anything more could be done. It was not feasible to amputate the wounded leg. Howse realised that no one of the general's advanced age could stand the shock of amputation, especially taking into consideration the already dramatic loss of blood and his very weakened condition. Indeed, Howse, together with other medical consultants, decided not to attempt it.[55] It wasn't long before the founder of the AIF had his final rendezvous with death, with Colonel Neville Howse beside him, caring for him until the last.

William Bridges died on 18 May 1915 from a sniper's bullet that severed his profunda femoris artery and femoral vein. On the hospital ship *Gascon*, his final words to Howse were that he regretted not being able to complete a dispatch recommending the withdrawal from Gallipoli. He wished that the dispatch be conveyed to the Australian Minister of Defence before dying. He then lost consciousness.[56]

The General and the 'Supernumerary' Medical Officer

Neville Howse was well aware of what he owed General

55 *Gallipoli Correspondent. The frontline diary of CEW Bean,* selected and annotated by Kevin Fewster, Allen & Unwin, Sydney, 67, 103.
56 Butler, 'Gallipoli Campaign', 158.

William Bridges in support of his military career as he sat beside him on his death bed as the hospital ship left the Gallipoli shores en route to Alexandria. No longer was he a supernumerary, but a vital cog in the wheel of the AIF's endeavour.

A deep friendship between the Major-General and the last-minute 'supernumerary' had developed on the long slow journey from Australia to Egypt in the first immense convoy aboard the flagship. The astute Bridges identified Howse's potential in his ideas, intensity and organisational and administrative skills that were close to his own. For obvious reasons, Howse sought to get close to the Anzac supremo. Quite simply, he had gained the complete confidence of the commander.

After Bridges' tragic death, it was Howse's well-hidden emotions of gratitude that guided his actions in remembering his most vital mentor during his brilliant, fast-gathering career. After all, Bridges had appointed him from the uncertain supernumerary status to that of assistant director of medical services of the 1st Australian Division with the rank of colonel in December 1914.

Howse had long been gravely perturbed by the inadequacy and even confusion of the Imperial forces' medical plans for the Gallipoli Campaign, both its landing and eventual evacuation. He took the initiative when it came to its inevitable ending to improve its medical plans. Over the exacting months of May to August 1915, Howse, both tired and worn, shared with everyone else on Gallipoli the frontline dangers and frustrations: the diseases, the personal discomforts and the privations and he was no longer a young man. Despite his energetic drive, he continued to be harassed by seemingly impractical instructions from medical Headquarters in Cairo. The same problems had existed in the Crimean War which his father had endured.

At the end of August with the prospect of the arrival of a severe winter with its added hardships, special provisions for the health and fitness of the troops caught in a stalemate were now absolutely necessary. Howse was appointed Deputy Assistant Director of Medical Services (DADMS) on General Birdwood's staff until he was to arrive from India. Like Bridges, Howse gained Birdwood's confidence. They related well to each other.

The impact of Howse's appointment was felt immediately. Everyone on the peninsula suffered at some time from intestinal disease. Howse rigorously tackled this problem, to some degree at least. He improved rations; made provisions for the retention of light casualties and for their return to their fighting units as soon as they were fit. He instituted the Anzac Medical Society to improve morale and teamwork amongst frontline medicos. This innovation did improve morale considerably. More than fifty medical officers met when an opportunity presented itself. He promoted the ideal of professional keenness and *esprit de corps*. There was frequent administrative discussion to develop team work co-ordination and co-operation in medical work on the Front.

He was able eventually to adjust medical service of Anzacs in the operational arena, but in Egypt confusion persisted for a time. There was a gross underestimation by the Army authorities of the predicted casualties and the accommodation at the base hospital and convalescent support proved drastically inadequate.

Later, Colonel Major-General Hubert Featherstone, acting Director of Medical Services, realised this when he arrived in the Middle East and had recommended that Howse be appointed as Surgeon-General, Director of Medical Services for the 1st AIF. A few days on, Howse received an urgent message to return to Gallipoli as it had been decided to evacuate.

While there were still major problems with medical services in Cairo, including shortages of accommodation for the wounded, Featherstone went on an inspection to Gallipoli where he had met Howse on 17 October 1915 for the first time and was highly impressed. He saw that Howse was right in his criticisms of all the shortcomings of medical support. But he was also impressed with the qualities of the man himself and his total grip on the complex, confused situation. His written recommendations on 25 October bear the clear marks of Howse's clear thinking and the concise manner of his expression.[57]

As Bridges would have realised if he had survived, Howse's ability and resourcefulness had now been decided and was urgently needed to handle the medical aspects of the hazardous venture of the entire evacuation from the Dardanelles as ordered by Kitchener. For once, the expected casualties had been grossly overestimated at 50 percent and his plans completely covered the needs and demands of this remarkably successful operation.[58]

57 Braga, *Anzac Doctor*, 212-3.

58 Norris, *Annual Post-Graduate*, 222-5.

Memories of the Gallipoli disaster lingered. Howse's most vivid memory and regret about his time there was the death of his friend Sir William Bridges on 18 May 1915 before any decision had been made to evacuate, although he expected it to happen before the end of 1915.

Sir William Throsby Bridges and the AIF

Bridges was very much an Empire man like Neville Howse. He was born at Greenock in Scotland on 18 February 1861. Greenock (meaning 'sunny knoll') was an industrial town on the southern shore of the Firth of Clyde, some two miles (35 kms) west of Glasgow in Inverclyde. It was a port accommodation for Royal Naval personnel of which his father was a member and a shipbuilding centre. So Bridges was the son of a Royal Navy officer, William Wilson Somerset Bridges, a Scot, and Mary Throsby, an Australian. He was educated at Ryde on the Isle of Wight, then at the royal naval school at Greenwich and, finally, he received two years training at the Canadian military college in Ontario when his family migrated to Canada. In 1879, he followed his now retired family to Sydney.

He entered the public service in the New South Wales roads and bridges department. He volunteered unsuccessfully for the Sudan contingent, but in 1885 obtained a commission in the colony's permanent artillery as a lieutenant and then sought a life in the professional military.

He pursued his ambition relentlessly, rather like Neville Howse. Promoted to captain in 1890, then major in 1895; lieutenant-colonel in 1902; colonel in 1906; brigadier-general in 1910 and major-general in 1914 – the highest rank in the Australian military. He was in charge of the forts on Middle Harbour in Port Jackson. At Middle Head barracks in 1893, a school of gunnery was established and Bridges had been made chief instructor. He had become a highly regarded expert in gunnery and other weapons.

Bridges volunteered, just like Howse, for the South African War which turned out to be a rehearsal for the Great War. He was attached as major to the artillery of the cavalry division and saw the relief of Kimberley and the fight of Paardeberg. He was invalided home with typhoid in 1903.

Bridges joined a newly-established federal headquarters staff as assistant quartermaster-general and in 1904 acted as deputy-adjutant-general and chief staff officer. He had long since gained a reputation for hard work and erudition and when, in the re-organisation of the federal defence force, a chief of intelligence was needed (1905-8), Bridges was the man who ably filled that role.

He became Australia's representative on the Imperial general staff in London (1909-10). The Federal Government was to recognise the significance of this experience in the work of the British Empire. Returning at the right time from London in 1910 to create the military college at Duntroon, Canberra, he was to succeed General Kirkpatrick as inspector-general of the Australian military forces.

At the outbreak of war in 1914, he was entrusted by the Commonwealth government with the organisation of an expeditionary force that had been offered for overseas service on 3 August 1914 to the British government. The plan had originally been to be integrated into brigades within the British Army.

As a nationalist, Bridges persuaded the Minister of Defence to offer an Australian Division instead and hinted that its organisation had already begun. Such an offer insisted that Australian troops would be a separate entity, destined later to grow into an army. Howse picked up from his mentor Bridges that the Australian medical services should also be a distinct entity throughout the 1914–1918 War.

When Bridges suggested another to command such an army, the Federal government chose – without any hesitation – Bridges for the part. He was given command of the prior training of the AIF once they were recruited and before they left for overseas.

When Bridges landed on Gallipoli on the first day, he soon became convinced, by the extremely steep landscape that could be easily defended by the Turkish Army, that the enterprise was a tragic mistake strategically. He was to convey this opinion to the closest of his staff officers, like Brudenell White and Neville Howse. He urged withdrawal, but was sternly overruled by British military authorities.

For the next three weeks, he visited the firing line on a daily basis, constantly exposing himself to danger until he was hit by a bullet from a Turkish sniper on 15 May. He died three days later on the hospital ship *Gascon* being treated, as already described, by Neville Howse as his personal surgeon.

He was being transported to Egypt when he died. His body was returned to Australia – the only war death to be so treated – and, after a service at St Paul's Cathedral in Melbourne, he was buried on the slopes of Mount Pleasant overlooking Duntroon military college, the academy he had created. The grave was supervised by the architect of

Canberra, the American Walter Burley Griffin. The simple inscription ran: 'A gallant and erudite soldier'.[59]

Becoming Major-General

In January 1917, Neville Howse had his position as Surgeon Major-General of the entire Australian Medical Services Corps confirmed. His headquarters were to be established in the centre of affairs in London. He was part of the AIF Administrative Head Quarters established in the substantial building of the former Methodist Training College with its distinctive quadrangle in Horseferry Road.[60]

Dr FA Maguire, Howse's colleague in the New Guinea campaign, put it all concisely when he wrote in 1930 in the *Medical Journal of Australia*:

> After the evacuation of Gallipoli the Australian Imperial Force was reorganized. Ultimately General [William] Birdwood was appointed General Officer Commanding the Australian Imperial Force. As an outcome, a Director of Medical Services for the whole of the Australian Imperial Force in Egypt, France and England [and other fronts] became a necessity. As the man who knew most about the problems, who had foreseen the necessity for the reorganization and who was best qualified from a military, professional and

59 'Bridges, Sir William Throsby (1861-1915)', Arthur Wilberforce Jose & Herbert James Carter (eds), *The Illustrated Australian Encyclopaedia, vol.1*, Angus & Robertson, Sydney, 1925, 202; Peter Dennis, Jeffrey Grey, Ewan Morris, Robin Prior & John Connor (eds), *The Oxford Companion to Australian Military History*, Oxford University Press, Melbourne, 1995, 120-1; Robert Likeman, *Australian Doctors on the Western Front*, vol 3, Rosenberg, Dural, 2014, 418.

60 Butler, 'Gallipoli Campaign', 809.

> personal standpoint to hold such a position, Colonel Howse was selected. He was promoted Surgeon-General on November 22, 1915, and appointed as 'Director of Medical Services, Australian Imperial Force'. From then on to the termination of the war General Howse administered the medical services of the Australian Imperial Force. The high standard of efficiency that he set and maintained was recognized by His Majesty the King when in 1917 General Howse was made a Knight Commander of the Most Honourable Order of the Bath and in 1919 Knight Commander of the Most Distinguished Order of St Michael and St George.[61]

The key words were the 'high standard of efficiency' that included highly innovative approaches in introducing surgical teams in the field and radically reorganising the field ambulance to increase their efficiency and mobility. By the time Howse had set up his own headquarters within the AIF headquarters in Horseferry Road, he had achieved an all-powerful, but complex position. He controlled all medical services in Egypt, Palestine, France and Belgium as well as those in England.[62] While Howse demanded the highest standards of medical care for Australian soldiers, he was able to keep them apart from the British patients. He was everywhere he was needed. His guiding principle was 'go ahead' and do what you believe should be done until someone stops the process.

---

61 'Dr FA Maguire writes', Obituary – Neville Reginald Howse, *Medical Journal of Australia*, 22 November 1930, 710.

62 John Ramsland, Dedication. *Neville Howse VC Rest Area. The War Veterans Remembrance Drive, Wingham-Wauchope NSW*, War Veterans' Remembrance Drive Association & the Manning Valley Historical Society, 16-17.

He had gained the absolute confidence of General Birdwood, supreme commander of the Anzacs (as he had done with General Bridges). He always insisted on direct access to the High Command in Horseferry Road. Birdwood was later moved to write in a reference:

> Since then [Gallipoli] he has been employed as DMS of the AIF, and in this capacity has been has been responsible for the whole of the administration of the Australian troops in England, France and Egypt. This he has carried out with complete success, and with the absence of friction. He so distinctly stands out for his magnificent work that I sincerely trust that this may now be fully recognised.[63]

Neville Howse's military career in World War I was a brilliant achievement. Under his authoritative care as Surgeon Major General to AAMC, he became second to none, given in what was a brutalising, destructive industrial war of stalemate till 1917-18 with enormous casualty rates on both sides.

Soldiers ventured into No Man's Land to gain a few yards of territory only to be cut to pieces by machine-gun and rifle fire. The wounded survivors depended on the efforts of the AAMC and their swiftness of support. Behind it all was the innovative director Neville Howse. In such a war, it was impossible to correct all the mistakes that could be made in such critical and chaotic encounters, but for Howse, engendered effective teamwork, overall structure and effective coordination were the essential keys. No doubt he

63 WR Birdwood, 'A periodical award (KCB) Surgeon-General Neville Reginald Howse, VC, CB', in Butler, *Official History of the Australian Medical Services 1914-1918*, vol III, 'Special Problems & Services', Appendix No 8, 1943, 1047.

made a few enemies on the way - those who did not accept his techniques of administration.

At AIF headquarters at Horseferry Road, London, Howse soon came to control all Australian medical services by effective communication. He made frequent visits to battlefronts to assess their peculiar problems. He was innovative and independent of other Allied medical systems, nevertheless coordinating and co-operating with them with tact. He was among the first to introduce surgical teams working closely together near the Front. Thus many lives were saved. He reorganised the field ambulance in such a way to increase its efficiency into what became regarded as an outstanding enterprise. He always aimed to expedite the recovery of the wounded so that they could return to their fighting units. He fought to control venereal disease and to resist strongly any attempts to lower physical standards of the AIF. Several of the recruits in the latter phase of the war were turned back to Australia after they had arrived.

Captain Neville Reginald Howse, VC, KCB, circa 1902 (AWM A02711)

He continued to sustain the work of the ANZAC Medical Society throughout the war which he had established on Gallipoli to disseminate up-to-date medical knowledge among medical officers. He emphasised the importance of an effective dedication to medicine as a calling, rather than just a job; the need to care for human life as a primary issue was emphasised amongst the chaos of brutal trench warfare; an acute sense of loyalty to colleagues who strive effectively was insisted upon; he emphasised the importance in warfare to act in a confident and decisive manner – a quality he looked for in medical officers at the Front or in recovery hospitals – and he saw that bravery, strength in persistence and so on were properly rewarded. In all of this, he believed in the importance of maintaining a sense of humour and the need to boost morale in difficult circumstances.

At first, Howse had to learn about the 'beast' that was the rigid military mind and the vast complex organisation of an army in a modern warfare, but, because of his South African experience, he learned particularly quickly what was needed or practical. He revealed the capacity to learn and grow with the magnitude of his task, as a good leader should. Mistakes had to be made, but he was quick to correct them. Howse appeared never to lack the confidence needed as commander. Some of it, of course, was theatre.

Sir Harry Chauvel of the Australian Light Horse, on Howse's death in 1930, commented:

> Sir Neville's personality and organising ability helped, of course, by the personnel with which he had to deal, made the Australian Army Medical Corps second to none in the forces of the Empire. The efficiency of the Australian hospitals was a constant source of admiration to the high commanders of the British and Allied forces in the war. Australia owes a great deal of gratitude to Sir Neville Howse.[64]

---

64 'Neville Howse. Surgeon, Statesman, and Hero. Close of a Splendid Life', *Sydney Morning Herald*, 22 September, 1930.

Another writer in the *Sydney Morning Herald* viewed Howse as keen and full of life, 'every inch a soldier' and a man of 'strong will, vision and quick decision'. At Anzac and beyond, he was everywhere and set the highest example by 'his contempt for danger'.[65]

As a World War I soldier, General Howse was the embodiment of the spirit of Empire. He did not spare himself of any exertion to carry out his duty. While his extraordinary ability marked him from the first as an outstanding candidate for higher office, his first thought was always the health of the troops in frontline situations. He believed they should be housed as well as circumstances would permit and cared for in sanitation, food and clothing at the highest possible standard. Such matters were foremost in his mind.

In his attitude to all people who suffered with depression in the war, Howse was kindly, approachable, full of sympathy and cheery encouragement. Why many viewed him as outwardly cynical, brilliant and often scathing in conversation, he was a past master of diplomacy in the inflexible military chain of command. But he had a dual love of the British Empire and nationalistically for rural Australia.

His life can be characterised as a devotion to both. He had the subtle ability to communicate to his most eminent superiors with an independent, but ever so tactful sense – he once dressed down Lord Kitchener for lack of medical planning on Gallipoli and Sir John Monash who attempted, unsuccessfully, to take over control of the

65 John Ramsland, 'Neville Howse VC, rural doctor and War Hero', unpublished talk, Hunter Postgraduate Medical Institute, 2 August 2014, Marina View Function Centre, Newcastle Harbour.

AAMC in 1918. Howse made absolutely sure it remained independent as a corps.

Howse was a master of men because he was master of himself and yet he admitted to any weakness. At the same time, he had the greatest sympathy and understanding for the frailties of others who always felt safe, happy and comfortable when he was nearby and in control during the Great War. His slogan was duty and hard work.

★ ★ ★

Howse's achievement as Director of Medical Services is backed by a wealth of official records and personal testimony. He administered a complex organisation with conspicuous efficiency and extraordinary economy. His department was the creation of a single mind of exceptional calibre. He moulded the organisation in his own image. His medical responsibilities focused on the physical efficiency – the fitness – of the Australian force between 1916 and 1919. His most important work in the war was his creation of an effective headquarters at Horseferry Road.The outstanding feature of his technique was the absence of any formality or 'red tape'. His team was personally selected to work smoothly as a team of shared responsibilities – men who knew the frontline and how it operated.

There were people who could readjust mistakes quickly and come up with practical solutions in the shifting chaos of war. He was ruthless in scrapping flawed plans and uncertain staff lacking in decision-making skills, or who did not have a reliable work ethic. He had a flair for discerning what is, and what is not, a medical responsibility. It was the first lesson his staff were required to learn and the keystone of his work. He and his staff did not interfere with military affairs beyond their medical responsibilities. He had tremendous energy to pursue his intentions. He lived for his work and retained a 'remorseless drive' on himself and on his officers. He had a small flat in walking distance from his headquarters. He spent many late nights in his office. He believed that his staff at Horseferry Road should work twice as hard, because they had been freed from the unpleasant discomforts and dangers of the frontline. He saw his headquarters only 'as a means of getting things done'.

Howse was generally wise in delegating responsibility. A good example is his relationship with the Light Horse in far-off Egypt where he trusted his medical staff on the spot to carry out his intentions. He created an atmosphere of mutual cooperation and respect.[66]

After the War

Neville Howse became the first and most able Federal Minister in charge of Repatriation as part of his Defence and Health portfolio in the Cabinet as the National Party member for the elected seat of Calare in the lower house.The 1920s, begun with the Influenza pandemic, was a troubled and grieving decade.We were a broken nation yet to recover from a disastrous war, especially in the human toll. Howse worked as hard as ever to see that thousands of returned men received a reasonable degree of social justice and care. He

66 Butler, 'The Gallipoli Campaign', 802-58.

made disabled veterans and public health his mission in his twilight years. Unfortunately, some fell through the cracks.

In 1920, Howse had been appointed the Director of Medical Services by the Commonwealth Government. As a public servant, he was not permitted to speak about broader controversial issues of public health. This restriction, in part, motivated him to resign the post in November 1922.

Standing for the Federal seat of Calare in the Central West of New South Wales, he was elected. From January 1925 until April 1927, he was Federal Minister of Defence and Health and similar portfolios. His own ill-health forced him to give up his portfolio in February 1928, but he continued to administer the repatriation program. The following year with the collapse of the Stanley Bruce-Earle Page Federal Government, he lost his seat in the Federal election closely to an unheard of Labor candidate GA Gibbons.

By 1930, Howse was a sick man. He went with his wife to London to consult a famous surgeon. But his medical problem was serious. Shortly after a second operation, he died of pancreatic cancer on 19 September 1930 aged sixty-six. He was buried in Kensal Green Cemetery, London, beside his father, Albert.

> It is characteristic of the man that at the time of his death, at the age of 66 years, he was pursuing medical studies abroad and endeavouring to bring up to date his already vast store of medical, scientific knowledge. Australia can ill afford to lose a citizen such as the late Sir Neville Howse.[67]

---

67 Sir Thomas Bavin, Premier of NSW, 1927-1930, in Dennis *et al.*, *The Oxford Companion*, 296-7; *SMH*, 22 September, 1930.

Like all of the First AIF, apart from his mentor General Bridges, he was buried abroad with his simple grave as a memorial.

John Ramsland (author) and Dr Charles Howse at the Dedication of the Neville Howse VC Rest Area, 24 July 2014 (photo by Marie Ramsland)

4

Monash's War: Gallipoli and The Western Front

> I have had plenty of opportunity of comparing them [the Australian troops] with the troops of British regular units and Territorials, and the British officers are the first to admit for physique, dash, enterprise and sublime courage, the Australians are head and shoulders above any others.
>
> John Monash, 16 May 1915[1]

An acute and typical observation made in a letter by Monash while on Gallipoli may have been devastating to the British, but like a good lawyer he had reliable witnesses : the British officers themselves. He held this opinion strongly and publicly until his death on 8 October 1931 at the age of sixty-six years.

General Sir John Monash, *Reveille*, Supplement, October 31, 1931

Overview

Lieutenant-General Sir John Monash GCMG, KCB, VD, MCE, BA, DC, LlD, MInstCE,

1 John Monash, *War Letters of General Monash*, Black Inc, Melbourne, 2015, 38.

Grand Officer of Honor, Grand Officer of the Order of the Crown of Belgium and holder of the American Distinguished Service Medal had, by the end of his life, garnered a multitude of distinguished civic and military awards, many more than the vast majority of Australians who fought in the 1914-1918 War.[2] He was, however, born in reasonably humble circumstances on 27 June 1865 at Dudley Street, West Melbourne.[3] Outstanding ability, hard work and a strong self-belief won for Monash a distinguished position in civil life, just as it had placed him in the highest position in the AIF during the Great War.

John Monash (1865-1931), engineer, businessman, citizen-soldier, administrator and public servant, was Australia's most outstanding military leader during the war of 1914-18 and Melbourne's most famous citizen. At his birth, he was trebly disadvantaged: he was **colonial-born** and the child of **Jewish-German** parents.

For most of his life, he strove to surmount these obstacles to public acceptance and he was so successful that, on 1 June 1918, he was appointed the commanding officer of one of twenty army corps in the Allies army on The Western Front.

After the war, he brilliantly organised the repatriation of Australian troops and then became the principal executive of the Victorian State Electricity Commission and an acknowledged leader of Australia's returned soldiers. In 1929, he was very belatedly promoted to the rank of general and, after his death at the age of 66, a crowd of 300,000 gathered in Melbourne to pay their last respects. Among the crowd

2 'Sir John Monash: His Career', *Reveille*, 28 February 1929, 4.

3 AWB, 'Celebrities of the AIF: No 81 General Sir John Monash GCMG, KCB, VD', *Reveille*, May 1927, 2.

were thousands of former soldiers of the 1st AIF who he had led at Gallipoli and in France and who regarded him as Australia's greatest national hero. They were intensely proud that the AIF, alone of all the corps to serve in Europe and the Middle East, consisted entirely of volunteers and had been eventually commanded by one of their own citizen-soldiers.[4]

In his controversial *Memoirs* (1958), Field Marshal Bernard Montgomery (Viscount Montgomery of Alamein), British hero of desert fighting in World War II, claimed extravagantly that the Great War might have ended sooner and with fewer casualties if Monash had been supreme commander of the British Armies in place of Field Marshal Haig.[5] Montgomery was not renowned for self-restraint, but he had a flair, not unlike Monash, for inspiring confidence in the troops under his command.[6]

While British historian AJP Taylor's famous assessment of Sir John Monash was that he was the sole general of creative originality in World War I, the word 'creative' on the surface may be misleading. The real measure of Monash's much celebrated genius, as one of his more recent biographers Grantlee Kieza[7] frequently points out in his massive tome, was that he learnt, not without mistakes, how to wring the full usefulness from every tool he was given in an integrated

4 Review of Geoffrey Serle, *John Monash: A Biography*, Melbourne University Press, Carlton, 1982, *Journal of the Australian War Memorial*, no 1, October 1982, 48.

5 Phillip Wellington, 'General Sir John Monash', *100 Famous Australian Lives*, Ure Smith, Sydney, 1968, 237.

6 'Montgomery, Bernard Law', *The Concise Dictionary of National Biography*, vol II, Oxford University Press, Oxford, 1992, 2071.

7 Grantlee Kieza, *Monash. The Soldier who shaped Australia*, ABC Books, Sydney, 2015.

way. He was brilliantly innovative at manipulating the modern industrial weapons of war – which he played no part in inventing. He took judicious departures from traditional military norms; he drew on every aspect of his engineering, legal, academic, military and socio-cultural education and training to shape his wartime strategies. He was able to communicate such strategies to significant others in the imperial command, like Haig.

Whatever the case, Sir John Monash was an outstanding Australian who served his country with distinction in war and in peace. He was an important product of a new era in development in twentieth-century Australia and, as a man who was close to the tides of history, he deserved a rich and exhaustive biography.[8] He did not receive this until well after the Second World War with Geoffrey Serle's magnificent *John Monash. A Biography.*[9]

John Monash was the son of one of the immigrant European pioneers of the gold-rush decade – the "Fifties".[10] A twenty-one-year-old Jew, John's father Louis arrived from Prussia in 1854. He was seeking his fortune on the Victorian goldfields, but soon after landing decided to turn his attention to retailing and commerce. He remained in the Colony for nine years, then returned to his homeland to secure a bride of the Jewish faith willing to migrate to Australia. He married Bertha Manesse in Prussia on 27

8 AD Spaull, 'Sir John Monash – A Vanishing Hero?', *RAHSJ*, vol 56, pt 3, 1970, 255.

9 Geoffrey Serle, *John Monash. A Biography*, Melbourne University Press, Carlton, 1985.

10 General Sir John Monash, GCMG, KCB, VD Statue Unveiled', *Reveille*, 1 February 1951, 7.

June 1865. They returned to north Melbourne.[11]

Growing up as John Monash

After John was born, Louis and Bertha had two daughters, Mathilde in 1869 and Louise in 1873. But Louis found making an adequate living was difficult as the economic and commercial boom of the goldrushes was tapering off. He suffered financially and decided to take his business to the Riverina, at first at Narrandera with his brother and then by himself at Jerilderie where he set up a general store.[12]

John was brought up bilingually (English and German), but never acquired Yiddish.

His first school was St Stephen's Church of England in Richmond. He attended there for three years until 1874. At Jerilderie in the wilder bush, however, he was a pupil at a small local state school for three years under a man in his early twenties, William Elliott, the teacher-in-charge of about seventy pupils. Now a genuine 'country schoolboy',[13] John was fortunate to have such a scholarly schoolmaster who became his mentor. Apart from being the legendary hero in saving many lives in the Jerilderie last stand of the Kelly gang of bushrangers, Elliott was an exceptionally good teacher. Under his tutelage, the young Monash did well and blossomed. He even became an unofficial apprentice teacher or class monitor. He lent a hand in teaching the younger and more backward children of the large class in the poorly-appointed timber classroom. The precocious, bookish and musically talented boy

11 AWB, 'Celebrities'.

12 Tim Fischer, *Maestro John Monash*, Monash University Publishing, 2014, 3-4.

13 Spaull, 'Sir John Monash', 251.

benefitted from the rough-and-tumble 'democratizing state school process'. By teaching individual pupils, he reinforced his own learning more precisely. Monash was to display well-honed teaching ability throughout his career.

For Monash, the experience at Jerilderie was a memorable and rewarding time as he was dealing with all sorts: boys of the land and bush, future pastural employees, railwaymen, country postal clerks, blacksmiths, storekeepers, miners and so on. He later saw this time as a critical part of his growing knowledge of Australian social life in a rural setting.[14] Later, he became a keen and regular bushwalker.

Elliott quickly recognised the boy's 'gargantuan appetite' for learning and delighted in the quick intelligence of his youthful, devoted protégé. This interpretation was made in 1936 by Dr Gershon Bennett, Monash's loyal son-in-law who had early access to Monash's extensive private archives. Bennett recounted in a lecture that William Elliott took a personal interest in the boy, 'teaching him many things outside and beyond the state school curriculum in the bush: particularly in higher mathematics', which he excelled in.[15]

Eventually, Elliott found his favourite pupil so responsive intellectually that he began to doubt his own capacity and ability to teach him much more. When John turned twelve, Elliott approached Louis and Bertha, John's parents, and urged them to take the boy back to Melbourne where facilities for a superior post-elementary education were readily available to those who could afford it.

And so, after his father had built a modest villa at Hawthorne,

14 Serle, *John Monash*, 9.
15 Spaull, 'Sir John Monash'.

John entered Scotch College, an elite Presbyterian secondary school, as a day student. On occasions, his father had to struggle to pay school fees.

John sang in the choir at the East Melbourne synagogue and celebrated his bar mitzvah there. Classically Jewish in their expectations for their first-born and only son, John's parents drove him hard academically in his early formative years. He soon became a precocious, articulate boy at ease in adult circles.[16]

In 1879 at the early age of fourteen, John matriculated for university. In his final year at Scotch College, he became equal dux of the school and topped mathematics and modern languages (French and German). For Melbourne University, he gained a Mathematics Exhibition that was to prove useful as his parents were struggling financially.[17] He was determined to study Arts and Engineering.

Throughout his academic career Monash lacked funds, but because of his huge youthful energy he found it not such a huge handicap. He even began his own course of concentrated reading in British literature at the Public Library of Victoria during his first year at University. In what spare time he had, he did individual coaching for matriculation of secondary school students in elite families. His teaching flair came into play to earn needed money.

Monash and Work

In 1884, he was compelled to suspend his University studies for a period of two years in order to earn his living.

---

16 Geoffrey Serle, 'Monash, Sir John (1865-1931)', *Australian Dictionary of Biography (ADB)*, vol 10, Melbourne University Press, Carlton, 543.
17 AWB, 'Celebrities'.

He obtained an appointment on the construction works of Melbourne's Prince's Bridge that was just commencing. Having studied some surveying at University, he became accustomed to challenging field-work. He thrust himself into it. During these two years, he rapidly advanced his position. His employers were well aware of his outstanding ability and dedication despite his youth. They soon delegated him highly responsible tasks at various bridgework along the river where they had contracts.[18] It was part of the practical educative process.

During his enrolment at Melbourne University, Monash was slightly restricted by a lack of funds, which he had the will and drive to overcome. He continued to coach students for matriculation as well as for music examinations allowing him to pay his way.

While absent from full-time studies at Melbourne University, Monash – demonstrating his high level of energy – joined the original University Company when it was just being formed under the newly-structured Victorian militia. Starting as a private, he rose steadily through the ranks to colour-sergeant.

When the Company was disbanded, he gained a commission in the garrison artillery. On March 6, 1887, he wrote enthusiastically in his daily diary: 'A combination of military and engineering professions is a possibility that is before me'.[19] It became his chief objective until the early 1920s.

Earlier in that year, Monash, at the age of twenty-two,

18 AWB, 'Celebrities'.
19 AWB, 'Celebrities'.

was employed by another Melbourne construction firm in charge of the city's Outer Circle Railway. With a better income, he was able to resume his studies.

In 1891 – after completing the requirements for the Bachelor of Construction Engineering (BCE) – he completed the Master of Construction Engineering. In 1895 by completing some required subjects, he managed to graduate in the Bachelor of Arts (BA) and the related Bachelor of Law (LLB).[20]

Even in the depression of the 1890s, Monash pursued a successful business career in private practice as a consulting engineer and patent attorney. Much of this work was carried out in other colonies accompanied by a great deal of travel. He gave a formidable performance in the courts. In 1896, he innovated with reinforced concrete which he pioneered in Australia and, by 1900, he successfully introduced reinforced concrete construction in Victoria, Tasmania and South Australia.[21]

The early twentieth century (1904-14) was a period of great commercial prosperity for Monash. Between 1912 and 1915, he was elected President of the Victorian Institute of Engineers as a trusted leader in his profession. He was even appointed to the Council of Melbourne University, a position he was to hold until his death in 1931.

The Saturday-Afternoon Soldier

During the pre-war period, Monash found the time

20 CEWB, 'Monash, Sir John', in Arthur Wilberforce Jose & Herbert James Carter, *The Australian Encyclopaedia*, vol II, Angus & Robertson, Sydney, 1926, 137.
21 AWB, 'Celebrities'.

to be a dedicated 'Saturday-afternoon soldier'. He had a strong attachment to military history and military technology.[22] This demonstrates the man's 'gargantuan appetite' for knowledge. The normal work day for Monash often consisted of attendance at several university classes, 'a visit to the Victorian parliament, a music or painting lesson and reading ... two or three books on topics ranging from military history or Jewish history to the classics'.[23] Such activities more than just suggest Monash's outstanding intellectual capacities. He was a competent amateur concert pianist who could present a satisfying repertoire of light classical music. He performed regularly at University Union socials and in private homes to smaller, but appreciative audiences. His star piece in performance was a Chopin 'Polonaise'.

Activity in the militia intensified. He was noticed by British inspecting officers, including Sir Ian Hamilton, because of the power of his keen lucid exposition in their presence. He had advanced to major in 1897, after which he became lieutenant-colonel in 1908 and colonel in 1913 in the Intelligence Corps, brigadier-general in 1914, major general in 1916 and lieutenant-general in 1918.[24]

The Outbreak of War

At the outbreak, he was posted to the command of the 4th Infantry Brigade, which developed under his intense training into a powerful fighting machine as evidenced by

22 Spaull,'Sir John Monash', 251-2.
23 Spaull, 'Sir John Monash', 252.
24 CEWB, 'Monash, Sir John', 137.

its proud record in Gallipoli and on the Western Front.[25]

From the 4th Brigade, Monash went to command the gallant 3rd Australian Division, from the time of its formation in England in 1916, and lead throughout its engagements in France until early 1918 when he was appointed Commander of the Australian Corps in succession of Sir William Birdwood, who had become General Officer Commanding of the 5th British Army.

Shortly after Monash's death in 1931, General Sir Brudenell White wrote:

> His ambition was certainly not a predominant factor in his career, although it had its influences. Sir John was a simple man, and, to my mind, his simplicity was his marked and perhaps his most charming characteristic. Had you asked him from what he received the most gratification – from tasks well fulfilled from honor, from power, from pride of place or from the plaudits of the crowd – I think he would have replied from all these he received less pleasure than from the greeting at the end of the day accorded him by a devoted grandchild. … he possessed a calmness of judgment and a tolerance which made reference for his advice a pleasure. His modesty was amazing. His speeches were rare, and, when delivered, were outstanding. His arguments were closely reasoned and logical: they showed they came from the brain of a master.[26]

The apex of Monash's military career came at the end

25 'Late Sir John Monash. A Great Australian' (National Broadcast Oration by Colonel AW Hymans, President of the NSW Branch of the RSL), *Reveille*, November 1943, 2.

26 'Late Sir John Monash. A Great'.

of May 1918 when he took supreme command of the Australian Corps. It was then that his great powers were on full display. In the Battle of Hamel in July, he brilliantly coordinated tanks with infantry, artillery and aeroplanes.[27] It was a stunningly successful experiment in which Monash showed great flair. Australian troops at Hamel defeated the Germans at a speed previously unknown and with minimum casualties. War historian CEW Bean was to call the 8th of August, 'Monash's masterpiece'.

The Opposition of Bean, Dyson and Murdoch

While strongly supported by the powerful notables in the British Army, like Field Marshal Douglas Haig, William Birdwood and Field Marshal Herbert Plumer, Monash had some who, up until the recapture of Hamel, strongly opposed his appointment as the Commander of the Australian Corps. These included the official war historian Charles Bean, war correspondent Keith Murdock, war artist Will Dyson and even, but to a lesser extent, the Australian Prime Minister William Morris Hughes, who changed his mind at the last moment. On 18 May 1918, the Australian Federal Government in the absence of Hughes, who was at the time sailing to England via North America, formally approved Monash's appointment as supreme commander of the ANZAC forces.

Bean, Dyson and Murdoch favoured the appointment of Brudenell White instead of Monash who they deviously argued would better suit an administrative role at the AIF head office in London. The success of Hamel put pay to the political gamesmanship of Bean and Murdoch and other

27 AWB, 'Celebrities', 2-3.

enemies of Monash at home. Hamel proved the turning point in Monash's career when he captured 177 machine guns causing the death of 2,000 German soldiers and taking 1,600 prisoners with 1,400 Allied casualties including 800 deaths. Monash called it: 'feeding his troops on victory'. He was well aware of the 'very serious anti-Semitic intrigue' against him and wrote home to his wife Victoria saying he would discuss the whole thing with Prime Minister Hughes.[28]

By talking to all the staff officers under Monash's command, Hughes changed his tune radically and stamped Monash 'as an outstanding figure of World War I'. Brudenell White declared that Birdwood made the right decision in appointing Monash as the Corps Commander. White was a friend of Monash and not involved in the Bean-Murdock conspiracy.

Remembering a great citizen-soldier

When Monash died in 1931, *Reveille* regarded him as 'the civilian who became one of the world's greatest soldiers, the soldier who became one of our greatest civilians. It is not too much to say that Monash was Australia's greatest son'. They claimed that this young nation had produced men of letters, artists, scientists, engineers who have been written large in 'the book of fame', but John Monash combined something of them all: 'Brilliant in war, brilliant in peace, a scholar amongst scholars, a lover of the arts, such was Sir John Monash'.[29]

It was not until 8 October 1950, however – nineteen years after his death – that John Monash's memory was at

28 Kieza, *Monash*, 433-47.

29 'The Thinning Ranks', *Reveille*, October 1931, 1.

last honoured by the unveiling in Melbourne of his statue by the Governor-General, the Rt Hon. William J McKell.[30]

For most of the time from 1919 to then, Australians had overwhelmingly favoured memorials to fallen Diggers rather than individual notables, like Monash. As Andrew Spaull once told us, Australian egalitarianism sought to foster a class of heroes, 'the diggers', rather than confer hero-status on the individual.[31] Monash himself would have agreed with this.

The real measure of Monash's much celebrated genius, as Grantlee Kieza points out in his biography, was learnt – not without making early mistakes – by extremely thorough preparation, to wring the complete usefulness from every factor in an organisational cleverly integrated way. He was brilliantly innovative at manipulating the modern industrial equipment, manpower and weapons. He thus drew on every aspect of his academic, engineering, legal, military and even musical knowledge and formal training, personal skills and experience to shape and re-shape his wartime strategies that he was able, and careful enough, to communicate to others in the imperial high command. Even as early as the Battle of Messines Ridge in Belgium under Sir Herbert Plumer's command:

> Monash constantly studies aerial photographs of the landscape around Messines and sends out 36 circulars on the planned manoeuvres. The machine-gunners' instructions come in seven parts. Each brigade practises its attack in a training area, and two large models [1/4 life-

30 'General Sir John Monash, GCMG, KCB, VD Statue Unveiled'.
31 Spaull, 'Sir John Monash', 247.

> size] are set up of the battlefield showing in miniature the trenches, wire, entanglements, streams, roads, and ruins.[32]

Monash's culturally-driven Jewish childhood, early formation and schooling were the seeds of his great success in maturity. He was inculcated with ideas, values and a classical knowledge and an Australian concept of political liberty, individualism and responsible citizenship in a rising colonial society.

At Scotch College, Calvinistic values of hard work and intellectual honesty had been readily absorbed by Monash. Being bilingual within the folds of his immigrant family was a strong intellectual advantage. The mentorship of William Elliott, together with the socialising Jerilderie bush experience became valuable assets in the leadership roles he was to play in war and peace.

ON GALLIPOLI

Weary 'ashen-faced' Men

> The roll is called – how heart-breaking it is – name after name is called; the reply a deep silence which can be felt, despite the noise of the incessant cracking of rifles and screaming of shrapnel – there are few of us left to answer our names – just a thin line of weary ashen-faced men, behind a mass of silent forms, once our comrades – there they have been for days, we have not had time to bury them.
>
> Signaller Ellis Silas, 16 Battalion AIF, 11 May 1915[33]

32 Kieza, *Monash*, 364.

33 Cited together with Ellis Silas' sketch in pencil of the roll call, also depicting the dead bodies lying behind the line of remaining men on the morning of 9th May 1915, Richard Reid, *Gallipoli 1915*, ABC Books, Sydney, 2002, 36.

Under the command of Colonel John Monash of the 4th Brigade AIF, between 25 April and 13 May 1915, the 16th Battalion suffered 757 casualties (dead, wounded and missing) out of 1,207 who had landed on the peninsula.[34] These were largely the results of the so-called Battle of the Bloody Angle, Gallipoli, at dawn on 3 March 1915. One of the signallers, Ellis Silas described how they sang "It's a long way to Tipperary" as they charged up the hill and that the 'cries of the wounded, the tremendous fusillade of rifles and screaming of shells was indescribable'.[35] The 16th Battalion was the first unit of Monash's 4th Brigade to be blooded in war and the results were not at all pleasant.

Monash, who became commander of the 4th Brigade in October 1914, had been previously appointed the Senior Military Officer of the Second Australian convoy. He sailed on 22 December 1914 in the flagship *Ulysses* which was one of sixteen vessels that transported 10,500 new troops that Monash had thoroughly trained before departure. His convoy was joined by three more transports from New Zealand carrying 2,000 troops. The New Zealand contingent had rendezvous-ed with the Australian ships at Albany as the port of assembly.[36]

The 4th Brigade under the command of Monash, from its beginnings four weeks after the outbreak of the Great War, was an Australia-wide brigade which had been organised and gathered at Broadmeadows, Victoria, where it was given elementary training before sailing. When they had reached

---

34 Read, *Gallipoli.*

35 Cited in Read, *Gallipoli*, 35.

36 PA Pedersen, *Monash as Military Commander*, Melbourne University Press, Carlton, 1985, 48.

Egypt, they had gone into camp near Heliopolis as part of Major-General Sir Alexander Godley's New Zealand and Australian Division. Godley and the corps commander Lieutenant William Birdwood were well satisfied with Monash's extremely thorough methods of training.

Monash did not belong by birth to that select band of country gentry – ' the solid core of the Australian Club in Sydney, the Melbourne Club, the Adelaide Club, the Tasmanian Club and the Weld Club in Perth'. His birth as a Jew had excluded him from these clubs and he was never fully accepted in such circles. He had, however, employed 'the vast talents which nature had planted in him in a drive for recognition by that coterie which had no intention of ever receiving him in their hearts, while exploiting for their own purposes his energy and his gifts'.[37] And yet, he was a pillar of Melbourne society as a contradiction in terms.

On the Voyage to Egypt

At Albany, Monash had complained bitterly of the lamentable arrangements for the voyage; the grave difficulties that he was struggling to overcome. No agreement had been reached with the Navy on inter-ship communication which he had viewed as being vital. Once at sea, signals were restricted to urgent navy matters. It was to Monash a chaotic situation from a military organisational point of view. Some vessels had leaking pipes or toilets that did not flush. Essential medical supplies were either inadequate or non-existent on some ships. Many men had been allocated

37 CMH Clark, *A History of Australia*, vol V, Melbourne University Press, Carlton, 1981, 391.

to the wrong ship and their whereabouts was unknown to their commanders. Too much secrecy by staff officers had created disorganisation.

Even so, somehow Monash managed to settle the 4th Brigade into a strict routine of training that was carried out throughout the voyage. The rank and file concentrated on musketry and theoretical work. NCOs received advanced instruction in evening lectures on responsibilities and leadership. Monash concentrated on the training of commissioned officers, including reconnaissance. In this, Monash revealed himself as a highly effective lecturer/teacher with outstanding skills that were to impress the whole officer class of the contingent. On the journey, Monash made certain that time was fully occupied in the waking hours for all the men on board each vessel.[38]

On 29 January 1915, the convoy entered the Suez Canal. Monash learnt that the AIF were to be placed under the supreme command of Major General William Riddell Birdwood, a professional English soldier, who had been born in India in 1865 as a son of the military. He had trained for the army at the Royal Military College at Sandhurst, 'the fortress of class privilege in the mother country and the empire at large'. Kitchener as Secretary of State for War had recommended him as Supreme Commander of the Australian and New Zealand forces. As an English gentleman-soldier, he was to give orders to the Australian Army, including John Monash. The Australians, to their surprise, adored him and called him "Birdie", but only among themselves, never to his face. He had a charisma as a leader, the 'gift of the gab'

38 Pedersen, *Monash*, 48-49.

and a 'bubbling warmth' that appealed to both the so-called boys of the bush and the men from the suburbs that had made up the entire AIF.

In Egypt after a vast amount of training, Birdwood inspected Monash's 4th Brigade. He told its commander that his men were the finest brigade in Egypt.[39] The brigade, however, and Monash were yet to be tested on Gallipoli. But Monash and Birdwood had struck up an excellent relationship from the very start.

Experiencing Gallipoli from start to finish

For Monash and the brigade, their baptism of fire was to be on Gallipoli rather than the Western Front. The brigade landed in dribbles and the 16th Battalion was to meet the enemy early as Signaller Ellis Silas portrayed in words and illustrations. Most of the 4th Brigade were in reserve and spread in different spots. Shortly after 8am on 26 April 1915, Monash landed with a bodyguard and immediately came under shrapnel fire. They bivouacked briefly on a sheltered part of the beach. Monash was given the highly difficult and vital left-centre sector including Pope's Hill and Quinn's Post to organise while the Turks constantly counter-attacked.

Soon Monash headed up Shrapnel Gully at the southern end of the beach, coming immediately under 'a hail of shrapnel and a chaos of cracking bullets'. The debris of battle was everywhere. His brigade was expected to hold the left-centre section of the perimeter near Pope's Hill and Quinn's Post from what soon became known as Monash Valley, the deepest of territory from the shore on the peninsula.

39 Clark, *A History of Australia*, vol V, 392.

By 30 April 1915, the 4th Brigade were still scattered to some extent, but Monash had a conference with his battalion commanders that day and things began to get better organised. The night offensive on Baby 700 of 2 May, which Monash had opposed, was disastrous according to Bean. Later, the 4th Brigade played a role in defeating the major Turkish attack on 19 May. On 29 May after the break in to Quinn's Post, a much depleted brigade was relieved to be rested in Reserve Gully.

Monash and the brigade's involvement came with the major August offensive, the Battle of Sari Bair, which was an attempt to outflank the Turkish position facing the Anzacs above them and to seize Sari Bair Ridge on the left hook of Hill 971 which overlooked them. Then, they were to press on across the straits to the narrows, to form the spearhead of the left assaulting column. After seizing the approaches, it was intended to take and consolidate Hill 971 (Koja Chemen Tepe) and Hill Q. It did not work as planned as the terrain proved too difficult.

In July, Monash received official word of his tardy promotion to brigadier-general at a time when he was well-aware of the wild rumours circulating in Cairo, London and Melbourne that he had been shot as a German spy and traitor. Earlier the previous October, there had been similar anti-Semitic campaigns in Melbourne.

At the beginning of this most ambitious assault, the 4th Brigade made a good start, but time was lost. Their night march was delayed. Things went awry. The guides lost their way at a vital turning and the maps were found to be unreliable. The men became exhausted. Dawn found them well short of their objective and uncertain of their position. Sensibly, Monash ordered them to dig in where they were to await events. They were scattered across the rough terrain.

The next day, 7 August, an attempt was made to renew the advance under the command of Colonel Harold Pope delegated by Monash who remained at his headquarters, but was out of touch since the telephone wire had been cut. The result was a fiasco. Pope was hopelessly confronted with a heavy Turkish reinforced force. Machine guns and artillery were killing the Australians in large numbers. The remnant of the 4th Brigade was, therefore, forced to withdraw on 8 August. Some of the dead and wounded had to be abandoned.

The morale of the brigade plummeted. It was not Monash's finest hour, but the whole offensive had been fatally flawed anyway. The task the high command had given the 4th Brigade had been beyond the capacity of any attacking force. Elsewhere in the south, the attack had also collapsed.

The role of the brigade had not ended there. There were orders, against Monash's wishes, to attack a small outcrop. Hill 60 was still held by the Turks and it was considered by the high command essential to take it and establish the link between the bridgeheads and secure them.

When they attacked, the Allied artillery from the British ships accidently fell on the attacking waves of the brigade killing them in large numbers. A second attempt four days later also failed. On 13 September, the remnant of the 4th were embarked for a rest on the island of Lemnos.

While in Egypt, Monash learned of his appointment as CB (the most honourable Order Companion of the Bath of the Military Division). The CB was introduced after the Battle of Waterloo specifically to acknowledge acts of bravery. It was a knighthood. He had become Sir John Monash.

After three weeks leave in Egypt, Monash returned with the 4th Brigade to a quiet sector on Gallipoli. There was to be no more heavy fighting, as in November 1915 a decision was made by the higher command to evacuate. Monash had learnt and absorbed many stern lessons.[40]

Nevertheless, the fact of the matter was the Anzacs, with limited resources, were faced with an impregnable Turkish stronghold. Bean linked the 8 August 1915 Battle of Sari Bair for the 4th Brigade on Gallipoli with the Battle of Fromelles on the Western Front as the two 'Black Days' of the AIF. His personal experience of what he had seen was that:

> ... so rugged was [the country in front of the 4th Brigade] that from the supposed starting-point [which the column had barely reached at the end of its calamitous advance] the climbing of Abdel Rahman Bair, even in daylight and in peaceful manoeuvres, would have taken troops, though at the acme of fitness and health, longer than the time allowed for the whole operation. Leaving out of account the fact that the brigade was intended to proceed up an exposed spur with the enemy possibly on several sides, the natural difficulties which were still in front of the column at day-break were considerably greater than the sum of those encountered by any column on the night of August 6.[41]

No one could have led a brigade to victory in such

---

40 'Monash, General John (27 June 1865-8 October 1931)', *The Oxford Companion to Australian Military History*, 404-06.

41 Cited by AJ Smithers, *Sir John Monash*, Angus & Robertson, Sydney, 1973, 124.

conditions. The casualties amounted to 22 officers and 743 other ranks, mostly wounded, but Monash had learned much about modern warfare.

Monash's mind pondered on the events: 'I am afraid it must be admitted that [Sir] Ian Hamilton's plan in its entirety has so far failed to achieve its main objective.'

He believed that the failure overshadowed 'the many minor successes and the brilliant achievement of the Australian troops and the New Zealanders'. He had come to realise that there were 'insufficient troops, inadequate munition, attempting more than was possible with the means available'. He realised that the Turkish losses, despite their success, were enormous. But the Australian and other Allied losses were heavy as well. He quickly came to the realisation that the 4th could do no more 'than hang on to what we have gained'. He and his men marched out of Reserve Gully with 3,350 men. The parade after the 6th of August assault numbered 1,037: two lieutenant-colonels, five majors, three captains and twenty-two lieutenants (out of a total of 136 officers). Some were 'lightly wounded' and sick from various infections, diseases and debilitating illnesses. Monash's loyalty to his men and to Australia was absolute: 'I am more than satisfied that after the destruction of the regular [British] army in France, no other troops at the Empire's disposal could have got and held a footing on Gallipoli except the Australians and New Zealanders'.[42]

When the evacuation was completed, Monash, on a bunk in the pantryman's cabin on the small transport

42 Cited in Smithers, *Sir John Monash*, 125-6; Serle, 'Monash, Sir John (1865-1931)', 543-6.

Arran, wrote in his diary his last impressions: 'It was a most brilliant conception [the evacuation plan], brilliantly organized, brilliantly executed, and will, I am sure, rank as the greatest joke – and the greatest feat of arms – in the whole range of military history'.[43] Monash was not given to any exaggeration here.

In Egypt and wearied with the experience of Gallipoli, but now battle-hardened, Sir John Monash began training his reconstituted brigade. He was profoundly distressed by the news of his wife's operation for cancer. At first, he received a cable from Melbourne saying that his wife was ill and required surgery, but not telling him the cause. He was asked to give his permission as husband for the operation, which he did, without knowing what it was all about. After, he discovered that it was a matter of life or death; Victoria had uterine cancer. He was overwhelmed and cabled furiously. He went to Birdwood and Godley asking for a release on compassionate grounds to travel home if his wife further deteriorated. They refused. He persisted only to be told that the War Office would not let him go. If he left for Australia, it would be 'a sacrifice of honour'; he would let the whole AIF down. He was still prepared to leave Egypt until he received a cable from his wife's surgeon on 1 February 1916 notifying him that the operation was successful and his wife's prognosis was fairly good. He did not leave, but monitored his wife's progress.[44]

The remnants of the 4th Brigade were joined to the 4th Division and then spent two months in defences east of the

43 Cited in Smithers, *Sir John Monash* 132.

44 Roland Perry, *Monash. The Outsider who won a war*, Random House, Nth Sydney, 2007, 238; Pedersen, *Monash*, 127.

Suez Canal. In June 1916, they were moved to France to the Armentières sector and were involved in an unsuccessful night-raid on 2 July.

That month, Monash was promoted to major-general in command of the new 3rd AIF Division that was arriving on Salisbury Plain in England for further training.[45]

THE WESTERN FRONT

A frail and tenuous mist lingers on baffled and intricate branches;
Little gilt leaves are still, for quietness holds every bough;
Pools in the muddy road slumber, reflecting indifferent stars;
Steeped in the loveliness of moonlight is earth, and the valleys,
Brimmed up with quiet shadow, with a mist of sleep.
But afar on the horizon rise great pulses of light,
The hammering of guns, wrestling, locked in conflict
Like brute, stone gods of old struggling confusedly;
Then overhead purrs a shell, and our heavies

Answer, with sudden clapping bruits of sound,
Loosening our shells that stream whining and whimpering precipitately,
Hounding through air athirst for blood.
And the little gilt leaves
Flicker in falling, like waifs and flakes of flame.

Frederic Manning, "Leaves"[46]

45 Serle, 'Monash, Sir John', 546.
46 Frederic Manning, *Eidola*, John Murray, London, 1917, 25-26.

How did they get to the Western Front?

When the Gallipoli campaign ended in December 1915, the AIF was hastily reorganised and expanded from two to five divisions and then readied for action.

The 3rd Division at first trained vigorously on Salisbury Plain in England. King George V inspected the division meeting Monash and, in November, they moved into the Amentières sector as part of Godley's II Anzac Corps and General Sir Herbert Plumer's Second British Army.

The term 'Western Front' came from the Germans who distinguished this battleline from their eastern front against the Russian Imperial Army. Australian, Canadian, Indian, French and other troops simply adopted the term as their own.

When the Australian Divisions entered 'the fray' in early June 1916, the Western Front had settled into an opposing stalemate line of trenches and fortifications stretching about 800 kilometres from the Channel coast near Ostend in Belgium to Belfort in the French-Swiss border. Despite massive casualties and slaughter, there were no great changes of this Front.[47] The awesome power of the artillery barrage – 'The hammering of the guns, wrestling, locked in conflict', as the Australian poet Frederic Manning put it – and the scything of deadly machine guns at 500 or 600 bullets per minute, favoured mere defence over attack. The impasse was unbroken until the massive German offensive of March 1918, apart from the gut-wrenching Battle of Passchendaele in Belgian Flanders to the north.

Monash's good fortune on his arrival in France with the 3rd

47 Peter Cochrane, *The Western Front 1916-1918*, ABC Books, Sydney, 2004, vii.

Division was to serve directly under Sir Herbert Plumer and his chief-of-staff, Major General Charles ("Tim") Harington. His first major battle was to be Messines in June 1917.

The Triumph at Messines

The Australian position was focussed on the southern forward slope of the Messines-Wytschaete Ridge and stretched from the Hill 60 region in the north to the Lys near Armentières in the south. Between Warneton and Frelinghien, the Lys River separated the line. It was an area of countryside on which there had been no peace since October 1914.[48] The key objective was the western heights of the ridge.

Plumer's Second Army held the Allies Salient which was almost surrounded by German guns on ridges. Nonetheless, he had made – in 'bulldog fashion' – the 'Salient a nut so hard to crack' that the enemy had not tried to take the position. Plumer had an extraordinary chief-of-staff in Harington. He was a highly competent senior officer of 60 years – cultured, wise, a cautious, well-organised planner with an 'extra dash' of imagination and verve and a brilliant eye for detail. Thus an ideal mentor for Monash to emulate and learn much from.

During two long, lean years, Plumer and Harington had hung on, constantly strengthening their defences and studying 'their terrain with microscopic thoroughness'. They planned on the salient to capture the occupied Messines-Wytschaete flank. Plumer's 'trump card' was a system of enormous land mines burrowed beneath the German Front. This work had begun in 1915, when Monash and

---

48 FM Cutlack, *The Australians: Their Final Campaign, 1918*, Sampson Low, London, 1918, 21.

the Australians were on Gallipoli, with the construction of shallow galleries about fifteen feet underground. In 1916, the idea of concentrating on a deep mining offensive with tunnels and charges nearly 100 feet below the surface was contemplated. But to penetrate secretly with galleries of substantial size seemed impossible in the saturated semi-liquid layer that made up the Flanders subsoil. On the face of it, it seemed an impossible task. Might there be a way?

The problem was examined by Lieutenant Colonel T Edgeword David, chief geologist of the British Expeditionary Force and the Engineer-in-Chief, Brigadier-General GH Fowke. Together they analysed the sand and clay layers of subsoil and variation in water in each. They recommended to go further down to the layer of heavy blue clay at 80 to 120 feet below, which could not be blown up accidently by enemy mortar fire.[49]

Secrecy was vital and time was of the essence. By January 1916, six tunnels had been started. Their entrances all had signs above them to deceive the enemy – 'Deep Wells' – and, during the year, twenty of the largest mines ever in the history of warfare were completed. Twenty underground communities of military miners or sappers had come into being so much nearer the cutting face to save time.

From the sandbagged entrance to each mine, long wooden staircases led almost vertically down to the sleeping quarters of the men. Below them again were planked passageways slanted to headquarters posts and thence to the actual three-by-six galleries in the bowels of the earth. There was

49 Leon Wolff, *In Flanders Fields. The 1917 Campaign*, Longman, Green and Co, London, 1960, 70-71.

a mole-like character to it all in the deep dark places. The hum of pumping engines to remove water worked on a twenty-four-hour basis. It was absolutely vital to remove as much water as possible. Thousands worked at the face with picks and shovels. They coughed in the dampness. Their skins were greyish white. The rate of work per day was ten to fifteen feet forward. They worked under the glare of electric lamps. As each gallery was completed, a powerful explosive mine was laid in place, and sometimes even two. These individual mines contained charges of ammonal of up to 95,000 lbs. Some tunnels were about half a mile in length. By 7 June, the total came to about a million pounds of explosives and five miles of gallery. The Germans were also mining in the opposite direction, but not anywhere near to the same extent.

The steep commanding ridge was occupied by the Germans who were expecting an attack on the ground, not from below. They sent out raiding parties that the 3rd Division had to deal with under Monash's careful direction.

Every tunnel had been given a name, including the Newcastle shaft, the Snout, the Sydney, Perth, Hobart and the Great Brisbane. By late evening, 6 June, the nineteen mines were fully in place under the occupied Messines Ridge and charged, their shafts were tamped down – some even six months before.

To the Allies, the German-held Messines Ridge seemed as lofty and arrogant as Gibraltar, flaming with bigger guns, webbed with row after row of sandbagged trenches, peppered with thousands of machine-gun emplacements, pillboxes and sharpshooters' nests. The Messines-Wytschaete section of the ridge was manned by four German divisions, with two more in reserve.

On 29 April, a spy advised the German High Command that the British would attack the ridge after stopping their main effort on the Arras Front, which was close to the truth of the matter. But not quite. The Germans reinforced their position opposite Plumer's Army, expecting an attack across the surface of the terrain.[50]

About 3.10am, each of the nineteen land mines exploded, almost in unison. The sound travelled across the Channel to London and was heard by Prime Minister Lloyd George – he always claimed – awake at the early hour in his study at No 10 Downing Street. At the same moment, Plumer had returned to his bedroom at his headquarters away from the rest of his staff and knelt at his bed in prayer. The huge explosion even caused panic in the city of Lille, fifteen miles away.

Nineteen volcanoes seemed to erupt almost at once as over a million pounds of ammonal completely tore apart the carefully-constructed German defences from which the Germans had dominated the Allied lines for the past two years. Whole villages completely disappeared. As the mighty pillars of smoke and flame billowed upwards into the sky from the earthquake with a red glare of Hell, the Allied artillery followed it by an unrelenting assault of all known German artillery positions behind the ridge. They were followed by the Allied troops of Plumer's Army.

Nine Allied infantry divisions, a total of well over 100,000 men – British, Australians, New Zealanders, Irish and Welsh – swarmed forward in a ten-mile line. There was

50 Wolff, *In Flanders Fields*, 75-79.

not a great deal of opposition on the ground; most of the German soldiers who had survived were too stunned, too dazed to react. The main obstacles to the Allies offensive came from German gunfire from well behind the Messines position using a mixture of high explosives and gas shells. Monash's 3rd Division, as they moved forward, were gassed, 500 of them.

General Plumer was too shrewd a leader not to consolidate. He skilfully directed troops to occupy vital positions as they moved forward. Over 7,000 prisoners had been taken and large quantities of German arms captured which had been carried by the surviving troops. The German official history gave their casualty figure (dead and badly wounded) as 23,000, not including the lightly wounded. The British Second Army casualties in the battle on the land was 23,000, over half of which were in the Anzac Corps,[51] especially from gassing and accidental friendly fire from British artillery.

John Monash absorbed Plumer's methods of thorough planning and preparation of troops for battle. In a letter home prior to the staged battle, he wrote on 19 May 1917:

> I am now in the thick of preparation for our forthcoming offensive operations [the Battle of Messines Ridge]. My job is to capture the southern spur of a famous ridge, and to form a defensive flank for our army. For weeks past, we have been making roads, building railways and tramways, forming ammunition-dumps, making gun emplacements and camouflaging them, preparing

51 Philip Warner, *Passchendaele. The Story behind the Tragic Victory of 1917*, Wordsworth Editions, London, 1999, 34-35.

> brigade and battalion headquarters and laying a complex system of underground cables, fixing the position of machine guns, heavy guns and howitzers...[52]

Using his commercial background in business life, he took account of the mass of field engineering work to complete with great efficiency in creating large dugouts, approach avenues, assembly and jumping-off trenches; volumes of written orders were produced containing notable clarity of expression to avoid confusion in critical moments. The movement and total control of 20,000 men as well as the carrying animals – mules and horses – was essential in Monash's overall plan. He addressed feeding organisation, transport organisation, ammunition supplies, cutters for the enemy barbed wire, preliminary destruction bombardments and, finally, the preparation of 12,000 infantry for the actual work of 'going over the top'.

Monash spent a full day with the brigade commanders going carefully through the details of his plan.[53] In other words, Monash at Messines did all he possibly could to ensure success in a set piece of a battle based on Plumer's pick-and-hold technique of carefully advancing into enemy territory and consolidating before moving on. There was no point in a rapid advance without securing limited objectives. Monash even had built, on a piece of land, a large-scale model of the whole battleground that the troops could observe the various concentration points and the terrain difficulties they would encounter, as well as the position of

52 Cited in Richard Travers, *Diggers in France. Australian Soldiers on the Western Front*, ABC Books, Sydney, 2008, 155-6.

53 Travers, *Diggers in France*, 155-6.

the barbed-wire barriers.[54] Nothing was left to chance.

The Battle of Messines was a huge success for the Allies. It regained public confidence in the leadership of the British Expeditionary Force, especially in General Haig. Monash had done well in his part of the attack on the German salient and had been noticed by British authorities. The Germans had suffered an immense setback, even though they were resilient.

The way was now clear for the British Expeditionary Force to drive on to Passchendaele to secure a passage to the coast of Belgium. That, anyway, was the plan in Haig's mind. At Messines, however, while the Allies won decisively, casualties surprisingly were about even on both sides. The British sustained 26,000 including 13,900 in the 3rd and 4th Divisions of the Anzac Corps.[55]

On to Passchendaele

With the dramatic clearance of the well-fortified German Messines salient, Haig claimed he had secured his right flank in Flanders (he took credit for it rather than recognising Plumer) in readiness to drive the Germans away from the Belgian coast around Ostend which they had occupied at the beginning of the war. His plan was to advance north-west from the ruined city of Ypres which the Allies held across the Passchendaele Ridge and then on to the coast. The Battle of Passchendaele, or Third Ypres as it was sometimes called by some historians, was the more famous name given to a series of eleven limited smaller battles in succession fought between 31 July and 30 November 1917. Haig

54 Documentary footage shown in *Monash. The Forgotten Hero*, Film Victoria, Screen Australia, ABC TV, DVD 2008.
55 Travers, *Diggers in France*, 157-8.

intended that the II Anzac would spearhead in at least five of these attacks – the third to the seventh inclusive. Instead of the brilliant Plumer, Haig put in Sir Hubert Gough to command the Passchendaele adventure. With Messines, Haig, via Plumer's work, had only cleared the first hurdle in 'his race against time and politicians'[56]. But his plan was a big gamble in Flanders field, with the odds against him.

In Gough, Haig had made a bad choice. He was a conservative ex-cavalryman, an impetuous forty-seven-year-old who was not interested in limited partial gains and careful consolidation, like Plumer or Major General Sir Henry Rawlinson. Gough had no understanding of the countryside in which he was asked to operate. He did not accept the step-by-step approach, but simply wanted to storm ahead.

The assaults in Belgium that make up the Third Ypres or Passchendaele, in which the Australians participated and distinguished themselves, included: the Battle of Menin Road on 20 September 1917; the Battle of Polygon Wood on 26 September, where Monash brought off one of the greatest AIF victories; the Battle of Broodseinde on 4 October; the weather had broken and Monash's 3rd Division suffered the mudded misery of Passchendaele on 12 October.

They then were withdrawn from the murderous battlefields of Flanders and rested for a while until the Battle of Cambrai.

Captain Clarence Smith Jeffries, a Victoria Cross winner on 12 October 1917, was recognised for 'deeds of supreme merit' in the ferocious second last year of the war of 1914-1918. He died in a deadly encounter with the enemy at Passchendaele. Courageous men and women were vital,

56 Wolff, *In Flanders Fields*, 83.

as John Monash saw it, to a young and emerging nation finding its own identity, as well as his military success.

★ ★ ★

Monash boasted publicly that the 3rd Division was 'one of the Crack Divisions of the British Army'.[57] It spent most of the winter quietly in the Ploegsteert sector. In November, it had at last gained the other divisions in I Anzac Corps. John Monash dined privately with Sir Douglas Haig, who let him know that he wanted him as a corps commander. At the New Year, Monash was appointed KCB – not a mere knighthood, but the Most Honourable Knight Commander of the Order of the Bath, which was founded in 1725 and reconstituted in 1815 to three military classes. Monash gained the top class.

The event of his investiture by King George V was one of Australia's most elaborate presentation ceremonies. It was held at Monash's headquarters and took place at the Front, at Bertangles Château in the open air at the entranceway above the steps on 11 August 1918. Documentary footage of the event survives, depicting the strict protocol that was followed before a large contingent of Australian

Lieutenant-General Sir John Monash knighted by King George V, Bertangles Château, August 1918; spoils of war (guns) exhibited in the background (AWM E0395)

57 Cited in Serle, 'Monash', 546.

troops at attention on parade. They were inspected by His Majesty in uniform, before the 'dubbing', attended at the top of the steps by prominent members of the High Command.[58] Movie cameras were there to record the event.

Monash, because of high security for a monarch at the Front, only received 24 hours' notice of the King's arrival at Bertangles at 3pm to invest him with his knighthood. General William Birdwood had requested it to take place on the Western Front. The preceding day, Monash had received glowing commendations in writing from Sir Douglas Haig.

Monash was able to gather 600 of his finest troops for the King's inspection and the main audience of the ceremony of the great event. A guard of honour lined the long drive at Bertangles from the iron gates with its coat of arms to the steps of the château's forecourt. Several items of war spoil were dragged in by Monash's staff: several hundreds of German artillery, howitzers, machine guns, transport vehicles, even searchlights. All of these large items were arranged 'artistically' for the filmed event in the château's quadrangle. Hubert Wilkins was the official photographer to record the event.

Charles Bean's anti-Semitism stirred up anger; he called it 'a lot of nonsense'.[59] Monash had organised the whole impressive occasion well, however, and had honoured the reigning monarch's bravery. Monash's star was in the ascendency, despite Bean's nasty opposition.

When the King's car came into view in brilliant sunshine along the kilometre avenue leading to the château, Monash

---

58 Major General Gordon Maitland, *Honours and Awards of the Army*, Playbill Military Publications, North Moore Park, Sydney, 2014, 233-5; Documentary footage, DVD, 2008.

59 Kieza, *Monash*, 484; Pedersen, *Monash*, 256.

called his men to attention. With Thomas Blamey, his chief-of-staff, and Brigadier-General Carruthers, he greeted the King who was accompanied by two aides. The King then took the royal salute, inspected the Australian troops with Monash beside him. They then walked up the steps of the château and into the reception area through the doors. Monash presented the owner Marquis de Clemont-Tonnerre, a very elderly French gentleman with a white beard who had recently lost his only son on the Western Front. Monash then proudly presented his five divisional commanders with whom King George chatted. After ten minutes or so, they moved outside to the piazza for the investiture. A sword, which had taken some time to find, lay on a small table and a footstool had been placed on a carpet for Monash to kneel on. With his staff looking on, his name was called out and he stepped up and stood at attention before the King.

'Kneel, please', said the King.

Monash went down on his right knee. The investiture ended with the King saying: 'Arise, Sir John'. He then handed Monash the insignia of Knight Commander of the Bath. It was placed around his neck. The King smiled, pumped his hand and made a little speech commenting on his work and that of the Australian troops under him. The onlookers applauded. Monash took the King around the outside of the château showing him the impressive battle trophies cleaned for the occasion.[60] Monash had received what he called his 'battlefield honour', but the war had not yet been won.

In a letter to his wife Victoria, Monash remarked: 'The whole ceremony lasted only a half-hour, and took place amid

60 John Monash, *War Letters*, 260.

brilliant sunshine, and our Australian Squadron aeroplanes circling overhead',[61] – a nice last touch for Monash as the shrewd showman who knew how to organise great occasions.

Monash as Corps Commander

What had lead up to his knighthood when Monash was the first in 200 years to be 'dubbed' in the battlefield?

When Monash became Corps Commander and replaced General William Birdwood, his responsibilities were numerous and complex. Always, he had had General Haig's complete backing for the appointment with open virulent opposition by some Australian journalists, led by Charles Bean who frequently expressed Anti-Semitic prejudice against him as a German Jew, rather than a native-born proud Australian, not of British descent.

Lieutenant-General John Monash outside the headquarters of his 3rd Division at Glisy, 25 May 1918 (AWM C1218)

As Corps Commander, he was in charge of five Australian infantry divisions, a fixed allotment of 50,000 corps troops, comprising the 13th Australian Light Horse Regiment, two Australian tunnelling companies, heavy and siege artillery, heavy trench mortar, signal and transport units and several administrative services. Also attached to his command on a permanent basis was the 3rd

61 Roland Perry, *Monash*, 383-4.

Squadron Australian Flying Corps for reconnaissance, artillery observation and contact patrolling (dogfights with the enemy). The administrative tasks included motor ambulance convoys and twenty labour companies.

Other units, distinct from the Corps, were available to him for specific purposes, like the 5th British Tank Brigade. In all, the Corps had a total of 166,000 men and was the largest by far in the British Expeditionary Force under the supreme commander General Douglas Haig.

Haig expected a lot from Monash and he never failed to deliver. Monash's command, he proudly claimed, was more than two and a half times the size of the British Army under the Duke of Wellington at the Battle of Waterloo, or even the French Army under Napoleon Bonaparte.[62] And it all was under the charge of a native-born Australian engineer from Melbourne – culturally, a gentleman fond of the Arts.

From the Battle of Messines, Haig had great faith in Monash. Birdwood had supported him as successor, taking Brudenell White with him as his Chief-of-Staff. White was the only viable alternative to Monash to command all the Australians on the Western Front. Haig's view progressively grew to a consistently favourable impression. Monash consolidated it by his successive achievements in key battles. And yet, Charles Bean had argued: 'Besides, we do not want Australia represented by men [meaning Monash] mainly because of their ability, natural and inborn in Jews, to push themselves'.[63]

Bean and war artist Will Dyson left for London on 18 May to discuss a cunning plot with Keith Murdoch to shift

62 Pedersen, *Monash*, 219.
63 Cited in Pedersen, *Monash*, 216.

Monash upwards from Corps Commander in the field and put Major-General Brudenell White in his place. Then Monash could be promoted further up the line to replace Birdwood as GOC AIF, a largely administrative position, beit higher up on the British Military chain-of-command. They believed Monash's ego would tell him to accept. The intrigue Bean started and persisted with became his greatest mistake. He was totally wrong because of deep-seated prejudice.

At this time, William Morris Hughes, Australia's Welsh-born Prime Minister, was *en route* to England for the Imperial War Conference. Keith Murdoch, a powerful London-based Australian journalist close to the Prime Minister, cabled him claiming falsely that he was representing the Australian Army. He proposed that Monash's current position, which had already been endorsed by the Cabinet of the Australian Parliament, be made only on a temporary basis with the intention of replacing him with White – in opposition to Haig's view.

On 29 May, one of Birdwood's staff Major Thomas Dodds 'positively assured George Pearce [Australia's Minister of Defence] in Melbourne that the views of Murdoch and Bean [both only war correspondents after all] did not accord with those of the senior officers in France he had consulted', and were 'entirely opposed to the feeling of the whole AIF who stoutly opposed control … of personnel from London by officers not serving in the field'.[64] Dodds said that Murdoch, who was lying, was an 'irresponsible pressman'. The damage, however, was done by Murdoch as Hughes had already acceded to his request. Geoffrey Serle called it: 'perhaps the

64 Cited in Pedersen, *Monash*, 216-7.

outstanding case of sheer irresponsibility by pressmen in Australian history'.

Hughes, a wily politician, eventually found he needed to do a backflip, although the sabotage, especially by Murdoch and Bean, had continued. On 1 July, Hughes and his deputy prime minister Joseph Cook arrived at Monash's headquarters at Monash's invitation. With Birdwood, who was also there, they inspected the troops. Both Hughes and Cook questioned, in private, all the commanders they could during their stay. Everyone to a man enthusiastically supported Monash as commander. Murdoch had gone too far in intimidating Birdwood and trying to get rid of him altogether. Monash was well aware of what was going on and it was an added pressure.

Three days later, Monash won his most significant battle of the war at Le Hamel. Afterwards, William Birdwood wrote to Monash saying that the battle had entirely justified his promotion. White rebuked Murdoch for impropriety, ignorance and dangerous meddling in military affairs. White had become embarrassed by the situation. Hughes now changed his tune and cabled the Australian cabinet telling them that he was impressed with Monash.[65] How could he not be after Le Hamel? Hughes had also spoken to General Plumer and Rawlinson of Messines fame who also supported Monash to the hilt and showed great faith in him as a Corps Commander.[66] Hughes then realised that he needed to leave it all alone. There was too great a political risk for himself in pursuing such a cause.

65 Serle, *John Monash*, 324-7.
66 Perry, *Monash*, 336-8.

The 'messianic' approach of Bean and Murdoch had ignored certain facts: Monash's popularity from the grassroots to the top of the AIF; the support of the British military establishment, especially Haig and King George V; the support of Birdwood and also of the modest White, who regarded Monash, his friend, as a better choice than himself for the vital role of being in charge in the field of all the Anzac forces on the Western Front.

For these reasons and more, the pressmen as kingmakers had failed. Haig had had the AIF commander's position earmarked for Monash from the beginning as soon as he had taken over the 3rd Division. Although King George could not openly support Monash, he was still his favourite son in the BEF.

While the Bean-Murdoch cabal had not worked, Field Marshal Haig had a simple solution if it did: he would appoint John Monash to command another army corps under his control. With this level of support, Monash had no need to defend himself. And yet he wrote home to his wife: 'It's a great nuisance to have to fight a ***pogrom*** of this nature in the midst of all one's anxieties'.

The reality of the entire matter, anyway, was Monash could not be removed or replaced as field commander of the new Australian Corps without his agreement, since his appointment had been confirmed by the Australian Government, beit in the absence of William Morris Hughes.[67]

The whole aggressive campaign against Monash was misjudged and deluded. Monash had stood his ground,

67 Ross Coulthart, *Charles Bean*, Harper Collins Publishers, Sydney, 2014, 314-5.

refusing to budge from the Australian Corps command. He also believed that he was the best man for the job anyway. Nevertheless, during the entire meddling, he had to fight to keep his job while planning one of the great set-piece battles of the war.

During his visit, Hughes witnessed an impressive four-and-a-half hour briefing by Monash who had memorised every aspect of his plan and knew all the details of units that would be engaged in it. Monash was able to draw powerfully from the teaching ability he had displayed from adolescence.

Later, Hughes gave a rousing speech to the Australian soldiers about to fight in the proposed Battle of Hamel. Within thirty-six hours, these men would be advancing under the bursting shells and be confronting machine-gun nests. Sir John Monash's performance at Hamel completely and utterly dispelled any doubts about his suitability for the fighting command appointment.[68]

One British historian, David Stevenson, in *With Our Backs to the Wall. Victory and Defeat in 1918*, was moved to write:

> The Australian divisions had recently been consolidated into an Australian Army Corps, and for the first time would fight with their own staffs and support services and under an Australian commander, Sir John Monash, allowing them to display **to the full their aggressive and democratic fighting ethos**. Monash, who was unusual among BEF officers both for being Jewish and for his civilian background, applied a clear brain and business experience to the problem of the Western Front ...[69]

---

68 Coulthart, *Charles Bean*, 316-8.

69 David Stevenson, *With Our Backs to the Wall. Victory and Defeat in 1918*, Allen Lane, Penguin, London, 2011, 120.

Stevenson had read Monash's *The Australian Victories in France in 1918* which was published in 1919 and had been written in the space of a month.

Hamel – the First Black Day for the German Army

> This battle [Hamel] was the first definite offensive on a substantial scale which had been undertaken by any of the armies of the Allies on any front since the close of the autumn campaign of 1917 and the opening of the German offensive in the early spring of 1918. Its success converted the whole thoughts of the Allies from an attitude of pure defensive to an attitude of offensive, and it begun to dawn upon the High Command that it was, after all, possible to do something else but sit down and take the cuffs and kicks of the enemy. The psychological effect of the battle of Hamel was electric and startling.[70]

So wrote John Monash. He was not one to hide his great achievement under a bushel. While writing his own propaganda, he was always close to the truth.

General Headquarters, in answer to the excited enquiries 'from far and near' asking how it was done in 93 minutes, published a special pamphlet describing the battle plan and the 'new methods' Monash had employed. It was used widely in the British Army as an instructional tool for training officers. Marshal Ferdinand Foch, the supreme commander of the Allies, was induced by it, Monash claimed, to undertake a counter-attack on 18 July 1918 which had the effect of

70 FM Cutlack (ed.), *War Letters of General Monash*, Angus & Robertson, Sydney, 1934, 275.

arresting the German rush towards Paris.

The enemy had pushed within forty miles of the capital, which was Germany's last success of the war. Under Monash, the Australians with other Allies in their counter-offensive went on to the capture of Mont St Quentin on 28 August; the capture of Péronne on 31 August; the capture of the Front system of the Hindenburg defences on 18 September and the capture of the main Hindenburg defences on 29 September to 6 October.

During this period, Monash's was a fluctuating command, varying from the five Australian divisions up to a total of eight divisions including, at times, two Canadian divisions, two American divisions and the British 32nd Division headed by General Lambert. During one phase, Monash had under his command 200,000 troops.[71]

But what of the Battle of Hamel that started it all going and frequently described by historians as John Monash's masterpiece?

> In the name of France I am happy to express to Australia the memory which we shall cherish of her incomparable soldiers.
>
> Marshal Foch, Anzac Day, London, 1919

General John Monash's surprise attack on the German defences at Hamel village and forest on 4 July 1918 took 93 minutes to take to victory – three minutes longer than he had carefully estimated it would take. It went like clockwork. The Australians in their first action as a corps won a near perfect victory. And it was a battle in which Monash had staked so much. He had achieved a sense of

71 Cutlack (ed.), *War Letters*, 277.

musical harmony for the first time between the use of the British tanks and the infantry in combination. They were under the same orders and, for the first time, on firm ground instead of mud. Brilliant use by the Australian Flying Corps was made. Tanks protecting infantry came through better than expected and better than they had ever before achieved – only three were put out of action by the German defence and even those three were repairable to be used again. Monash ensured the tanks were well protected by artillery. The Australians collected 1,500 prisoners. While there were, at the first count, 800 Australian casualties, most, it appeared, were walking wounded who would fight again. Hamel had involved American troops for the first time and, on 4 July – United States national day!

In a highly mobile battle, Monash had used planes to drop ammunition to the machine gunners successfully and it reduced the risk to ammunition carriers to machine-gun emplacements on the ground. Time and life was saved efficiently.

From the Inter-Allied War Council meeting in Versailles, William Morris Hughes sent a telegram, which included a message from Haig to Hughes as Australian's Prime Minister: 'Will you please convey to Lieutenant-General Sir John Monash and all ranks under his command, including the Tanks and the detachment of 33rd American Division, my warm congratulations on the success which attended the operation carried out this morning, and the skill and gallantry with which it was conducted.'[72] Warm praise indeed from the British supremo!

72 Cited in Perry, *Monash*, 356.

Hamel could be described in a sentence as 'a dawn attack against a ridge by two brigades of mainly Australian troops and some Americans, with no prior bombardment but supported by sixty tanks and a creeping barrage. It achieved complete surprise and attained all its objectives in ninety minutes'. The open, dry and uncratered countryside was excellent for the use of tanks and the movement of troops with them.[73] The Hamel operation on 4 July was also the debut for the new Mark V tanks, all 60 of them.

Hamel was the first set-piece operation entirely planned and conducted by Monash, as newly-appointed commander of the Australian Corps, and proved politically significant for that reason. It became a model and famous for a so-called ***all-arms*** battle, even though in World War I terms, it was a reasonably small-scale affair. Monash's thorough and meticulous planning was universally praised. His use of conferencing as a means of both informing and consulting subordinates led to a new standard of coordination-in-action of General-ship which was to be emulated subsequently across parts of the Western Front with, sometimes, similar success.

Little was left to chance in Monash's methodology. Its real purpose was to straighten the frontline by carrying it eastwards by about two kilometres on a frontage of 6.5 kilometres. Covering the movement were 650 heavy guns with the advancing infantry supported by the British 5th Tank Brigade of the 60 Mark Vs. The success of this overcame the Australians' unhappy experience of working with tanks at the First Battle of Bullecourt.

They accompanied the assault troops in a co-ordinated

73 Stevenson, *With Our Backs*, 118.

manner on this successful occasion immediately behind the creeping barrage, operating under infantry control to break down the barbed-wire obstacles encountered and dealing with troublesome enemy strongpoints, especially machine-gun nests. To mask the sounds of tanks moving into position during the night of 3 July with the Allied aircraft, Monash had organised to bomb Le Hamel and the enemy rear areas.[74] This kept the element of surprise alive for the dawn attack.

Tanks were also used to bring forward supplies. The attack started at 3.10am and was over in barely 90 minutes. In broader terms in the wider operation of the occupied Hamel forest and of Hamel village, the final tally of casualties reported was 1,062 Australians (not just 800 as first counted), 176 Americans plus 142 involved in a diversion elsewhere that helped the surprise element of the main assault. German casualties (both wounded and killed) were considerably more than 2,000 as well as 1,600 taken prisoner. About 200 enemy machine guns as well as trench mortars and some anti-tank weapons were captured.

Amiens, or the Third Battle of the Somme

The Battle of Amiens on 8 August 1918 delivered a severe blow to the German Spring assault and advance. It was stopped in its tracks. The operation was complex involving the British Fourth Army and the French First Army. The Australians were south of the Somme and north of the Amiens-Chaulnes railway line. The vigorous Canadians were on the right between the railway line and the Amiens-Roye Road. Under Monash, the Australian Corps was augmented

74 Coulthardt-Clark, *Australian Battles*, 148-9.

by the return of its 1st Division from the Lys Front. 430 British tanks were assembled – their noise masked by using aircraft noise as Monash had done at Hamel.

A British creeping barrage signalled the start of the advance at 4.20am. In little more than three hours, the enemy front trenches were overrun. In the Australian sector, the 4th and 5th Divisions passed through in opposite directions, the 2nd and 3rd Divisions, who had originally led the assault until then, pushed ahead to the second line of objectives, another three kilometres further on. By mid-afternoon, these had been reached and taken. By this method, Monash was able to rest his troops.

Meanwhile, the British Corps had been slower and fell behind, exposing the Australian 4th Division's left flank. Fire came from German forces north of the Somme around Cérisy on the Chipilly Peninsula. Despite this, the Australians were able to press their advantage to the second objectives. They caught hundreds of German support and reserve troops in the Morecourt Valley as prisoners, then continued on to the third and final stage, still with the enemy firing heavily into their flank and rear.

By nightfall, the Allied Armies had reached their final objectives south of the Somme. It was a shattering blow to the enemy, who suffered 27,000 casualties, including 16,000 prisoners, 7,925 of these taken by the Australian Corps. 450 guns were captured. All this had been won with 9,000 Allied casualties (about 2,000 being Australians).

General Erich Ludendorff famously wrote that the 8 August had been the 'black day' of the war, which is universally quoted by historians. The final outcome was now inevitable.[75]

Ludendorff's offensive had had one good result despite its evident danger, in that it frightened the often jealous Allied leaders into uniting under one commander and, for the rest of the war, they fought under the leadership of Field Marshal Foch, the great French supremo.

Péronne and St Quentin, 29 August to 2 September, 1918

As historian Roland Perry put it: 'Monash's obscure object of desire was Mont St Quentin'. He believed it had to be taken as quickly as possible along with Péronne, an ancient fortress river town that was heavily fortified by the German Army which lay one and a half kilometres to the south.

Mont St Quentin was 110 metres at its height and did not stand out particularly in the landscape. It protected the northern way into the town of Péronne. Monash argued that possession of it meant control of approaches from all points of the compass on the Somme. Mont St Quentin was really a hill rather than a mountain and was riddled with German-built underground galleries and huge well-furnished German shelters or dugouts. Domination of it would command both stretches of the river.[76]

Monash persistently laid before his army commander, General Sir Henry Rawlinson, a daring, aggressive plan to transfer the main strength of the Australian Corps to the northern side of the Somme and then to assault Mont St Quentin with three battalions. Rawlinson was very cautious, but Monash assured him it could be done. Finally, Rawlinson

75 Coulthard-Clark, *Australia's Battles*, 151-2.
76 Perry, *Monash*, 397-8.

gave in: 'What presumption! However, I don't think I ought to stop you! So go ahead and try, and I wish you luck!'[77]

After the usual thorough planning, Monash launched his most daring attack. The Australian Corps crossed the River Somme to take Mont St Quentin and Péronne. There was no available artillery. There were no tanks to be had. The target was a bald hill, covered with wheat fields on its surface and yet, in three days, it was taken. The crops were grown from the base of the mount almost to its summit which was partly covered in woods. On the wheat fields there were no or very few trees. Assaulting troops had to find what protection they could in the sunken roads and the folds in the hill. Otherwise they were in the open.

As was his well-established habit, Monash called a preliminary conference on 21 August 1918 both to instruct and to consult. He told his men there was to be an attack on the tributary valley that ran from Herleville to Chuignes. This would be carried out by the 1st Division under Brigadier General William Glasgow and by the 32nd British Division under General Lambert attacking side-by-side.[78]

While Rawlinson was initially sceptical, he changed the direction of his army's advance and conformed to Monash's plans. The going was to be hard in spots as the Germans were well aware of the advance and the importance of Mont St Quentin for their cause. They garrisoned the hill strongly with reinforcement troops, including the elite 2nd Prussian Guard Division.

77 Cited by Peter Firkins, *The Australians in Nine Wars*, Rigby, Adelaide, 1971, 140.

78 Travers, *Diggers in France*, 300-01.

With precision, Monash prepared for swift assault. He employed his engineers with their work team to build a new bridge over the Somme and repair old ones damaged by earlier bombardments. On 29 and 30 August, the 3rd Division advanced along the northern bank of the Somme clearing the enemy from most positions with fierce, passionate fighting, consolidating as they went. They drove the Germans out of Cléry which allowed the 2nd Division to pass through. The enemy still held on to about a mile of ground on which the main attack by the Australians would be launched the following day.

The 20th Battalion, 5th Brigade cleared the way for three battalions to be used in the main attack. They swiftly hammered through the German mile-deep trench system and, finally at night, reached the starting point in Monash's plan for the next day. They had taken 120 prisoners and captured eleven machine guns in the process, but the casualty rate on both sides was high in the open countryside. The three battalions (17th, 18th and 19th of the 5th Brigade) moved into position created by the 20th Battalion.

The 20th Battalion had 70 officers and 1,250 other ranks. They were badly knocked around by earlier fighting. As the shell-fragments of their artillery barrage was still falling on the German position, the Australians rose out of their trenches in the pre-dawn darkness. It was cold, but they 'yelled like fiends' and kept up a rapid fire in order to make the Germans believe they were being attacked by a much larger force.

As a keen historian of war, Monash wrote that he used the same methodology as that perfected by Stonewall Jackson in the American Civil War: sudden onslaught followed by a swift turning movement during the dark to deceive the enemy as to the direction of the attack.[79]

Suddenly, the Australians burst through the enemy defences. Lacking numbers, they used sheer speed and individual savagery. It happened like lightning before the Germans could fire a shot.

On the right flank, the 19th Battalion ran into heavy opposition by enemy troops hidden in a ruined sugar factory at St Denis – on the main road between Péronne and St Quentin – but by 7am the three battalions had overwhelmed the ancient fortress. Monash telephoned Rawlinson, while he was shaving before his breakfast, about the victory.

Nevertheless, the elite Prussian Guard did not accept defeat so easily. They reorganised and launched a savage counter-attack that drove the Australians out of the thinly-held Mont St Quentin village on the hill's crest. Reinforcements were hurried to them while they grimly held on outside the village just below the summit. They were then relieved. During the day, they had taken the stone fortress, beaten back five counter-attacks and taken 800 prisoners. But it was all at a fearful loss of lives. Only eight officers and 75 men of the 17th Battalion plodded wearily back down the hill.

The next day, the 2nd Brigade of the 2nd Division advanced beyond Péronne and Mont St Quentin while the 15th Brigade of the 5th Division consolidated the capture of Péronne. It was all done in three days of supreme courage and tactical skill. Six Australian Victoria Crosses were won in three days, but there had been 3,000 casualties. Rawlinson,

79 Firkins, *The Australians*, 141.

in his Order of the Day, stated:

> The capture of Mont St Quentin is a feat of arms worthy of the highest praise. The natural strength of the position is immense and the tactical value of it, in reference to Péronne and the whole system of the Somme defences cannot be over estimated. I am filled with admiration for the gallantry and surpassing daring of the 2nd Division in winning this important fortress, and I congratulate them with all my heart.[80]

For General Rawlinson, it was an unusually passionate speech and came sincerely from the heart. And yet, there was no exaggeration in it.

The 2nd Division were led by Major-General Sir Charles Rosenthal as commander. Rosenthal was an Australian architect by profession and was promoted to command the division by Monash in May 1918, a position he held to the end of the war.[81] He had been wounded twice on Gallipoli.

Rosenthal, a Wesleyan Methodist of Scandinavian antecedents, had proved to be one of Monash's great performers. He was a talented man who had designed several Sydney churches and was an accomplished musician. But he was not Jewish, as Charles Bean had labelled him along with Monash expressing the same racial sentiments – 'not one of us'.[82]

On to the Hindenburg Line

The Hindenburg Line was the most formidable example of defence in depth. It ran along the northern and central

80 Cited in Firkins, *The Australians*, 142.

81 Travers, *Diggers*, 338.

82 Perry, *Monash*, 152.

sectors of the Western Front. In August 1916, the period of attrition on the Somme, Germany's Chief-of-Staff General Erich von Falkenhayn was replaced by the third supreme command of Field Marshal von Hindenburg and General Ludendorff. They decided to build a new defensive system some 32 kms (20 miles) behind the existing lines.

The aim was simply to shorten their Front so that it could be held with fewer troops. It was the Allies that soon called it the Hindenburg Line.

Work began on it in September 1916. Its construction signified that Germany was struggling to wage war on two Fronts – the Western Front and the Eastern Front against Russia.

While the two Fronts existed for the Central Powers, they were at the time unable to make a major offensive in the West. Russia's defeat and withdrawal from the war allowed Germany to strengthen their situation in the West and attempt the nearly successful Spring Offensive in 1918 which was stopped only by the Battle of Amiens.

Earlier in late February and early April 1918, the Germans had largely withdrawn to the new and much stronger position in the Hindenburg Line between Arras and Soissons, leaving behind wasteland of flattened villages, ruined bridges and smashed roads to add to their defensive notion.

By 27 September, Field Marshal Haig expected a hard fight now that his assault troops – what was left of them – faced the formidable Hindenburg Line. He hesitated about what was to be the final Allied attack. Haig and Monash did not see eye-to-eye about it. Monash wanted to go ahead and attack and as soon as possible before the winter closed in. He was, however, left to watch from the heights above Biache to observe the enemy's major withdrawal across the eight miles of undamaged countryside that lay between his new successful positions of Péronne and Mont St Quentin and the Hindenburg defences. Clouds of smoke from burning dumps carried out by the retreating Germans ascended gently into the skies of the high summer. It was the traditional scorched-earth policy. But Monash had much work to do in improving communication over the country behind him and in entertaining his VIP guests.

Lieutenant-General John Monash seated on a chair from Bertangles Château, his Australian Corps Headquarter with his staff: Capt Aubrey Moss (l), Monash's nephew and Aide-de-Camp (r) Major Walter Berry, Camp Commandant (AWM E0275; Lib of Vic H42079)

The price of fame for Monash were visits from Sir Douglas Haig, Sir William Birdwood, Winston Churchill, Lord James Milner MC, the writer Ian Hay (pseudonym for John Hay Berth) and the famous author Sir Arthur Conan Doyle who had lost a son in the war. There was also a profusion of artists, photographers and journalists he found he was required to meet and entertain with his usual courtesy and, sometimes, good food and wine.

Nevertheless, in any waking time he had left, he relentlessly planned for a major assault with what was left, because of casualties in the drastically-reduced Australian Corps. To help him through this difficult period, he had the able support of his two Aides-de-Camp – Captains Audrey Moss and Paul Simonson – both intelligent and highly efficient and very faithful to their leader.

After meeting John Monash at his headquarters at the magnificent Bertangles Château, Sir Arthur Conan Doyle wrote:

> … an excellent soldier who had done really splendid work, especially since the advances began … He showed that the long line of fighting Jews which began with Joshua still carries on. One of the Australian Divisional Generals, Rosenthal was a Jew and the Headquarters Staff are full of eagle-nosed, black-haired warriors.[83]

Clearly, apart from expressing perhaps a strong anti-Semitic sentiment, Doyle was dead wrong about Rosenthal who, as already mentioned, was an Australian-born Wesleyan Methodist of Scandinavian origins. Other division commanders, like Sinclair-MacLagen, Gellibrand, English and Glasgow, had Scottish roots like Doyle himself.

Doyle's visit, however, was mutually cordial – one of the most cordial, as Monash remembered it. Doyle had found that Monash had an 'undemonstrative charm'; his words were well chosen, precise and inspiring. He found him to be the greatest of all generals he had met on the Front during his VIP tour that resulted in a book. Doyle saw that Monash had 'an attractive aura', a charisma and 'a rare compelling personality whose dark flashing eyes and swarthy face might have seemed more in keeping with some Asiatic conqueror

---

83 Sir Arthur Conan Doyle took the opportunity to address 12,000 Diggers and he reminded them, as an Empire man, that 72% of them were 'Englishmen of England', that is born in England before emigrating to Australia.

than with the prosaic association of the British Army'.[84]

While Monash had had serious problems with unpleasant inference from Prime Minister Hughes, giving leave to all veterans of 1914 in the Australian Corps at a vital time, thus weakening the Corps of its most experienced and hardened troops. Monash was ready for the final assault a week after he had won the Battle of Mont St Quentin and Péronne. He was at the peak of his military power despite Charles Bean, Keith Murdoch and William Morris Hughes who continued feeble attempts to white-ant him in various ways.

The Hindenburg Line, or Siegfried Line as the Germans called it, lay ahead, a frighteningly 80 kilometres long and nine kilometres wide – a well-designed, complex system of trenches and fortifications. It was an immensely solid barrier of barbed wire that could be manned by a minimum of soldiers so that a maximum number could go ahead and attack the Allies in front of it or elsewhere.

On 16 September, Monash brought together his divisional commanders, Glasgow of the 1st and Sinclair-MacLagan of the 4th. Tank commanders were also present for the in-depth exhaustive discussion and analysis. (The divisions of Rosenthal, Gellibrand and Hobbs had exhausted themselves and were resting after the judgement days of Mont St Quentin and Péronne.

Monash had received a huge boost due to the capture on another Front of a German truck containing vital detailed plans of the Hindenburg Line as well as documents describing how the defence system worked. He had been

84 Arthur Conan Doyle, *The British Campaign in Europe, 1914-1918*, Geoffrey Bles, London, 1928, 104.

able to base his own plans of attack on these most valuable finds after studying them closely.

In the heavy rain, the 1st and 4th Divisions attacked after a preliminary artillery bombardment. The enemy did not have any elite Prussian guardsmen on this occasion, only conscripts. On the main, many German troops surrendered or ran away, but others stood fast and put up a grim defence. Monash's old brigade of the 4th took the hamlet of Le Verguier after some stiff opposition. There were several feats of extraordinary bravery by individual Australians.

Sergeant Gerald Sexton

AIF Maurice Vincent Buckley (alias Gerald Sexton) VC, DCM shakes hands with Private Francis Miles VC, Gloucestershire Regiment, after the ceremony at Buckingham Palace in 1919 during which George V awarded both men their medals for gallantry. Both had launched successful solo attacks on field-gun and machine-gun emplacements, Miles at Bois-l'Evêque (23 October 1918) and Buckley at Le Verguier north west of St Quentin (18 September 1918)

The 13th were led by Sergeant Maurice Vincent Buckley (alias Sexton), in the dawn attack as the smoke and fog cleared, firing his Lewis gun from the hip. He took out a field gun and its crew and then flushed out the headquarters of the German 58th Infantry Regiment. He deserved and was awarded the Victoria Cross, even though it was much harder to achieve towards the war's end.

In *The Australian Victories in France in 1918*, to illustrate 'the nature of the individual fighting carried out by the Australian Corps in 1918', Monash featured in his appendix: 'No 6594 Sergeant Gerald Sexton, 13th Battalion AIF', together with his citation for the award of the Victoria Cross.

Monash was proud of Sexton for his deeds of gallantry – he was one of twenty-nine men named in his book. Such men reflected Monash's own glorious achievements in 1918 as the Corps Commander – especially how he inspired them to carry out such amazing deeds.

What he failed to realise, perhaps, as he took only a month to write his book, was that Gerald Sexton was really Maurice Vincent Buckley. To complicate matters, another Australian, Alexander Henry Buckley 54th Battalion, temporary corporal, had won the VC at Péronne on 1 September 1918. Another Buckley was also featured in Monash's book and his VC citation quoted.

Maurice Vincent Buckley (Sexton), the son of a bricklayer, was born on 13 April 1891 in urban Melbourne at Hawthorn. He worked as a coach trimmer before enlisting on 18 December 1914 under his own name. He was posted to Egypt in the 13th Light Horse Regiment, but was returned home for medical reasons – in disgrace as he was diagnosed with venereal disease at the Australian medical unit under Doctor Neville Howse. He was admitted to Langwarrin Camp on 25 September 1915. He walked out of the camp on 21 January 1916 and was posted AWOL, declared a deserter and taken off the AIF's roll.

He re-enlisted on 6 May 1916 using the false name of Gerald Sexton and fought using this pseudonym for the rest of the war. Gerald and Sexton were the given names of his brother who had died six months earlier, shortly after joining the AIF. Sexton was his mother's maiden name. Clearly, he had an intense desire to clear his family's reputation. He was happy to join the 13th Battalion on the Somme in January 1917. That year, he fought bravely at Bullecourt, Polygon Wood, Ypres and Passchendaele and, in early 1918, at Hébuterne and Villers-Bretonneux.

On 6 July, now a temporary sergeant, he was wounded in the Battle of Hamel, but recovered in time to participate in the Battle of Amiens. There, on 8 August, he was awarded the Distinguished Conduct Medal.

When his company was blocked by deadly machine-gun placements during the advance from Hamel toward Morcourt, Sexton/ Buckley silenced each enemy post by using his Lewis gun with great skill, killing as he went.

On another occasion when his unit was advancing through tall crops, a hidden German gun caused several casualties. Sexton/ Buckley stood up in full view of the enemy and very calmly identified the position of the hidden gun from the flashes and, firing from the hip, put it out of action.

He was confirmed as sergeant on 28 August. Revealing his true name of Buckley, he was invested with both the Victoria Cross and the Distinguished Conduct Medal at the same time by King George V at Buckingham Palace on 29 May 1919.

Buckley returned to Australia on 8 September 1919 and was discharged as medically unfit in December of that year.

He began work as a road contractor in Gippsland, Victoria. In February 1920, as a Catholic educated in a Christian Brothers School, Abbotsford, he was a member of a delegation that approached the Melbourne City Council requesting permission to hold a traditional St Patrick's Day march the following month. Several anti-Catholic and anti-Irish groups and individuals in high places of the Protestant Ascendency in Melbourne wanted to stop the march which had not been held for many years due to the troubles in Ireland. Speaking in support of the march, Buckley said his Victoria Cross was his 'most treasured possession; yet I pledge it to you [Melbourne City Council] that we will loyally abide by your ruling'. Buckley and the others won the day. It turned out to be a memorable occasion that included 10,000 ex-service men and women led by fourteen Victoria Cross holders from around Australia who were of Irish ancestry. The march was intended to honour Archbishop Dr Daniel Mannix.[85] With the Archbishop – a bitter opponent of the Prime Minister William Morris Hughes over Irish-Australian political issues – in the lead role and with the whole performance directed by prominent wealthy entrepreneur John Wren, it was the most spectacular St Patrick's Day ever held in Melbourne; it recognised the loyalty to country of ex-service men and women of the Catholic faith.

Buckley and the other VC winners were each mounted in the parade on white horses at Wren's expense. They acted as a guard-of-honour for Mannix in his open vehicle. All fourteen in uniform were photographed with Wren and the Archbishop in the grounds of his Melbourne Palace.[86] It was a proud day for Maurice Buckley and his family, but short-lived. At the age of 29, he died tragically from injuries

85 Staunton, *Victoria Cross*, 181-3; Hamilton, *Victoria Cross Heroes*, 343.
86 See Chapter 7, 'For Ireland's Freedom' in Brenda Niall, *Mannix*, Text Publishing, Melbourne, 2015, 146-79.

sustained in a riding accident beside a railway crossing. He was buried at Brighton Cemetery where Sir John Monash was also buried in 1931. At Buckley's funeral, ten VC holders were his pallbearers.[87]

By 10am on 18 September 1918, Monash had won back the old British Front of 21 March 1918. It was taken in three and a half days restoring the status quo. (The Hargicourt Line was 1,700 metres further on.)

The Australians' success at Mont St Quentin-Péronne and the simultaneous success of the British Third Army to the north had led to Ludendorff's decision to retire to the Hindenburg Line, which had been held by the Germans prior to the German Spring Offensive. The Hindenburg outpost line ran generally a kilometre or two west of the main Hindenburg Line and at the same distance east of the old British outpost line. On 14 September 1918, the 1st and 4th Australian Divisions attacked towards the Hindenburg Line. The 4th Division's 4th Brigade successfully took the occupied village of Le Verguier and the 13th Battalion attacked with success south of the village.

On 18 September, battle began at 5.30am with Monash's 1st and 4th Divisions. In the carefully worked out set piece, they reached their objective by 10.00am. The 1st under General Glasgow made its way to the outpost line. The 4th under General MacLagan pulled up 500 yards shorter. The 4th then rested while the artillery was brought up behind. At 11pm, they advanced again into what appeared to a be a rendezvous with certain death with a rain of machine-gun bullets flying around them.

87 Hamilton, *Victoria Cross Heroes*.

Casualties underline the grim situation. The 1st, who attacked with 2,845 men, suffered 490 killed or wounded. Nevertheless, they captured 1,700 prisoners with unknown numbers of Germans killed or wounded. The 4th attacked with 3,048 men and suffered 532 killed or wounded, but captured 2,543 prisoners with unknown numbers of Germans killed and wounded. They also captured about 80 guns.[88] It was a huge victory for Monash on the figures alone, but costly in human life on both sides. It was the last battle of the war for the 1st and 4th Divisions.

Monash kept hammering the Hindenburg Line with what remained of the Australian Corps with strong, and needed, American support of two divisions. His attack was fixed for 29 September 1918 at 5.50am. The going was difficult, especially for the less-experienced American troops. On 30 September, the 3rd and 5th fought on together reasonably successfully. During the night of that day, the Germans decided to cease their fierce attempts to retain contested territory and began running away. For them, they knew the war to be over. On 1 October, the operation had been completed and all objects had been gained by Monash's men. This was the last battle of the war for the 3rd and 5th Divisions.

It now remained for the 2nd Division alone to attack the heavily-fortified Beaurevoir Line, associated with the Hindenburg Line. On 3 October, they captured the line and went beyond it, rounding up about 1,000 prisoners and numerous machine guns. On 4 October, they continued to harass the broken enemy, taking another 800 prisoners. Lieutenant Joseph Maxwell's feats in capturing successive

88 Travers, *Diggers in France*, 314-5.

machine-gun nests beyond the huge wire entanglements at Beaurevoir were extraordinary and he won a well-deserved VC to add to his MC and Bar and his DCM.[89]

★ ★ ★

For the Diggers, the fighting was over. The major battles they had fought in were Gallipoli 1915; Fromelles, Pozières and Mouquet Farm in 1916; in 1917 Bullecourt, Messines, Menin Road, Broodseinde Ridge, Polygon Wood and Passchendaele; in 1918, most notably Villers-Bretonneux, Hamel – 8 August – and Mont St Quentin and Péronne.

Monash's significance in all of this is attested by a series of major biographies grounded on both primary and secondary sources. The prominent historian Geoffrey Serle was the first to have access to Monash's most extensive collection of private papers released by his son-in-law. They were an extraordinary near-complete record of the life of an Australian individual. Monash was meticulous in the keeping of his diaries, letters and so on – a vast collection of written records and memorabilia. The result was *John Monash. A Biography* by Serle in 1982, which is universally regarded as an outstanding literary historical achievement. It was preceded by AJ Smithers' very soundly accurate military biography published in 1973 entitled *Sir John Monash*. But Smithers did not have access to Monash's papers and so had to rely on the more standard official records available to the public. Then, following on Serle's work came PA Pedersen's

89 See John Ramsland, *Venturing into No Man's Land. The Charmed Life of Joseph Maxwell VC World War I Hero*, Brolga Publishing, Melbourne, 2012.

Monash as Military Commander in 1985, Roland Perry's award-winning *Monash. The Outsider who won the war* in 2004 and Tim Fischer's *Maestro John Monash Australia's Greatest Citizen General* in 2014; in 2015 Grantlee Kieza's huge study *Monash. The Soldier who shaped Australia*. The titles of the more recent tomes about Monash are noticeably more extravagant than the more measured ones of Smithers, Serle and Pedersen and may have slightly embarrassed Sir John Monash had he been alive when they were released. He never claimed to have won the war, despite a sizeable ego. But these works and several others have made it more certain that he has now ***not*** been forgotten and the Western Front and Australia's efforts there have been given their rightful place in the history of war.

Monash is no longer 'The Forgotten Anzac'. The Monash studies no longer provide merely prosaic accounts of military history, but more successfully 'life analysis', encompassing childhood development, cultural and physical influences, social outlooks, literary interests, sex life, public persona and aspirations and personality flaws and mistakes. They are now not just 'the skeleton of a man'.[90] Monash's popularity has reached folk-hero proportions, but he was much more than that and much more complex.

Sir John Monash was certainly an outstanding Australian who served his country with distinction in war and peace. He was an exceptional product of a new era in Australia's development and a man who was close to the tides of history. He richly deserved the noteworthy efforts of his biographers.

90 Spaull, 'Sir John Monash – A Vanishing Hero?', 240.

General Sir John Monash leads the 1931 Melbourne Anzac Day. His health was declining and he died on 8 October 1931 (AWM A03451)

5

The Aboriginal Presence, 1914–1918

Research on the Indigenous commitment in the Great War remains fragmented and, at best, very much a work-in-progress. Military historians on the main have most frequently left it alone, following the tradition established in Charles Bean's weighty six-volume *Official History of Australia in the War of 1914–8*, although there are excerpts found in academic journals. Bean held some unenlightened notions of Anglo-Saxon racial superiority. Bean's prejudices took on a eugenics character about physical fitness: 'As it was for many Australians of his generation it would be the shock of Adolf Hitler's barbaric racism and anti-Semitism that dispelled for ever Charles Bean's notions of white Australian racial superiority.'[1]

Aaron Pegram's work is an exception to many military historians' work,[2] and Michael Wenham's yet unpublished PhD thesis, '"My own darling laddie". In search of George Wenham: an Aboriginal Anzac and the History of Denial' (University of Newcastle, 2015), break fresh ground. Pegram is a senior historian at the Australian War Memorial and Michael Wenham is an independent family history researcher who has presented papers at learned conferences on military history.

1 Ross Coulthart, *Charles Bean*, HarperCollins, Sydney, 2014, 364.

2 See Aaron Pegram, 'Under the Kaiser's Crescent Moon', *Wartime*, issue 76, Spring 2016, 32-37.

In a brief comment on the 1914–18 war, Robert Hall claims that there were over three hundred identified Aboriginal and Torres Strait Islanders who served in the 1st AIF, despite the existence of formal legislative barriers to the service of non-Europeans. 'Over 300' is now a wild underestimation. The 'barriers' were, to a good extent, ignored by nature of the Attestation Papers which did not require of the volunteer an ethnic identification, such as 'Aborigine' or 'Part-Aborigine'. The European family associations were considered sufficient.

Hall is able to identify briefly Aboriginal fighters in the 1914–1918 war who displayed outstanding courage: Corporal Albert Knight (43rd Battalion, a so-called 'part-Aborigine') from Bourke NSW who won, not as Hall claimed the Distinguished Conduct Medal, but the Military Medal (MM) in 1918; Private William Reginald Rawlings, who was described by Hall as 'a full-blood' from Purnim in Victoria. He also won the Military Medal at Morlancourt, France on 28-29 July 1918.[3]

Dr Robert Hall is Executive Director of the Australian Defence Force Academy with a strong interest, unlike Charles Bean, in Aboriginal and Torres Strait Islander involvement in war. He was a former Lieutenant in the 8th Battalion, The Royal Australian Regiment.

Three charge at dawn

Hall also pointed to yet another 'part-Aborigine', Corporal Harry Thorpe from Orbost, Victoria, who had been involved in October 1917 in a mopping-up operation near Ypres and

3 Robert Hall, *Fighters from the Fringe*, Aboriginal Studies Press, Canberra, 1995, 5-6.

leading his men against a strong German resistance. Thorpe and Rawlings did not survive the war. With Knight, Rawlings and Thorpe, Hall provides us with tantalizing examples of Indigenous courage, initiative and enterprise on the Front, but provides little background about them.

Pte Reginald Rawlings MM Corporal Henry Thorpe MM
are buried in Harbonnières Cemetery, killed in action, 9 August 1918
(AWM P01695.001) (AWM P01695.002)

Reg Rawlings, Henry Thorpe and another Aborigine John Firebrace all had rendezvous with death in action on the same day – 9 August 1918 and on the same Front. They now lie buried close to each other in a military cemetery at Harbonnières, France. In life, these three Victorians had never met each other. Within days, another member of the Firebrace family met his death on the same Front. Both Rawlings and Thorpe were distinguished winners of the Military Medal.

Henry Thorpe was born in Orbost in 1887. On 12 February 1916, he volunteered in the larger town of Sale. Two months later he had completed basic training and sailed from Melbourne for overseas as a member of the 7th Battalion who were fighting in the trenches of the French Belgian border.

Reginald Rawlings was born in December 1890 on Framlingham Aboriginal Mission about six hundred kilometres from Thorpe's home town. Thorpe's Aboriginal family were illustrious; his father had been a very well-regarded athlete and his sister was the great grandmother of the world champion boxer Lionel Rose. Another sister Ina was the grandmother of Reg and Harry Saunders – Second World War AIF heroes.

The fight that Thorpe was part of was a bloody stalemate most of the time, fought from frontline trenches in frantic, hopeless 'over-the-top' charges across a blasted landscape of No Man's Land. The loss of life on both sides was enormous:

The dead leaves float in the sighing air,
  The darkness moves like a curtain drawn,
A veil which the morning sun will tear
  From the face of death – We charge at dawn.

Patrick Macgill, "Before the Charge"[4]

On 21 August 1916, Henry Thorpe was wounded during a charge. By January 1917, he had recovered reasonably well and was promoted to lance corporal and, on 29 April, he was again wounded.

In early October 1917, the Allies launched a massive offensive in the hope of dislodging the German Army from around the strategically important Belgian town of Ypres and to the east. The advance seemed to be going reasonably successfully, but the slowly retreating German Army fought tenaciously and skilfully. Pockets of Germans stayed behind

4 In Lyn Macdonald (ed.), *Anthem for Doomed Youth. Poets of the Great War*, Folio, London, 2000, 77.

fighting last ditch-stands to slow down the Allies advances. The whole operation involved Anzac troops made up of the 1st, 2nd, 4th and 5th Australian Divisions.

On 4 and 5 October 1917, Henry Thorpe and platoon were given the difficult task of mopping up highly dangerous German fortress pill boxes, their dugouts and their deadly machine guns. Thorpe began to show conspicuous courage as an inspiring leader of the men. It was no surprise to comrades that he was awarded a Military Medal (MM) which they all supported. His citation tells the story in some detail in inspiring language:

> Near Ypres on 4/5 October 1917, L/Cpl THORPE displayed great courage and initiative in mopping up enemy dugouts and pill boxes. In the capture of Battalion Objective he was conspicuous for his courage and leadership, handling his men with skill and materially assisting his Company Commander. By his splendid example and disregard of all danger he inspired those under him.

The key words and phrases of this type of military citation are 'great courage', 'initiative', 'leadership', 'splendid example' and, as implied, inspirational while following orders: 'materially assisting his Company Commander'. These were all qualities the AIF were looking for. As a result, Thorpe was promoted to corporal on 5 October 1917.

Thorpe fought on through to late July 1918 when the war was only a few months from its disastrous journey's end. Thorpe, Rawlings and Firebrace found themselves separately among the Australian troops fighting near the Belgian border.

Allied commanders were still planning a final breakthrough. Australia had five divisions (approximately 75,000 troops) stationed in France. All were thrown into the final battles of the Great War.

In the thick of it, Reg Rawlings was engaged in the same type of daring mopping up actions that Thorpe had experienced in the previous autumn of 1917. Rawlings was in the dangerous position of first bayonet man in a bombing team. Each man was given a particular function in the assault. The citation for Military Medal for Rawlings at Morlancourt Ridge on the far side of the Somme on the 28/29 July 1918 is his remembrance memorial, his requiem:

> … Pte Rawlings displayed rare bravery in the performance of his duty [as first bayonet] killing many of the enemy, brushing aside all opposition and cleared the way effectively for the bombers of his team. His irresistible dash and courage set up a wonderful example for the remainder of the team. [5]

Only a few days later, Reg Rawlings MM was killed in action. On the same afternoon, Henry Thorpe took a fatal bullet in the stomach, in a situation where the air was thick with deadly machine-gun bullets.

The stretcher-bearers found him still alive, but gravely wounded. He asked for water and was refused as the stretcher-bearers understood what damage water would do to a such a wound and that water would cause unbearable pain in a man close to death. Thorpe was taken to the dressing station where the staff did their best to make

5 Alick Jackomos and Derek Fowell, *Forgotten Heroes. Aborigines at War from the Somme to Vietnam*, Victoria Press, Melbourne, 1993, 5-8.

him comfortable before going to another emergency. He cried out again for water. When they returned, they found Thorpe in mortal agony. It was suspected, with justification, that some well-meaning bystander in the field station had answered his pleas for water. Soon after, Henry Thorpe of Lake Tyers Aboriginal Mission died.

Before the day's end, Lance Corporal John Firebrace, a twenty-two-year old, was also dead.

Above: Roll of Honour 1914 - 1918, Lake Tyers Mission Church
Right: Roll of Honour St Mary's Mission Church, Lake Condah

★ ★ ★

Aside from the work of Alick Jackomos and Derek Fowell in *Forgotten Heroes* and a few other researchers on Aboriginal involvement in the 1st AIF, this important subject had been very patchy indeed. Jackomos and Fowell captured the deeds of Thorpe, Firebrace and Rawlings well, derived from official sources in the Australian War Memorial. The best advances now on Aboriginal involvement in the Great War appear to come mainly from family historians like Michael Wenham in Newcastle and regional historians like Trevor Munro in Dubbo.

Professional military historians appear to be more interested in the presence of professional and citizen Aboriginal soldiers in the Second World War, the Vietnam war and beyond, as is the case with Robert Hall's *Fighters from the Fringe*, since the documents are more accessible.

In his interrogation of service records for his Doctoral thesis, Michael Wenham demonstrated conclusively that Indigenous servicemen did play a significant role in the 1914-18 war despite the Bean-influenced silence about them. Wenham found they were members of fifty-nine of the sixty battalions in the 1st AIF. They fought in most theatres of war from Gallipoli to the Western Front. They were present in the First Bullecourt tragedy, the success of Messines and the protracted agony of Ypres/Passchendaele. They were at Villers-Bretonneux and, as the tide changed to victory, at Le Hamel and Amiens as well as Mont St Quentin and the breakthrough of the Hindenburg Line.[6]

This is the reality that has yet to be told fully for the truth to be shared.

Private Albert Bonser, 18th Battalion

In *Digger*, Trevor Munro tells the story of Private Albert

6 Michael Wenham, ' "My own darling laddie". In Search of George Wenham: an Aboriginal Anzac and the History of Denial', PhD (History), The University of Newcastle, 2015, 110-11.

William Bonser (6429), known widely by the nickname of "Wagga".[7] Albert was born on 9 November 1899 to Bertie and Matilda Bonser in Bourke. He was one of over a thousand Indigenous men to join the 1st AIF as volunteers. He enlisted on 5 June 1917 at the age of twenty-six; his brother "Tunna" had enlisted about a year before. Albert or "Wagga" described his occupation as a 'colt breaker'. Several other Aboriginal soldiers were horse breakers by occupation. He was looking for work at Wilcannia at the time of enlistment.

His initial medical examination was conducted by a stern local medico who noticed he had bad teeth and required him to have dental treatment before he was permitted to go overseas. His complexion was described as 'clear' by the medico. Like his brother "Tunna", "Wagga" was described in his attestation papers as having brown eyes and hair.

"Wagga" arrived at Dubbo to undergo basic training conducted in the local showground where buildings and space were available for both accommodation and training, like a number of other larger rural centres. The training at Dubbo lasted two months. Private Bonser then went on to the Liverpool army camp at Holsworthy on 19 September 1916 where he was eventually placed in the 18th Battalion reinforcement. He was upgraded to acting corporal.

On 11 November 1916 after further intensive training, Bonser left on the troopship *Suevic* for England. The ship arrived at Devonport on 30 January 1917. In a draft of about one hundred men, "Wagga" was sent to Rollestone for even more training. His rank reverted to private and he continued

7 Trevor Munro, 'Private 6429 Albert William Bonser, 18th Battalion', *Digger*, no 40, September 2012, 34-6.

heavy training until early May that year.

On 13 May, Bonser and his comrades crossed the Channel and eventually joined the 18th Battalion at the Front. At the time, the 18th were out of the trenches training at the village of Fricourt where they were billeted at the back of the Front. The same day, "Wagga" witnessed General William Birdwood's visit. While on parade, several men in the battalion were presented by the General with medals and decorations. "Wagga" was suitably impressed with the show.

On 18 May, the battalion moved to Contay where they continued training for the rest of the month – frequent route marches! They marched to Puchevillers and entrained to a tented camp near Bapaume. Training continued as usual, but the battalion was also supplying working parties for dangerous duties close to the Front. Through July, the 18th remained at No 2 Camp near Bapaume and continued training via route marches in particular as well as fierce mock battles with other units.

On 28 July, they marched firstly to Beaucourt and then on to St Omer. They were sent the next day to a tent camp at Malhove and, on 31 July, they were in Bouvelinghem – now at the Front. They were assigned a sector of trenches near Joncourt and Etricourt.[8]

On the night of 2 October 1918, the 18th Battalion was aware that it was to be part of a major attack on the Beaurevoir-Fonsomme Line. The attack was launched the following morning, 3 October at 0600 hours.

Bonser was under the strong leadership of Lieutenant Joseph Maxwell MC and Bar, DCM, who was to win the

8 Munro, 'Private 6429'.

Victoria Cross on that day. Corporal Albert Bonser, who was by this time his company's leading Lewis gunner, provided Maxwell with his sole and essential backup on that occasion in a dashingly courageous effort.

Between 3 and 5 October, due mainly to their joint efforts, the Beaurevoir Line was overrun. The process took longer than had been hoped because of the firepower of the masses of machine-gun nests behind the wire – at least 200 of them in one village alone!

In this situation of 3 October, Maxwell was forced to take command of the company when his commander was killed soon after the jump-off. When the enemy wire was reached by Maxwell's company, they were met by a deadly hail of machine-gun fire and suffered considerable casualties.

After getting the company into safer situations, Maxwell went forward alone under the wire that was six belts thick. He was soon followed under the wire by Bonser who was to provide backup with his trusty Sten gun which he mounted under the wire. He provided Maxwell with cover fire to keep the heads of the machine-gunners of the other side in their nests. Maxwell attacked the first machine-gun nest and killed three of its crew with his revolver. Some of his command then followed him through the wire.

Bonser's cover fire from a dangerous spot helped to save Maxwell's life as he went on to take out other German machine-gun nests on that day, capturing many prisoners. While he won the VC, Bonser was awarded a Distinguished Conduct Medal (DCM),[9] but he also received a serious

9 John Ramsland, *Venturing into No Man's Land. Joseph Maxwell VC World War I Hero*, Brolga, Melbourne, 2012, 143-8.

gunshot wound in the thigh. After hospitalisation in England, he was returned to Sydney on 20 December 1918 and was discharged on 25 March 1919.

Bonser worked for the Post-Master General in Sydney for several years after the war and then returned to his hometown Bourke, where he was involved with the RSL and Bourke sporting clubs as well as the local Church of England. He was highly respected by all locally. He died at the age of 84 on 15 July 1974 and was buried in the Bourke Cemetery.[10]

Douglas Grant Remembers

At the age of forty-six on 27 March 1931, Douglas Grant told his own story of his war service during World War I in a succinct, admirable prose style which demonstrated the accuracy of his memory:

> I was a **prisoner of War in 1917-1918.**
>
> I was captured on the **11th April, 1917, at Bullecourt** in France. I was then taken to **Lille, to the firing line**. I carried down shot and shell in the German lines. This was reprisal against the French, who had German prisoners behind the French firing line.
>
> **We only had one plate** [a day] of sauerkrauet [*sic*], one slice of bread, and no meat whatever. I took sick. We had absolutely no meat.
>
> **We left Douai** on the **25th August, 1917**, and I took sick in the German Concentration Camp at **Dülmen in Westphalia.** They inoculated us there, and we were then sent to **Wittenberg in Saxony**, where I worked in the coal mines from the latter end of September until February,

10 Munro, 'Private 6429'.

> 1918, and then I took sick there. I was sent up to a place they call **Zossen**, to the Brandenberg Concentration Camp, 40 kilometres from Berlin. I remained there until **22.12.18**, and I was **in charge of all the coloured section** of the Concentration Camp. I was really the **President** of the British Section of the various coloured races there, Indians, &c. I had to see to the sick and the wounded, and I had to wait until everyone had left. That was after the Armistice, and I left on the **22nd December, 1918.**
>
> I had a touch of 'flu there. They inoculated us with serum in the left breast and in the arm.
>
> It didn't affect me until I came to Australia.[11]

In this study of the Aboriginal presence in World War I, the linear or chronological narrative sequence is secondary to a circular approach where the present recoils upon the past and the future is inherent within the present. Such an approach is familiar in Aboriginal oral storytelling where everything is gathered together in a coherent whole to communicate meaning.

Douglas Grant in POW uniform (AWM 2016.400.1)

Douglas Grant was an intelligent, well-spoken and well-educated man in the Scottish manner of friendly disposition. He wore his clothes with dignity and style, both in his private's uniform of the 1st AIF during World

11 Extract from Douglas Grant's Patient Case Records (18304), Callan Park Mental Hospital, Rozelle, 27 March 1931, NSW State Archives, Kingswood. (Bold for emphasis by author).

War I and in civilian clothing after the war back in Australia. Some of his nasty racist contemporaries claimed that he dressed above his station in life. He was, as they branded him, what was commonly called a 'full-blood Aborigine'; a black member of what they believed to be a dying race of primitive barbarians. The role that was assigned to him and others of his race by many in Australia after the war was as an unskilled farm or manual labourer and capable of nothing more in the workplace.

Grant, a 30-year-old highly skilled mechanical draftsman, enlisted in the First Australian Imperial Force on 13 January 1916 at the New South Wales country town of Scone in the northern Hunter Valley while living on the pastoral property Belltrees.[12] By today's standards, he was a small man (5ft 3 ½ inches or 160 cm) in height and weighing 8 stone 4 pounds (53 kg) on enlistment. He spoke in a modulated Scottish brogue and had the marked ability to play the bagpipes well. He was also an outstanding Rugby player. These were but a few of his distinguishing features that tended to startle those who met him.

Becoming Douglas Grant

Sadly, as an infant survivor of a massacre inflicted on his traditional clan in the dense mountains of north-eastern Queensland by the punitive Queensland Mounted Native Police armed with carbines,[13] Douglas Grant knew

12 Greg & Sylvia Ray. *The Hunter Region in the Great War*, self-published, Newcastle, 2017, 134-5 & 248 ; John Ramsland, *The Legacy of Douglas Grant.A Notable Aborigine in War and Peace*, Brolga, Melbourne, 2019, 25-8; Douglas Grant, 13th Bn Enlistment Papers, National Archives of Australia (NAA).

13 See Ramsland, *The Legacy of Douglas Grant*, 33-53.

nothing or very little of his original native community's rules, customs, taboos and language.

He had been rescued from what was in reality the crime scene of a massacre by Robert Grant, a Scottish immigrant and his Scottish wife Elizabeth who were in the vicinity on a collecting expedition for the trustees of the Australian Museum in Sydney. The couple formally adopted the child. At the time, they were childless.

Before volunteering for the Museum expedition, Robert Grant had trained in Scotland as a taxidermist, an ancient Scottish craft and art. On arrival in the colony, he had first worked in the coalfields of industrial Lithgow, just beyond the Blue Mountains to the west of Sydney. He had, however, further aspirations as a taxidermist and naturalist in connection with the Australian Museum.

The entire Grant family had arrived in Australia from Scotland as assisted colonial immigrants in 1879 aboard the *Clyde*. Robert's parents were Henry and Elizabeth who were aged forty-three when they arrived. Robert was twenty-three, his brother Richard was eleven, his sisters Elizabeth, seven, and Janet, nine. They settled in coalmining jobs in Lithgow and soon became a prominent Presbyterian family in the Lithgow town community.[14]

As an adult, Douglas was to maintain strong relationships with members of his adoptive family, visiting and staying with them on many occasions in Lithgow during his lifetime after the Great War. They provided him with accommodation in the family homes when he was working in the Lithgow Small

---

14 Family history information supplied to the author by Carl Kirwin, a Grant family relative and a foster cousin of Douglas.

Arms Factory. In a real sense, they replaced his Aboriginal family and community which had been lost to him forever.

Soon after the tribal clan massacre, Robert and Elizabeth brought the destitute infant by ship to Sydney concealed in a blanket. Since they were contracted to a second expedition specimen collecting for the Australian Museum in another remote situation in the outback, they took Douglas, who was not yet speaking English, to Lithgow to live temporarily with his adoptive grandparents where he was to learn the first fundamentals of English, albeit with a strong Scottish accent. His tribal language disappeared into the deep recesses of his mind. He was sent to the local Eskbank Superior Public School where, at an early age, he showed promise as a scholar. He was quick to learn.

After Robert and Elizabeth completed the commissioned expeditions for the Museum, Robert was rewarded with more permanent employment within that organisation as a taxidermist and museum guide. The couple then obtained good terrace housing in the leafy suburb of Annandale in Albion Street and recalled their adopted child to their new home there.[15] Here, Douglas attended Annandale Superior Public School immediately graded into third class (3A) and always performed well, both in the primary and the secondary sections, as did his white brother Henry Sneddon, who was four years younger. Both Douglas and Harry (Henry) were particularly intense products of the strict Scottish upbringing provided by Robert and Elizabeth Grant.

When Douglas reached early manhood, a family friend

15 'Brief Life History of Douglas Grant, Queensland Christian Aborigine', *Messenger*, 1922.

found him a permanent position as apprentice mechanical draughtsman at Mort's Dock Company and Engineering Works in the nearby waterside suburb of Balmain.

Mort's Dock

Mort's Dock Company and Engineering Works formed the most extensive and important undertaking of its kind in the Australian colonies. Situated about two miles west of Sydney, the private dock was about 300 feet in length that could receive vessels from Sydney Harbour in a continuous natural waterway. Adjoining the wharf was a vast array of workshops covering five acres which, in full swing, employed 700 hands in the iron and brass foundries, boiler making, locomotive making, engine making and ship-building works. Many locomotives were supplied to the colonial governments.

It was a busy, crowded industrial site. Several large steamers had also been manufactured there, including most of the fleet for the Australasian Steam Navigation Company.[16] The mechanical engineering drafting office lay at the heart of the vast enterprise and this was where Douglas Grant skilfully carried out the design of valuable plans.

He remained there for ten years proving to be a smart, innovative and capable employee, graduating to a good, hard-working central position in the drawing office. He became a general popular favourite with all the staff at Mort's Dock because of his fine disposition.[17]

While working at Mort's Dock, Douglas began to show his prowess in district sport and social activities, especially in

16 *New South Wales in 1881*, published by govt authority, Thomas Richards (ed.), 2nd issue, Sydney, 1882, 75.

17 'A Plea for the Australian Aborigine', *Sydney Mail*, 11 July 1917.

rugby union and cricket. In 1908, he was starring as a member of the premiership Balmain District First Grade Rugby Union team in the Sydney and suburban competition.[18] As an astute rugby captain, he led the team to victory. Every single item, like Grant's trophy for the Balmain Rugby Club, has a pregnant historical meaning revealing something more about the subject – in this case his sporting fame.

Sojourn at Belltrees

Then a desire to lead a more quiet and outdoor life attracted him away from the heavily crowded industrial works at Balmain. Having good references led him to a position at Belltrees near Scone, the vast homestead owned by Henry Luke White and his brothers.

Here, he remained for two happy years under the mentorship of "H.L." who made use of his skills in taxidermy taught to him as a boy by his father Robert. White had a large collection of birds' wings and eggs – the best in Australia – and called on Grant's expert assistance in preparing the collection for exhibition and private display.

While on the station, several of the employees volunteered for active service and Douglas, as a thirty-year-old, was moved to go along with them to the nearby town of Scone to join up.[19]

Douglas Grant joins up

A photograph of this event has been discovered. It appeared in the *Sydney Sun* on 31 January 1916 under the

18 His premiership trophy medal of 1908 is now held in Carl Kirwin's private collection of Grant's memorabilia. Kirwin is related to the Grant family on his mother's side.

19 Their names appear in the Belltrees chapel.

banner: 'Upper Hunter's Boast'. It showed the latest batch of eager recruits declared proudly to be the last eligible single men of the district, including Grant, who had answered the Empire's calling. The men, mainly in formal dress, are standing proudly posed in front of the store of Rowland and Dodd Auctioneers which was used as the town's recruiting rooms.[20]

Douglas Grant, dressed in a neat suit, sits at the front of the group, his light-coloured stylish hat placed on the ground in front of him. The recruiting officer in full-dress uniform sits beside him in a Scottish regimental uniform of one of the NSW militias. Grant is the only Aborigine in the group of white men from the bush.

Similar group photographs, in many country towns and even in Sydney suburban centres, frequently reveal the Aboriginal presence, indicating their gathering acceptance as the war went on and deaths in frontline involvement steadily increased. Many are now unknown and unidentified, especially itinerant workers in country settings.

Serving the Empire

In Hobart's *Weekly Courier* of 5 July 1917 under the heading of The Empire's Call, a full central page (p.24) of photographic portraits of Tasmanian men in uniform, all captioned with their individual details. By this time, they were all serving overseas in the 1st AIF in various theatres of war. Curiously, a portrait of a young Douglas Grant of Annandale appeared in the same compilation, but not in an AIF uniform; rather he wore the Scottish uniform of the

20 A newspaper scrap provided by Margaret Ashford from her grandfather's family history collection in Scone NSW.

Annandale pipe band playing the bagpipes. Thus, he stood out on the page. He was the only Aborigine in a set of nineteen individual portraits that filled the news sheet and the only man not from Tasmania. Why was this so?

His caption read:

> 8 – Douglas Grant, an Australian aborigine, who is serving the Empire. Adopted son [*sic*] of Mrs [Elizabeth] Grant, mother of Mrs J Simpson of Railton. Was adopted by Mrs Grant as a child of 18 months and brought up as her son. He is with the A.I.F. in France and is first lieutenant [really only a private]. Was wounded recently.

The caption contains a generational inaccuracy. Mrs J [Janet] Simpson was the younger sister of Robert Grant, Douglas' adoptive father and the youngest daughter of Henry Sneddon, the elder, and Elizabeth Grant. When she married, Janet went to live on a farm at Railton, Tasmania. She most probably donated the photograph from her private collection.

Indigenous Diggers like Douglas certainly made their now-forgotten mark in World War I, but when the war first broke out those who tried to sign up were occasionally rejected if their Aboriginality was revealed, because they were not regarded as British subjects or citizens under the 1909 amendment to Australia's Defence Act: 'Persons who are not substantially of European origin or descent, of which the medical authorities appointed under the Regulations shall be judges', were to **be exempt from compulsory military service.**

In the first few years of the war, *The Instructions for the guidance of Enlisting Officers* openly stated: 'Aboriginal half-castes, or men with Asiatic blood are not to be enlisted'.

Apparently, this applied to all coloured men. This actually happened to Douglas Grant.

Sergeant Douglas Grant, 34th Battalion, April 1915 (Lithgow Library)

On 1 May 1916, Douglas Grant became a sergeant (No 1146) in the 34th Battalion, 1st AIF. He was suddenly removed from the troopship HMAT *Hororata* on the eve of its departure from Watson's Bay for overseas and discharged. The next day – 2 May 1916 – *Hororata* sailed without Douglas. However, he soon joined up again and left for France on 22 August 1916 aboard the HMAT *Wiltshire* as a member of A Company with the reinforcements to the 13th Battalion. His rank had been reduced to private and he never regained his stripes.[21]

Yet in spite of these sometimes theoretical restrictions, several slipped through the net, some deliberately. Grant was one of about 1,500 or more Indigenous men who did eventually succeed in enlisting in the 1st AIF, some after several attempts and some on the very first occasion of enlistment.[22]

As the war chewed up more and more men from Australia, recruiting authorities across the island continent nation began to find practical ways to avoid such regulations against

21 Ramsland, *The Legacy of Douglas Grant*, 27-28.

22 Michael Wenham, unpublished address reviewing Ramsland's *The Legacy of Douglas Grant*, United Service Club, Newcastle, 3 October 2019.

Aborigines. Many, who were knocked back for the first time, tried again successfully the second time under new conditions and ended up on one of the war Fronts.

Indigenous soldiers from the Hunter Valley of NSW

The best known and legendary Aboriginal Digger, of course, was Douglas Grant. Others of Indigenous descent in the Valley also demanded their right to fight for the country within the fervour of continuing volunteer recruitments.

In the Hunter Valley a number of known Indigenous men successfully managed to enlist:

John Brenell of Cessnock was killed-in-action in February 1918 leaving his wife Rachel a widow.

Archibald and Charles Benjamin Johnston of Boolambyte – a black community near Buladelah – served on the Western Front. Archibald was taken prisoner, like Douglas, but at Villers-Bretonneux in April 1918, where he served a briefer time in a concentration camp until Armistice in November of the same year.

John and William Jonas were two other Hunter Valley Diggers in World War I. William James was a 27-year-old horse breaker who was mentioned in despatches; his brother John was an older bushman (35) when he enlisted. He was working at Allworth near Booral in the Central West of New South Wales.

Alister Roy Lester, an 18-year-old manual labourer on enlistment, was from Mount Olive, an Aboriginal fringe settlement near the town of Singleton. He died on the Front in April 1918. His brother Augustus was killed "somewhere in France" on 23 August 1918. These two Lester brothers have unknown graves, but their names are now recorded on the Australian National War Memorial at Villers-Bretonneux.

Harold Maher, a 22-year-old manual labourer from Karuah, Port Stephens, joined the 20th Battalion as a private. He was wounded in August 1918, but survived the war.

Leaving Forster, also to join the 20th Battalion, was 30-year-old Alexander Slater who was married. His body now lies in Warloy-Baillon cemetery on the former Western Front in Flanders.

Albert Edward Stow became a lighthorseman and later a field engineer. His two brothers Arthur Henry and Frederick Williams were both infantrymen. The three came from the Underbank Aboriginal settlement near Dungog.

William John Swan was a 27-year-old from the small town of Denman when he signed up.

Daniel Syron joined up aged 19 as a lighthorseman from Cape Hawk. He was a fisherman.

James Henry Morris, who fought in the 33rd Battalion, lived on Purfleet Aboriginal Reserve near Taree after the war.

William Francis, also known as Billy, Swan was from the Aboriginal Inland Mission Home near Singleton. He was gassed and wounded in France.

Forster's well-known William Simon signed up in 1916; by 1918 he was discharged as medically unfit and returned to Australia.

Of the shadowy or obscure military careers of these Indigenous men in the vast Hunter Valley, the Belltrees woolclasser Douglas Grant's is by far the best known as a press celebrity.[23] Most other Aboriginal soldiers of the First World War throughout Australia became obscure figures.

The Overall Indigenous commitment

Private Alfred Lovett and wife Sarah and two sons; one of five brothers who fought overseas in the 1st AIF, Alfred fought at Pozières (AWM P01651.001) & Trooper William (Willie) Allen, 11 Light Horse Regiment; originally from Darwin, he enlisted on 10 December 1917 and returned home on 20 July 1919

It is difficult to identify how many Indigenous men served in the Great War, partly because of the enlistment papers for volunteers. The men were routinely described in the medical annotations on these papers as 'dark', but these were not precise or reliable descriptors of ethnicity. As

23 Ramsland, *The Legacy of Douglas Grant*, 369; Greg and Sylvia Ray, *The Hunter Region in the Great War*, self-published, Newcastle, 2017, 134-5; Tony Griffiths, *Douglas Grant : that Black Digger from the Scottish Mob*, Friends of Callan Park, Rozelle, 2019; Tom Murray & Hilary Howes, 'Douglas Grant and Rudolf Marcuse: Wartime Encounters at the Edge of Art', *History and Anthropology*, vol 30, 13 May 2019; Pegram, 'Under the Kaiser's Crescent Moon'.

well, there were multiple and often confusing definitions of Aboriginality.[24]

In the case of Douglas Grant, he is described in many newspaper articles as 'full-blood', a surviving child of the massacre of a traditional clan of Aborigines in their original tribal state, but this type of description does not appear at all on his enlistment papers.

In answer to the question: 'Are you a natural born British subject …', Douglas answered 'natural'. The examining medical officer simply described his complexion as 'Dark'; eyes 'Dark'; hair 'Dark Brown' and his religious denomination as 'Presbyterian', with no reference to his Aboriginality.[25]

It is certain, that at least 124 Indigenous men were to die during the Great War; 75 or 61% were killed in action (KiA); 29 or 23% died of wounds (DoW) and 20 or 16% from disease (DoD). The majority of Aboriginal men perished on the Western Front: 68 or 55% in France and 32 or 26% in Belgium. In the Dardanelles campaign seven died at Gallipoli and one in Egypt. Two died in the campaign in the Middle East, five in hospital in the United Kingdom and a further six back in Australia. During their evacuation to Australia two died at sea. The data for Indigenous men thus largely reflected that of the First AIF as a whole[26] and they were integrated into the same battalion, not separated

24 Joan Beaumont & Alison Cadzow, 'Serving Our Country', Beaumont & Cadzow (eds), *Serving Our Country. Indigenous Australians, War, Defence and Citizenship*, NewSouth, Sydney, 2018, 12.

25 Douglas Grant AIF Attestation Papers of Persons Enlisted for Service Abroad, No 1126, 13.1.1916.

26 Wenham, '"My own darling laddie".

as in the American and Canadian forces.

This latter factor always gave Douglas Grant a strong sense of belonging, of mateship with non-Indigenous soldiers; to him they were all comrades-in-arms with absolute loyalty to each other. In fact, they were a strong part of his adopted and perceived identity throughout his life.

Grant, who became a champion rifle shot at the AIF Camp at Rutherford in the Lower Hunter Valley, served in the 13th Battalion. On 8 February 1917, he arrived in France with his battalion reinforcements.

Strategical incompetence at Bullecourt

Some time after, on 11 April 1917, the 13th were involved in the First Battle of Bullecourt.[27] This attack was hastily planned as a diversion to the Battle of Arras and resulted in disaster. The Australians suffered 3,300 casualties and 1,170 Australians were taken prisoner – the largest number captured in a single engagement in the war. Among them was Douglas Grant who was wounded in the open battlefield near the German-occupied village of Riencourt slightly east of Bullecourt.[28]

English military historians give less attention to the 1st Battle of Bullecourt than do Australian military historians. Even *The Oxford Companion to Australian Military History* (1997) does not include an entry, perhaps because it was an inglorious defeat. It is mentioned in the same volume in half a sentence in the entry on the highly

---

27 Chris Coulthard-Clark, *The Encyclopaedia of Australia's Battles*, Allen & Unwin, 2001, 125-6.

28 Wenham, 'Unpublished Address'.

-decorated Lieutenant-Colonel Henry "Harry" Murray VC.[29]

The Battles of Bullecourt do not appear in the Index of *Serving Our Country* (2018) about Indigenous Australians in wartime, even though there are narrative sections dealing with the experiences of Douglas Grant himself. They do not mention Bullecourt.[30]

Popular military historian AK Macdougall, in his general history of *Australians at War* (2012), gives the two battles of Bullecourt some highlighted space under the heading of '1917 Wars of Attrition'.[31] He points out correctly that General Birdwood pleaded for a postponement for the first offensive at Bullecourt without success. He foresaw that his men would be needlessly slaughtered. But the British commander General Hubert Gough was mistakenly, but entirely convinced that the Germans were at the point of a full withdrawal, because the occupied village in the distance could be seen burning. He believed that the Germans were on the run – a completely wrong assessment.

Gough had been convinced by tank commanders that, instead of a preliminary barrage, the twelve new tanks at his disposal could go forward before the attacking infantry and crash through the elaborate wire reinforcements that

---

29 'Murray, Lieutenant-Colonel Henry William (1 December 1880 - 1 January 1966)', in Peter Dennis, Jeffrey Grey, Ewen Morris, Robin Pryor (eds), *The Oxford Companion to Australian Military History*, Oxford University Press, Melbourne, 1997, 413.

30 Eg 126-9; 134; 326. Under the sub-heading "The Tragedy of Douglas Grant", historian John Maynard mentions only the first battle of Bullecourt in half a sentence, 127.

31 AK Macdougall, *Australians At War. The Illustrated History*, The Five Mile Press, Scoresby, 2012, 131-3.

the Germans had set up. The strategy was a failure, partly due to weather and environmental conditions; the assault troops shivered on the sloping open field; the twelve Mark I tanks went forward to lead the breakthrough only to break down from mechanical failure or to suffer a direct hit from the heavy and accurate German barrage. Some got lost in the snow. By 7am on 11 April, all the tanks were burning wrecks littering the battlefield, only four reached the enemy wire and just one got to the first trench line.[32]

The failure of the tanks left the assault troops, like Douglas Grant, nakedly exposed in the field and ready for the massacre. They were subjected to relentless crossfire of well-placed machine-gun nests.

It could be assumed that to be successful any offensive in 1917 would require, as an absolute prerequisite, a heavy concentration of artillery with plenty of reserves of ammunition for the guns. In the First Battle of Bullecourt the Allies had neither and the alternate strategy of the tanks failed miserably.

The Strength of the Hindenburg Line

As a major superstructure of the famed Hindenburg Line, the salient village of Bullecourt was surrounded by innovative fortifications: deep zig-zagging trenches, elaborate eight foot high rolls or bands of barbed wire – one after the other and three deep – thus almost impossible to penetrate without serious loss of life.

The wire entanglement of the Hindenburg Line was eventually known to be the most formidable ever constructed;

---

32 Coulthard-Clark, *The Encyclopedia*, 125.

the aerial photographs taken by the Allies bear witness.[33]

As part of the Line, there were large, elaborate and well-designed German dugouts housing reserve or relief troops that could be quickly brought into battle at a moment's notice when needed. Members of the formidable 27th Württemberg Division were able to emerge from these deep shelters, even on the flanks and from the rear of the Australian assault waves. A little while after midday, survivors began to limp back from their untenable gains.[34] The entire new German defensive structure of fortification was needed for the new strategical theory of 'elastic defence'. Machine-gun nests were cleverly positioned to provide a wind of bullets from three directions that caught opposing troops in a deadly cross-fire.[35] German infantry under the 'elastic defence' idea could move in an orderly manner in attack and then retreat to a more protective location. Fewer German lives were thus lost than the Allies in 1917.

Action in the 1st Bullecourt

The Australian historian AK Macdougall captured the battle melodramatically, but realistically:

> At 4.45 am on 11 April 1917 the first two Australian battalions went forward, without a preliminary bombardment. They quickly walked past the three remaining tanks and amid a storm of bullets threw themselves against the wire. 'Come on boys, bugger

33 George Franki & Clyde Slatyer, *Mad Harry, Harry Murray VC, CMG, DSO & Bar, DCM, C de G, Australia's Most Decorated Soldier*, Kangaroo Press, Pymble, 2001, 86-87.

34 Coulthard-Clark, *The Encyclopedia*, 125-6.

35 John Ramsland, 'The Legacy of Douglas Grant, 13th Battalion', *Digger*, no 64, September 2018, 13-23; 16.

the tanks!' shouted Major Black, VC, before he was killed. Incredibly they managed to seize the first line of trenches. Thinking the town had been taken, Gough sent in his cavalry, who were decimated. The full weight of the German counter-attack fell on the Australian brigades in their tenuous positions, and they were withdrawn amid shellbursts and constant enemy grenade attacks. Rollcall revealed the hideous casualties. The 4th Brigade, 3,000 strong, had lost 2,339 men; 12th Brigade had lost 950.[36]

Earlier, the 13th Battalion, with the well-known Aborigine Private Douglas Grant, had bivouacked at Favreuil village on the outskirts of the town of Bapaume about eight miles behind the jumping-off point in a railway cutting for the proposed attack of 10 April, some 1,200 yards of open farmland. The battalion moved off from Favreuil beginning at 10pm on an extremely cold night and took up behind the 16th Battalion at the railway cutting close to the village of Ecoust-Saint-Mein for the proposed jumping-off time at 4.30 the following morning of 11 April 1917.[37]

The Australian 14th and 15th Battalions were also in readiness, lying out in No Man's Land, sheltered in a sunken road about 700 yards from Bullecourt. All were ready to go forward then at 4.45, but the tanks to lead and support them had not yet arrived and would not, in time for the beginning of the prepared attack. The decision was then made to call off the attack, just as dawn was breaking on the cloudy grey sky.

36 Macdougall, *Australians at War*, 132.
37 Franki & Slatyer, *Mad Harry*, 94-5.

Lieutenant Colonel Durant CO of the 13th Battalion ran out to tell his company to inform the commanding officer, ordering him: 'Get back for your lives!' Grant and the rest wasted no time in doing what they were told. At that moment, the Australians were exposed to a sudden unexpected German artillery barrage as their presence had been detected by enemy intelligence. Luckily, a snowstorm began which provided them with cover, obscuring them from the enemy as they retreated.

The 13th were route marched quick-step eight miles back down the road to Favreuil. They then waited, exhausted, standing close together for warmth, but shivering in the icy cold. They had used up precious energy uselessly – stolen for many from their future lives, but Grant was to be a survivor, the second time in his life: the first from a north Queensland massacre, at the age of two or so, perpetrated by Mounted Native Police operating the dispersal policy.

At 6pm, the 13th were ordered to return, again on the double, to the railway cutting at Ecoust. They were told that the attack was to go ahead at 4.30 the following morning of 11 April 1917. By that time, the Australians had endured two sleepless nights in the cold, mainly on their feet, and were now in poor condition. Some were on the point of collapse and had to be carried away to the field hospital.

As most of the men advanced in the open farmlands at about 4.45am, a terrifying machine-gun and rifle fire enveloped the leading 4th and 12th Brigades. They had walked into a well-organised death trap! Men of the 13th Battalion who followed fell dead before the endless storm of lead.[38]

Lying on the ground for cover, Douglas later claimed about

38 Ramsland, *The Legacy of Douglas Grant*, 103-111.

it all ending there. As it was such an onslaught, it reminded him of his infant experience in north-eastern Queensland. The German machine-gun nests were having it all their own way. Douglas made the next hundred yards at a dog trot, bent forward, and then fell forward in the snow with bomb wounds to his back and neck from flying shrapnel. Some 825 metres had been gained temporarily on the Western Front at a huge sacrifice of Australian men – all with a rendezvous with death.

Bullecourt 1, on 11 April 1917, was a military blunder of immense magnitude by General Gough who had totally miscalculated the strength and strategic power of the German Army. In a single day, 3,300 Australian infantry of the 4th Division were casualties with 1,170 being taken prisoners, including Douglas. When General Birdwood gave his usual after-battle talk, hard-swearing, hard-faced officers from the Dardanelles campaign broke down with uncontrollable tears.

Grant had escaped death by good fortune – there was an advantage in being short in the hail of machine-gun bullets. While being wounded in the back and shoulder by grenade fragments, he had reached Riencourt further to the east of Bullecourt – most had not even got as far. He was one of the last left on the battlefield when the triumphant German stretcher-bearers came to remove him through tunnels in the barbed-wire defences of the Hindenburg Line. At first, Grant was handled roughly, but then he was taken to a German field hospital for treatment. His war was over; his wounds were attended to.

He was operated on by a German surgeon in another hospital to remove all the grenade fragments. After recovering sufficiently, he was released and spent two months as a manual labourer and slave in the occupied town of Douai in northern France close to the Front and in the heart of the occupied coal belt on the railway south of occupied Lille.[39]

Allenby and the Battle of Arras

To some historians, 1 Bullecourt was only an adjunct to the much better known Battle of Arras (9 April – 15 May 1917), the first major attack by the British Expeditionary Force (BEF) in 1917 where the Allied troops fought under Field Marshal Edmund Henry Allenby (1861-1936) in the east of the city of Arras. Bullecourt was intended to divert German troops from engaging in Allenby's massive assault.

Allenby was one of the few successful British generals of the First World War. His reputation rests on three great battles: Arras in France, Third Gaza and Megiddo in the Middle East. Arras was one of the most costly British offensives of the war, but 3,300 Germans were captured as well as twenty-three big guns.

The Canadian troops scored a great victory storming the difficult German defences on Vimy Ridge. By the end of the first day in the spring of 1917, Allenby's army had advanced three and a half miles and the momentum was sustained for the following three days despite bitter fighting at the fortified village of Monchy-le-Preux. It was a breakthrough of between twelve and fifteen miles. The technique of breakthrough had been mastered, but the technique of how to exploit that breakthrough had not.[40] At the same time, Bullecourt I stalled with Australia suffering its worst ever losses on the Western Front.

---

39 Ramsland, 'The Legacy', 15-17.

40 Simon Innes-Robbins, 'Allenby and the Battle of Arras', *Military History Matters*, issue 110, November 2019, 18-24.

Slave-labour at the Front

For Douglas at Douai, life was hard and food was poor and in short supply. As he recalled in 1931: 'We had absolutely no meat'.[41] He was still suffering from his wounds and the dangerous work requirements in terrible outdoor conditions so close to the Front frequently placed him on the receiving end of Allied bombardments. His life was often in mortal danger.

As his wounds healed, he felt hungry all the time. He thought up feverish, far-fetched ideas about escape, but he and the other POWs were closely guarded. As well, he had a noticeable appearance in a sea of European live bodies.

Back in Sydney, his adoptive parents Robert and Elizabeth and their younger son Henry or Harry were in deep despair – they had received official notice that Douglas was lost or missing in action,[42] believed dead.

Removal from Douai

Douglas was no doubt relieved to be removed from Douai with its fear of Allied bombardment and death. In August 1917 at the slave-labour camp of about 180 men – mostly Australians – they were issued with an official printed leaflet from German authorities explaining that they were required to work in conditions close to the fighting Front to punish the French Army for treating German POWs in the same way. The document claimed that many German prisoners-of-war had been killed in the crossfire.

Eventually, through negotiations between the two sides, the POWs were recognised as such and removed to

41 Extract from Douglas Grant's Patient Case Record, NSW State Records, Kingswood.

42 They were not informed of the location.

Germany under safer conditions. They were issued with postcards and invited to write home to their families. Grant did so immediately through the efficient German postal service. For Robert Grant and his family, it was a great relief to receive news from Douglas himself; he had survived and was still alive.

Dan Cooper (1890-1917), son of William Cooper, Cummeragunja Mission, killed in action. William Cooper of the Australian Aborigines League wrote: 'I am father of a soldier who gave his life for his King on the battlefield as did thousands of coloured men in the AIF' (Jackomos & Fowell)

Douglas was placed in hospital in Dülmen in Germany where he received further treatment of his wounds and influenza and a compulsory inoculation that he blamed for the continued pain and weakness in his left shoulder and chest (for which he received a small army pension after the war). When he was sufficiently better, he was removed from Dülmen by train under guard to Wittenberg in Saxony where he worked as a labourer in the coalmines for eight months. His physical condition actually improved with better food and persistent heavy exercise in the mines. He wrote to his family at home, reassuring them:

> I am well and comfortable as circumstances will permit ... Do not worry; I am quite fit. The Australian Red Cross sends me three packets of groceries a fortnight ... also I get loaves of bread and a tin of biscuits [once] a week from the Red Cross in Switzerland.

> I have good boots, shoes, slippers, socks, shirts and a prison uniform … I get letters to cheer me up.
> [published in full in the *Sydney Mail*, 20 March 1918]

In Australia, Douglas Grant had become the most famous Indigenous solder in the 1st AIF. It was frequently claimed in Australian newspapers that he was the only so-called 'full-blood' Aborigine in the Australian fighting forces, which was not correct.

At the Crescent Concentration Camp

Eventually, Grant was moved to the 'Half-Moon' or Crescent Concentration Camp (*Halbmondlager*) in Germany for coloured prisoners-of-war from the English, French and Russian armies, many of whom were Muslim in faith. The camp was between the villages of Wünsdorf and Zossen at forty kilometres south of Berlin. A wooden mosque had been built within the camp's boundaries – the first in Germany – in an attempt to provide for religious freedom and to invite Muslims to fight for the Central Powers alongside the Turks.

In the 5,000-strong camp, Douglas was soon appointed as inmate-in-charge of the coloured soldiers section because of his good level of Western education and leadership qualities. He revealed his heroism by acting as an advocate for other prisoners and was able to save lives in difficult circumstances. He became the President and chief organiser of the British Help Committee within the camp, constantly caring for the sick and wounded.

When a large number of prisoners staged a hunger strike,

Grant took swift action. He conducted a huge amount of urgent correspondence with the international ameliorating charitable organisations operating in World War I. As a result, he was able to persuade the British Red Cross to support the regular supply of specialised food parcels for Muslim and Sikh prisoners. They sent him, on request, vital medical supplies by consignment from the neutral Dutch port of Rotterdam into Germany. He also achieved vital help from the Invalid Comfort Fund for Prisoners, the British Help Committee, the Merchant Seaman's Help Society, a German Lutheran Charitable men's group and other organisations. He wrote many compelling letters to these organisations. The hunger strike, which was of great concern for the authorities, was thus quickly brought to a happy end. For Douglas, this was a singular achievement and a high watermark in his professional life's journey.

While in the camp, Grant and a couple of other Australian Aboriginal prisoners, became objects of intense interest to German academics: Social and Physical Anthropologists and linguists. These men were interested in 'exotic' indigenous societies of the South Pacific; they were unable to carry out field work because of the war. A revolving door of scholars and artists visited the Crescent Concentration Camp to meet and examine Douglas Grant and another Australian Aborigine POW, Roland Carter, in particular.

Grant had his photographic portrait taken by Otto Stiehl along with Roland Carter (51st Battalion) from South Australia. Portrait artists Thomas Baumgartner and Max Beringer painted oil portraits of both men – such was the intense interest in their 'exotic' qualities. Grant sat for the renowned German-Jewish sculpture Rudolf Marcuse who produced a bronze bust of him that has been located in a private collection in England.[43]

Sculpture of Douglas Grant by Jewish sculptor Rudolf Marcuse (photograph Tom Murray) Private collection, Rupert O'Flynn, England

Private Roland Carter, from Point McLeay, South Australia, a fellow POW with Douglas Grant (AWM2017.727.1.3)

Repatriation and Post-war Neglect

Repatriated at the war's end while waiting for transport back to Australia, Grant paid a joyous visit to his surrogate Grant family in a small Scottish village. He returned to Australia on 1 June 1919 and was discharged from the 1st AIF.

For Aboriginal people, twentieth-century Australia did not reflect improvement. Following the war, the racism that seemed to have avoided Douglas before the war began to impact on him with increasing severity. Racism, so widespread in country and city, was a deep scar on social life in post-war Australian society. Despite Grant's comparative level of education and status in the army as a comrade-in-arms or Digger, his qualifications as a mechanical draughtsman,

43 Pegram, 'Under the Kaiser's Crescent Moon'; Murray & Howes, 'Douglas Grant & Rudolf Marcuse'.

taxidermist and woolclasser (a significant occupation in the Australian wool industry) were ignored as well as his leadership and administrative clerical skills that he had demonstrated so ably at the Crescent POW Camp. Despite recent publicity in Australia that he was received as a military hero, the only work he could gain, both in the country and the city despite many efforts, was as an unskilled, temporary labourer.

In a highly-stratified and racist society, he continued to be viewed merely as an Aborigine – fit only for work as an unskilled, lowly-paid labourer. Australia of the 1920s and 1930s was a place where racial intolerance toward Aborigines was mainstreamed and the accepted norm.

Over time as the supportive members of his adoptive family passed away, he became increasingly alone and lonely, depressed and sometimes resorting to bouts of heavy drinking. As with many returned servicemen, he suffered from post-traumatic stress from his wartime frontline and imprisonment experiences.

How Douglas became a patient, Callan Park

In late February 1931, Douglas Grant was 'Found wandering and threatening people with a razor in East Sydney'.[44] In the information accompanying his transfer to Callan Park Hospital for the Insane, it was noted that he had spent six days in the Darlinghurst facility and was in a 'miserable & depressed' state, but was 'quiet and clean'. At this stage of the six days, he was not under any treatment

---

44 Order made for the Medical Hospital, Callan Park to accompany patient Douglas Grant, from the Reception House, Darlinghurst, 2/3/1931, NSW State Records, Kingswood.

(apart from incarceration) and was not taking 'stimulants', and not refusing food. There was no indication of suicidal tendencies. He had, it was noted, so-called 'alcoholic excesses' extending over years. A physical examination revealed scars on both legs and upon his abdomen.

The admission process used was the most common, that is via a public arrest if a person showed signs of what was considered to be insanity, in this case in the streets of East Sydney. As with many so-called lunatics, Douglas was homeless and seemingly friendless, although several friends were to come forward in support of him when they heard about his dilemma. Any signs of violence, as in Douglas' case of holding a razor in his hand and seeming to threaten people in the street – at least from the observer's viewpoint – was sufficient grounds for arrest. There was no evidence of any sign of violent behaviour directed to others. According to the records, there was no evidence in Grant's case that he was 'directly deposited' by family members or friends to a police station, or that he was simply abandoned at a police station.[45] The police chose the option of arresting him in the street and placing him into the custody of the Darlinghurst Reception House where he was to spend six days being examined. He was not charged with a criminal offence. Under the *Lunacy Act of 1898 – Third Schedule*, two medical doctors at the Reception House examined Grant 'Draughtsman' of 'no fixed address'. They 'deemed' it 'necessary' – as he had been found 'wandering at large' in 'Insane and indigent circumstances' – to incarcerate him at Callan Park Hospital for the Insane to

45 Sarah Luke, *Callan Park. Hospital for the Insane*, Australian Scholarly, North Melbourne, 2018, 87.

provide him with treatment.[46] The Order of Conveyance was signed on 2 March 1931. Douglas was quickly removed to Callen Park.

Under the *Lunacy Act of 1898 – Fifth Schedule*, an official at the Reception House diligently filled in a pro-forma Statement about Douglas: he had no children, was a draughtsman by profession, a native of Queensland (that is, born in Queensland) with no 'fixed' home and a Presbyterian. His supposed cause of insanity was stated: 'Alcoholic excesses'. There was no record of any insane attack before the present one. It was the only accountable attack in his life. He did not have any insane relatives. He had never before been an inmate of any institution for the insane. He was not subject to fits, nor did he appear suicidal. In the question: 'was he dangerous to others', the handwritten reply was a hesitant, 'maybe'. His nearest relation was recorded as 'Foster Brother. Henry Sneddon Grant c/- Sydney Museum College Street, Sydney'. The whole document was signed by the Assistant Superintendent, The Reception House, Darlinghurst – a qualified medical doctor.[47] The two medical doctors who examined Grant did so separately under the rules governed by the Lunacy Act.

On his arrival at Callan Park, his first examination by the medical doctor, who was from the Medical School of the University of Sydney, noted as part of the first Medical Certificate:

(1) Patient is so persecuted by delusions of fear &

46 Order of Conveyance to a Hospital or Licensed House, Douglas Grant's Patient Case Records, 2 March 1931.
47 Statement, Patient Case Records, undated document.

> persecution that he cannot carry on normal life. He says to me "voices follow me through the city" & when he was at work which repeat "We've got you" —
> That he cannot sleep because of these accusations. He cannot name the owners of the voices. He states he has taken alcohol to xs [excess], but not lately. He can give a good a/c [account] of his life – & altho an aboriginal, speaks good English & says he is a draughtsman. He appears unduly depressed, & on being questioned thereon – says he has no interest in life, feels he is doing wrong all the time.
>
> …
>
> They call him "vile" names never leave him alone. He is emotional at times.[48]

This was a careful assessment through the use of interviews, but the impact of his war experiences and the traumas they had produced seem to have been ignored in what was a purely clinical approach consistent with its time in psychiatric institutional care. The impact of racism, though vaguely noted, was not explored in terms of its effect on well-being.

Authorities were aware that Douglas had a history as an alcoholic. In the first five days or so, he had made no improvement. He was not sleeping well and he complained of being continuously persecuted by voices day and night, continually calling him "vile" names, as he put it in his own words.

By early February, he was observed as being restless and

48 Medical Certificate & Personal History of patient, Order or Request for Reception into a Hospital or Licensed House, Patient Case Records.

worried. He still had delusions of persecution. "Voices" still followed him wherever he went. He still heard the words: "We'll get you". He was still observed to be emotional at times. He was now very frightened to be left alone.[49]

Several other records described the same behavioural patterns with little or no change as observed by medical authorities at Callan Park. Douglas was carefully monitored. On many occasions over time, he was labelled as an alcoholic.

In early 1930, Douglas Grant began to speak out against the treatment of Aborigines since the 1914–1918 war. He was granted a daily leave-of-absence from Callan Park to do so on 25 May 1933.[50] In a talk to a small think-tank, 'Questions Circle of the Balmain Methodist Church', he made an extremely powerful plea to allow Aborigines to have their own territory and create their own colleges and schools as had the native Americans (he called them in the fashion of the time – Red Indians).The fact that Callan Park authorities allowed him daily leave indicated that they saw him as being no danger at all to society outside the asylum.

The following day, his talk received wide-spread recognition in the national daily press which provided some background to Grant himself in introducing him to the public: 'Mr Grant, who was adopted when he was only 18 months old and educated to a standard fitting him for the position of draftsman in a Sydney dockyard, served with the A.I.F., and was a prisoner of war in Germany for 22 months'.

In his talk. he argued forcefully that if Aborigines of the day were given opportunities to develop, free from

49 Medical Certificate, Patient Case Records, 2 March 1931.

50 Leave-of-absences bundle, Douglas Grant's Case Study file.

'white influences', with the high communal spirit of the pre-settlement days, he could be used usefully 'to occupy the outposts of the continent where at present Europeans could not go'.

He argued that Aborigines should be allowed to develop naturally, 'not merely stop around missions, whose gifts of tobacco and drink made him lose his head'. 'Let him become an asset instead of a drag', he emphasised. His ideas meshed with those of David Unaipon, the celebrated Aboriginal scholar and inventor.[51]

Grant forcefully pointed out the racist views in white society, in which Aborigines were portrayed 'as one of the lowest types of the human race', was totally wrong, whereas their communal life was of a far higher standard morally than was 'much European life today'. He emphasised the importance in Aboriginal communal life of male initiation ceremonies, of 'different grades and ordeals'. That is, he pointed out, 'the girls were taken in hand by the women of the tribe and taught to make blankets from bark, to tan and treat skins, to gather food and all the domestic requirements of a nomadic race'. He argued that there were still native groups 'living the same primitive life which the natives had lived from time immemorial' in the centre of the continent.

Instead of fostering this spirit, the White man, he argued, had broken up communal life, which was on a 'high plane' of civilisation. The penalty for the violation of the communal moral code in traditional Aboriginal society, he added in his address, was death.

---

51 John Ramsland and Christopher Mooney, *Remembering Aboriginal Heroes. Struggle, Identity and the Media*, Brolga, Melbourne, 2006, 1-2, 15-26.

Grant exhibited to his audience several 'chip-back knives, chipped from suitable stone on the mountains and carried to the coast for barter'. He noted: 'Along the shores of Leichhardt Bay ... were still to be found middens or kitchens of the natives with chip back knives, stone tomahawks and so forth buried beneath.'

'Many other marks of the primitive race were to be found', he said. He gave examples of the original civilisation found at Kurnell under the sand dunes.[52]

Grant's ideas followed on those of David Unaipon who he was featured with in a 1917 article in the *Sydney Mail.* In that article, both of their photographic portraits were presented.[53]

★ ★ ★

By 1934, Callan Park reports about Douglas had begun to change. They were now 'Records of Progress'. On June 1937, he was described as fairly well mentally, but far too irresponsible to look after himself in the outside world. But he was working as a clerk for Callan Park's manager. Nevertheless, he sought alcohol on 'every possible occasion'. By 18 August 1935, he was observed as 'behaving well lately' and working for the institution's manager. And yet it was claimed he was, 'Quite unable to look after himself away from the hospital', even though he had been granted several day-leaves.

While he worked well for the manager, he always had 'an alcoholic thirst'. By 23 August, it was observed that he had

52 An unidentified newspaper clipping dated 27 April 1933 with the heading : 'Abo Plea. Communal Life. Own Colleges. Racial Standard', placed in Douglas Grant's file at Callan Park, circa early 1930s.

53 'PSA', 'A Plea for the Australian Aborigines', *Sydney Mail*, 11 July 1917.

been 'on his best behaviour lately, does some office work'.

One report in 1935 revealed:

> He obviously looks depressed although he states he feels alright. He states he was brought here [Callan Park] because he was a bit lost & does not know why he is being kept here. Slightly aggressive in speech lacking some insight into his condition weight into his condition. Admits worrying but says it is natural to worry. He says he is in a groove & can't get out of it.[54]

His alcoholic 'lapses' appeared to be commonplace during his stay in Callan Park Mental Hospital and never clearly resolved, even though he signed the pledge several times, in 1933 and on other occasions under the influence of Anglican Missionary Reverend Hammond.[55]

On his file at Callan Park dated 21 November 1933 was the following typewritten statement:

> I Douglas Grant HEREBY PROMISE
>
> that I shall never in future consume any alcoholic substances.
>
> I am fully aware of the terrible results of alcoholism, and whatever may happen to me in the future I shall keep this promise.
>
> (sgd) Douglas Grant [handwritten]
>
> Date 21.11.33[56]

On the other hand since admission, it was officially reported that Douglas had lost his acute depression 'and had adapted himself to his environment, being usefully occupied assisting in clerical and draughting work required

54 Record of Progress, Douglas Grant, 5 Patient Case Records.

55 Record of Progress, 5 December 1933.

56 From Douglas Grant's case file, Callan Park.

at the Hospital'.[57] Thus, after the Great War, Callan Park Hospital was the only institution or employer to return Grant to his skill level of work and his professional training and education. In this, they showed respect for the man. The drawing work he was assigned included the design of the ANZAC Bridge memorial.

Once Grant's deep depression was substantially cured (apart from his ongoing drinking problems), he was allowed day-leave from Callan Park.

Leave-of-Absences

During the year 1932, he was granted day leave on six occasions only. On the first occasion, the Medical Superintendent granted him leave-of-absence 'to obtain an advance from his [war]pension, if available'. He was granted up to £1 to meet the 'reasonable expenses' of his visit, probably lunch money and bus travel.[58] He would have had to visit, on this occasion, the office of the Commonwealth Department of Repatriation. Douglas carried the typed statement with him as a kind of licence or passport on the streets of Sydney to show police or government officials, especially as he was a well-known identity.

His second leave-of-absence was officially granted for 2 November 1932. The document supported his request for another monetary advance as the period fell in the Christmas and New Year holidays – his allowance of 10/- for the quarter ending 31 January 1933.[59] Thus the first official leave

57 Typed report, undated, Case study file.

58 The Deputy Master in Lunacy, Chancery Square, Sydney, from the Medical Superintendent, Callan Park, 30 June 1932.

59 Deputy Master in Lunacy, 2 Nov. 1932.

granted was to deal with money – his allowance from his war pension which was, to a large extent, usually absorbed into the costs of his board-and-lodgings at Callan Park.

Douglas Grant's third day release on 25 November 1932 was to make a few purchases for himself in the early morning and then to visit the Sydney Cricket Ground to watch England play against New South Wales. He was successful in asking for 15/- for the expenses of the day which would have included lunch at the Cricket Ground.

On 16 December 1932, Douglas was granted extended leave to visit his family and friends at Lithgow in prior preparation for the Christmas and New Year period. By 30 December, the same leave was granted yet again in a second document that called for a money advance to be given to him.[60]

In the following year, there were eleven leave-of-absences given to Douglas. In the first eight of these between January and April, his destination was unstated, but he received 16/- or so expense allowance on each occasion.[61]

On 2 June 1933, the ninth leave took him to the Sydney Cricket Ground to watch a football game – Rugby League – and he was granted £1 expenses allowance. It is known that Douglas had been an outstanding Rugby Union and League player.

For the rest of the year, the destination was not stated, except one to buy items for personal comfort. On 30 June, he received 30/-; on 11 August, £2.0.0; on 22 September, £2.10.0; on 30 October, 25/-; and 15/- on 3 November.[62]

60 Deputy Master in Lunacy, 16 & 30 December 1932.

61 Batch of Leave of Absences for 1933, Grant Case Study file.

62 Batch of Leave 1933.

These amounts clearly enabled Douglas to have a few drinks. His nurses began to complain officially that, on several occasions, he had returned to the institution intoxicated, while on other occasions, sober.

In 1934, Grant received eighteen leave-of-absences; in 1935 – fifteen; in 1936 – nineteen; 1937 – also nineteen and in 1938 – twenty-three. Finally, eight were granted – the last on 20 June 1939, not long before Grant left Callan Park forever. On most of these forms, his destination was not identified, but an allowance was usually stated. The daily expense allowance commonly rested at 15/- or 16/- and frequently, for some reason, 16 shillings and 9 pence. Sometimes it was more: 33/-, indicating he was travelling further to an unspecified destination.

It appears Callan Park had given up on his drinking problem, as long as he didn't drink on the premises. On 1 February 1939, a different sort of form was issued with stricter requirements. Leave was granted to Douglas Grant strictly from 9am until 4pm. A note in handwriting above stated: 'Granted on the understanding that no more leave will be given for six months if anything goes wrong'.

In February 1939, Douglas Grant escaped from Callan Park only to give himself up and into its care at the Reception House in Darlinghurst at 6.45pm on 19th of that month when he stated 'that he had escaped' … It was observed that the patient 'had been drinking'. He stayed three days at the Reception House and was treated with 'Mist Pot Brom with three doses daily'. During that time, he was 'Quiet and Well Conducted' and showed no suicide tendencies – his 'Bodily condition: Good and clean'. After three days had elapsed, he was returned in good condition to Callan Park at Rozelle.[63]

★ ★ ★

Douglas Grant had been living at Callan Park for eight and a half years – a relatively long time – when he was, discharged on 23 June 1939, never to return. His discharge was recommended by the Medical Superintendent of Callan Park and approved by the Inspector General of the Insane, New South Wales.64 He had first been admitted to Ward H3 on 3 March 1931 and transferred to War H4. By 10 April, he was placed in Ward B. His final assessment was: 'He is an incorrigible alcoholic with mild alcoholic dementia and will never improve'[65] – but could still work for a living.

One of Eleven

Douglas was one of eleven inmates of Ward B, Repatriation Cottages at the bottom of the hill overlooking Iron Bay. The numbers in the Ward fluctuated as a group between about ten to twenty. One report revealed the nature of the mental conditions of the eleven men:

> 'He is a case of an advanced Dementia Praecox and will never recover' (Pte, 6th Btn);
> 'He is an incorrigible alcoholic with mild dementia and will never improve' (Douglas Grant, Pte, 13th Btn);
> 'He is a long standing case of Paraphrenia and will probably always be unstable' (Pte, 34th Btn);
> 'He is a case of advanced alcoholic dementia and will

63 Reception House Statement, 22 February 1939.

64 Patient Case Records, 23 June 1939.

65 Medical Superintendent to Deputy Repatriation Commissioner, 18/3/1939, Patient Case Records.

never recover' (Cpl, 53rd Btn);

'He is a case of mild deficiency with added Confusional Psychosis and will never improve' (Pte, First L.T.M.B,);

'He is a case of very advanced Dementia Praecox and will never improve' (Dvr. 5th F.A.B.);

'He is a case of Confusional Psychosis and will never improve' (Spr – 1st D.Sig.Co.);

He is a case of Confusional Psychosis and will never improve' (Pte, 4th Btn);

'He is a case of advanced alcoholic dementia and will never improve' (Pte, 4th Btn);

'He is a case of very advanced alcoholic dementia and will never improve' (Pte, 18th Btn);

'He is a case of secondary dementia due to alcoholism and will never recover' (Pte, 18th Btn).[66]

This deterministic prognosis in March of 1939 of all the men patients of Ward B, who were permanent residents, demonstrates Douglas Grant's charismatic leadership powers to encourage such men in a range of positive occupational therapy activities: building an innovative war memorial; manufacturing soap; gardening; playing cricket, golf and other outdoor sporting activities. As a patient, Grant became something of an amateur therapist who knew how to make a contribution and is reminiscent of his achievements in the Colours Camp of World War I. Although Grant had spent most of his time in Callan Park in Ward B, he was confined on several occasions to isolation sections of the mental institution for treatment.

66 Medical Superintendent of Callan Park to Deputy Commissioner, Repatriation Commission, 15/3/1939.

The ANZAC Bridge War Memorial

In 1931, Douglas Grant was admitted to Callan Park Mental Asylum to the Repatriation cottages or wards for disabled veterans and subject to the Park's Master of Lunacy while remaining in facilities under the Repatriation Board. Again, in a bright spot in his life, he showed his leadership skills with his design and supervision of the construction – along with other patients – of an innovative Anzac Bridge War Memorial featuring a replica of the Sydney Harbour Bridge and a fish pond. It was built in the open air and still stands undisturbed on the flats of Callan Park near the former Ward B building in sight of Iron Cove.

After Release, 1939-1951

For the next twelve years after his release, Grant's condition slowly deteriorated.

In 1945, he was found working as a general labourer in a large cardboard factory and he worked hard. He had already wandered around the countryside in temporary outdoor labouring jobs and at the Small Arms Factory in Lithgow owned by the Federal Government. The Government reserved some employment there for ex-servicemen from World War I.

Douglas Grant was one of several Aboriginal war veterans who returned to a nation that promised much, but delivered little.

★ ★ ★

Grant was a living example of the government's confused state and Federal policies of Assimilation. His lonely death on Bare Island, La Perouse, in the Veterans Home there, shows its flaws. Douglas Grant is a type of tragic hero. The events of his life in war and peace showed with clarity the flaws of the policy. Despite the love and equality given him by the Grant family, he never successfully assimilated into white society. At the same time, despite his racial origins due to circumstances, he had been irreversibly separated from his traditional culture.[67]

A Scottish brogue and his ability to play on the bagpipes all the 'tunes of glory', now can be seen more a symptom of an unfulfilled life of tragedy – which, nevertheless, is somehow supremely and undeniably heroic. Human beings like Douglas Grant are always more complicated, brave, long-suffering that we can ever guess. *He* would not regard his own life as necessarily tragic.

67 Wenham, unpublished address.

6

Sydney University Soldiers

Irony is the attendant of hope, and the fuel of hope is innocence. …

Never such innocence again.[1]

These Sydney Doctors were answering an urgent call from the British Empire for 100 medical men to send to join the Royal Army Medical Corps as surgeons with the rank of lieutenant. These fifteen men were nearly all Sydney University graduates. Twelve other Sydney men had already left to join the steamer at Adelaide to depart for England. All together, the University of Sydney provided thirty-two graduates in response to this special call. Other universities in the British Empire were doing the same. In one sense, this call deprived the First AIF of needed medical staff.[2]

1 From 'MCMXIV' by Philip Larkin, in Paul Fussell, *The Great War and Modern Memory*, Folio, 2014, 20.

2 'Sydney Doctors for the Front', *Sydney Mail*, 24 March 1915.

This chapter mainly examines responses to the First World War in *Hermes*, the magazine of the University of Sydney, calibrated against other sources. The responses reflect the impact the war had on life at the university. The institution was psychologically embedded in the British Empire. 'The War Records of the University of Sydney', compiled by John Le Gay Brereton provide a valuable source of information about the wartime biographies of Sydney University men on the warfront in the various theatres during the Great War. These narratives of intellectual youth are analysed in terms of social class and educational background.

> An unimaginative labourer may be pardoned if he is deaf to the piteous appeals that have wafted across long stretches of ocean ..., but the educated man should need no incentive to the performance of his duty. Would that we could all feel the emotion that stirred the breast of France's greatest poet ... in December of 1870, on a late battlefield strewn with its ghastly victims, he cried:-
>
> "*O morts pour mon pays, je suis votre envieux!*" [You who have died for my country, how I envy you].
>
> Ours is an age of ... great events; and he who passes through the turbulent events of this great war, sharing all its suffering and misery, will feel a thrill like to that of Wordsworth, when looking back to a time no less pregnant with spiritual meaning, he cried:-
>
> "Bliss was it in that dawn to be alive,
> But to be young was very heaven."[3]

Recently, such sentiments were expressed – not exactly

3 'The War', *Hermes*, vol XXI, no 1, May 1915, 5.

in the same terms: 'What a momentous year in which to graduate – the beginning of the first global war, a war that changed the course of human history'.[4]

Hermes May editorial distinguishes between the imagined responses of the so-called labouring classes and the University man, thus establishing an elitist position found in other editorials of the same journal. Reference is then made to the French poet's reaction to the Franco-Prussian war so as to place the Great War in a historical sequence. Wordsworth is used to bring the discourse to an imperial standpoint about youth and a British version of Western Civilisation. That may not be what Wordsworth intended – ironically implying that the blissful youth in 'very heaven' was ready to bear arms against the Empire's enemies.

The editorials echoed messages by school authorities. The propaganda at the elite Sydney Boys High, which provided matriculated students for Sydney University, was crystal-clear after compulsory military training for the nation's youth had been introduced in 1911:

> The early part of the year saw the inauguration of a system of Compulsive Training. Australia's citizens have determined, at the cost of personal inconvenience and self-sacrifice, to fit themselves to assert their national strength in the hour of crisis. It is a system which affects us nearly, for it is principally upon the boys ... that the burden will immediately fall. Nevertheless, no one will look upon it as such for one moment when he reflects that here is offered to him an opportunity of doing

4 Professor Stephen Garton, Talk at Golden Graduate Lunch, The Great Hall, The University of Sydney, 10.4.2014.

something personally for the defence of the Empire. Conscription it will never be called.[5]

The last sentence conjures up the notion of enthusiastic volunteerism for overseas service for King and Country. Other public and private schools expressed similar sentiments of unreserved patriotism. For a boy matriculating to University, there was a smooth transition of military training (Junior to Senior Cadet Training), a preparedness for an international war against the Empire's enemy 'in the hour of crisis'. Sydney High's purpose, like private colleges, was to prepare students for university through an examination system with a classical curriculum.[6]

Cadet training psychologically enfolded adolescent boys and youths. They were seduced by the smart uniform, rifle practice, camping and a feeling of masculinity. Kings, Newington Grammar, Sydney Grammar, North Sydney Grammar, all had cadet corps. Local militias and rifle clubs across the social spectrum, in both the city and country, had multiplied. British-style uniforms were all the go.[7] Schools and university reflected the society at large.

The University of Sydney Volunteer Rifle Corps was established in the South African War as part of the colonial

---

5 'Editorial', *The Record. The Magazine of the Boys' High School*, Sydney, vol II, no 3, June 1911, 1.

6 Latin was required for all students entering the University of Sydney in the first half of the twentieth century. Educational historian Dr Alan Barcan has described the State's intensely academic curriculum in the early part of the 20th century as being based on a humanist/realist compromise: Latin, English, Mathematics, History, French, Science and Physical Education (and sometimes Geography and German); Alan Barcan, 'The Classical Curriculum in Australian Schools', Fritz-Peter Hager *et al* (eds), *Aspects of Antiquity in the History of Education*, University of Hannover, 1992, 137-61.

7 For example, the Richmond River Lancers of northern New South Wales.

Military Forces of New South Wales. Sydney Boys High cadets were founded earlier in 1883 as a voluntary organisation, but it was compulsory from 1911 for all fit boys at the school.

In 1903, the University Volunteer Rifle Corps changed to Sydney University Scouts and became compulsory for all physically fit undergraduates in 1911 and increased to a full military battalion. Later in the Great War, they became the Sydney University Company and then the Regiment.[8]

With the war's outbreak, over sixty percent of the University Scouts volunteered in the Australian Imperial Force, such was the peer and societal pressure. They served in all the major theatres of war. Most became commissioned officers as they were, on the main, from socially-elite families and were well-educated, qualified and trained in the cadets.[9]

The University Scouts were to have a persuasive influence on University life. In 1911, it had become the law of the land supported by University authorities. This was detailed in 'Soldiers All' in *Hermes*. It was 'no toy scheme' and was not to be taken lightly. It was a means of preserving life; the learning that took place could save the individual faced with warfare. It was argued patriotically that it was to preserve 'the freedom of the nation'. These were commonplace justifications.

Scout training was not just a matter of 'shooting and drill'. It was conceded that discipline could not be enforced unless the subject was willing. In the past of the colonial period,

8 Craig Stockings, 'Khaki in the classroom junior cadet training in Australia 1911-31', *History of Education Review*, vol 37, pt 1, 2008, 16-33; 'SHS Cadet Corps', *Record*, vol II, no 2, April 1911, 21-2; www.army.gov.au/who-we-are/Division-and-Brigade/Forces-Command/2nd-Division/5th-Brigade/Sydney-University-Regiment>, accessed 20 May 2013.

9 John Ramsland, *The Other Side of No Man's Land. Arthur Wheen, World War I Hero, Scholar and Pacifist*, Brolga Publishing, Melbourne, 2015, 3.

the volunteer citizen "soldier" was less willing and became nicknamed the "bloomin' old smooth-bore" among professional barrack soldiers. But the notion of volunteer militia was fading; a new form of discipline was necessary in the hour of crisis – 'self-discipline'. A man needed mastery over self. It was argued that it was surely not too much to expect the individual to govern himself in such an important international critical situation. University Scouts were needed to be violently reincarnated 'to drive home the festive bayonet'. Thus a compulsory training system, rather than outmoded voluntarism, was vital.

The writer believed a soldier's chest measurement should be greater than his waist.[10] It was argued at the "Varsity' to 'work our sport and soldiering together without either suffering was essential', as they were both 'indisputable to our existence, the one by nature and the one by law' so that 'we' may be 'both good sports and soldiers'. This Arnoldian theme was repeated in editorials appearing in *Hermes* during the war and immediately after. It was prominent in the prose of Brereton's biographies of University men. He emphasised his subjects' sporting prowess.

' John Le Gay Brereton, BA, Professor of English Literature, The University of Sydney. *The Arts Journal*, vol 4, no 1, Lent Term 1921

'Soldiers All' concluded with an imperialistic sentiment: 'To the recruit one would say: "read Kipling more assiduously than your physics even, and having

10 This measurement was carried out in all Australian recruitment procedures.

acquired the habit of thinking Tommily your education has begun"'.[11] If there were students who were opposed to such sentiments, they were not to find expression in *Hermes*.

By May 1915, the University community was proud of its enlistment rate in the AIF in comparison with other sections of Australian society. Both undergraduates and graduates had responded to the Empire's call entailing sacrifice to careers. The Medical Faculty had shown a pre-eminent sense of duty: they had sacrificed 'all chance of preferment' to minister to 'stricken soldiers' in the Australian Army Medical Corps and less familiarly with the Royal Army Medical Corps. Engineers had shown equal enthusiasm. Indeed enthusiasm for joining up had 'permeated' every faculty.

So-described German atrocities in Belgium, according to *Hermes*, had been confirmed by responsible sources, 'whose accuracy is unimpeached' and yet there had been many unofficial stories of barbarity which were false. Thus the author presented a Janus-like argument. 'Popular imagination seemed to have a hunger for the ghastly and the terrible'. The author dismissed 'as idle and pernicious' a large proportion of the descriptions of cruelty. Nevertheless, there was left a 'woeful series of crimes against honour and humanity':

> Belgium is ... an inferno of woe and desolation, such as only a Dante could describe. Reflection on the scenes of wanton pillage and rapine, murder and violation in what was but ten months ago a happy centre of quiet industry becomes well-nigh intolerable.

Thus was discourse at the colonial academy blended with pro-war propaganda and a subtle recruitment drive, using

11 "E.S.R.", 'Soldiers All', *Hermes*, vol XIX, no 1, June 1913, 15-16.

literary and classical references to engage scholars. The civilised British notions of honour and liberty were underlined. The Germany of 1915 was no longer the Germany of Goethe and Beethoven and lacked a moral compass unlike that of British Empire civilisation where there was 'the love of liberty and justice'. The 'moral courage of the Briton' was building up to a 'world embracing empire, offering it as a sacrifice on the altar of Liberty'.[12]

Hermes and a Call to Arms

The journal *Hermes* was persistent in its call to arms and placed a great emphasis on its role in supporting the British Empire in the Great War that was unfolding:

> Amid all the fearful accompaniments of a world-war, its ghastliness, its cruelties, its crimes, there is yet time for reflection on a boon which it brings in its train to humankind. It has been called patriotism, but it is not that. Some have called it **the impulse of duty**, driving men to the physical justification of right. But duty implies a moral basis, and this is not characteristic. Rather is it an indefinite, all-absorbing, **all-contagious** passion, which suffuses the souls of men, fires their imagination, and carries them into **a heaven of exultation**. The present war, based on the strength of two antagonising principles, is swept along in the whirlwind of emotion such as we describe. That emotion finds its parallel in the devotion to every great cause, whether it be an intellectual new-birth or **the dawning of a great religion**.

12 'The War', 4.

> The greatest wonder of this war is the metamorphosis it has produced in our fellow-men. Our dearest friends have changed from quiet professional or business men into the protagonists of **a great cause.** They have **become soldier-missionaries** of a world-doctrine of **liberty and justice** which part of the world has wilfully transgressed.

They were highly sophisticated arguments on an elite, middle-class audience of intellectuals, of university men who belonged to the British Empire.

The unnamed author – probably Le Gay Brereton – claimed that such changes were seen in 'thousands of faces'. He carries on elaborating his theme of the righteous, sacred cause:

> … to-day we see him fighting, struggling, suffering, **rejoicing in his manhood** and his strength, and willingly giving the last **meed of sacrifice** to a cause which he cannot define. Yet that cause is vividly real. It has the beauty of poetry, the potency of truth. Under its influence a man becomes at once as fierce as a tiger and as gentle as a lamb. Nature seems to have changed her quiet tints into colours of **savage grandeur.**

In this editorial of August 1915, words and phrases stand out as key notes in a evocative emotionally-charged symphony of not so subtle persuasion in favour of enlistment, of being a true Empire man: 'impulse of duty'; 'all-contagious passion'; 'a heaven of exultation'; 'a dawning of a great religion'; 'a great cause'; 'become soldier-missionaries'; 'liberty and justice' and 'savage grandeur'. At the same time, most Australian newspapers were full of the same thing in simpler form, the sort of straight-out war propaganda – sometimes in cruder, even racist terms.

After much more about the perils to civilisation and the

so-called 'death struggle' in Europe comes the final classical exhortation: 'It is as though we heard again the words of the Athenian: "Go, every man of you, into the ranks!"'[13] And many of 'the sons of the great University' searched their hearts and did.

The University began its toll of dead on the battlefront by August 1915 on a decorated *Hermes* memorial page:

NEW GUINEA

Capt. B.C.A. Pockley, M.B.

DARDANELLES

Brig.-General H.D. Mclaurin, B.A.

Lieut. M.P. Smith, M.B.

Lieut. R.K.S. May, Med. I

Pte A.D. Mitchell, Law I

Sgt-Major D.N. MacGregor, B.A., Sci. I

Capt. S.E. Townshend, B.A., LL.B.

Lieut. L.W. Street, B.A., Law II

Pte N.L.W. Reid, Arts II

FLANDERS

Lieut. J.S. Rich, Med. I

Of these first ten reported killed-in-action, six had commissions, four held Bachelor of Arts degrees and one was an Arts undergraduate; two were graduates in Medicine and one an undergraduate in First Year Medicine; one was a graduate in Law (LLB), two were Law undergraduates and one Arts graduate was enrolled in Science I.

Brian Pockley's death in the German New Guinea Jungle

Brian Colden Antill Pockley was killed in the assault by the Naval and Military Expeditionary Force on the German

13 'The Call to War', *Hermes*, vol XXI, no 2, August 1915, 43-45.

wireless station in Kabahaul. He was a son of an ophthalmic surgeon of Macquarie Street, Dr Francis Pockley, who later lost a second son, Lieutenant John Pockley, on another war front. Joining the AN&MEF, Pockley was appointed as a captain in that first expeditionary force. He had the dubious distinction of being the first in the Australian Army to be killed in action in the war, as well as the first Sydney University man to be killed. He died on 11 September 1914 – the first medico from Australia to die. Several others were to follow.

The day war was declared, Pockley was a residential medical officer at Sydney Hospital. He volunteered successfully as being fit for active service as well as applying for a commission which was promptly granted.[14] Brereton's biography revealed Pockley as the model University man: he had received a classical education at North Sydney Church of England Grammar School and was a student at St Paul's College while completing his Bachelor of Medicine. At school and university, he proved an outstanding sportsman and scholar. In his final year in Medicine, he won University Blues in Rugby and Athletics. He was a representative for the New South Wales Rugby team in fixtures against Queensland in 1914.

In New Guinea, Pockley, who had qualified as a surgeon six months before, was in the thick of the sporadic battle. When, with bullets flying about him, Pockley provided assistance to a German Sergeant-Major of Police, Mauderer; he quickly amputated his hand. Without treatment, Mauderer

14 Pockley, Brian CA, Application for a Commission & Personal File, 1st AIF (ANMEF), National Archives of Australia (NAA), Canberra.

would have died. He extended his arm and bit on a cigar as Pockley performed the amputation. Witnesses claimed that Mauderer's 'face did not betray ... the pain he endured'. He was taken to SS *Berrima* as a prisoner-of-war.

Meanwhile, as Able Seaman Billy Williams started down the road, a shot rang out from the trees. The round entered the right side of his chest and exited on the left. Stoker William Kember carried him half a mile towards the beach. Hearing of Williams' wounding, Pockley set off to find him. When he did, he saw the wound was mortal and instructed Kember to carry him to the beach. In an act of selflessness, Pockley removed his Red Cross brassard and tied it to Kember's hat to give him safe passage. Kember and another man carried Williams back to the staging area.

Pockley's gallant action was fatal. While attending to another wounded man in an unmarked officer's uniform, Pockley was mortally wounded through the abdomen by a high velocity German bullet, punching a hole through his back and shattering several vertebrae. Later back in Sydney, the German police prisoner described Pockley as a very brave, cool and 'very humane man'. Pockley and Williams were transferred to the *Berrima*. Pockley died just after 2pm, followed by Williams soon after.[15] Ironically, the German

15 'Captain Brian Colden Antill Pockley, The War Records of the University of Sydney', *Hermes*, vol XXIII, no 1, May 1917, 31-2; War Service Record, Pockley, Brian Colden Antill, NAA; 'Medical Heroes ...Late Captain Pockley', *Sydney Morning Herald*, 23 December 1915; Michael Kelly, 'First to Fight', *Wartime*, issue 67, Winter 2014, 48-9; John Connor, 'The Capture of German New Guinea', in Craig Stockings & John Connor (eds), *Before the Anzac Dawn*, NewSouth, Sydney, 2013, 283-303; Michael Piggott, 'Stonewalling in German New Guinea', *Journal of the Australian War Memorial*, vol 12, 1988, 3-15.

prisoner survived the war and settled in Australia.

Brigadier-General Henry N MacLaurin

Not all Sydney University graduates joined the University Scouts. Henry Normand MacLaurin, the son of the former Chancellor of Sydney University Sir Normand MacLaurin, had been educated at Blair Lodge School in Scotland and graduated as a Bachelor of Arts at Sydney University in 1899. At eighteen, he joined the Scottish Rifles of New South Wales as lieutenant. By the outbreak of war, he became lieutenant-colonel of the 26th Infantry from which he was appointed to command the First Infantry Brigade with the rank of colonel. He was killed in action as a brigadier-general leading the landing party at the Dardanelles on 25 April 1915 at the age of twenty-six.[16]

Henry Normand MacLaurin appeared as the first death under the DARDANELLES heading on *Hermes* decorated memorial list of August 1915, under Captain Pockley of the New Guinea expedition. (His surname was misspelt as McLaurin.)

MacLaurin, the son of Normand MacLaurin (1835-1914), physician, company director and University administrator, was born on 31 October 1878 as a member of a highly distinguished wealthy Sydney family. He was already a well-known young barrister and part-time citizen-soldier who had been promoted to lieutenant-colonel in July 1913 in the militia. He joined the 1st AIF in mid-August 1914 and was given command of the 1st Infantry Brigade at the outbreak of war with the rank of colonel. Charles Bean, who met

16 *Hermes*, XXIV, 2, August 1918, 111.

him on Gallipoli and in Egypt, described him as 'a man of lofty ideals, direct, determined with a certain inherited Scots dourness … an educated man of action of the finest type that the Australian Universities produce'. Bean and MacLaurin were of the same social class and intellectual closeness.[17]

While many other ranks on Gallipoli – those who survived – quickly became battle savvy, some of their officers still appeared reckless in exposing themselves to the enemy. As a model seemingly of courage that came with breeding, General Bridges had shown the way at Anzac by receiving a fatal wound from a sniper. Major Francis Irwine, a regular British officer attached as brigade-major to Colonel Henry MacLaurin, was a similar consequence. He was told by some of his more astute men at Steele's Post to keep his head down because of the accuracy of known Turkish snipers; Irwine promptly replied it was his job to be sniped at. He only took another breath, when a shot from the rear on Russell's Top killed him instantly. Some minutes later, MacLaurin, standing on the ridge that was to bear his name, was also shot and killed in a similar fashion.[18] Authorities placed on their maps where he had died as MacLaurin's Hill in his memory.

In November 1915, the second listing of University men killed in action appears in *Hermes*: two in Flanders and thirteen on the Dardanelles. This was just in the space of less than two months. Above their names in a second elaborate

---

17 Ann M Mitchell, 'MacLaurin, Sir Henry Normand (1835-1914)', *Australian Dictionary of Biography (ADB)*, vol 10, Melbourne University Press, Carlton, 1990, 327-9.

18 Harvey Broadbent, *Gallipoli the fatal shore*, Viking Penguin, Camberwell, 2995, 122-3; *The Oxford Companion to Australian Military History*, 374.

memorial frame was the declaration:

Blow out you bugles, over the Dead!
They brought us, for our dearth,
Holiness, lacked so long, and Love and Pain.
Honour has come back, as a King to earth,
And paid his subjects with a royal wage;
And Nobleness walks in our ways again;
And we have come into our heritage.

In November 1916, Brereton compiled a consolidated 'Honour List' after other progressive lists that year. It demonstrated an extraordinary rate of deaths of Sydney University men and dramatically illustrated comprehensive involvement of undergraduates and graduates from all faculties in frontline fighting. Most were killed in action or died of wounds, but a few died of illnesses or accident as well. Seventy names appeared showing the extent of the University's involvement in a dangerous devastating war. They died in all major theatres of war. In France those killed in action, or had consequently died of their wounds, amounted to thirty-one. In the Dardanelles, there were twenty-three, including one who died of an illness. In Flanders (Belgium), six were killed-in-action or died of their wounds and one of an accident. Three others were reported as killed-in-action, but no location was provided. One person died of an illness in Mesopotamia and another died at sea. In effect, the University of Sydney was emptied out of its menfolk in nearly all faculties.

The preponderance of the seventy men on the 1916 November list were commissioned officers – mainly lieutenants and captains – forty-eight of them. In World War

I, the death rate at this level of junior officer rank was high since they led assaults and advances in exposed positions. They also included Brigadier-General Henry MacLaurin BA; Lieutenant-Colonel Ernest Brown killed on the Dardanelles in August 1915; a graduate of Duntroon Military College with a Diploma in Military Science and four Majors. While the great majority fought in the Australian Imperial Force, a few fought with the British Expeditionary Force: two were identified as such, but there may have been several others whose Force was not identified of British nationality.[19] The cream of University medicos had been taken up early in the British Army by the Royal Medical Corps.

In defining courses studied, the Faculty of Arts at 29/70 had the most killed made up of two holding a Master of Arts (MA); fourteen with Bachelor of Arts and thirteen undergraduates. The Faculty of Medicine had 23/70 deaths made up of thirteen MB with seven holding a ChM, as well as three undergraduates. The Engineering Faculty had 11 deaths (7 graduates and 4 undergraduates). In Law, there were ten: two holding a BA/LLB, two with BA and undergraduate Law studies and six enrolled in undergraduate Law. In Science, there were two graduates and two undergraduates; in Economics, three undergraduates and in the Diploma of Military Science, two. These numbers included those holding two degrees, or one plus the study of an undergraduate course. These figures would reflect enrolment numbers in each faculty which was quite variable in the early 1910s. There were 39/70 who held University degrees and were of officer rank. A few undergraduates in Medicine and Law also

19 'Honours List', *Hermes*, vol XXII, no 3, November 1916, 82-3.

held officer rank. The rest were in other ranks.

The establishment of Royal Duntroon College had been very recent. Economics was a new emerging discipline. The Honour Lists in *Hermes* would have shown to its readers the seriousness of the loss of life as well as the early loss of potential academic and professional contributions to Australian society that could have otherwise been made. As the war dragged on, more names were added to the lists. The Australian elite or financially comfortable classes were not protected from the dangers of industrial frontline war – their lives were constantly risked with other strata of society, despite some rhetoric to the contrary. Some conditions of the officer class were fractionally better than for other ranks, apart from the actual fighting and its associated dangers, like bombardments.

Captain Marks MC: 'cool, capable and courageous'

Douglas Marks was accepted into Law as a mature-age student at the University of Sydney after the war was over. He deferred for twelve months to study Latin which was a matriculation requirement at the University at the time for entry into degree studies in all faculties. At the same time, he was employed as manager of the Continental Paper Bag Company of Sydney. An act of extreme bravery meant he was never to complete his degree.

At Palm Beach on 25 January 1920 in heavy seas, Douglas Marks attempted to rescue a drowning stranger in the surf. They were both lost at sea. Marks' body was never recovered. His memorial service at St James Church of England, Sydney, overflowed, mainly with ex-servicemen of his battalion and other wartime friends and associates who knew him. Lieutenant-Colonel Harry Murray, Australia's most honoured Victoria Cross winner of the First World War, was present. He said of Captain Marks: 'We love Douglas Marks for his indominable spirit, his dash and daring … no truer comrade ever lived'.

During his wartime exploits, Douglas Gray Marks was mentioned in despatches on four separate occasions: 'In his planning he was consistent, resourceful and thorough; under fire he was cool, capable and courageous, and took every care to ensure the safety of his men'. Lieutenant-Colonel AM Durant pointed out: 'He was loyalty itself to his commanders and he governed with universal fairness and humanity'. High praise indeed and carefully based, mainly on his wartime record.

* * *

Douglas Marks was born on 20 March 1895 in the country NSW town of Junee to Montague Marks, a local shopkeeper, and his wife Elizabeth (née Plunkett). He did well in primary school and was accepted into a selective state high school, Fort Street Boys in Sydney. After high school, he became a bank clerk and studied mining engineering part-time at Sydney Technical College, Ultimo. In June 1914, Marks was commissioned a second lieutenant in the 29th Infantry, Australian Rifles, an important militia. In November, he enlisted in the 1st AIF and was immediately appointed second lieutenant in the 13th Battalion which sailed for Egypt in December 1914. On 25 March 1915, he was promoted to full lieutenant.

After landing on Gallipoli on 26 April, the 13th moved up

to Quinn's Post and Pope's Hill with the difficult task ahead of clearing the fortified Russell's Top. In fierce fighting, the 13th suffered heavy losses. On 2-3 May in the attack on Baby 700, the battalion temporarily captured the Chess Board and the ominously-named Dead Man's Ridge.

Marks had gained a precise personal knowledge of the enemy's dispositions and this materially assisted his commanding officer Lieutenant-Colonel Burnage significantly. Having been acting adjutant on 20 July, Marks was promoted to captain on a temporary appointment, but on 8 August, he was wounded in the left foot and evacuated. For his outstanding service on Gallipoli, he was awarded the foreign Serbian Order of the White Eagle, awarded for bravery in the battlefield. (The award lasted from 1882 to 1915.) Marks was then among the last recipients of this honour. The medal, a knight's badge, displayed a double-headed white eagle with a white cross in the centre and a crown above. The ribbon was red with a grey border.[20]

Serbian Order of the White Eagle, Knight's badge awarded to Capt Douglas Gray Marks for bravery on Gallipoli (*Medal Year Book* 2018)

On 20 January 1916 in Egypt, Douglas Marks was promoted to captain on a permanent basis. Soon after, on 1 February, he was appointed adjutant of his battalion which sailed to France in June. After the unit's two operations at the Battle of Pozières in August 1916, Marks was awarded the Military

20 *Medal Yearbook 2018*, Token Publishers, Exeter, 2018, 374.

Cross for his consistent and energetic work as adjutant; he rendered significant and 'conspicuous valuable work frequently under heavy shellfire'. He was promoted to major on 11 November and second-in-command to Lieutenant-Colonel Durant, who he assisted in planning the attack on Stormy Trench near Gueudecourt on 4-5 February 1917 where Lieutenant-Colonel Harry Murray famously won the Victoria Cross. Murray became the highest decorated frontline soldier in the 1st AIF, closely followed by Lieutenant Joseph Maxwell VC. Just before the Battle of Stormy Ridge near Gueudecourt, Marks designed the successful attack led by Murray in an inspirational manner.[21]

At the first Battle of Bullecourt, Marks suffered a bad chest and leg wound when a shell hit the 13th Battalion's headquarters. He was coughing up blood and close to death when he struggled through the snow on foot to the casualty clearing station. He survived his first rendezvous with death, just barely. He was eventually evacuated to England where he recovered sufficiently and was returned to the Front.

He rejoined the 13th on 5 December, was promoted to lieutenant-colonel and replaced Durant in charge of the battalion. Durant went on leave. At the age of 22, Marks became one of the youngest commanding officers in the 1st AIF. For his work between September 1917 and February 1918, including at the Ypres Salient operation, he was awarded the Distinguished Service Order (DSO).

Under Sir John Monash (see Chapter 4), Marks' 13th Battalion led the 4th Brigade advance to halt the reported

21 Robert Hamilton, *Victoria Cross Heroes of World War One*, Atlantic Publishing, 2015, 190.

breakthrough at Hébuterne. The town was secured and the enemy thrust halted. Following the Villers-Bretonneux operation in April, the battalion took part in the assault on Monument Wood and, in July, on the attack on Hamel, the success of which owed much to Marks' detailed planning and rehearsal for the 13th, under Monash's brilliant overall scheme.

In other words, Marks had become one of Monash's most trusted and capable field commanders. In the Allies offensive on 8 August and operations on 23 August, Marks' unit captured many prisoners-of-war near Morcourt and Vauville. In the assault on the Hindenburg Line on 13 September, the battalion took its objective as planned near Hargicourt which was its last major battle of the 1914–18 War.

Douglas Gray Marks returned to Australia via North America and his AIF service was terminated on 20 February 1919. Soon after, he was accepted into Law at Sydney University…[22]

The experience of Lieutenant **Laurence Whistler Street** was illustrative of the sacrifices being made in the officer class from Sydney's prominent families. Laurence was the second son of Mr Justice Street of the Supreme Court of New South Wales and was born in 1893. He was educated at Sydney Grammar School like a number of his peers. He graduated Bachelor of Arts in 1914, after being active in the University's undergraduate life playing cricket, football, hockey and rowing. He was an associate to his father, as well as studying Law II. He volunteered and obtained a commission as a second lieutenant in the 3rd Battalion 1st Infantry Brigade.

He landed at Gallipoli on 25 April 1915 and was soon

22 R Sutton, 'Marks, Douglas Gray (1895-1920)', *ADB*, vol 10, 410-11.

promoted to first lieutenant. On the night of 3 May, the Turks made a fierce attack on MacLaurin's Hill, Anzac Cove. Street was in charge of an unfinished sap on which Turkish fire was concentrated. Many casualties resulted. At dawn on 19 May, Laurence Street was shot through the head shortly before the Turks retired. They had been unsuccessful in the assault. Lieutenant-Colonel Owen wrote to the grieving family: 'Your son was a gallant soldier. He had done splendid work, and I have specially reported him. He was a great loss to the Battalion and to me personally'. Street had performed various acts of conspicuous gallantry between 26 April and 19 May 1915. He was mentioned in despatches 'for conspicuous gallantry in defending a dangerous portion of a sap, and bravely remaining at his post until he met his death'.[23]

Major Archibald McKillop, DSO

Archibald McKillop was born in Goulburn in the Monaro Highlands of NSW, the son of Dr Robert McKillop, the Government Medical Officer there, and his wife Mary Theresa (née Macdonald). Archibald was sent to Sydney as a boarder at the elite Jesuit school, St Ignatius College, Riverview. He succeeded academically and matriculated to Sydney University's Medical School, completing the MB in 1908 and ChM in 1909. He had followed in his father's footsteps.

After graduating, he moved to Queensland where there was a shortage of medicos in most country regions. He was appointed Medical Superintendent of the Warwick Hospital in 1909. In 1910, he moved on to Blackall and, later, to

23 'Lieut Laurence Whistler Street', *Hermes*, vol XXIII, no 1, May 1917, 32-3.

Dalby gaining valuable experience in rural Australia.

He was commissioned in mid-1915 and sailed to Egypt with reinforcements for the 1st Australian General Hospital. In January 1916, he was posted briefly to the 2nd Field Ambulance and then transferred to the 9th Battalion as the Regimental Medical Officer. He moved on to France with the battalion at Rouge de Bout near Fromelles in April and was badly wounded in the buttocks while bending over dressing a casualty. He was evacuated to the 3rd London General Hospital in England and transferred later to the 4th Australian Auxiliary Hospital at Welwn. He was recommended for mention in despatches: 'This officer particularly distinguished himself during a bombardment when the Bn first arrived in France in April 1916'.

Sufficiently recovered, McKillop returned to France in September that year and rejoined his battalion the following month. He remained with the 9th until after the first Battle of Bullecourt and then transferred to the 3rd Field Ambulance. He was again recommended for mention in despatches after the operation at Le Barque in March 1917 and, in June, he was promoted to major. He served with the 3rd Field Ambulance through the Third Battle of Ypres and then transferred to the 1st Field Ambulance in October 1917. He was again recommended for the DSO, especially for conduct during the German breakthrough in April:

> The Division took up a position at Strazeele for the defence of Hazebroucke. Major McKillop organised Aid Posts and Relay Posts with great rapidity, regardless of the fact that the enemy was attacking strongly the whole time.

Archibald McKillop did receive the recognition he

richly deserved. He was mentioned in despatches twice in October and December 1918 and was duly awarded the DSO in January 1919.

He was granted study leave in the AIF and worked at the Hammersmith Hospital in western London for two months. His return to Australia was marred and then derailed by an attack of the influenza pandemic in May 1919. When he finally returned to Australia, he set up a practice in the NSW country town of Temora. He was basically a devoted country doctor, well-loved and respected locally, even though it was not well-known that he was in attendance at the famous battles the Anzacs fought in at Fromelles, Bullecourt, Ypres and Hazebrouck as well as other places on the Western Front.[24]

★ ★ ★

Emile Cammaerts wrote a poetic tribute in French in *Hermes* to his friend Sergeant Jacques Bouvier who, at the age of twenty-three, was killed at Dixmude, Belgium,

> while trying to rescue a comrade buried under his dugout:

Il n'est pas mort.	He is not dead.
Il est parti.	He has left.
Il a forcé la porte	
de sa vie.	He forced the door of his life.
Il a franchi,	He crossed
D'un bond, le seuil	
de son sort.	The threshold of his destiny,
	in a rush.
Il n'est pas mort.	He is not dead.
Il est sorti	He has gone

24 Robert Likeman, *Australian Doctors on the Western Front*, Rosenberg, Dural, 2014, 50.

D'un monde qui	
était trop petit pour lui.	From a world that was too small for him.
Couvrez le tambour	
d'un voile noir	Cover the drum with a black cloth
Couvrez son corps	Cover his body
Du drapeau de la Victoire.	With the flag of Victory.
…	…
Battez le tambour à	
petits coups las,	Beat the drum slowly and gently,
Portez son corps	Carry his body
A petits pas.	Slowly and gently.
Il n'est pas mort,	He is not dead,
Mais nous mourrons	But we will die
Chaque fois que nous	
songeons à lui,	Each time we think of him,
Et que nous nous	
souviendrons	And when we remember
Que nous ne l'avons pas	
suivi.	That we did not follow him.
Il n'est pas mort.	He is not dead.[25]

Not all had their bodies covered with 'the flag of Victory', especially at Fromelles and Pozières.

Short *Hermes* Biographies to Inspire

Brereton also provided short biographical investigations into those University men who survived the war. Nevertheless, their young lives were forever changed. **Lieutenant Alexander Jarvie Hood Stobo** was a case-in-point. He was in first year Medicine when he enlisted in

25 Emile Cammaerts, "Epitaphe" (trans. by Marie Ramsland), *Hermes*, vol XXIII, no 2, August 1917, 77.

October 1915 and embarked on the *Medic* on 6 January 1916. He crossed to France. Shortly after arriving, he was in the fighting of the first half of 1916, before he was wounded at Fleurbaix. Two months later, he was gassed at Pozières.

After attending an Officers Cadet School at Balliol College from November 1916 to February 1917, he was granted a commission and was soon back in France. He took part in Bullecourt in May where he was again wounded. Between August and December that year, he held the rank of Brigade Musketry Officer and, from September 1918 to February 1919, he acted as Intelligence Officer. He returned to Australia in May 1919 and his appointment in the AIF was terminated. Brereton was able to check his account of Stobo's military career with the man himself as he had resumed his medical studies.

Captain Ronald Butler Hinder MC matriculated from Maitland High School where his father was headmaster. He studied Engineering. In 1911-1912, he played fullback in Sydney University's First Fifteen Rugby Team in the Sydney competition. After graduating, he worked at Cobar copper mines in the far central-west of New South Wales. When the mines closed down, he worked for the New South Wales Public Works Department, Sewerage Construction Branch and remained in the public service until May 1915 when he enlisted. He transferred to the engineers and joined Professor Edgeworth David's Mining Corps on its formation. He left Australia as second lieutenant. He was again promoted and immediately crossed to France with David's Corps. He performed important tunnelling work at Messines Ridge, Belgium, taking part in the famous Hill

60 'stunt'. Early in 1918, he was promoted to captain and, in January that year, was awarded the Military Cross. He remained with the Corps until the signing of the Armistice after which he returned to Australia.[26]

Brereton considered the living and the dead, undergraduates and postgraduates, administrative and academic employees of the University.

University men realised the social and environmental devastation the war caused well before TS Eliot's "The Waste Land" was published. One Art's undergraduate officer, **Captain Raymond Kershaw** MC, wrote for *Hermes* before the war's end in June 1918:

> Before us lay the silent, unpeopled valley of the Somme, looking through half-closed eyes like the grey-green ridges of some mighty untraversed sea. Down the deepest valley crept the poor twisted [river] Ancre; here and there blown out of its course and spreading amid fallen trunks and broken pathways, in forlorn and stagnant little pools. Who can make of this savage wilderness the quiet spacious countryside it was before this thunderbolt came? I do not doubt that the energy, power, that went in to wreck this region, were if consolidated in one terrific thrust, could shake this tormented earth in its orbit.

And yet the 'hungry, wet tired' soldier on the line did not have time to contemplate all of this. What Kershaw valued most was 'the incomparable spirit of comradeship that the mutual endurance of hardship fosters'.[27] On his return to the

26 *Hermes*, 123.

27 Raymond Kershaw, 'A Course of Philosophy on the Somme', in 'From the Front', *Hermes*, vol XXVI, no 1, June 1918, 56-8.

Captain Raymond Newton Kershaw MC, Rhodes Scholar 1918 (*Hermes*)

University, Kershaw was awarded the Rhodes Scholarship to Oxford for 1918 which he took up in 1919. As an expatriate, he became an executive of a London bank.

The University created a bronze plaque listing University World War I veterans that stands at the entrance of the Quadrangle under the clock tower and, in 1928, completed a war memorial carillon in the tower. About two hundred names of those who died during the 1914–18 War are cast there in bronze.[28] This unusual memorial carries, in addition to the names provided by Le Gay Brereton, names that have no acknowledgement elsewhere in Australia. Some students and graduates were overseas when the war broke out and enlisted in the British, French and Canadian Forces. As they did not enlist in an Australian military unit, they appear on no other Australian war memorial.[29] Others on the memorial did not attend University until after the war, thus they do not appear in any of Brereton's *Hermes* listings.

There was debate in the early 1920s as to the nature of the University's proposed war memorial. Some argued for a memorial swimming pool; others for a sports oval. A memorial military drill hall was another proposal given consideration. All these proposals denoted sectional interests. Finally, the suggestion by the Evening Students

28 A mural tablet at the head of the stairway of the original Fisher Library was only intended as a temporary memorial.

29 Garton, Talk.

Association for the installation of a carillon appealed to the majority. It became the first of its kind to be erected in Australia. The idea for the carillon originated from those in the Belgian towns. The parents of University servicemen were overwhelmingly in favour of the carillon to remind them of their sons' sacrifice.[30]

In August 1918, Le Gay Brereton prepared a ROLL OF DISTINCTION of honours and rewards for service in the field.[31] These reveal the names of many who produced high levels of gallantry in the face of the enemy, as shown particularly by the large number of Military Crosses and Bars awarded by June 1918, as well as an impressive array of other bravery decorations, along with others for military leadership. Only one woman appears: 'Surgeon Martha I Ormiston MBE, ChM', who received the Montenegrin Red Cross and Orders of Danilo and the Nile.

Isabel Ormiston, MB 1907 (*Conversation*, 16 March 2015)

Surgeon Martha Isabel Ormiston, the Intrepid one

She was known by her second name Isabel. An intrepid, lively medical graduate, she left Sydney for London six months before the war broke out and had exciting experiences serving both in the Red Cross in London and the

30 'Editorial. The War Memorial', *Arts Journal*, vol I, no 3, 1923, 59-61.

31 John Le Gay Brereton went to the University in the 1890s and gained a BA. He joined the library staff in 1902, becoming University Librarian in 1914. In 1921, he became the first Professor of English Literature. He was an Elizabethan scholar and a poet.

French Red Cross. She distinguished herself in Belgium. After Ostend was captured, she maintained her duties at the Ostend Hospital with Dr Emile Van de Watte and Matron Patton-Bethune despite the rest of the staff having fled. The wounded Belgian soldiers, who were too ill to take part in any flight, needed tending and these three brave individuals showed their devotion. They had watched 70,000 enemy troops march into Ostend and were treated with great respect by German authorities even when a British warship opened fire on the hotel, watched coolly by Ormiston from her balcony as a German gun immediately below returned fire. She refused to retreat despite the desperate pleas of German officers. Luckily, she survived.

After another two weeks, the Germans decided that the three should be evacuated to neutral Holland. Dr Ormiston quickly returned to London. 'Having collected funds, motor cars and anything she could lay her hands on', she went to Europe to take up duties between 1914 and 1915 at the Queen of the Belgians Hospital, five miles from the firing line. The hospital held the wounded from all nations. Later, she was sent by the Wounded Allies Relief Committee to a hospital in Montenegro, a small Balkan country that became independent of the Ottoman Empire in 1878. There was a serious typhoid outbreak there. Ormiston also served in the Wounded Allies Relief (WAR) hospital in Limoges.

Martha Isabel Ormiston had graduated from University in 1907 and became Medical Inspector of Schools in Tasmania for four years when she took leave-of-absence so that she could do hospital work and further training in London where she was when World War I began.[32]

Roll of Distinction, June 1918

The breakdown of distinctions to June 1918 was:

VC	1
CB	1
CMG	7
OBE	1
DSO	49
Bar to DSO	1
MC	111
Bar to MC	7
DCM	3
MM	4
Bar to MM	1
Foreign orders	12
Total	198[33]

Percy Storkey VC: 'as cool as an Arctic iceberg'

Percy Valentine Storkey had the unique distinction of being the first and only Sydney University man to be awarded the Victoria Cross in the AIF in the Great War. It made him a celebrity in Australia for the rest of his life. A fellow officer said: 'In any emergency he was always as cool as an Arctic iceberg and always maintained a keen sense of humor [*sic*]–

32 *Cowra Free Press*, 5 May 1914, 2; *Examiner*, 23 November 1915, 7; Jennifer Baker, 'Australian Women who served in WWI', <https://sites.google.com/site/archoevidence/home/ww1womendoctors >.

33 VC (Victoria Cross); CB (Commander of the Order of the Baltic); MCG (Commander of St Michael and St George); OBE (Order of the British Empire); DSO (Distinguished Service Order); MC (Military Cross); DCM (Distinguished Conduct Medal); MM (Military Medal).

a priceless possession in war as well as in peace'.[34]

Storkey was born at Napier in New Zealand, in1891. He was the son of a journalist Samuel and his wife Sarah. Percy was educated at Napier Boys High School where he was a cadet colour-sergeant and became dux. He went on to the Victoria (University) College where he completed his first year of Arts. He then set out for Australia arriving in Sydney in 1911. His first position was in the Orient Steamship Company. He then went on to the administrative staff of Sydney Teachers College and the administrative staff of the University, partly so he could attend lectures at the Law School. He enlisted in May 1915. He had had five years previous experience with the Wellington militia.

When news reached the University on 8 June 1918 of his honour, there was great jubilation about the twenty-seven-year-old administrative officer of the University:

> 'Which was Storkey?', asked a [prominent] University man in the midst of the excitement on the morning the news came through. 'You remember the lad in the office, dark hair and eyes, with a laughing face and such dare-devil, happy-go-lucky ways, that's Storkey, V.C.'[35]

He enlisted in the 19th Battalion as a private, but before the year's end, was promoted to second lieutenant on 24 September 1915. On the Western Front, he was wounded on the first day. He was promoted to first lieutenant on 18 December 1916. On October the following year, he was again wounded, at Passchendaele. He was awarded the Victoria Cross at Hangard Wood near Villers-Bretonneux on

34 'Celebrities of the AIF: No 64 Capt PV Storkey VC', *Reveille*, 1 December 1935, 15.

35 'Lieut Percy Storkey, VC', *Hermes*, vol XXVI, no 1, 1918, 55.

7 April 1918 and promoted to captain. He returned to Australia on 23 September 1918 and his appointment was terminated on 31 January 1919.[36] He then resumed his studies in Law III and soon graduated. *Hermes* argued that Storkey had brought honour to his *Alma Mater* and celebrated his achievement with a page presentation containing his smiling portrait and an illustration of his Victoria Cross, accompanied by its citation.[37]

Lieutenant Percy Storkey VC outside London Headquarters, 1st AIF, Horseferry Road.

The German Spring Offensive ended on 5 April 1918 on the Somme mostly held by Australian troops. The Australians resumed the offensive on 7 April to clear up Hangard Wood south of Villers-Bretonneux. Two companies from the 19th Battalion (with Percy Storkey) and the 20th Battalion had been assigned to push through Hangard Wood and dig in along a road that skirted its western side.

While waiting for the Allied barrage, the exhausted Lieutenant Storkey had fallen asleep and roused himself to find his company had moved out. He hurried to overtake it as it crossed about 400 metres of open country sloping down to the wood. There was no opposition directly ahead, but murderous fire from unseen machine guns within the wood on the right flank had killed or wounded three officers and hit at least twenty-five percent of the company, before

36 War Service Record, Capt Storkey, PV, NAA.

37 'The University's First VC', *Hermes*, 41.

its leading group reached the wood and scrambled through a wire fence into the thick undergrowth.

Storkey used his initiative to take over the ten men and one remaining officer and lead them back through the brush to locate the rear of the enemy force that had fired on the company. He made an instant decision to lead the charge just as the hundred or so Germans had begun to turn their machine guns around to face the small assault. He beat them to it. Storkey's confident leadership led to the taking of many prisoners and the killing of others. He completely blotted out the significant German defensive position. Those who survived fled.[38]

Storkey completed his Law exams at the University while holding a position as Associate of Mr Justice Sir Charles Gregory Wade of the Supreme Court, the ex-Premier of New South Wales. After Wade died suddenly in September 1922, Storkey was appointed Crown Prosecutor for the circuit bounded by Goulburn, Albury, Deniliquin, Hay, Wyalong and Broken Hill.

As the holder of the highest gallantry decoration within the gift of King George V, Storkey carried to his profession the highest of ideals. One observer made this estimate:

> Manner polished but no mannerisms. Just plain common sense. If Percy Storkey will not put anything over on the accused, he sees that the accused puts nothing over on him. ... No kid gloves for a witness who shuffles or is manifestly lying.
>
> Unruffled temper, restrained in language but always

38 Anthony Staunton, *Victoria Cross. Australia's Finest and The Battles they Fought*, Hardie Grant Books, Prahran, 2005, 121.

enough emphasis. Interesting to see him in action at all stages of the case.[39]

As a RSL member, Storkey was the first president of the Vaucluse sub-branch. Between October 1938 until June 1939, he served for a while in the Army Legal Department. He was elevated to the District Court bench and was judge of the northern district court until his retirement in December 1955. On 15 April 1922, he married Molly Burnett. They moved to Teddington, Middlesex in the United Kingdom and he died there on 3 October 1969.[40]

Storkey's Victoria Cross was bequeathed to Napier Boys High and the machine gun captured in the charge he led is in the collection of the Australian War Memorial. An oil painting portrait by Max Meldrum hangs in the Archives Building in Wellington, New Zealand.[41]

Captain Patrick O'Shea, a publican's son as hero

Patrick Joseph Francis O'Shea (1892-1952) was one of the highest decorated military medical officers in the 1st AIF. He was born in the Sydney inner-city working-class suburb of Ultimo, the fourth son of the local publican Daniel O'Shea and his wife Margaret (née O'Leary). Of Irish descent – both parents were born in Ireland – he was educated at St Joseph's College, Hunters Hill. After finishing the Bachelor of Medicine (MB) at Sydney University in 1916, he completed residency at Sydney Hospital in Macquarie Street and even sailed for England in the 1st AIF

39 Cited in John M Ward, 'Wade, Sir Charles Gregory (1863-1922)', *ADB*, vol 12, 340-2.

40 Staunton, *Victoria Cross*, 123.

41 Lionel Wigmore, *They Dared Mightily*, Australian War Memorial, Canberra, 1986, 116-7.

in the same year. He was commissioned as a captain. Clearly, he was anxious to get to the Front as quickly as he could.

After a brief period with the 2nd Training Battalion on the Salisbury Plain attached to medical camps at Parkhouse, Lark Hill and Durrington, he went to France on 4 April 1917. After a week of orientation at the 2nd Australian General Hospital, he was posted to the 2nd Field Ambulance. He was then detached from there to 1st Division and to the 56th Casualty Clearing Station (CCS), but led the bearer division of the Field Ambulance on the Menin Road and Polygon Wood. He was quickly awarded the **Military Cross** for his remarkable courage and energy while in charge of the stretcher bearers. He ordered the stretcher-bearers essential work under heavy shellfire on 19 November near Ypres and was responsible for saving many lives.

Only a week after, he was detached to the 8th Battalion for the assault on Broodseinde Ridge, in which he dressed casualties in the open 'with a fine disregard for personal danger in spite of experiencing, in the process, mild gas poisoning'. He attended the wounded under heavy fire, yet again saving many lives. For this action, he was awarded a **Bar to his MC**. His gallantry clearly deserved the award of a Victoria Cross.

In December 1917, he was posted to the 1st Battalion as Resident Medical Officer (RMO) and was again gassed near Ypres in March 1918. This gassing was much more serious and he was evacuated to the Brook War Hospital in England in Woolwich on the Thames for treatment.

He returned to France at Wimereux and the Australian General Hospital in June 1918 as RMO in the 8th Battalion and remained working with them until the Armistice. In

August 1918, he had been awarded a DSO and had been again mentioned in despatches for his courage at Herleville Wood near Chuignes when he 'was always in the hottest part of the line ... cleared all the wounded of two battalions when other medical officers in the sector became casualties ... and handled the enemy wounded without the slightest rest of three days and nights in the open', with little or no sleep.

In April 1919, Patrick O'Shea – a truly outstanding hero of great energy and commitment – returned home to Australia. He accepted a Senior Residential Medical Officer position at St Vincent's Hospital, Darlinghurst, Sydney, and completed his ChM degree in 1921. He remained full of energy and drive. But his war injuries prevented him from continuing in such a demanding position.

He went into private practice in the Sydney suburb of Burwood for a less strenuous life, but fell victim to tuberculosis and was admitted to the special sanatorium in Leura in the Blue Mountains to convalesce. He spent a difficult eight years with his recovery being complicated when he developed a common form of war neurosis or Post Traumatic Stress that manifested itself as aphonia; his speech loss lasted six months.

Historian Stephen Garton described him as a short, stocky man with thick grey hair, a round cheery face and glasses. His manner with patients was very supportive and he was much loved and respected. He married a nurse, Shirley Sybil Robinson, at St Canice's Catholic Church, Ultimo, on 2 March 1921. They had two children, a boy and a girl. His favourite interests were golf, cricket and Rugby League.

Through his personal experience of psychotic problems brought on by war neurosis, O'Shea developed a passionate interest in psychiatry and, by 1928, was well enough to apply to join the NSW Department of Mental Hospitals. He began work on 13 June at Bloomfield Mental Hospital at Orange in the Central West of NSW and was senior medical officer there from 1932 to 1935. The climate at Orange together with his wife's careful and caring nursing improved his health. After Orange, he was appointed Deputy Medical Superintendent at Gladesville Mental Hospital in Sydney from 1935 to 1944.

In June 1944, Shirley died. He resigned from the Department and set up a private practice in psychiatry in 1944 in Macquarie Street, Sydney. He was often called to provide expert testimony in criminal trials in Sydney. On 24 October 1946, he married Cora Naylor Sheridan at St Mary's Cathedral in Sydney. They had no issue.

In 1952, his tuberculosis returned and he died from meningitis at Concord Repatriation Hospital. He was buried in the Northern Suburbs Cemetery.[42] His wife Cora and his two children from his first marriage survived him.

* * *

John Le Gay Brereton's meticulous work on the War Records have provided valuable insights into the schooling of enlisted University men at the primary, secondary and tertiary levels. With few exceptions, these veterans had been educated in academically elite private and public high schools and colleges and belonged to socially prominent, and even wealthy families. Most parents were well-educated and many fathers belonged to professions like medicine,

42 Stephen Garton, 'O'Shea, Patrick Joseph Francis (1892-1952)', *ADB*, vol 11, 105-06; Likeman, *Australian Doctors*, 63.

law and engineering. Some were prominent landowners and graziers. All of the veterans had had military training in school and university cadets or elsewhere and had been inculcated with imperial King and Country/Empire ideals.

Sydney University Company Flag 1914-1918 (formerly Sydney University Scouts from 1903 and, before that, University Rifle Corps)

They realised that, when Britain was at war, the Empire was automatically at war. They knew they had to play their part and prove themselves worthy of the race from which they had sprung. Like men from other sectors of society, they came to volunteer 'from city and suburbs, from town and village and country far remote' to take 'their share in the Great World War'. Instilled in them was the belief that they were fighting with Britain 'to preserve righteousness, honour, justice and liberty'.[43] They belonged to a classical education tradition that provided the values and culture of Greece and Rome coupled with the English concept of political liberty and citizenship.[44]

The sum total of evidence showed that many Sydney University men displayed the spirit of extraordinary heroism in all the theatres of war. But they left a major gap in the life of the University that was never recovered. The loss of Australia's best and brightest was incalculable. Alan Barcan, 'Latin [45] Many served with great distinction – over 240 decorations were

43 AE Mills, 'Some Lessons of the War', *Hermes*, November 1920, 232-3.
44 Alan Barcan, 'Latin and Greek in Australian Schools', *History of Education Review*, vol 22, no 1, 1993, 40-1.
45 Garton, Talk.

awarded. Fifty medical students and graduates alone were killed during the war. Over 200 University men from all Faculties and Schools died. Their names are cast in bronze on the University's memorial. And some served with other nations.

In the last year of the Great War, Ethel Turner, the popular writer of juvenile fiction, captured the social implication of the war for young women:

"The Cry of the Girl Children"

"Oh Mother when they're trampling past, before the sun climbs up the sky.
Tramp, trampling down the startled roads, we push our windows very high,
And lean far out, and shout and wave,
And call, 'Fight well – be very brave,'
Yet when we're back in bed again, – we wonder why, – oh, tell us why, –
Since we know none, not one, of them – we simply cry and cry and cry?"
"You cry because those trampling feet that wake and make you start from bed,
Not only trample down the road but through your lives," the mothers said,
"Those are your husbands' feet that go,
Swinging away, row after row,
You see your lives, grey piteous lives, that wander lonely far ahead,
And sob yourselves to sleep again, soft, tender things that might have wed."[46]

46 Ethel Turner, "The Cry of the Girl Children", *Hermes*, vol XXVI, no 1, June 1918, 28.

7

The Last Days of the Red Baron

He was a killer. The von Richthofens were landowners and hunters, and Manfred regarded fighting as his duty and saw killing as an extension of. blood sport. He didn't appear to hate his enemies, nor did he suffer from a romantic view of war. It was simply his business, his true vocation. Once, as a young cavalry officer on the Eastern Front, he'd locked a village priest in a church and politely informed him: 'At the first sign of hostility from your villagers you will be executed'.

Dan Hampton, *Lords of the Sky*, William Morrow, 2014

Baron Manfred von Richthofen's funeral attended by the Australian Flying Corps and 1st AIF infantry. Australian chaplain leads (photo by Sgt John Alexander, *Lords of the Sky*)

Baron Manfred von Richthofen known to all as the Red Baron

A notable incident occurred on 21 April 1918 in the frontline sector controlled by the 8th Brigade, 5th Australian Division. Cavalry Captain Baron von Richthofen and his flying 'circus' of aeroplanes were airborne in the vicinity engaging Allied planes.

The German press had recently announced the brilliant German aviator ace's 80th aerial victory or 'kill'.[1] This had made him the most successful fighter or combat pilot of the 1914–1918 War on either side. He was shot down as his famous red-painted three-winged supremely manoeuvrable DI Fokker fighter plane was just cresting Morlancourt Ridge.[2]

Australian airmen, soldiers and medical officers played a largely unacknowledged, but important part in the Red Baron's last day.[3]

The reason von Richthofen died in his distinctly-coloured triplane has remained controversial and something of a mystery that has never quite been solved, but the details of his funeral were well published and even filmed and photographed by the Australians:

> Richthofen was buried with full military honours on the afternoon of the day after his death. From the tent hangar, a plain black-stained wooden box, containing the remains, was carried on the shoulders of six fighting pilots of the Royal Air Force, who acted as pall-bearers.
>
> The coffin was placed in an open Army tender

---

1 Alexander D Ellis (Capt. 29th Battalion), *The Story of the Fifth Australian Division*, Hodder & Stoughton, London, 1920, 290-91.

2 Tony Holmes, 'The Red Baron', in Allan Burney (ed.), *Famous Fighters of World War I*, Key Publishing, Stamford, 2014, 82-83.

3 Thomas Faunce, 'The last hours of the Red Baron', *Wartime*, issue 32, 2005, 18-21.

and covered with floral tributes that came from all neighbouring air squadrons. Preceded by a guard of Australian infantrymen, who carried their rifles reversed, the cortège proceeded slowly down the road beside the aerodrome. To the left of the road, the hum and roar of motors told of the arrival and departure of fighting planes to and from the front. The war continued as usual, but the busy war traffic on the road slowed up for once to the pace of a solemn funeral.

The procession arrived at the cemetery on the outskirts of Bertangles. There, at the foot of a tall poplar tree, an open grave awaited. The black box was placed beside the grave while the pall-bearers stood bareheaded at the foot. At one side were stationed two files of Anzacs, standing rigidly with bowed heads and the muzzles of their rifles grounded. French children and old civilians beyond the years of military service attended, while Australians from the ranks ranged themselves behind the hedge fence on the road.[4]

From the east, the thunder of guns could be heard as a dramatic backdrop while a Church of England chaplain in a white surplus read the words of the burial service. Then:

The coffin is gently lowered into the grave by the pall-bearers. The quiet is broken by a sharp order from an officer. The double rank of Australians snaps to attention. Another order, and they raise their rifles. Three volleys – a parting salute – are fired over the remains of a respected fallen foe. The grave is filled.

4 Floyd Gibbons, *The Red Knight of Germany*, Cassell and Company, London, 1931, 386-88.

On the day after the funeral, a British pilot flew low over Richthofen's old aerodrome at Cappy. He threw down a metal container attached to a streamer. It landed in front of the hangar near where the German ace had paused to pat their puppy mascot. Then, three days before, he climbed into the cockpit of the three-winged red Fokker and had flown off on his final flight to a rendezvous from which he never returned. The metal container carried a photograph of the funeral party firing its parting salute over the grave at Bertangles cemetery. It also contained a simple message:

> To the German Flying Corps
> Rittmeister Baron Manfred von Richthofen was killed in aerial combat on April 21, 1918. He was buried with full military honours.
>
> From the British Royal Air Force.[5]

The German press carried long obituaries of the fallen ace. All of Germany was soon mourning their most famous military hero.

* * *

Manfred Freiherr von Richthofen was born on 2 May 1892 in the lower Silesian town of Kleinberg near Schweidnitz. His father was a retired career army officer and Manfred seemed destined to follow in his footsteps.

At the tender age of eleven, nearly twelve, Manfred entered the Silesian Cadet Institute, a military academy at Wahlsatt. He then moved on to the Lichterfelde Military Academy at Potsdam from where he graduated in 1909 as an officer in the Silesian Uhlan cavalry in 1911. When the war broke

5 Gibbons, *The Red Knight*, 388.

out in 1914, he was called to the Eastern Front and then to the French Front and, like several other cavalry officers, he requested transfer to the German airborne troops. He was officially granted the transfer as an observer. He flew for the first time in 1915 and completed his pilot training in December before joining the Jagdstaffel 2 where he took command in January 1917 before forming a new unit – the Jagdeschwader 1, a mobile nomadic fighter group known as the 'flying circus' which shifted constantly along the Western Front until it became well-known, even legendary, everywhere. Earlier, he spent time fighting on the Eastern Front in Russia. His mentor was the leading ace Oswald Boelcke. Boelcke did much to promote his career.

He rewarded Boelcke's faith in him by downing an FE.2B near Cambrai on 17 September 1916 while flying an Albatros D.II – the momentous first of an amazing number of eventual aerial battles or 'kills'. After Boelcke's death on 28 October 1916, Richthofen famously showed in the German press his enormous potential when he downed the DH2 of Major Lanoe George Hawker, Britain's premier fighting ace and tactician on 23 November for his eleventh victory or 'kill'. Thus, on 10 January 1917, he was made commander of Jasta II and, two days later, he received the uplifting news that he was to be awarded the coveted *Pour le Mérite* – the famous Blue Max which followed on his amazing 24th claim of an aerial victory.

* * *

Called 'the British Boelcke' after the famous German air ace, on 30 June 1916, Hampshire-born Major Lanoe George

Hawker (1890-23 November 1916) – as Captain – posted the following notice to his pilots in No 24 Squadron, Royal Flying Corps (RFC): 'STANDING ORDER OF the Day: Attack Everything'.[6]

Hawker, from a distinguished military family, had joined the RFC from the Royal Engineers and began the 1914-1918 War as a pilot. Before the war, he attended the Royal Naval College at Dartmouth and then became an officer cadet in the Royal Engineers. He had discovered a keen almost obsessive interest in flying and gained his aviator's certificate in 1913. He was a brilliant natural at it.

On 18 April 1915, Hawker took off in his BE-2c and, by himself, attacked the German Zeppelin base at Gontrode with a bag of hand grenades and three melinite bombs. To defeat the German powerful anti-aircraft defence at the base, he spiralled down around the side of the tethered Zeppelin, throwing grenades at it. He was able to blow a hole in the Zeppelin's skin after several tries and the huge blimp 'waffled to the ground'.

Through a hail of ground fire bullets, he destroyed a new huge hangar with his last bomb. He then managed to escape back to his base. This heroic exploit quickly established Hawker as a flying ace. Largely due to his spectacular efforts, as an example of what could be done, the 'bogeymen' of the early air war – the Zeppelins – were largely prevented from efficiently attacking targets in England, of killing civilians and of affecting homefront morale. Such fears were soon removed.

---

6 Dan Hampton, *Lords of the Sky. Fighter Pilots and Air Combat from the Red Baron to the F-16*, William Morrow, New York, 2014, 42.

Hawker's feat earned him the Distinguished Service Order (DSO) and much public acclaim. He was a superb airman and an innovative thinker; he fixed a Lewis gun to the top wing of his Bristol Scout which led to his perfection of the double drum magazine permitting the pilot to fire ninety-seven rounds before reloading. His engineering ability came to the fore in fine-tuning the existing gunsight design. He invented a new 'ammo belt' based on disposable links that practically eliminated jamming on most occasions.

On 25 July 1915, Captain Hawker was flying alone, hunting the skies, when he attacked three German aeroplanes in succession above Flanders. A new weapon, a flamethrower, had been used with devastating results by German infantry to break the line along the Menin Road, about two miles east of Ypres. Ground anti-aircraft fire was heavy, as reconnaissance flying patrols were everywhere.

Major Lanoe George Hawker (1890-23 Nov 1916) VC (Hamilton, *VC Heroes*)

Late in the afternoon of that day, Lanoe Hawker attacked a two-seater Aviatik over Passchendaele so fiercely that the German dove to the ground and crash landed. At dusk, he found an Albatros C and sent it spinning into the Houthulst Forest which was behind the British Front. With the light fading over cheering British and Commonwealth infantry witnesses in the trenches, Hawker – diving from 10,000 feet – put a thirty-round burst into the belly of another Albatros C and sent it, spectacularly, down in flames over the Front at Hooge. Both the German pilot and observer died in flames.

He went on shooting down enemy planes in a dramatically spectacular fashion until he was recalled to England to be promoted to major and to be awarded Great Britain's highest award for bravery, the Victoria Cross. In February 1916, Major Hawker took command of the newly-formed 24 Squadron, equipped with DH-2 single seat fighters. He and his men took control of the skies from the Germans, but not for long.

While Hawker went to work killing more German aviators, the bug-like DH-2 began to show its limitations. Its propeller was behind the pilot, thus providing a clear field of view for firing, but it placed the pilot in a very vulnerable position. He was an easier target for the enemy pilots who were accurate gunners. Nevertheless, the DH-2 became known amongst members of the RFC as the 'Spinning Incinerator' – a form of very black humour which was also realistic.

Despite the appallingly heavy casualty rate on both sides for pilots in the struggle in the air supremacy over the Western Front, the air battle retained some of the glamour that had been quickly lost in the land battles. On both sides. 'aces' were claimed as national heroes and both Hawker and Richthofen were outstanding examples. They became household names.[7] And on the whole, aerial combat retained some elements of chivalry, or a semblance of it.

---

7 John Percival, *For Valour. The Victoria Cross: Courage in Action*, James Methuen, London,1986, 77.

From June to October 1916, Hawker's 24 Squadron, while suffering heavy losses, destroyed 80 German aircraft (the same number as the Red Baron's total number of 'hits'). As far as known, Hawker was responsible for more than half of the Squadron's 'kills'.

On the cold night of 23 November 1916 between Bapaume and Albert, Major Hawker was prowling over the Western Front when he saw five Albatros fighters in the Red Baron's squadron close to Bapaume. Not hesitating a second, he went on the attack, concentrating on the leader von Richthofen. For over thirty compelling minutes, Hawker and his able opponent fought a 'twisting, looping gut-wrenching dogfight'.

The Albatros was more powerful and armed with superior twin Spandau guns while the British DH-2 was lighter, and, therefore, more manoeuvrable. At 2,000 feet, the two aircraft continued attacking several times into each other. Round and round they went, each trying to outturn the other and to get into a firing position.

Often they were close enough to see each other clearly. Hawker waved on one occasion to his opponent. As time went on, the fateful wind pushed the dogfight deeper into German occupied territory. Hawker was running short of fuel. Passing the Red Baron, he pulled into the vertical in an attempt to use altitude for a tighter turn, intending to get behind the German by this device.

Coming down out of the loop, he fired off a long burst of bullets from his Lewis gun and then dove for the ground. As Dan Hampton, the American author, has written:

With ten victories behind him, Manfred von Richthofen

was confident, dangerous, and he clearly realized that he was fighting no ordinary pilot. The Baron wasn't the gifted flyer that Hawker was, but his calm, cold nature and superb marksmanship made him an extremely lethal fighter pilot. The superior performance of the Albatros also helped as he followed the DH-2 around and down, his faster machine rapidly closing the gap. Just above the trees, a bare 100 feet behind, the German cleared a gun jam and fired a double burst with the last of his nine hundred rounds of ammunition.[8]

It is not certain that the English hero was killed outright or grazed and knocked unconscious. Richthofen later claimed he shot him in the back of the head. Hawker's plane bounced end over end across shell holes in a No Man's Land of shattered debris and mud, and finally came to rest.

Major Lanoe George Hawker, VC, DSO was buried south of Ligny, off the Flers Road, by a squad of silent German grenadiers. Afterwards, the Red Baron wrote: 'My eleventh Britisher was Major Hawker, twenty-six years old and the commander of an English squadron … He gave me the hardest fight I have experienced so far.'

According also to one official report, Hawker was shot in the head and thus killed. He is remembered on the Arras Flying Services memorial in the Faubourg d'Amiens Cemetery in northern France. His VC is held at the RAF Museum in Hendon, north London.[9]

The legendary battle between Major Hawker and Baron

---

8 Hampton, *Lords of the Sky*, 45-46.

9 Hampton, *Lords of the Sky*, 42-46, 48, 64-65, 73, 77-78, 98; also, Robert Hamilton, *Victorian Cross Heroes of World War One*, Atlantic publishing, Hertfordshire, 2015, 89; Gibbons, *The Red Knight*, 396.

von Richthofen was a 'meeting of champions in the air'. They were truly Lords of the Skies. 'It was a battle of eagles, each determined upon the other's death …' It had taken place high above the battle lines between Albert and Bapaume and had been watched by thousands of mud-grimed infantrymen from inside their trenches.

The Red Baron was to exploit the event as propaganda for his publisher Ullstein and Company. He described the event in detail to the German public referring to his opponent as a fine sportsman, a fighter, a brave man and a 'plucky devil'. As the final touch, von Richthofen wrote: 'His machine-gun rammed itself into the earth, and it now decorates the entrance over my door'. He had been able to rescue it from the wreckage of the British plane as soon as he landed.

Thus, above the door to his room, Manfred von Richthofen was to hang a gruesome trophy that represents a death struggle in mid-air, but it was also in a position of honour over the door to his separate bedroom in his military accommodation. For the Red Baron, the trophy was from an English place where bullets had sent many German airmen to their death.[10]

And it was the weapon of the first English ace. As was his usual practice, von Richthofen had called his jeweller to manufacture a small engraved silver cup in memory of his eleventh victim and of his battles in the sky. Such silver cups were placed on the shelf above his fireplace. Eventually, the jeweller was to fashion eighty tiny silver cups with the names of his conquests and the dates when such personal victories occurred. Killing opponents to the

10 Gibbons, *The Red Knight*, 7-9.

Red Baron was very much a blood sport.

★ ★ ★

As a Staffelführer, von Richthofen proved to be an outstanding skilful leader, trainer and organiser. He was a fighter pilot heralded in the German press as a national hero. He was promoted to the rank of Rittmeister (Captain) on 6 April 1917. By the end of what was called "Bloody April", he had surpassed his idol Boelcke's score with 53 victories, and his Jasta II was famous throughout Germany.

His leadership of Jagdgeschwader I was soon interrupted by a near fatal injury on 6 July 1917.[11] One RAF pilot reported it in a matter-of-fact way:

> The struggle increased daily in bitterness, extent, and losses. Four days after he killed Whatley and Pascoe, Richthofen himself went hurtling down from a fearful height with an English bullet-wound in his head.[12]

Sergeant Hubert A Whatley and Second Lieutenant FGB Pascoe, as pilot and observer in a British fighter, were hunted and killed by the Red Baron on 2 June 1917 in his 57th aerial victory at Deulemont. Richthofen spent time in hospital recovering, but he returned to service as quickly as he could and made his next and 58th 'kill' on 16 August 1917 – the name and fate of the occupant unknown.[13]

Writing to Hubert Whatley's mother, Sergeant Randall Kay, who was wounded in Queen Mary's Hospital, said:

---

11 Holmes, 'The Red Baron', 82-83; 'One of the military aviator heroes Manfred von Richthofen, the Red Baron', *The Visitor's Guide to the Battlefields*, Somme Tourist Bureau Board, undated, 20.

12 Gibbons, *The Red Knight*, 302.

13 Gibbons, *The Red Knight*, 400.

> With regard to the exact spot where Hubert is buried, I can say that he fell about 1,000 yards north-east of Messines about 10.30am, July 2, 1917, and was buried near there by some of the third division Australian infantry. His observer's name was Lieutenant Pascoe, but I do not know where his home was. I have made many inquiries, but this is about all the information I can get.[14]

Such situations made Richthofen a spreader of inconsolable grief.

The severe head injury was the first wound the German ace had received in almost three years of war. Floyd Gibbons wrote: 'Richthofen was never the same after that English bullet dented his skull and sent him tumbling down two miles to earth.'[15] Gibbons' opinion is commonplace amongst German and English historians.

The RAF pilot who shot Richthofen down that fine July morning was Flight Commander Albert Edward Woodbridge – second lieutenant at the time. Woodbridge was acting as an Observer for Pilot Captain DC Cunnell, commander of a wing of the 20th Squadron, Royal Flying Corps (RFC).

Cunnell was killed six days later, but Woodbridge survived the war. Woodridge, who was eighteen at the time, described the encounter ten years after the war had ended in a most lively manner:[16]

> Of course, neither Cunnell nor I had any idea that it was the Baron himself with whom we were exchanging pot-shots, and, for that matter, I don't know it yet,

14 Gibbons, *The Red Knight*, 300-01.

15 Gibbons, *The Red Knight*, 316.

16 Gibbons, *The Red Knight*, 303-09.

> but I must say that Richthofen's account of the fight coincides exactly with our reports made at the time and my recollections of that damned busy forty minutes we had with his flock of red Albatross [*sic*] scouts...
>
> It all fits in ... and it seems conclusive that the Baron had Cunnell and me picked out that day, and also that some of our shots sent him down ... I remember it now as clearly as though it happened two hours ago.

The No 20 Squadron that Cunnell and Woodbridge belonged to were quartered at Marie-Chapelle not far from the road between St Omer and Cassell.The principal weapon on their plane was manned by the Observer (Woodbridge in this case) mounted on a movable pivot.A second Lewis gun was fixed to the side of the forward cockpit and could be fired by a trigger on the pilot's control. A third Lewis gun was fixed on a tall pivot rising from the Observer's cockpit. Woodbridge continued:

> Two of them came at us head-on, and I think the first one was Richthofen. I recall there wasn't a thing on that machine that wasn't red, and Gosh, how he could fly! I opened fire with the front Lewis, and so did Cunnell with the side gun. Cunnell held the FE to her course, and so did the pilot of the all-red scout. Gad, with our combined speeds, we must have been approaching each other at somewhere around 250 miles an hour.
>
> Thank God, my Lewis didn't jam. I kept a steady stream of lead pouring into the nose of that machine. He was firing also. I could see my tracers splashing along the barrels of his Spandaus [machine gun] and I knew the pilot was sitting right behind them. His lead came

> whistling past my head and ripping holes in the bathtub [cockpit].
>
> Then something happened. We could hardly have been twenty yards apart when the Albatross [*sic*] pointed her nose down suddenly and passed under us … We saw the all-red plane slip into a spin. It turned over and over and round and round. It was no manoeuvre. He was completely out of control … I figured I had at least wounded him. As his head was the only part of him that wasn't protected from my fire by his motor, I thought that was where he was hit …
>
> … it was Cunnell and I who winged the flying Baron that day …

The Red Baron managed to bring his machine safely to the ground, but he was thrown head first into a briar bush driving nasty thorn points into his skull wound. The sergeant who attended him had shaved his scalp, cutting off the tops of the thorns in his head. But this left the fine sharp points still embedded in his torn scalp which could cause infection. In the Courtrai hospital, the Baron had the best surgeon and doctors that Germany could supply to attend him and operate.[17]

Thus, as related, the dominant opinion was that von Richthofen was not quite the same after he returned to the battlefront. Nevertheless, he continued his splendid success of 'kills' in a frenetic manner. It was apparent that the ace was still suffering from the effect of his head wound. At the time of his death, he was clearly Germany's most decorated hero.

17 Gibbons, *The Red Knight*, 318.

Aside from the *Pour le Mérite*, he was awarded the Order of the Red Eagle, the Iron Cross of the First and Second Class, the Order of the House of Hohenzollern, the Bulgarian Cross for Bravery, the German and Austrian Pilot Badges, the separate and highest Orders of the States of Mecklenburg, Bavaria, Guttenberg, Coburg, Saxony, Hamburg and Bremen, as well as three Turkish decorations for bravery.[18]

Captain & Flight Commander Alfred Youdale, MC

The Red Baron, throughout his military career, was up against some outstanding pilots on the side of the Allies, including several Australians. One was Captain Alfred C Youdale of Ashfield, one of Sydney's important suburbs. When Youdale was awarded a bar to his Military Cross for bravery on the Western Front, he was promoted from lieutenant to captain and Flight Commander of the Royal Flying Corps.

Before the war, he worked in a soft goods warehouse in York Street, Sydney.

Captain Youdale MC, AFC; left, pointing to the bullet hole in his biplane (*Sydney Mail*, 7 Nov 1917)

The British Empire – related the *Sydney Mail* on 7 November 1917 – had produced many such men like Youdale who had completely confounded the German theory that 'no nation of shopkeepers can ever raise a big army

18 Gibbons, *The Red Knight*, 352.

or create great generals'. The *SM* also reported that the daring Youdale had returned from one flight in his biplane with thirty bullet holes in the machine.

Youdale was the third son of Mr and Mrs JB Youdale of Ormond Street, Ashfield. Initially at the outbreak of war, Alfred Youdale enlisted in the Australian Light Horse just as Manfred von Richthofen had enlisted in the German cavalry. After a period of training on horseback in Menangle in outback New South Wales, Youdale went horseless onto Gallipoli and saw seven dangerous months of service there reaching, through gallantry, to the rank of sergeant-major.

Later, he received his commission on the field, but was struck down with enteric fever before he was able take up his lieutenancy. He was invalided back to Australia and he tried to regain his commission with a view of studying at Duntroon, Canberra's pioneering military college, but he was turned down.

Rejoining his unit at Menangle, he was soon returned to Egypt where he was able to obtain a transfer to the Royal Flying Corps. He then proceeded to England for flight training. A few months later, he was specially chosen to perform 'flying evolutions' before King George V when His Majesty inspected the Australians at the training camp of Salisbury Plain.

In France, he was awarded the Military Cross 'for materially assisting in the capture of a strongly fortified position on the Western Front'. His bar was for another act of outstanding bravery.

Captain Youdale had three brothers on active service: Sergeant Stanley Youdale, Warrant Officer Roy Youdale of the Army Service Corps and Sergeant Eric Youdale of the Army Medical Corps.[19]

Second Lieutenant John Hay

Second Lieutenant John Hay, Australian from Gunningbar sheep station in NSW. The Red Baron's 17th kill, 23 Jan. 1917 (*Wartime*, no 2, 20)

Manfred von Richthofen recorded on 23 January 1917 that he pumped 150 rounds into Second Lieutenant John Hay's FE 8 from about fifty metres. This was more than enough to rupture the plane's system, sending petrol spraying onto the hot spinning engine and engulfing the frail plane and its pilot in flames. Hay was the Red Baron's seventeenth victim and an Australian to boot! Hay's flaming aeroplane plunged into the snowbound mire of No Man's Land. It was after a fierce and terrifying air battle with uneven odds – an obsolete machine versus an up-to-date Fokker DRI with its distinctive three layers of wings.

John Hay, known as Jack, was born in Sydney on 22 January 1889, but grew up on Gunningbar, an outback sheep station in north-western NSW. He was successful in matriculating to Sydney University via the NSW Leaving Certificate to enrol in the Bachelor of Arts. On the property, he met Emma a'Beckett, a school friend of his younger sister. Emma and

19 'Captain and Flight Commander Youdale MC of Sydney', *Sydney Mail*, 7 November 1917.

Jack soon became regular partners at local country dances and other country events like the Agricultural Shows. They developed a close loving relationship as a young couple.

The outbreak of war in 1914 turned Jack's happy, comfortable life upside down. He decided to suspend his Sydney University Arts degree to join directly the Royal Flying Corps, unlike others who came through the ranks of the Australian Light Horse, like Youdale and several others. Hay sailed for England on 25 September 1915, but continued a passionate correspondence with Emma throughout the war until his horrific death by fire.

He reached England in early November and immediately began pilot training. On 4 January 1916, he was successful and appointed second lieutenant in the RFC. Pilot training, however, had been a hurried affair. There was a shortage of pilots on the Front, partly because of the high death toll.

Jack's enthusiasm for flying got him through difficult conditions. In June 1916, he was appointed to No 40 Squadron that was using the notoriously difficult FE 8. Its design had already been outmoded.

Jack had proposed to Emma by correspondence and she had eagerly accepted. From France, he sent her an engagement ring that she was to wear for the rest of her life. She never married.

In August, Hay's squadron were transferred to Treizennes near Lens in France. To the south, the Battle of the Somme was in its closing stages, but the northern area No 40 patrolled was still held by the British 3rd Army.

On 22 October, Jack Hay claimed his first aerial victory shooting down an enemy aircraft. As the winter of 1916 closed in, weather conditions heavily reduced the number of operations for Hay's squadron as well as for the Germans. Meanwhile, Emma had persuaded her parents to let her travel to England so that she would be able to meet Jack on leave. Her departure date was 27 January, but tragedy was to intervene – on the 23rd of the same month.

The German Jasta II was having very little success, so Germany's premier ace von Richthofen was put in charge and took over tactics. His successful leadership regenerated the German squadron even though the bad weather and snow continued through most of January. The 23rd of that month was clear enough for the Red Baron to take six pilots over the Lens area for the first time.

In response, Hay was left behind with engine trouble when his squadron as an escort took off. After a delay, he took off by himself to search for his squad. He then scored his second 'kill'. Not long after, he met a hostile plane – an eye-catching red triplane, the trademark of the Red Baron. But they did not engage. For Hay, it was a near miss – a glimpse.

That afternoon, Hay took part in another patrol over La Basse. They encountered a flight of thirteen Albatros. Jack was able to shoot down his third and last victim. As his wing flew toward Lens, they spotted a flight of Jasta II that had avoided combat that morning. The Red Baron had scored two victories on Lieutenant Edwin Benhow and Captain Gregory. In both cases, their guns had malfunctioned. Then, he closed in successfully on Hay. Hay had put up a gallant fight against all odds. But his machine could not match the all-red Fokker DRI.

On snow-covered, marshy No Man's Land, a party of No

40 Squadron recovered Hay's charred body and returned to Aire. His propeller was cut down to form an unusual cross. A round brass plaque was placed in its centre and engraved with the words: 'The earth holds not a braver gentleman'.

Jack Hay was laid to rest in what is today the Aire Communal Cemetery.

The aftermath of Jack's death was full of tragedy and vibrated to other loved ones. Emma wore his engagement ring until her death in 1973.

The plaque on Hay's grave was given to his mother Isabella Hay. She kept it all her life on display in her home and it was finally passed on to the Australian War Memorial through other relatives.

In 1924, Isabella Hay donated £615 to the building of the University of Sydney's carillon memorial which paid for a bell that would bear her son's name permanently. The carillon is a memorial of all those who died in the 1914-1915 war who were members of the University of Sydney.[20] Emma and Isabella would have regarded the Baron as a ruthless murderer, not a heroic figure.

John "Jack" Hay's grave, Aire Communal Cemetery

20 Chris Goddard, '"The earth holds not a braver gentleman". The life and death of John Hay', *Wartime*, no 2, April 1998, 20-23.

Australian Air Squadron Fund (AASF)

On the Australian Home front, one philanthropic and patriotic fund, the AASF, raised money to provide battle planes as their gift to various air forces of the Empire. Between August 1916 and September 1918, individuals, families and local communities banded together to raise one or more subscriptions of £2,700 – the cost of building and equipping a fighting plane for the various theatres of war. Some were to meet with the Red Baron – the Angel of Death.

The scheme's founder was Charles Alma Baker who was a wealthy owner of plantations and mines in Malaya. He also had large interests in Australian and New Zealand cattle stations and properties. His scheme in Malaya produced 53 battleplanes; four he purchased himself.

In Australia, the AASF provided 41 aircraft. New South Wales contributed 30 including 8 donated by the State Government (matched with private donations pound for pound); Queensland provided four; Victoria three and Western Australia and the Northern Territory one each. Two came from South Australia with money donated by Sidney Kidman, the Cattle King.

In the Riverina district of NSW, money was raised in its country towns to provide an aircraft called the "Narrandera-Jerilderie". Raising the necessary money took two years. As No 19, the "Narrandera-Jerilderie" was shot down over France on 12 April 1918 while operating with No 3 Squadron. There were rumours that Richthofen had carried this out. But rumours about the Red Baron were floated everywhere with the drop of a hat.

Most of the Australian battleplanes were donated by

wealthy pastoralist families like the White family of Belltrees in the Upper Hunter Valley of New South Wales. They alone funded four planes of the thirty provided in New South Wales: No 1 "White Belltrees"; No 2 "White Edinglassie"; No 4 "FJ White"; No 22 "White Belltrees (No 2). The other pastural families is like a roll-call of the great property owners: the Macintyres of "Katunga" station near Muswellbrook, NSW; the Ramsays of "Umbiram", Queensland; the Butchers of "Boolathana" on the Gascoyne River of Western Australia.

Many families who were donors had also given sons to the war. The four sons of Richard Capel of "DerraDerra" near Bingara in New South Wales all enlisted, two volunteered in November 1914 and two in January 1916. Three served in the Australian Light Horse. One, Kenneth Capel, transferred from the Light Horse to the Royal Flying Corps after being wounded on Gallipoli and evacuated to hospital in England.

Some of the donated planes quite simply gave their source name: No 3 – "Mrs P Kirby and Son"; No 9 – "Tweed" (river, NSW); No 16 – "Upper Hunter" of NSW; No 20 – "Tamworth and District"; No 26 – "Manning and Wallambi District"; No 28 – "Sydney and North Sydney" and in South Australia, No 1 – "Sidney Kidman" and No2 – Mrs Sidney Kidman.

"Victory" – the last aircraft donated – came two months before the war ended. The donors were the Loyal Volunteer Farmers and Settlers, Residents of Collarenebri and Wahroonga.

In all, there were 94 gift battleplanes that fought in the

1914–1918 war, all technically presented to His Majesty's Imperial Government: Australia forty-one; Malaya fifty-three and sixteen of these were presented by His Highest the Sultan of Johore, and one by His Highest the Sultan of Kedah.

The communities did not pledge to a particular type of aircraft, but were credited with one of the latest as it came off the production line because of the rapidity of technological change in the design of the aircraft industry as fighting machines.

★ ★ ★

In February 1930, *Reveille*, the magazine of the Returned Soldiers and Sailors League in New South Wales, highlighted the issues about the Red Baron by the use of a title to their article on him: 'Richthofen's Death: Importance of the Controversy' (previously referred to). The photograph used on the front cover of the same issue was supplied by the Australia War Memorial showing Richthofen's wrecked plane and Australian pall-bearers removing the body of the German ace airman. In turn, the photograph came from the drawing by Lieutenant Henry Fullwood, an eye-witness and an official artist attached to the 5th Division 1st AIF. Fullwood was convinced that the shot that killed Richthofen was fired from the Australian lines:

> He saw no third 'plane at the time Richthofen crashed, and mentions that the 'plane, in flight, shown in his picture, was the one that Richthofen was pursuing. That 'plane later landed, and the airman put in a claim that it was he who had shot down Richthofen, but the

Diggers who had gathered, and who were well aware of the facts, told him to run away and not be silly.[21]

Thus, the controversy in a nutshell! *Reveille* argued that the controversy had grown from 'the exaggerated and unfounded claims of Capt [Arthur] Roy Brown, the Canadian airman'. The magazine claimed to be intervening with the article to vindicate the merit of the Australian claims and to show 'how Brown's case was built, not on facts, but on flights of fancy'.

Sopwith F I Camel flown by the Canadian Arthur Roy Brown in the last encounter with the Red Baron (*Journal of the AWM*, no 9, 49)

It also claimed that Brown denied the Australian gunners even 'a share of the credit' for the shooting down of Richthofen. By 1930, the controversy was still a burning issue. 'Who killed Richthofen?' was of more moment than the question, 'Who won the war?'

The big question was : Who fired the fatal shot?

The Australian War Memorial's all-red Fokker DRI is not the triplane flown by the Red Baron, merely a replica officially handed over at Canberra airport by Neil Cottee, a wealthy Sydney businessman, who had had the machine

21 'Richthofen's Death: Importance of Controversy', *Reveille*, 28 February 1930, 2.

built in the United States based on the plans of the original Fokker factory. The War Memorial is rich in Richthofen memorabilia: the Red Knight's flying boots; items from his plane's wreckage – the number-plate, the compass, the control column, pieces of metal, red fabric and timber, several declarations from eye-witnesses of the crash and photographs of the wreckage and the military funeral.

The legend of the Red Knight of Germany, who was seen by many as the Angel of Darkness, has continued unabatedly to be a major fascination in the eyes of the public, especially because of the continuing controversy about the circumstances of his death. Much research has been carried out and numerous books and articles in journals and magazines have been published on the life and the still mysterious death of Baron Manfred von Richthofen, the much acclaimed Red Knight of German. It is still a controversy worthy of examination.[22]

Remarkably, the Red Baron continues to be well-known to the public at large, 125 years after his death – one of the very few – unlike other formidable figures of World War I. General Erwin Rommel, the German Desert Fox of World War II, is also well-known.

Apart from his spectacular career as an air ace with 80 recorded aerial victories in dog-fights, much attention has been given to Richthofen's last flight which has become a legend in itself, mingled with romantic ideals about the nature of war. To many, it seems likely that the Red Baron had fallen in a dangerous aerial combat, rather than at a

22 Dennis Newton, 'Spectre of the Red Baron: part 1', *Journal of the Australian War Memorial*, no 8, 1986, 46.

low level, 'blundering into a fatal storm of ground fire' from the Australian machine-gun batteries assembled on that section of the Front. It seems, as John White has put it, that it constantly raises the blood pressure of historians, amateur or professional, the world over.[23]

An eminent well-researched British magazine, *Military History Monthly* conducted a survey among its professional historians to determine the TOP FIVE WW1 PILOTS. They selected five of the most decorated. Number 1 was Manfred von Richthofen:

> Nationality: German
>
> Awards: Prussian Order pour le Mérite, Prussian Order of the Red Eagle 3rd class with Crown and Swords (and many more).
>
> Widely regarded as the top ace of WW1, the Red Baron – as Richthofen was known – was officially credited with 80 air-combat victories. The commander of a squadron of elite pilots, Richthofen was not an aggressive or acrobatic pilot. He was, instead, a brilliant tactician, often diving from above to attack with the sun behind him.
>
> The Red Baron was finally shot down in his red Albatros on 21 April 1918. He was buried on the following day in a cemetery near Amiens, where a guard of honour fired a salute and wreaths were laid.[24]

The other top pilots were: No 2 William George Baker

23 John White, 'The Unbelievable Truth: The "Red Baron" controversy 1918-1998', *Wartime*, no 2, April 1998, 16-19. (White is Senior Curator of Military Heraldry and Technology at the Australian Museum.)

24 'TOP FIVE WWI PILOTS', *Military History Monthly*, issue 47, August 2014, 82.

VC, DSO and Bar, Military Cross and two bars, the French *Croix de Guerre*. Baker was a Canadian. Between 1917 and 1918, he became, in his Sopwith Camel, the most successful fighter pilot in the history of the RAF by shooting down 46 aircraft and balloons.

No 3 was a French pilot Charles Nungesser with the *Légion d'Honneur* and other French bravery awards. By the end of 1916, he claimed 21 air kills. His lack of respect for authority, rugged good looks and appetite for fast cars and beautiful women made him the archetypal fighter -ace pin-up to rival, at least temporarily, von Richthofen.

No 4 was Billy Bishop, another Canadian with a Victoria Cross and other eminent awards. His fifth victory made him an air ace. His lone wolf style helped him to achieve 12 victories in April 1917 which eventually gained him the VC.

No 5 was Grahame Donald, the sole Britisher in the list. A potential international rugby player, he entered the Royal Navy Volunteer Reserve in 1914 as a surgeon probationer. He made some death-defying escapes from his Sopwith Camel. He won the Distinguished Flying Cross and the Air Force Cross.

★ ★ ★

Richthofen and his airmen of the crack Jagdstaffel II squadron, Fighter Wing No 1, known as the "Flying Circus" had its principal aerodrome just east of the little village of Cappy. The night before his final flight, he had slept there. His flyers were full of congratulations for his eightieth victory the previous day. He was looking forward to the prospect of up-coming leave and a game-hunting expedition in the Black Forest with his close friend Lieutenant Hans Joachim Wolff. They would probably travel there by the railway in the event of bad weather. They had already purchased tickets. For Richthofen, it was intended as an escape from celebrity and the crowds of fans.

After a light breakfast, the famous German ace stepped out of his quarters to find a loud regimental band playing, as it commonly did to build up martial spirits. On this occasion, it had been sent there to offer a serenade to congratulate him on his 80th victory. He smiled, although he didn't like the music – it was too loud. And he really hated it and felt embarrassed.

On that day – 21 April 1918 – the weather was unusually cold. With his friend Hans Wolff, he walked away from the sound of the band. There was just a tiny touch of Spring in the air. Richthofen noted the wind was coming unusually from the east. This was not good for German air tactics on the Western Front. The ace, always thinking about tactics, knew that the heavy westerly wind that prevailed a lot of the time had the advantage of the wind behind a disabled plane limping back to base. As well, with a westerly, it was more difficult for an Allied plane to set back across the frontline to the safety of the Allies zone.

At the door of the hangar that housed his famous bright red Fokker triplane, the ace stopped to play with a friendly puppy called Moritz.[25] A press photographer standing by to catch a glimpse of Germany's war hero snapped him in this act. It was to be the last photograph taken of him alive.

25 Faunce, 'The last hours', 19.

German flyers believe it to be bad luck to be photographed just before departing for a battle in the air.

A mechanic in the hangar came forward with a postcard addressed to his son back home. Politely, he asked Richthofen to sign it. With a friendly smile, the great man did so, signing his name for the last time.

By 11.30am German time or 10.30 English time, the clouds lifted and the planes left the base to fly east to engage the enemy on the Western Front. The squadron flew in two groups of five planes each. The ace led the first group which included his cousin Lieutenant von Richthofen who was a beginner under the ace's wing. The other pilots in the Red Baron's command were Lieutenant Karjus, Lieutenant Wolff and Sergeant Major Scholz. Staffel 5, also under the Baron's command, had taken to the air at the same time. They flew as a wing towards the Front.[26]

The constant presence of German fighters above any sector of the battlefield made it clear an attack on the ground on that sector was soon to take place. As Richthofen and his wing of ten were in the skies it seemed likely. At least, there may be an epic battle in the air.

Earlier in the morning, just before he had taken off, two slow moving Australian RE.8s from No 3 Australian Flying Corps were on a reconnaissance mission over the Somme. By 10.45 the Australians were taking photographs over the contested village of Le Hamel, then in German hands. Looking above, they saw the sun glint off some tiny specks coming from the east. These tiny objects became brightly coloured German attack aircraft.

26 Gibbons, *The Red Knight*, 368-70.

Soon six Fokker triplanes were diving on the Australian airmen. White streams of tracers streaked towards them from their noses. Lieutenant Alfred Barrow fired 120 rounds from his Lewis gun in bursts which drove off two of the enemy. Lieutenant Edmond Banks fired 200 rounds with sufficient accuracy to cause four of the German planes to withdraw. The men of No 3 squadron showed great daring in their antiquated machines.

At the same time, Richthofen and his flyers encountered five British Sopwith Camel fighters. Richthofen believed he would soon be onto his 81st kill. One of the Sopwith Camels was flown by the inexperienced Lieutenant Wilfred May. The Royal Flying Corps had just been renamed the Royal Air Force by the King. They were over the heavily-manned Australian sector of the Somme frontline. Arthur Roy Brown, a Canadian in the same squadron as May, took off after Richthofen with the blood-red painted Fokker on his tail. Brown poured a stream of bullets into the Fokker and believed he had hit the German airman in his cockpit. It is probable that he had just crouched over for a moment, as Bean later explained.

According to historian David W Cameron, Richthofen continued tracking May, firing into the scout aircraft. May took desperate evasive action by flying very low into a valley and a river, but the Baron followed him. There, a number of Australian Lewis and Vickers gunners of the 52nd Battalion blasted away at the brightly coloured Fokker as it came in low and just cleared a hill east of Corbie above the valley. Riflemen with .303s also took potshots as the red plane sped past close to the ground. May later recalled:

> Richthofen was very close on my tail. I went around a curve in the river just near Corbie. Richthofen beat me to it and came over the hill. At that point I was a sitting duck. I was too low down between the banks to make a turn away from him. I felt that he had me cold, and I was in such a state of mind at this time that I had to restrain myself from pushing my stick forward into the river as I knew that I had had it.

Nevertheless, many Australian eyewitnesses saw May's machine skim very low over the houses of the nearby town followed by a 'German red three decker'. Suddenly, all saw the triplane swerve and literally fall from the sky. Richthofen seemed to manage to bring the aircraft down, nevertheless, near a brick kiln about 500 metres from Bonnay. He died a few seconds later. This reconstruction was presented in David W Cameron's 2018 book.[27]

Who then did kill Richthofen?

In the mid-1930s Charles EW Bean, the official Australian World War I historian, finally reported on a much earlier commission to make a thorough investigation into the death of Richthofen and to come up with some answers. It was, in fact, the day after Richthofen's death that he was asked to do the investigation, but he spent many years patiently gathering evidence in between other more important work. Bean carried his research out with great care and published his findings, partly based on many interviews with eyewitnesses, as an appendix in Volume 5 of his official history under the

27 David W Cameron, *Australians on the Western Front 1918*, vol 1, Viking, Melbourne, 2018, 274-78.

heading : Appendix No 4 The Death of Richthofen.[28] As far as possible, he provided an abstract of the 'relevant first-hand evidence' available and came up with the same conclusion as more recent historians, like Cameron in 2018.

Bean provided the clearest description over many historians of the real nature of the only wound found on the ace aviator's body: 'The four medical officers' at the first examination of the body 'agreed that Richthofen had been hit by only one bullet, which entered at the right armpit at the level of the ninth rib, passed through the body from right to left and came out a little higher in the front of the chest', about half an inch below the right nipple.[29]

Bean's Conclusions

Bean concluded that the Canadian pilot, Arthur Roy Brown's claim was a mistaken impression where Richthofen merely crouched and Brown saw nothing of the continuing chase between Richthofen and May that ensued. Richthofen actually went on chasing Lieutenant May for almost a mile, attempting to follow his manoeuvres and firing bursts from his machine gun. He could not have done this if he had been mortally wounded by Roy Brown. As Richthofen started to rise to cross the ridge, he was brought into the presence of numerous Australian batteries of machine-gun companies beyond it and he came under extremely heavy fire from the ground. He suddenly abandoned the chase of May, swerved to the right and seemed to come down. A

28 CEW Bean, *The Australian Imperial Force in France During the Main German Offensive of 1918*, vol V, seventh edition, Angus & Robertson, Sydney, 1940, 693-701.

29 Bean, *The Australian Imperial Force in France*, 699.

third plane was not in anyway involved, nor was it sighted by eye-witnesses on the ground.

Of all those in the batteries, Bean believed Sergeant Cedric B Popkin (No 424) of the 24th Machine Gun Company, a carpenter from Palmwood, Queensland,[30] was in such a position to fire the fatal bullet in a second burst. This was confirmed by Private Rupert F Weston who was helping Popkin. He confirmed that the second burst fired by Popkin 'was fatal'. Popkin stated that he 'observed at once that my fire took effect'. Sergeant Popkin was using a Lewis gun and was in the 53rd Battery.[31]

Immediately after Popkin fired successfully at the bright red machine, it arched upwards, then side-slipped down into a beet field near the St Colette brickworks. It made a heavy, bumpy landing, but apparently did not crash as the Australian official historian recorded. Richthofen was still alive and conscious when the first Australian soldier reached him. He was reported to have said: '*Alles Kaput*' (It's all finished). He died a minute of two later.

The Australian first there remarked on his closely cropped blond hair, striking blue eyes and the fact that the blood was pouring from his mouth as well as a cut on his chin, which had apparently struck his machine gun butt in the rough landing.[32] It seems that the famous ace had calmly switched off the plane's engine before he died. A discharge shell was jammed in the breech of each of his guns. The engine cylinders of the plane were undamaged indicating they had not been powered and rotating on impact, which

30 Popkin was born in North Sydney on September 1890.

31 Bean, *The Australian Imperial Force in France*, 700-01.

32 Faunce, 'The last hours', 20-21.

indicated that Richthofen was in control of the plane in the last moments throughout the landing.

Cedric Popkin was twenty-five and eleven months when he enlisted in Brisbane on 6 May 1915. He was married with two children. His wife Mrs Nellie Popkin was his next-of-kin. He was 5 foot 6 inches tall and weighed 150 lbs. His complexion was dark, his eyes were brown and his hair black. He survived the war and was awarded the 1914/1915 Star, the British War Medal and the Victory Medal.[33]

Not one, but two official autopsies were conducted on Richthofen's body – one by a team of British doctors and the second by a team of Australian doctors who were senior officers in the Australian Medical Corps.

Australian Stretcher bearers carrying Richthofen's body from his Fockker (painting by AH Fullwood AWM ART 02495)

The body had been transported to Poulainville where it lay in a section or enclosure of galvanised iron in one of the hangar tents of No 3 squadron, Australian Flying Corps (AFC). On the evening of 21 April, the day the ace had been killed, Corporal EJ McCarthy was ordered to clean and prepare the

33 Attestation papers, Cedric Bassett Popkin, National Archives of Australia.

Baron's body for the autopsy the next morning. He removed the uniform, flying gear and a wallet from the left breast inner-pocket of the flying jacket. A spent bullet fell out in the process which McCarthy kept as a souvenir. He noticed that the bullet had exited the body through a large jagged hole on the left breast and had entered in a neat small round hole on the right side under the arm. The aviator's head had been badly battered by the impact of the crash landing.

McCarthy noticed that, if the bullet had not killed the Red Baron, the impact of the crash landing most probably would have.[34]

The first autopsy carried out by medicos in the British Army in front of about twenty witnesses found that the single bullet on its way through also struck, they claimed, the spinal column. They noted that there was a compound fracture on the left side of the lower jaw and severe facial bruising caused by the impact of the crash. Importantly, they did not offer an opinion about who fired the fatal shot.

Early the next morning, the second official autopsy was conducted with Australian medical officers: Colonel GW Barber, Deputy Director of Medical Services, Australian Medical Corps; Major CL Chapman of the Australian Medical Corps and Major D Blake with the presence of Captain EG Knox, No 3 Squadron, Australian Flying Corps. In his examination, Barber denied the rumour that the body was riddled with bullets – there was only one bullet hole and one wound through the heart and chest. He concluded that the bullet had to be fired from the ground

34 Dennis Newton, 'Spectre of the Red Baron: part 2', *Journal of the Australian War Memorial*, no 9, October 1986, 47.

because of the angle of the wound and that it had hit the pilot while he was banking his aircraft. The other examiners agreed that the bullet had come from ground fire.

The two different conclusions were the beginning of a controversy that has blazed on to the present day. The question remained open: Who fired the fatal shot? As Dennis Newton put it: 'for the spectre of the Red Baron, there can be no rest'.[35]

The following night after the funeral, French villagers desecrated Richthofen's grave, because they saw him as the Angel of Death. General Sir John Monash had to reprimand the local mayor and had the grave restored. Four days later, the Australians successfully captured Villers-Bretonneux.[36]

Earlier, after Richthofen's body was carried on a stretcher from the plane to the Poulainville aerodrome, the red triplane was brought back on the rear of a lorry. Many souvenir-hunters from the Australian troops arrived and the plane soon became a skeleton with very little of its red painted fabric remaining intact. Even General Sir John Monash obtained a section of the fabric and a propeller which he sent back to his home in Toorak, Melbourne.[37]

Today, in dozens of Australian homes a fading piece of red fabric is still proudly on display in hallways or living rooms – the remnants of a legend.

How many airmen did the Red Baron Kill?

The list of Richthofen's victories started on 17 September near Cambrai where the pilot, Second Lieutenant LBF Morris, and the observer Lieutenant T Rees both died of wounds.

35 Newton, 'Spectre of the … part 2', 52.
36 Faunce, 'The last hours', 21.
37 Faunce, 'The last hours'.

Richthofen's last victory – his 80th – took place north-east of Villers-Bretonneux where DE Lewis became a prisoner-of-war in Germany. Between his first 'kill' and his last, Richthofen was everywhere on the Western Front: in the vicinity of the Somme, Lagnicourt, Bapaume, Lens, Vimy, Thelus, Mazingarbe, Zonnebeke, Acheville, Loos, Souchez, Roclincourt, Bailleul, La Folie Forest, Oppy, Neuville, Givenchy, Nieuport, Farbus, Lembras, Quincy, Mercatel, Willerval, Noyelle-Godault, Méricourt, Pelves, Lecluse, Inchy, Foucaucourt, Chignolles, Moreuil, Villers-Bretonneux, Hangard, Bois de Hamel and so on. He was everywhere at different times across the map of France and Belgium with his elite wing. On many occasions, he killed two men in one aerial victory, the observer and the pilot; on other occasions, his enemies were captured and became POWs, thus put entirely out of action. For each of his 80 'kills', Richthofen had a jeweller make a small engraved trophy cup that he put on display in his quarters.

Flying Circus commemorated in New Zealand with replicas in flight. Colour photograph by Gavin Conroy

In sum, during his eighty aerial victories, 71 British and Dominion (including Australian) airmen were killed and 27 became prisoners-of-war for the duration. A few others walked away from their wrecked plane to fly again. Some escaped across the Front into France. Others were not identified.

So, 92 – or probably at least 100, if every case could be identified – British and Dominion airmen were removed entirely from the war against Germany.[38] It is no wonder that Richthofen was named The Red Knight of Germany, its greatest airman.

"*Alles Kaput*" – but, paradoxically, the legend lives on. For the spectre of the Red Baron, there may not be any final rest.

38 Gibbons, *The Red Knight*, Appendix. List of Richthofen's Victories, 395-402.

8

Harry Chauvel and the Lighthorsemen

Light Horse Patrol riding by night to Jifjafa (AWM A00221)

A wounded man in the desert knew a kind of hell, peculiar to the modes of transport that the exigencies of the country made necessary. The sand cart with its wire-mattress flooring gave a small degree of comfort, but even here the inevitable jerking over sand hills caused agonies, which, however, were light compared with those of the cacolets, which were two chairs in which a man could lie slung, one each side of a camel. The camel had a rolling gait that moves these chairs with a jerky action, inflicting hellish torture upon the wounded. Many died of it; but nothing could be devised to serve the conditions; so it was a chance whether a man died of his wounds or the transport.

Donald Black, *Red Dust*, 1931[1]

1 Adapted for *Digger*, no 70, March 2020, 24.

This was the reality rather than the romance of being wounded in the Light Horse. The desert was a different kind of hell from that of a wounded man in the mud, despair and rain of Passchendaele, but transportation to a field hospital was just as torturous and many died on the way. This is where it ended for many, but how did it all start – and end? And what part did Harry Chauvel of the Australian Light Horse play?

General Sir Harry Chauvel

When Henry (Harry) George Chauvel took his last salute on 16 April 1930 and formally retired from the Australian Army in which he had served for some forty-four years, it was almost the end of the story of the Light Horse Cavalry as a viable fighting machine. Motorised vehicles were in the process of taking over in military life. Chauvel's retirement was not to be an absolute break. He was to return to military duties and affairs from the middle of the 1930s to the Second World War. In the 1940s, he suffered failing health.

★★★

Henry George Chauvel was born on 16 April 1865 on the Upper Clarence River of northern NSW at his father's property of 96,000 acres (39,000 ha) near the small village of Tabulam. He was the second son of grazier and cattle breeder Charles Henry Edward Chauvel and his wife Fanny Ada Mary (née James). His family was part of a larger clan of Chauvel descendants from French Huguenots who had left the Loire Valley and settled in England after the Edict of Nantes was revoked. They were refugees from the religious wars in France. Several male members of the family became officers in the Indian Army and then emigrated to New South Wales, having been granted land in 1837, thus becoming landed gentry.[2]

From early days, he was always known as Harry. His early education was conducted in Mr Belcher's private venture boarding school near Goulburn in the Southern Highlands of New South Wales. Still a boarder, Harry went on to Sydney Grammar School for his secondary education from 1874 to 1880 and spent the school holidays at Tabulam, where he soon learnt to ride and become highly skilled on horseback. While at Sydney Grammar, he served in their school cadet unit with great enthusiasm with the rank of lance corporal. When his family began to move, under financial stress, to a smaller property on the Darling Downs in Queensland from 1881 to 1882, he continued his secondary education as a boarder at the elite Toowoomba Grammar School. In 1888, Harry moved back to the family home.

During Harry's time at Sydney Grammar, his father was given permission, on 14 March 1886, to raise two troops of cavalry at Tabulam after much preliminary work in the local community. Charles Chauvel was commissioned as captain of the Upper Clarence Light Horse, referred to, at first, as the Upper Clarence Lancers. (This unit formally escorted Lord Carrington, the State Governor, when he

2 Stuart Cunningham, *Featuring Australia. The Cinema of Charles Chauvel*, Allen & Unwin, North Sydney, 1991, 1.

opened the railway at Tenterfield in 1886.)

Harry soon found his way into military activity on Saturday afternoons under his father's influence. In his second year in the Upper Clarence Light Horse, he was commissioned as a second lieutenant.

Harry's real ambition was to travel to Sandhurst and train as an elite cavalry officer. This expensive dream could not be fulfilled, because his father was finally forced to sell his property at Tabulam, in 1888 after a series of droughts in northern New South Wales, to pay off his debts. Thus he invested in a smaller property of 12,000 acres (4,900ha) at Canning Downs on the Darling Downs, Queensland, and settled the family there. Nevertheless, as a young man, Harry Chauvel embarked on a solo Grand Tour of Europe, visiting Venice, Rome, Florence, Paris and London. He even watched military manoeuvres near Aldershot in the presence of Kaiser Wilhelm II of Germany who was visiting his royal cousins in England at the time. Harry returned after his tour and resigned his commission in the NSW Military Forces when his family moved to Queensland.

Harry Chauvel's first commission in the NSW Light Horse was as second lieutenant. He was then commissioned in 1890 in the Queensland Mounted Infantry as lieutenant; captain in 1896 with the Moreton Regiment; major in 1899; lieutenant-colonel, in 1909; colonel in 1913 and brigadier-general in 1917. But this does not tell the whole story of an ambitious and able professionally dedicated military man.

During the 1914–1918 war, General Sir Harry Chauvel became a household name throughout Australia and the

Empire as a whole and with the Allied military staff in Europe, in particular. When he first donned the Queen's uniform, he was already a polished horseman and a lover of the soldier's life.

Chauvel had served with distinction in the South African War as a major in the 1st Queensland Mounted Infantry – his first taste of violent, life-threatening war, rather than the repetitious simulated training on weekends and at annual camps. He took part in the relief of Kimberley, the advance on Pretoria and the Battle of Diamond Hill. At the Vet crossing, he personally captured a dangerous Boer machine gun that had troubled the Mounted Infantry. He was mentioned in despatches on this and other occasions. The whole experience was a rehearsal for the Great War of 1914–1918.

He was a man that seemed destined to higher rank and this was borne out by his steady rise in the military in peacetime and then in war. In 1899, when he was appointed to the Queensland permanent military staff and went to the South African war as adjutant of the First Queensland Contingent, he soon rose to command a mounted infantry battalion popularly known as "Chauvel's Mounted Infantry" and the 7th Commonwealth Light Horse on Edward VII's ascension to the throne after the death of Queen Victoria:

> But soldiering in those early days was a primitive affair – particularly in Queensland, where men learned to ride hard, to shoot straight and to imbibe the lessons of the text books derived from the experiences of the numerous 'little wars' which at intervals interrupted the

quiet tenor of Queen Victoria's reign.[3]

The South African 'adventure' was Harry's first taste of warfare and he was to thrive on it. He returned to Australia with an enhanced reputation as a brilliant cavalryman and he became famous in the popular press. In 1902, he obtained a brevet lieutenant-colonelcy. In 1903, he was made a staff officer for the Light Horse regiments in South Australia.

On 16 June 1906, Chauvel married Sibyl Campbell Jopp. They had two sons and two daughters. His sons graduated from the Royal Military College, Duntroon, and served in the Indian Army, thus fulfilling their father's early ambition. One daughter Elyne Mitchell became a well-known author – in 1978, her book *Light Horse. The Story of Australia's Mounted Troops*, was published.

In July 1937, Charles Edward Chauvel, pioneering film director – inspired by the distinguished war record in Palestine of his father, Lieutenant James Allan Chauvel of the Australian Remount Unit, and in the AIF in Sinai and Palestine, his uncle General Sir Harry Chauvel and his first cousin Sir Michael Bruxner – began preparations for his feature film *Forty Thousand Horsemen*, a tribute to the Australian Light Horse in the campaigns of World War I. The film was made mainly in the sand-dunes at the back of the Southern Beaches of Sydney, representing the Palestinian desert. It was released in Sydney on 26 December 1940 and was an immediate success with the public and critics as a romantic war saga. When released

3 'Prominent Personalities. General Sir Harry Chauvel, GCMG, KCB', *Table Talk*, 10 April 1930, 13.

overseas, it helped form popular American and British attitudes to the Australian 'digger' and to the international fame of General Henry Chauvel.[4]

Elsa Chauvel, Charles Chauvel's wife and collaborator, was able to explore family history of the Chauvel family in her book which explain Harry's fascination with military life and his devotion to the cavalry. Charles George Temple Chauvel, Charles Chauvel's great, great-grandfather:

> (a retired Indian Army Officer) gave up … his homeland England to take up a new life in the faraway Colony of New South Wales … with his family … in 1838. They made their first home near Mudgee, later in 1842 buying Tabulam Station. It was on this property that his son Charles Henry Edward Chauvel [Harry's father] set up his standard and persuaded his farflung neighbours … to join the mounted troop which he had organised, equipped and financed at his own expense. It was called 'The Upper Clarence River Lancers'.[5]

The volunteer cavalry movement spread through Charles Chauvel's influence to troops of cavalry being formed at Tenterfield, Acacia Creek and Warwick.

It grew nationally in other colonies in country districts. The term 'Lancers' changed to 'Rifles' to 'Infantry', then to 'The Light Horse' in the 1914-1918 War in Sinai and the Holy Land. Two of CHE Chauvel's sons, the grandsons of Charles George Temple Chauvel, were to hold rank in this

4 AF Pike, 'Chauvel, Charles Edward (1897-1959)', Bede Nairn & Geoffrey Serle (gen. eds), *Australian Dictionary of Biography*, Melbourne University Press, vol 7, 1979, 623-4.

5 Elsa Chauvel, *My Life with Charles Chauvel*, Shakespeare Head Press, Sydney, 1973, 79.

'great force': Harry, later General Sir Harry, Chauvel – as its famed commander in the Holy Land – and Major Allan Chauvel, OBE, Charles Chauvel's father. Allan was fifty-three when he arrived in Egypt.[6]

Historically, the Chauvel family were part of the Huguenot diaspora fleeing France after the revocation of the Edict of Nantes and finally arriving in New South Wales in 1838-9 by way of India and the British Indian Army. As part of the landed gentry, they had a keen sense of *noblesse oblige* which permeated Harry Chauvel's entire life.[7]

In 1911, Harry Chauvel became adjutant general to the Australian military forces and, in 1914, he was sent to the British War Office as Australia's military representative, but he had not reached London when the Great War broke out and he was immediately appointed to command the 1st Light Horse Brigade by General William Birdwood, supreme commander of the Anzac forces.

General Sir Harry Chauvel GCMG, KCB (*Table Talk*, Illustration by LF Reynolds, 1930)

The Great War came suddenly to Harry after a stretch of peacetime service in the 1900s and he stepped naturally into his new role of command. He was to make military history. In particular, it was his report on the unprepared state of the winter training camps on Salisbury Plain brought

6 Chauvel, *My Life*, 80.
7 Prof Frank Molloy, 'Charles Chauvel', *Huguenot Times*, no 26, 2015, 8.

to Lord Kitchener's attention by Sir George Reid, High Commissioner of Australia in London and former Prime Minister, that procured the decision to train the Australian forces in Egypt instead of them continuing on in England.

Harry Chauvel was able to join the 1st Light Horse Brigade on its arrival in the first convoy in Egypt where he trained it most thoroughly. He then took it as a dismounted corps to Gallipoli where he was to gain a fine reputation for shrewd leadership. On 6 December 1915, he was given temporary command of the 1st Division.

After the evacuation from Gallipoli, Harry was given his choice of taking the 1st Division to France or remaining with the Light Horse in Egypt. Without any hesitation, he chose the latter. Thus, on 16 March 1916, he took command of the Anzac mounted division. The opportunity to demonstrate his gifts as a leader came with the campaign in Palestine that gave such a commander ample scope.[8]

Sir Harry Chauvel of the Light Horse, portrait by McInnis

As a Boer War veteran of both New South Wales and Queensland state regiments, Henry George Chauvel formally enlisted for the Australian Army on 2 May 1902 at the age of 37 at the beginning of King Edward VII's reign. To the question on his enlistment

8 'Prominent Personalities'; 'Chauvel, Sir Henry George', Arthur Wilberforce Jose & Herbert James Carter, *The Illustrated Australian Encyclopaedia*, vol 1, Angus & Robertson, Sydney, 1925, 253; Peter Dennis *et al*, *The Oxford Companion to Australian Military History*, Oxford University Press, Melbourne, 1997, 142-4.

papers:. 'What is your trade or calling?', he quite simply answered 'Soldier'. He declared that his military service by 1902 was already 15 years. He was a member of the Church of England.[9] Permanent address was Brisbane, Queensland. Complexion was described as 'fresh', meaning fair, his eyes were grey, hair brown and he stood at 5 feet 8 and ¾ inches in height. His attestation papers were filled in for the '7th Battalion Australian Commonwealth Horse for Service in South Africa'. He was still a member of the Australian forces by the outbreak of World War I. He was not required to re-enrol or re-enlist.

The Formation of the Light Horse

> From the early months of 1916 until the end of October, 1918 the greatest cavalry exploit in military history was enacted. The campaigns of the British Desert Mounted Corps under the command of Lieutenant-General Sir Harry Chauvel in the deserts of Sinai, in the dust and heat of the Jordan Valley, and in the bitter wet and cold of the mountains of Moab, provided the most gruelling test to which horse-flesh *en masse* was ever subjected. It was the last great horse-mounted adventure in the history of warfare, and it set the seal on the fame of the Australian horse.[10]

The essential half of any cavalry was the horse. In the South African War, Australia contributed 16,357 horses to

9 Many Huguenot families joined the Established Church (C of E) when the King offered one of his chapels as a place of worship as long as they used the Prayer Book liturgy that had been translated in French.
10 Douglas M Barrie, 'The Australian Horse at War', in Elyne Mitchell (ed.), *Stories of Australian Horses*, Currey O'Neil, South Yarra, 1983, 100.

mount the Lancers, Mounted Rifles, Commonwealth Horse Bushmen Corps. Horses of 16 hands or more were rejected; 15 hands was the preferred size. The type of horse sought by army authorities was one of a strong constitution, resembling a blooded stockhorse and strong enough to carry a trooper of 16 or 17 stone, day after day on a continued basis.

While in South Africa, the Australian Bushmen, in particular, earned a reputation for independence, their mounts provided the ideal type on the high veld; one unit travelled more than 4,000 miles in every part of the Transvaal – including a forced march of 76 miles in one night – with little loss of horseflesh. Such horses evolved to what were called walers, named after the place of their main evolution, country New South Wales.

The typical waler stood between 15 and just below 16 hands, with 'clean legs', showing a good density of bone, 'hard feet', muscular sloping shoulders and the 'unmistakable stamp of his thoroughbred ancestry', together with the mixture of the Australian brumbies. Almost without exception, the horses of the Anzac Division were got by thoroughbred sires. Their stamina and courage were superb. Carrying heavy loads, they performed feats of endurance in the most trying of conditions.[11]

After the Boer War, the waler emerged strongly, during a revival period of breeding with a thoroughbred influence, to resource the many volunteer cavalry units being established during the 1900s. This included, for example, the Upper Clarence Lancers.

With the outbreak of World War I, Australia became an

11 Barrie, 'The Australian Horse', 100-02.

important supplier of horses together with the United States and Canada, the Argentine as well as, but to a lesser extent, India and North Africa.

The Australian War Horse able to carry a 15 stone lighthorseman 100 miles. A waler bred in NSW as a saddle horse for Egypt and Palestine (*Sydney Mail*, 7 November 1917)

For the AIF, 39,348 were initially shipped from Australia, besides a further 81,976, the bulk of which went to Indian troops. This was a total of 121,324 fine thoroughbred and mixed-bred horses. There were 46,000 horses and their replacements that carried the Allied advance from the Sinai Desert up to the Palestinian Plains. The Desert Mounted Corps included various commands: Australian, New Zealand, British, Indian and French, so not all of the 46,000 horses used were from Australia.

The other half of any cavalry were the horsemen – the men who rode the thoroughbreds. During the South African War, the Australian mounted troops were not known generally then as the Light Horse and did not fight as one unit, but were integrated into British forces. The Lancers were with Lieutenant General Paul Sanford Methuen at Modder River; the Queensland Mounted Infantry galloped with Major-General Sir John French to Kimberley; the Victorians with Colonel Clements at Elands River Post; the Bushmen from every colony were with General Herbert Plumer's force. All fought, then, under British commanders. There were Mounted Infantry, Mounted

Rifles, Lancers and Bushmen who all took part in nearly three years of mounted warfare.

By the outbreak of the Great War, these disparate units had been combined, as the 1st AIF took shape, into the 1st Light Horse Brigade consisting of three regiments from the former Lancers, etc: 1st (NSW), 2nd (Queensland) and 3rd (South Australia and Tasmania) and they were placed under the command of Harry Chauvel, who (as already related) was in England representing Australia on the Imperial Staff. He was to meet them when they arrived in Egypt in the convoy. Chauvel was one of the few Australian commanders who was a professional soldier in the Australian Forces, like General Bridges. He was not from the citizen-soldier ranks and tradition, like John Monash, who led the 4th Infantry Brigade, and Neville Howse who came to the charge of the Australian Army Medical Corps as surgeon-general,[12] although his very early experience was similar.

Chauvel arrived in Egypt soon after the 1st Light Horse Brigade had landed. He seemed ideal to direct their training, because of his wide experience in handling mounted infantry from his time in the Boer War and his long peacetime service in the 1900s. But when it came time to lead them into action, ironically, it was as a dismounted formation.

The Light Horse on Gallipoli

The three Light Horse regiments took place in the later landing at Gallipoli in May 1915 and remained on the peninsula for the rest of the Dardanelles campaign. Chauvel was not to lead them as a combined mounted

12 AK Macdougall, *Australians at War*, Five Mile Press, Scoresby, 2012, 42.

troop until the battle at Romani in 1916.

On Gallipoli, Chauvel assumed responsibility for some of the most dangerous sectors of the line. The Light Horse dismounted were called upon to provide 1,000 reinforcements. The entire mounted brigade without their horses were shipped to Anzac Cove. Chauvel's sector consisted of Pope's Hill and Quinn's, Courtney's and Steel's Posts, all above Monash Valley. Chauvel, with great care, reorganised the defences of the section, appointed permanent commanders of the posts and formed special sniper groups from expert riflemen to suppress the Turkish snipers, making it safer for mule trains carrying supplies and the wounded up and down Monash Valley. From their arrival, Chauvel's brigade were under particularly heavy fire and pressure from the Turks.

On 9 July, Chauvel was promoted to brigadier-general, backdated to when he assumed command of the 1st Light Horse Brigade on 10 December 1914. In hospital with pleurisy, he spent six weeks in Egypt, but returned to Gallipoli in time for the August offensive, for which he was mentioned in despatches. He became acting commander of the New Zealand and Australian Division for a short period in September and October in General Sir Alexander Godley's absence. Then, on 6 November 1915, he became commander of the 1st Division and was promoted to major general. He commanded this division through the final phases of the Gallipoli campaign, the evacuation and, then, the reorganisation in Egypt in February and March 1916.[13] His role in the Gallipoli campaign was recognised by his

13 Henry George Chauvel, Attestation and Enlistment Papers, 7th Battalion, National Archives of Australia (NAA).

appointment as a Companion of the Order of the Bath. Chauvel had held the vital sector against all the great surges in the Turkish attacks until he was sent to a quiet sector in September.

Ion L Idriess described the appalling situation in his notes of 2 September 1915:

> In a charge, the 1st Light Horse lost a lot of men. Their wounded lay in front of the trenches for days and could not be brought in. Two wounded men in particular were lying close to the Turkish parapet. Five of their mates went out to get them but were shot. One man managed to crawl back after two nights and a day, and told how the Turks had thrown biscuits and water-bottles out to them. The other man lay there for four days and wrote with charcoal on a board that he was hit by the cap of a shell and unable to move. But they could not get him. One morning he had disappeared. The Turks must have taken him into their trench ...[14]

While Idriess, a sharpshooter or sniper of the 5th Light Horse, recognises the huge death toll of the light horsemen in No Man's Land, he also recognises the common humanity in the Turkish troops in the diary he kept throughout the engagements in the Middle East against the Ottoman Empire allied with the Central Powers, Austria-Germany.

Chauvel had been shrewd in positioning his best snipers in various good vantage points in the hills around the Post under his charge. One such trooper was Idriess who later wrote about their exploits. Another trooper was associated

---

14 Ion L Idriess, *The Desert Column*, 13th edition, Angus & Robertson, Sydney, 1944, 42-43.

with Idriess who was commemorated in his famous diary:

> ...I 'spotted' awhile for Billy Sing this morning. Billy and I came down on the same boat from Townsville. He is a little chap, very dark, with a jet-black moustache and a goatee beard. A picturesque looking mankiller. He is the crack sniper of the Anzacs. His tiny possy is perched in a commanding position high up in the trench. He does nothing but sniping. He has already shot one hundred and five Turks. He has a splendid telescope and through it I peered across at a distant loophole, just in time to see a Turkish face framed behind the loophole. ... Billy fired. The Turk vanished instantly, but with the telescope I could partly see the motion of men inside the trench picking him up. So it was one more man to Billy's tally.[15]

Indeed, 'the crack sniper of the Anzacs'!

In the list of Australian Victoria Cross winners in the Great War, only one, surprisingly, was awarded to a member of the Light Horse Brigade and that was on Gallipoli, on 29/30 August 1915, to Hugo Vivian Hope Throssell, who was seriously wounded, of the 10th Light Horse Regiment, 3rd Light Horse Brigade, New Zealand and Australian Division.[16] One author headed the section on Throssell as 'Hill 60: The only Light Horse Victoria Cross Award'.[17] There were plenty more candidates in the Light Horse that seem to have been totally and unjustly ignored by authorities.

---

15 Idriess, *The Desert Column*, 37-38.

16 'List of VC Winners', in Robert Macklin, *Bravest. Australia's greatest war heroes and how they won their medals*, Allen & Unwin, Sydney, 2008, 260.

17 Anthony Staunton, *Victoria Cross. Australia's Finest and the Battles they fought*, Hardie Grant Books, Prahran, 2006, 39.

Hill 60 or Kaiakij Aghala was a prominent feature of landform on the tangled and precipitous fighting Front of the Gallipoli campaign. Australian, New Zealand and British forces had attacked Hill 60 on 21 August 1915. Although the attack was partly successful, another consolidating attack was launched on 27 August to complete the capture of the hill. The hand-to-hand fighting was particularly bitter and brutal for both sides in which the 4th and 5th Australian Mounted Brigades and the New Zealand Mounted Rifles, as well as the 5th Battalion Connaught Rangers took part. The summit was gained by the Allies, but, before the newly-won position could be consolidated by reinforcements, the Turkish Army counter-attacked fiercely and drove the Connaught Rangers from their very shallow and inadequate trenches. The New Zealand Mounted Rifles managed to hold on and the Australian 9th Light Horse Regiment attacked fiercely to regain lost ground. The 9th made a gallant attack, but it was out-bombed by the enemy and could not retake the lost ground.

John Masefield's classical book written in 1916, *Gallipoli*, details the horror, the heroism of the disaster and points out that the Allied success of the 'two thrusts' made by the 'men of Anzac in the latter days of August' on Hill 60 secured an important well and a Turkish stronghold: 'This last success made the line from Anzac to Suvla impregnable'.[18]

After this, no big attempt could be made by the Allied troops and no big attempt was made by the enemy. The fighting settled down into trench warfare on both sides.

18 John Masefield, *Gallipoli*, New Holland Press, Sydney, 2011, first published in 1916 by Rigby Ltd, 168.

At 10pm on 28 August 1915, the 10th Light Horse, fighting as infantry, were ordered to make another attempt to oust the Turks from their stronghold, starting from the dug-in New Zealand positions. Their objective, some 140 metres of Turkish-held trench about 70 metres distant. It was to be captured, deepened, barricaded and held. In this situation, Hugo Throssell, a second lieutenant, gained the sole VC awarded to the Australian Light Horse.

Jumping-off positions consisted of breast-high trenches on the New Zealanders' left. Every second man was given a bag of bombs. The attack commenced at 1pm on 29 August and, within seconds, the lighthorsemen were engaged in a furious hand-to-hand conflict with the Turkish enemy in their trenches. They succeeded in driving the defenders back. About 30 minutes later, the Turks counter-attacked with fury and succeeded in overwhelming the Australian barricades in the trenches, driving the lighthorsemen back. The Australians attacked again at 3pm and a bloody fight took place. Despite overwhelming odds, the 10th pushed the Turks out of the trench. Just before daylight, the 10th beat back still another attack. At dawn, the Turkish counter-attacks ceased. Reinforcements were brought in and the Australians at last were able to consolidate their position with a sense of completion.

Hugo Throssell VC

For the first time belatedly in the Gallipoli Campaign, Australians had received an adequate supply of manufactured grenades instead of makeshift devices put together by themselves. Hugo Throssell, as second lieutenant, boldly led a party of spirited fired-up men and held an exposed position during the violent counter-attack. He and his men were almost continuously employed in throwing grenades – Australian ones – as well as quickly throwing back Turkish grenades to the enemy. Throssell was heavily wounded in the action, but refused to leave his post for medical aid until all danger for his comrades had passed.

Captain Hugo Throssell VC, 10th Australian Light Horse (Portrait by George Lambert, official war artist); Throssell was awarded the Victoria Cross during operations on the Kaiakij Aghala (Hill 60) at Gallipoli on 29-30 August 1915 and was severely wounded. His war experiences turned him into a pacifist (AWM ART 02797)

When he had his wound dressed, he returned to the firing line until ordered out of the action by the medical officer. Throssell's leadership largely saved the situation at a critical stage. He was thus awarded the Victoria Cross for his gallantry and devotion to duty in the battle for Hill 60.[19]

Hugo Vivian Hope Throssell, popularly known by his mates as "Jim", came from a privileged background as some of the Light Horse did, like Harry Chauvel. Born in Northam, Western Australia, on 27 October 1884, Throssell was the son of George Throssell, a self-made Irish immigrant, who had served as the second state premier of Western Australia at the turn into the 20th century. His mother was Annie Throssell. Hugo attended the exclusive Prince Alfred College in

19 Staunton, *Victoria Cross*, 39.

Adelaide as a boarder in South Australia. There, he excelled in cricket and football. He was the school's champion gymnast and athlete and captained the school football team while learning a little Latin from the grammar school's classical curriculum.[20] He then returned to Western Australia and farmed at Cowcowing. Seemingly, he had the world at his feet as a grazier and part of the rural gentry, just like Harry Chauvel. His father gave him his own horse and trainer and he picked up prizes at picnic races and sports events. He boxed and wrestled the visiting champions, hunted kangaroos with his brothers in the scrub country beyond Northam and acted with the town's amateur dramatic society.

His six-years prior service with the 18th and 10th Regiments of citizen forces contributed to his promotion to sergeant on 6 October 1914 and his commission to second lieutenant on 5 February 1915 in the Light Horse of the AIF.

Throssell did not embark with his unit the 10th Light Horse, but joined it later on Gallipoli two days before the fierce fighting at Walker's Ridge early on 7 August 1915. On that day, the 3rd Light Horse Regiments charged toward the Turkish position at the Nek. Throssell went over the top with the fourth wave which had seen three other waves cut to pieces. He got through unscathed.[21] War was to be a life-changing experience for Hugo as for many others.

On 5 October 1914, both Hugo and his brother Frank Eric (Ric) had enlisted in the fledgling AIF and were posted to the state's first mounted squadron, the 10th Light Horse,

---

20 Ric Throssell, *Wild Weeds and Windflowers. The Life and Letters of Katharine Susannah Prichard*, Angus & Robertson, Sydney, 1990, 38.

21 Lionel Wigmore with Bruce Harding, *They Dared Mightily*, Australian War Memorial, Canberra, 1986, 120.

then being raised as part of the first AIF contingent. Like others, Hugo was full of ideals and vitality. His baptism of fire was when he found himself hurled into Gallipoli's mincing machine in the summer of 1915. He arrived in time to take part in the disastrous August attack at Nek. Wave upon wave of Anzac troops, including the Light Horse, fell in the assault which Throssell's commanding officer tried to have aborted once he had witnessed the carnage. When the request was denied, he apologised to the men and ordered them over the top. Many bade their comrades farewell as they were about to commit suicide on such a mission.

The *London Gazette* of 15 October 1915 recorded the citation for Throssell's award:

> For most conspicuous bravery and devotion to duty during the operations on the Kaiakij Aghala (Hill 60) in the Gallipoli Peninsula on 29th and 30th August 1915. Although severely wounded in several places during a counter-attack he refused to leave his post or to obtain medical assistance till all danger was passed, when he had his wounds dressed and returned to the firing-line until ordered out of action by the medical officer. By his personal courage and example he kept up the spirits of his party, and was largely instrumental in saving the situation at a critical period.[22]

In one encounter on Hill 60, Throssell coolly shot five Turks, one after another as they attacked round a bend in the trench while his unit was trying to build a barricade. As other Turks threw bombs at the barricade, the Western Australian lighthorsemen replied with their own. A Turkish

22 Cited in Staunton, *Victoria Cross*, 41.

bomb blew up the barricade, forcing the Anzacs back. The Turks rushed through, but they were met by the equally determined lighthorsemen led by Throssell. The hand-to-hand fighting was desperate and brutal. Even though pushed back, the Turks kept up their counter-attacks throughout the night. Throssell was wounded twice, but refused to leave his post. The bomb count continued as men in the way lost limbs – hands and arms, blown away. Throssell and his men repelled four more counter-attacks before the Turks finally gave up at daybreak on 29 August.[23] By that time, there had been over the whole period 2,400 Allied casualties at Hill 60.

Sergeant Macmillan, a trooper in the 10th Light Horse, in a letter published in Perth's *Daily News*, provided a tribute to Throssell and referred to his own involvement in the battle on Hill 60:

> The day I got my little lot [wound], poor old "Jim" Throssell got his hit. If ever a man won distinction on the battle field it was our officer [Throssell] that day. He took all kinds of risks, and he is such a tender-hearted chap! Every time one of his men fell "Jim" would insist on returning and doing his best for the poor beggars. He simply took no care of himself at all. And when he got potted …, he said, 'Oh, I'm going back. I'll gallop better with the colors up'. And gallop he did. He was fine to watch – never faltered. 'Come on boys, we'll get 'em; good old 10th', he called until he was knocked about so much, he was ordered out of action. His biggest grief was for his men, and he always made light

23 Harvey Broadbent, *Gallipoli the fatal shore*, Viking, Camberwell, 2005, 237.

of his own wounds.[24]

Such sincere accounts led to the shaping of a heroic and iconic myth, but based solidly on an eye-witness account. Lieutenant HVH Throssell was awarded the Victoria Cross by King George V at Buckingham Palace for conspicuous bravery at Hill 60 Gallipoli on 15 August 1915.

By this time, he had met his future wife, the intrepid Katharine Susannah Prichard, then an Australian journalist and novelist living in London. She visited him in hospital on several occasions when he was slowly and painfully recovering from meningitis and his wounds. She intended to write a newspaper article about the action in which he had won distinction, but she later abandoned the project when Sergeant MacMillan and several others published theirs in London. While MacMillan's article was later published back home in the *Daily News*, it first found its way into London's *Daily Mail* under the banner heading 'The Man I Want to Follow'.

Throssell, the acclaimed war hero, and Katharine continued to get to know each other and became romantically involved at the height of the war. Three years after their first meeting, Throssell was to marry Prichard back in Australia.[25]

Throssell's wounds had necessitated hospital in England. While a patient, he contracted cerebrospinal meningitis, an illness that nearly killed him. He hovered between life and death for a time and never fully recovered. He paid a price for the fame that the Victoria Cross brought him.

He was invalided to Australia in April 1916 and allotted

24 '"Jim" Throssell, VC, His Heroic Conduct', *Daily News* (Perth), 21 October 1915, 4.

25 Throssell, *Wild Weeds*, 36.

'light duties', but instead he worked strenuously in the recruiting campaign which brought more fame, but heavy responsibility. His promotion to lieutenant was gazetted on 26 February 1916.

He persuaded authorities to allow him to rejoin his unit. He arrived in Egypt after the evacuation of Gallipoli. On board, he was in charge of Light Horse reinforcements when he embarked on 22 January 1917. By April, he was back with his beloved 10th just in time for the second Battle of Gaza in which his brother, Frank Eric Throssell, was killed in action. The loss of his brother Eric (or Ric), who was a close friend, affected him deeply.

In tragic disillusionment, "Jim" Throssell searched every inch of the battlefield he could for his brother near Gaza. He called for him; whistled the notes that had been their rallying-cry in their boyhood. He 'found only the nameless dead and dying'. He then began to realise there was no glory in war. He was faced with the horrible reality of war, not the strange joy of battle that had inspired him and his men on Hill 60.[26]

He served with his unit in the operation in Sinai and Palestine that culminated with the capture of Jerusalem in 1918.

On 15 August 1917, he was promoted to captain and had the honour of commanding the ceremonial guard at Jaffa Gate through which General Edmund Allenby made his formal spectacular entry into the ancient city.[27]

Throssell's physical and mental health broke down badly

26 Throssell, *Wild Weeds*, 38.
27 Staunton, *Victoria Cross*, 41.

and he was returned to Australia. His appointment was terminated on 13 February 1919. With his wife Katharine, he settled on a 16-heactare mixed farm in Greenmount near Perth which was not financially viable. Throssell became an advocate acting as a soldiers' representative on the Returned Soldiers Land Settlement Board. Beset with debt, bad health, physical pain and post-traumatic stress, he shot himself on his farm verandah on 19 November 1933 at the age of 47 years.

Throssell had been profoundly disillusioned about the Great War. At a hometown victory parade, he had announced on a public stage: 'I have seen enough of horror of war and want peace. War has made me a socialist and a pacifist.' With the conservative local crowd, he had made himself a *persona non grata* and was deserted by friends and even the family. He felt he was an outcast. He knew he was viewed with suspicion by the State in the secret service, because he joined the Communist Party. The last decade of his life was a lonely, bitter struggle.

Katharine gave birth to his son Ric (named after his beloved brother). At one point, Hugo tried to pawn his medal, the Victoria Cross, but was offered only ten shillings. The government's Repatriation Board refused the cost of spectacles he needed, even though his sight was impaired by metal fragments from the war. After his death, his son Ric sold the medal and gave the proceeds to the nuclear disarmament campaign.[28]

To the people at large in Western Australia, he remained

28 'The pariah VC Hugo Vivian Hope Throssell 28 August 184-19 November 1933', in Robert Hamilton, *Victoria Cross Heroes of World War One*, Atlantic Publishing, Herfordshire, 2015, 96-97.

Captain Hugo Throssell, 'a dashing romantic figure', though many were shocked by his announcement at the victory celebration in 1919 that the 'war had made [him] a socialist'. Katharine, a founding member of the Communist Party of Australia, had written to her friend in Melbourne, the writer Nettie Palmer:

> Peace day at Northam was an event! Jim [Hugo Throssell] led the procession in that little country town – looking very splendid on a great bay charger. The crowd cheered and cheered him. And then at night, my dear, he said his say. The Premier on the platform. Northam's [the] chief town of his constituency and he's an old friend of Jim's. You could have heard a pin drop. Jim himself was ghastly, his face all torn with emotion. It was terrible – but magnificent. Now Mitchell [the Premier] is wondering about his seat. It's the opinion of most people that Jim could have it as easily as he liked, if he liked. But he doesn't want to go into Parliament – at any rate not yet – if ever.[29]

In June 1933, Katharine Susannah Prichard, by this time internationally recognised as a socialist author, or at least an author of social issues in Australian society, was formally invited to attend the Soviet Union for literary celebrations. She travelled by ship, visiting London and Paris before Russia.

While she was away, Hugo Throssell, in some financial difficulties, came up with a scheme to get the sale of some land on Greenmount moving at the end of the Great Depression. He would organise a grand rodeo that would include buckjumping, exhibitions of stock-whip cracking,

---

29 Throssell, *Wild Weeds*, 38-39.

boomerang throwing, pony rides through the bush. He believed it would draw huge crowds prepared to pay a two-shilling coin as an entry fee. He thought he would 'make a packet' and then unload the Greenmount land to a wealthy buyer. He built stockyards and other facilities to entertain the weekend crowds. Two thousand people streamed to the opening of the "Lazy H Ranch" and it seemed a success, at first. But the crowds dwindled and Throssell lost very heavily financially on the deal.[30]

It was not long after that Hugo Throssell committed suicide after becoming deeply depressed.

The day before his suicide, he re-wrote his will bequeathing the whole of his effects, real and personal, to his wife. On the back of the will was written: 'I have never recovered from my 1914-1918 experiences, and, with this in view, I appeal to the State to see that my wife and child [Ric] get the usual war pension. No man could have a truer mate'.

The Department of Veteran Affairs confirmed that HVH Throssell VC had received a 50% pension since his discharge. The Repatriation Commission then determined, on the evidence of his service history and medical record, that his death would be regarded as 'due to War Service'. Katharine's granted war widow's pension became her only source of income in the many lean years when her own literary work could not provide a living. Hugo's son Ric came to an understanding 'of the reasons why my father believed that the only way out of debt, unemployment and his own sense of failure was to destroy himself'.[31]

30 Throssell, *Wild Weeds*, 69.

31 Throssell, *Wild Weeds*, xiv-xvi.

Oh, yes, the spring fulfils its magic everywhere:
a native cuckoo calls.
But neither sun nor bird calls
wake you now,
and I must live alone.
How could you leave me so,
to take the beauty of the world with pain,
because you are not here, my love?

Katharine Susannah Prichard[32]

★ ★ ★

The Dardanelles Campaign of 1915 was conceived as an alternative to the stalemate that had set in on the Western Front. By the time of the battle of Hill 60, it too had become synonymous with deadlock and heavy losses, especially those for the Light Horse Brigades dismounted on Gallipoli. Winston Churchill, the First Sea Lord, one of the proponents of the campaign, resigned from the Admiralty when the decision was made to withdraw.

At least, the December withdrawal was a spectacular success, but the campaign had cost more than 250,000 lives for the Allied forces on Gallipoli. Turkey's success in preventing the Allies from gaining any access to the Black Sea and link up with the Russian Army – their ally – was the Ottoman Empire's most significant contribution to the Central Powers' war effort, but costly in human life.

Even so, the lighthorsemen were back in the saddle. They were reunited with their horses. In June 1917, Field Marshal Edmund Henry Hynman Allenby took supreme command

32 Throssell, *Wild Weeds*, 80.

of the Egyptian Expeditionary Force. As a cavalryman, he invigorated the troops, including the lighthorsemen with the focussed support of Harry Chauvel and, in October, attacked the Turks, breaking through at, but not capturing Gaza and eventually driving them northward beyond Jaffa, capturing Jerusalem on 9 December 1917.

The Battle of Romani, 4-5 August 1916

> For miles over the desert the sands told of hundreds of lonely fights to the bitter end.
>
> Ion Idriess, *The Desert Column*, 93

> We stand ready by our horses, awaiting the word to mount and move off. The last rays of light are passing as we form the column and ride into the night. For hours we ride, not a word is spoken, not a cigarette glows. The only sound the chink of bits and the low swishing of hooves on the ground; occasionally varied by the click of a kicked stone, or a whispered word as an order is passed along.
>
> Pte John Gray 6th Light Horse[33]

In a nutshell, after the brilliantly-conceived withdrawal from Gallipoli in December 1915, the 1st AIF were sent to France, but the Light Horse remained in Egypt for further training and to be reorganised – especially for replacement troops shipped from Australia under an Australian, Major-General Harry Chauvel (later Lieutenant General Sir Henry). Broadly speaking, under his command they spear-headed the fight. In turn, Chauvel was under the supreme

33 Cited in Juan Mahony (compiler), *The Digger's View – WWI in Colour*, self-published, New Lambton, 2014, 107.

command of General Allenby against the Ottoman Empire in Sinai and Palestine.

On 15 March 1916, they initially defeated the Turks at Romani.[34] But it was much more complicated and difficult than that. General Allenby later spoke of the Light Horse as being 'the spirit of the Army'. The evidence of the whole campaign indicates clearly that this was no empty diplomatically political statement to please the Commonwealth of Australia. Allenby, "the Bull", was not given to diplomacy.

Some of the lighthorsemen were disappointed by not being sent to France and the Western Front, but having to endure seemingly endless training in Egypt to allow new recruits the time to gain essential skills.

When Ion Idriess was reunited with his old regiment in Ma'adi, after a more comfortable convalescence in Alexandria – 'quite a happy stay' – he had an initial feeling of loneliness which overwhelmed him:

> It was real lonely, wandering down the old familiar lines, looking for familiar faces, and saddening to find only an odd one here and there. I think the boys of my regiment [the 5th] were the nicest lads in the world. The regiment is filled up with reinforcements. We landed on the Peninsula nearly five hundred strong. Our casualties were eleven hundred and forty-five. As fast as the reinforcements dribbled across, they were knocked. Only two original officers survived right through the Peninsula without being casualtied away. In my own troop, there are only four old hands left, and two of

34 Monty Wedd, *Australian Military Uniforms 1800-1982*, Kangaroo Press, Kenthurst, 1982, 95, 98.

them are first reinforcements who came over with us.[35]

At Ma'adi, Idriess found 'it was the same' old drill which made him wish 'this damned war was over'.

In training, Chauvel was insistent on the slightly flamboyant cavalry sense of uniform: the slouch hat with the brim turned up on the left side showing a khaki puggaree (or hat band) of seven folds, the centre fold being the distinctive Regimental colour, white. Some states favoured emu or cock's plumes; the 11th Light Horse adopted an eagle's feather.

In full kit, they carried a 90 round bandolier with four extra pouches on a leather waist-belt containing an extra 40 rounds. The water bottle was worn under the left arm to prevent it flopping around while riding. They wore heavily-corded serviceable khaki riding breeches and highly polished brown leather leggings and plain-toed boots.[36] Directing training, Chauvel insisted on a range of horse drills to foster obedience as well as the fitness of the horse in fighting action.

The Middle East and Egypt were crucial to the Allies war effort because of the Suez Canal, the major supply route to India and the Pacific, including Australia and New Zealand, and was highly vulnerable to attack by Turkish troops based in neighbouring Palestine.

The situation has its origins symbolically on 14 November 1914 in a speech given in Constantinople, the centre of the Ottoman Empire, by Sheikh-ul-Islam, a senior Muslim cleric. He declared a holy war – a Jihad – against the Allies: Britain, France, Montenegro, Serbia and Russia. As well, he preached that Muslims, who lived in Allied countries

---

35 Idriess, *The Desert Column*, 58.

36 Wedd, *Australian Military Uniforms*, 94.

or under the sphere of influence of England or France and who did not heed the call, would burn in hell, suffer painful torment. Much of this anti-Allied sentiment had its origins in a well-received visit to the Middle East by Kaiser Wilhelm II in 1898. Secret agents had been stirring anti-Christian feelings in Muslim communities in Allied countries.

Turkey's military attacks on the Allies in late October 1914 prompted the British government to annex Cyprus on 5 November and send battle cruisers to shell Turkish forces in forts at the entrance to the Dardanelles on the 35th. They then declared their sphere of influence in Egypt a protectorate on 18 December. This was to protect the French-built Suez Canal that was vital to Britain and France and their world-wide Empires. British and Empire troops soon arrived to defend the canal. General John Maxwell was placed there to command.

Strategies in the Battle of Romani

In early 1915, the Turkish forces with 22,000 infantry made attempts to capture the Suez Canal. They set out from Beersheba in Palestine on 14 January successfully crossing the waterless Sinai Peninsula with the support of the German General Friedrich Kress von Kressenstein and some German officers. The Turks then attempted to cross the canal on pontoons on 2-3 February, but this attack was easily broken up. They withdrew to Beersheba.

For the rest of the year, the canal remained a backwater to the war, mainly because both sides were heavily involved in the Gallipoli campaign and in Mesopotamia.

Battles over the Suez Canal resumed after the Allied

withdrawal from Gallipoli. Maxwell's replacement, General Archibald Murray, pushed the canal defences into the Sinai Peninsula and set up various forts in the desert with a system of supplying water to them, vital in the harsh environment. This was carried out without the Turks responding, although there were some savage skirmishes with the Light Horse, as Idriess had poetically described it: the 'sands' that 'told of hundreds of lonely fights to the bitter end'.

With the end of Gallipoli, there were larger fights. In one such encounter, a 3,500-strong desert force was led by the German officer von Kressenstein.

In July 1916, the Turks, freed up from Gallipoli, finally amassed 16,000 experienced fight-hardened troops to disrupt Murray's defensive system, supported by well-made German-manufactured machine guns, artillery and anti-aircraft detachments together with a dozen aircraft. By mid-July, a large Turkish force was assembled outside Romani, a town about 32 kms (20 miles) east of the canal.[37] It was far too close for comfort. There was a need for the Australian Light Horse to spring into action under Chauvel's direction. The Turkish force were getting close to the northern extent of Murray's advances.

The Battle of Romani was to cost the Turkish Army about 8,000 casualties and the Allies a few more than 1,000 infantry and mounted troopers. The Allied victory removed the Turkish threat on the Suez Canal. In the popular press, Romani created a legend of reckless valour for the Light Horse that mightily impressed the imagination of the

37 Ian Westwell, *The Ultimate Illustrated History of World War 1*, Hermes House, Leicestershire, 2011, 102-3.

homefront. It was a rare victory after the disaster of Gallipoli.

Murray, the British Commander-in-Chief, had ordered the Light Horse into the forward zone and placed Harry Chauvel in command of all operations. It was in the first phase of the desert campaign to earn him the reputation of being the finest leader of mounted troops in the Great War and the last of the mythical cavalry leaders.

Chauvel's available force eventually consisted of the 1st, 2nd and 3rd Light Horse Brigades and the New Zealand Mounted Rifle Brigade. At first, they engaged in a bloody series of deadly skirmishes in the midsummer desert heat. Bodies were left to rot in the sun in hurried hit-and -run operations.

On 18 July, aerial reconnaissance by the Allies planes located the presence of four large bodies of Turkish troops only a few days beyond the line of British outposts above Romani. Some short time later, it was established from prisoners-of-war taken in a desert skirmish that a reinforced division of about 14,000 Turkish troops commanded by the German General von Kressenstein had been assembled.

By this time, the Light Horse were not only providing a garrison role, but sending out small patrols to engage the Turks in small disruptive skirmishes that were mainly successful. General Murray noted to the War Office: 'I am assuming that you are leaving the three Australian Light Horse Brigades and the New Zealand Brigade with me otherwise I shall be deprived of the only reliable mounted troops that I have'.[38] Even this hearty endorsement may

38 Cited in Peter Firkins, *The Australians in Nine Wars. Waikato to Long Tan*, Rigby, Adelaide, 1971, 80.

have been an underestimation of their value.

The four large formations of Turkish troops, about 8,000 strong, were continued to be observed by Allied aircraft, plodding slowly through the awful desert heat towards Romani. The 2nd Light Horse harassed them continually on their way, using hit-and-run tactics on horseback. Fast riding was the order of the day. But the Turks moved steadily, yet slowly, closer toward their objective. The Australians patiently waited for a coming climax of a battle with keen expectation and readiness. Chauvel carefully and gradually surrounded the oncoming force which was being drawn into a well-organised trap. The attacking Turkish force had no water supply, as the Light Horse were heavily defending the oasis areas.

After the decisive battle, Chauvel wrote home:

> I am writing at present under an improvised shelter erected by Godfrey White [his batman] composed of two Turkish waterproof sheets and some date palm leaves, I don't know whether you have heard … but we fought and won a great battle, and my men put up a performance which is beyond all precedent although worn out with watching and harassing an advancing army day and night for a fortnight. My old Brigade (1st), under Meredith, held an outpost line of three miles against the enemy's main attack for four and a half hours, in the dark, until joined by me with Ryrie's Brigade (2nd) under Royston.[39]

The battle to hold Romani lasted two desperate days. The Turks, many fanatic Muslim fighters, had pushed the Light

39 Cited in Mitchell, *Light Horse*, 48-49.

Horse Brigades to their limit, but they calmly held firm. They knew they had to because Romani was essentially their base, especially in terms of a railway depot with a water pipeline well under construction. It was, indeed an important communication hub for the desert war. It was also – and importantly – the psychological entrance to the Suez Canal and, even more importantly, Egypt as a protectorate of the British Empire with its major training facilities for newly-arrived troops from different parts of the Empire. The Light Horse could in no way let the Turkish force succeed and they didn't! Romani was a tactical triumph for Chauvel. He had shown himself as a master of strategy.[40]

The Problem of Gaza

The capture of Gaza was much more difficult, in two major attempts: First Gaza on 26-27 March 1917 and Second Gaza on 19 April 1917. Both battles were unsuccessful with things ending in serious disruption for the Allies. By dawn on 28 March, they had had to withdraw and then, once again, in the April attempt. The whole effort was a dismal failure. The Turkish coastal fortress strongpoint at Gaza, thirty-two kilometres inside the border of Palestine, stood firm, while the rest of the Turkish garrisons, on the main, within Sinai had been cleared by the Allies. The British were ready to strike deep into the Turkish-held territory,[41] but for the problem that Gaza presented.

In the failed struggle to take Gaza, there were over 6,000 Allied casualties : 5,000 infantry, 547 in the Imperial

40 Firkins, *The Australians*, 79-85; Chris Coulthard-Clark, *The Encyclopaedia of Australia's Battles*, Allen & Unwin, Crows Nest, 2001, 118-9.
41 Coulthard-Clark, *The Encyclopaedia of*, 124-5; 126-7.

Mounted Division, 345 in the Camel Corps and 105 in the Anzac Mounted Division under Chauvel. The attack never seriously threatened the Turkish defence of Gaza.

Gaza was large and virtually on the Mediterranean Sea. It was heavily fortified and thick hedges of prickly pear had been grown around the town to slow attempts by riflemen on horseback as well as infantry. The Australians had hacked their way through the cacti, shooting and being shot at by the strong Turkish defence armed with German-built machine guns. The Anzacs, nevertheless, almost achieved their objective to break into outer parts of Gaza when the order came through – amazingly – from the British high command to retreat and withdraw in First Gaza because of the extreme difficulties that the British infantry were having elsewhere in the Gaza Front.

The Second Gaza seemed to be forced by the British Prime Minister David Lloyd George who wanted Jerusalem eventually captured to improve British homefront morale, because of the relative failures against the German Armies on the Western Front. Despite the Prime Minister's demands, everything went wrong in Gaza.

Sir Archibald Murray had made unfortunate blunders and was recalled. Perhaps he was a scapegoat! General Sir Edmund Allenby was brought to the Middle East to take over. Allenby's dash brought a new hope to the Middle East campaign. He was confident of success; he disliked incompetence and had a deep appreciation of the fighting men under his supreme command. And he was decisive. He made whirlwind unannounced visits to forward areas and showed a genuine interest in the welfare of the troops. In turn, they held him in great respect and awe,[42] and fought even harder.

Allenby's forceful personality was soon well known to the troops who called him "the Bull". His arrival brought 'an astonishing change' for the better for the British troops on the desert. For some time, they had felt neglected and forgotten. Now British troops, guns and, 'above all', up-to-date aeroplanes to spot the locations of enemy troop concentrations arrived and the Bull knew how to use them. They now believed that victory, more than just possible, lay before them. It seemed almost in their grasp.

Murray's central achievement, despite blunders and heavy loss of life, was that he had secured the safety of Egypt and the Suez Canal. After reconnoitring Palestine, Allenby, more aggressive and decisive than Murray, moved the headquarters of the Egyptian Expeditionary Force from Cairo to near Rafa and then proceeded to radically organise his command.

So after other major reorganisation of lines of communication and provision of stores, etc, he formed the Desert Mounted Corps, made up of the three brigades of the Australian or Anzac Light Horse and the British Yeomanry Mounted Division, also of three brigades.[43] Major-General Chauvel AIF was given the command of the lot. And Allenby appointed several other new leaders as well in other areas of the Expeditionary Force.

---

42 Kathrine Bell, *The Australian Light Horse*, Murray David Publishing, Australian History Series, Davidson, 2009, 19-23.

43 Colonel RM Downes, 'The Campaign in Sinai and Palestine', in AG Butler, *Official History of the Australian Medical Services 1914-1918*, Australian War Memorial, 1938, 627-9.

The Triumph of Beersheba

After the twin debacle of First and Second Gaza, Allenby was swift to devise a new plan with which to defeat the Turkish Army as quickly as possible by by-passing Gaza through the desert. The wells at Beersheba dated from the days of the Old Testament patriarch Abraham. The name in English means "The Well of the Oath".

An intelligence officer on Allenby's staff, Major Richard Meinertzhagen – of Danish ancestry – was the brains behind the new plan to deceive the enemy: the Turks and their German advisors. Under his influence, the Allied planners believed that an attack on the desert town of Beersheba would be a back-door method of finally capturing Gaza and solving the problem of the lack of water supply for a military force. Beersheba itself possessed reliable substantial wells if action could take place quickly before they were blown up and destroyed by the Turkish defence.

The plan was to deceive the enemy. Meinertzhagen rode out into the desert in the regions where Turkish patrols were common. He took with him a false set of documents in a briefcase describing British military intentions about large troop movements to Gaza as well as a false letter from his wife to provide the authenticity of the bundle of documents. The bag of documents was dropped in a place where a Turkish patrol passing by would inevitably find it, as though it had been lost. It was hopeful that the ruse would work – and it did! Major Meinertzhagen's dropped papers convinced the Turkish commander at Beersheba that they would **not** be subjected to a major British attack. Instead, another major offensive would be made on Gaza.[44] In reality, this was not about to happen.

After a gruelling night's route march, the British infantry attacked to the south and the west of Beersheba at dawn on 31 October, while the Desert Mounted Corps under Sir Harry Chauvel circled into the waterless desert countryside to the east and launched their attack on horseback from an unexpected quarter.

For the whole operation to succeed, Beersheba needed to fall in a single day, otherwise the huge British force would completely exhaust their vital water supply. As sunset fast approached, most of the infantry's objective had been reached reasonably well, but the Light Horse advance had been delayed by dogged Turkish resistance from some strongpoints in its defensive system in the desert.

Chauvel and his commanders conferred and the decision was made to charge Beersheba with two Light Horse regiments (4th and 12th with the 11th in reserve). Most of the walers had been watered about 26 to 30 hours before. Some had been without water for 48 hours – thus, it was a chancy situation.

There were other pressures on Chauvel. The impatient Allenby was beginning to get annoyed about delay. "Banjo" Paterson believed Chauvel's successor was even waiting in the wings as Allenby had already made so many changes.

Such was the situation which prompted the remarkable idea that the Light Horse would stage a sudden, decisive cavalry charge. Chauvel knew this would be costly. Nevertheless, he was confident that it would succeed.[45]

44 Bell, The *Australian Light Horse*, 23.

45 Ian Jones, 'Beersheba: The light horse charge and the making of myths', *Journal of the Australian War Memorial*, Canberra, no 3, October 1983, 26-27

Most historians capture the legend, but mix it with reality:

> The Light Horse men moved off at the trot, to that strange and thrilling symphony which may never be heard again: the drumming hooves, clinking metal, and creaking leather of a cavalry brigade going into action. As each troop rode to the top of a ridge and looked down a long, shallow valley towards Beersheba, they knew that the main Turkish defences lay in front of them and that the fate of the battle was in their hands.
>
> They rode forward at the same steady trot until they could see the main Turkish trenches and the first bullets cracked overhead from rifles and machine guns along the sloping sides of the valley. Then the pace quickened, with each man leaning forward like a jockey and urging his horse into the gallop. The tight formations were becoming strung out now, and the thunder of galloping hooves seemed to be echoed by the roar of rifle and machine gun fire as the horseshoe of trenches ahead of them and along the slopes on their flanks exploded into action. Horses and men went down in kicking tangles on the hard, dusty ground, but as the pace increased the Turkish fire became wild and high.[46]

So excitingly wrote historian Peter Firkins.

The first to reach the Turkish trenches were two scouts, Troopers Healy and O'Leary. The main body of the Brigade were eighty yards behind. O'Leary jumped clean across the trenches and galloped on alone. He paused to take out a machine gun single-handed. He leapt off his horse into the

46 Firkins, *The Australians*, 110.

trench and took on the occupants with his bayonet. The thundering mass of Light Horse arrived immediately after. The dazed Turks were forced to cower in their trenches with the onslaught and as the horses jumped over them. The Light Horse dismounted and charged with rifle and bayonet. They shot and bayonetted the confused demobilised Turkish foot soldiers who were no match for their fury. The 12th Light Horse Brigade trotted into Beersheba just in time to prevent the Turks from blowing up the vital wells.

The ambitious Allenby now had the kind of victory he was seeking. He had made heavy demands on the Egyptian Expeditionary Force.

By this time, Harry Chauvel's small force of Anzac cavalry had grown into an army of five divisions, the Desert Mounted Corps which included British, French and Indian units as well as Australians and New Zealanders. It was the largest body of cavalry ever assembled under a single commander in modern warfare times.

In the Beersheba charge, the men galloped over three kilometres under fire, before jumping the trenches and dismounting to fight the shocked defenders hand-to-hand and confident of victory.

Historian Russell Ward pointed out: 'It was Chauvel's faultless planning and synchronisation of the work of his scattered columns which continually surprised and finally overwhelmed the enemy'.[47]

---

47 Russell Ward, *The History of Australia. The Twentieth Century*, Harper & Row, New York, 1977, 118.

The Shaping of a Legend of Beersheba

As an iconic legend, the Charge of the Light Horse Brigade at Beersheba has become unstoppable in Australian popular culture. Harry Chauvel's filmmaking nephew Charles Chauvel added to its longevity by his hugely popular film *Forty Thousand Horsemen* (1940 release), at first conceived in real terms in the late 1930s.

Charles Chauvel had tried to raise the financial backing for the film feature with documentary elements in dramatic form since the beginning of the decade, hampered by the Great Depression. The plan began to crystallise in early 1937 when Chauvel was visiting Hollywood. He met with an old Australian friend Frank Baker, the brother of the famous "Snowy" who supplied a storyline for the film project. Returning to Australia, Charles developed the story with EV Timms, then a prominent and prolific writer of self-published historical romances about Australia.

Then Charles expanded the whole into a working script with his wife Elsa, a former actress and now his collaborator. Hector McIntyre of Universal Pictures in Australia stepped in and financed the film for £5,000. First, they shot a so-called 'shop window' sequence to attract funds from some other sources.

On a day in February 1938, Chauvel directed a section of the film's climax, the Light Horse charge at Beersheba, using four cameras and the sandhills of Kurnell, south of Sydney, to represent the sand dunes surrounding Beersheba. He used a real cavalry division of five hundred horsemen to heighten the authenticity as well as the excitement. They were professional lighthorsemen of the AIF staying in

Sydney for the parades of the sesquicentenary celebrations. The exciting film sequence was successful in attracting more funds from both private and government sources.

The film went into full production. A complete Arab village, constructed by Cinesound carpenters, was built on the Kurnell sandhills. In the filming, its street was packed with hundreds of extras, dressed realistically as desert Arabs, as well as camels, donkeys and geese. Further action sequences required a fulltime contingent of a hundred expert horsemen in Light Horse uniform, many of whom had actually served in the 1st AIF as lighthorsemen.

Arab village & mosque in the Kurnell sandhills; actor "Chips" Rafferty (*Forty Thousand Horsemen*)

Chauvel worked from a flexible shooting script prepared by Elsa. He innovated with the development of dialogue and added new scenes all with the intention of heightening authenticity and creating history in a dramatic filmed form. He worked with leading actors yet largely untried on film – Chips Rafferty, Grant Taylor and Pat Twohill took part in several extensive Middle East campaigns against the Turkish Army. After several exciting war sequences, the film climaxed with the Light Horse charge at Beersheba, which was brilliantly filmed by photographers, such as the famous World War I veteran Captain Frank Hurley, official 1st AIF photographer, who dug a pit in the sand in which to film the charge from below, with horsemen leaping over the supposed Turkish trenches.

This went a long way towards making *Forty Thousand Horsemen* the first Australian film of genuine international status. It was a huge box office success in Australia, the United Kingdom and even in America.[48] In a broad sense, Art imitated Life with a romantic legendary edge.

As the co-script writer and an experienced stage and screen actor herself, Elsa Chauvel provided drama coaching to the raw performers in the film, striving for naturalistic authenticity. She did much to shape the adventurous intrepid heroic qualities of the character of young Frenchwoman Juliette Rouget (played by Betty Bryant) that turned *Forty Thousand Horsemen* away from being merely a succession of masculine images of larrikin, 'beery, blokey faces' of folk-heroes of the bush tradition sticking to their mates 'through thick and thin', as historian Russell Ward described them.[49] 'A womanless world',[50] as Bill Gammage once defined the battlefront, was modified on the silver screen by Elsa Chauvel. The French merchant's daughter Juliette Rouget is very much in the midst of the frontline action disguised

48 Graham Shirley & Brian Adams, *Australian Cinema. The First Eighty Years*, Angus & Robertson and Currency Press, Sydney, 1983, 161-3.

49 Russell Ward, *The Australian Legend*, Oxford University Press, Melbourne, 1974, 2.

50 Cited in Ken Inglis, 'Mateship', Graeme Davidson *et al* (eds), *The Oxford Companion to Australian History*, Oxford University Press, Melbourne, 1998, 416-8.

as an Arab boy daringly spying on the German officers of the Turkish Army. It is, after all, a melodramatic film story. Juliette had witnessed her father's hanging as a spy by the Germans and vowed revenge. She takes up dangerous undercover work. To Elsa Chauvel, women characters on screen should not be passive decorative symbols of national purity, of wholesome womanhood. Juliette becomes sexually involved with the leading character, the impulsive Red Gallagher, played vigorously by Grant Taylor in an explicit naked love scene out of the rain in an abandoned hut. Instead of the middle-class English accent of many earlier Australian films, Elsa and Charles Chauvel insisted on strong natural Australian accents for their film. Elsa does not set masculinity and femininity apart as bipolar opposites. The character Juliette receives the same 'exposure to risk or potential risk' as the male heroic protagonists. The male body is not seen as superior to the female body,[51] as is sometimes commonplace in Australian films.

Forty Thousand Horsemen manages to mythologise a triumphal war event that is hegemonically masculine in some respects, but in an authentic manner. The film powerfully explores the role of warrior and the importance of loyal mateship as a military strategy for survival. Several scenes depict the lighthorsemen's close bonding with their horses – scenes that are caringly and touchingly sentimental – but very close to the historical truth. In one scene, Red gives his horse a drink from his hat in the desert heat before he

51 Katerine Agostino, 'Men, identity and military culture', Stephen Tomsen & Mike Donaldson (eds), *Male Trouble, Looking at Australian Masculinities*, Pluto Press, Melbourne, 2003, 108-31.

drinks himself and he is reprimanded for it by an Empire-type middle-class officer.

Historian Russell Ward provides a pen-picture of the characteristics of the myth of the bushman/soldier: 'rough and ready' manners, avoidance of a great show of affection, capacity for great exertion in emergency, being taciturn rather than talkative, propensity towards a binge of drinking and gambling on occasions for celebration, defiance of authority, fierce independence, hospitality, loyalty to friends and a propensity to be a 'rolling stone', somewhat nomadic.[52]

All such features are present in *Forty Thousand Horsemen* and are convincing realities in the frontline desert. Chauvel draws heavily on all these Anzac characteristics in dialogue, action and verbal and physical expression. The film is replete with romantic masculine images that have a strong association with Rayner Hoff's famous sacrificial ANZAC sculptures of the early 1930s.[53]

The film's nationalistic sentiments glorified Australian manhood in war in an understated form. The Anzacs' achievements in battle hit the right note with audiences in 1940 when the feature film was released soon after the declaration of World War II. It was seen widely as a magnificent tribute by Charles Chauvel and his filmmaking team to the Australian soldier of World War I and found stirring emotion in every detail that Chauvel shaped, even the lighthorsemen proudly singing "Waltzing Matilda" as they began to ride into battle.[54]

52 Ward, *The Australian Legend*, 1-2.

53 For example, in the Hyde Park War Memorial.

54 Andrew Pike and Ross Cooper, *Australian Cinema 1900-1977*, Oxford University Press & The Australian Film Institute, Melbourne, 1980, 250-4.

One of the main characters in the film was described (Red Gallagher) in the screenplay as :'There was a jauntiness about him, an aggressive disposition well camouflaged by dry jokes and ready grins'. Popular Australian historians and filmmakers like Charles Chauvel generally emphasised the characteristics of 'jauntiness', 'aggressive disposition', disguised by 'friendly smiles' and laconic jokes – the larrikin spirit made large.

These ordinary lighthorsemen protagonists of Chauvel's film, with its recreation of the battle for Beersheba from the Australian viewpoint, overall represents an iconic vision of the heroic soldier. Chauvel's task supported by government funding was intended to lift the morale of the homefront of cinema viewers in 1940. *Forty Thousand Horsemen* provided an optimistic charm and nationalistic sentiment in the time of war. Rural individualism is embodied in the characterisation and was profoundly influenced by the Chauvel landed gentry and grazier background; the three friends are all from the bush. Symbolically, Australians are understated, modest speakers who, in their actions, tend to exclude others that are foreign or alien to them. Two of the three characters die in battle in a foreign land – watered with the blood of their heroic sacrifice – and a third returns home. Mateship is then replaced by a love relationship between a man and a woman, marriage and settling down. Chauvel is thus well aware of the death toll in the Middle Eastern War under the demands of General Allenby and his uncle Harry Chauvel.

These days, young Australian backpackers gather in their hundreds on Gallipoli on Anzac Day and they are pumped up tearfully. The live televised occasion throbs with emotion and communal nationalistic warmth. Such occasions still play an important part in Australia's popular culture.

In his film, Chauvel drew constantly on the digger/mateship concept already embedded in the Australian psyche. His film confirmed values that were already there. He was also driven by his own family military history for inspiration, beit a conservative perspective.

Charles Chauvel was born in 1897 on his father's property in Warwick, Queensland, and he had a vivid memory of his father James in his early fifties joining the Australian Remount Unit in Egypt and later serving in Sinai and Palestine under Sir Henry (Harry) Chauvel, who had become renowned in what was regarded as the greatest cavalry force of the twentieth century. He was full of admiration for the Desert Column that Harry commanded, at first dismounted on Gallipoli and, after the evacuation, remounted for the Sinai Campaign.[55] It was encrusted on his personal understanding of family history.

55 Pike, 'Chauvel, Charles Edward', 623-4.

But the legend had been nurtured from at least the beginning in 1917. The *Sydney Mail*, 7 November 1917, had a double page illustration by the paper's artist Scaccia Scarcifoni, based on a photograph taken on the spot by an Australian trooper. It depicted a vast panorama of desert dunes and hundreds of the Desert Column on the move in single file in the endless desert unto the horizon. This exciting war image was one Chauvel was able to recreate impressively on Sydney's southern coastal sand dunes. The caption under the paper's illustration informed the homefront readers of an already shaped legendary version of war:

> … news of an important British success, in which the Anzac Mounted Division, under General Chauvel, played a prominent part. General Allenby, Commander-in-Chief of the British Forces, reports:– 'After a night march, we attacked Beersheba on Wednesday morning. While the infantry attacked the western and south-western defences the mounted troops made a wide turning movement through the desert and approached the town from the east. We occupied Beersheba in the evening in spite of a determined resistance'.

General Allenby was a master of understated military propaganda. The imagery of the legend of the Australian warrior goes back a long way, even and especially to the South African War. Charles Chauvel as a filmmaker drew extensively from it.

There were those like Captain John Oswald Stevenson of the 7th Light Horse who participated in the charge and was moved, on 19 February 1918, to write home to his family about how he experienced the real-live charge. They had started from Tel-el-Fara to get to the back of Beersheba and after two nights travel reached Khalasa, an ancient Christian ruin which was the jumping off point for the mounted troops. They left Khalasa at 5pm to get around Beersheba travelling all night and all the next morning and by 10pm they were in position for the charge. It had been a bright moonlight night and they had travelled along wadis all the time covered in dust, never above the skylight at any time. The wonderful long snake – a single column of men, horses, transport and guns, beginning miles ahead and ending miles behind, then working backwards and forwards through the hills closing in on Beersheba.

> … only two squadrons from each of the 4th and 12th were immediately available for the charge. Imagine the stupendous impudence of 450 men charging a town fortified with trenches, redoubts, and a position which has never before been taken in history, and armed only with a [*sic*] bare bayonets in their hands. The bluff was colossal, yet they charged yelling, cooeeing, and hooting like ten thousand devils raked like hell with artillery, machine guns and rifle fire. They cantered two miles and galloped three straight at them and right up through the town – a magnificent, a wonderful sight. Forty men of B Squadron of the 12th were alone in the town with captured guns and about 600 prisoners! No assistance reached them for half an hour. Yet one might say, 'How they must have suffered in casualties?' But no; they had less casualties than on the 19th April [in the Battles of Gaza], when they accomplished nothing.[56]

56 Cited in Mahony (compiler), *The Digger's View*, 118-9.

On to Damascus

For two and a half years from the Battle of Romani, through the problems of Gaza on to the final push to Damascus and Aleppo, the Australian Light Horse were a military elite always in the forefront of fierce fighting. Even after Armistice, they remained. Battles over, hundreds died of disease. More died in the Egypt uprising protecting British interests.[57] And their beloved horses never returned with them to Australia.

There was a shortage of medical units and a medical crisis in Damascus with 625 Allied patients and 3,006 Turkish wounded as well as widespread sickness among medical personnel. During the advance from Jaffa to Aleppo, the battle casualties had been 149 killed, 49 missing and 438 wounded. During these nine weeks, the mobile section of the field ambulance admitted 10,346 to the Damascus hospitals and between 1,400 and 1,500 died. This number represented only a small part of mortality of the entire Desert Campaign. There were major outbreaks of malaria and influenza.[58]

★ ★ ★

The Australian Light Horse, actually mounted after Gallipoli, provided the British Expeditionary Force with a most reliable, well-trained and consistent core. They spearheaded the crossing of the Sinai and, in 1917, mounted their famous charges to take Beersheba during the Third battle of Gaza. They saw fierce fighting in the Trans-Jordan raids in early 1918. And

57 Neil Dearberg, 'Aussies on Horseback', *Military History Monthly*, issue 36, September 2013, 57.

58 Butler, *Official History*, Ch XII, 'The Advance Through Syria', 729-51.

they crowned their part in the Palestine campaign fighting in the Battle of Megiddo in September 1918 and then captured Damascus, the capital of Syria, on 1 October 1918.

Were they first into Damascus? This was not shown in David Lean's film epic *Lawrence of Arabia*, rather the contrary, apparently because the director was not fond of Australians. The reason for this not being recognised by some British historians as well lies in the politics surrounding the Palestine campaign where the British were attempting to promote the Hashemite Arab ally, Prince Feisal, by giving him Damascus, which meant it had a terrible effect on Turkish wounded prisoners-or-war left behind in that city.

Under the Sykes-Picot arrangement of 1916, Syria and Mosul were meant to pass into a French zone of influence after the war. Palestine was to be internationalised. Britain began to feel that the 1916 agreement was inconvenient. So the 3,000-strong Northern Arab Army of Feisal, operating on the extreme right of Allenby's army, was to be allowed to take Damascus to assist Britain in excluding France from Syria politically. Britain was after more clout at the Paris Peace Conference and help, to provide for longer-term stability of the British Empire.

The Australian Mounted Division with the 4th and 5th Indian Divisions, all under Sir Harry Chauvel's Desert Mounted Corps, with Allenby's supreme command, were riding towards Damascus after the victorious Battle of Megiddo.

Manning Clark, the eminent Australian historian, wrote that the war news from the Middle East was promising:

The Australian Light Horse, under the command of

Harry Chauvel, were slowly driving the Turkish forces out of Palestine and Syria. The men ... were the epitome of the Australian bush legend, men of courage and audacity, with the will to endure, who accepted the idea that men must endure until agony was beaten out into joy.

When Jerusalem surrendered and the Light Horse stormed the Mount of Olives against heavy machine gun fire, the women of the town 'strewed palm leaves in front of the Australians as they entered the ancient city'.[59] The Australians were ordered on to Damascus from 25 September 1918 as the Turkish defeat in Megiddo became apparent.

The taking of Damascus was a complicated political and military affair. But to dispute contradictions of some British historians of eminence, as well as filmmaker David Lean, the facts of the matter are relatively simple. This is even though history has been falsely written in favour of Britain's secretive support of Prince Feisal and his northern Arab Army, with the intention of excluding France from Syria. Allenby's senior staff instructed the British officers working with Feisal to let him know there was 'no objection to Your Highness entering in DAMASCUS as soon as you consider that you can do so with safety'.[60] But Feisal's army was completely unable to take the town on their own, so the

59 CMH Clark, *A History of Australia*, VI, 1916-1935, Melbourne University Press, 1987, 83-84.

60 Cited in Matthew Hughes, 'Australians and the fall of Damascus, 1 October 1918', *Journal of the Australian War Memorial*, no 26, April 1995, 27.

Egyptian Expeditionary Force cavalry had to do all the work of securing the hostile approaches to the town strongly held by the Turkish Army.

Nevertheless, they were instructed to avoid entering the town if at all possible, unless it was absolutely necessary to do so on strategic military grounds, because of hostile Turkish resistance in other parts of the township. The facts are simple as inscribed in a stone rock face in Syria that was still preserved, at least until 1995:

THE DESERT MOUNTED CORPS
COMPOSED OF
BRITISH AUSTRALIAN NEW ZEALAND
AND INDIAN CAVALRY
WITH A FRENCH REGIMENT OF
SPAHIS AND CHASSEURS D'AFRIQUE
AND THE
ARAB FORCES OF KING HUSSEIN
1 OCTOBER 1918[61]

The inscription grants the Desert Mounted Corps with the achievement of ceremonially entering the gates of Damascus first. This achievement can be backed up by an array of reliable sources. Beyond them, Matthew Hughes, an eminent British historian of King's College London, supports the claim absolutely in a meticulous analysis.

On the eve of General Sir Harry Chauvel's retirement from the AIF in 1930, the well-researched journalist of *Table Talk*, in an insightful profile of the great man based on an interview, wrote:

In the preliminary stages of the grand sweep, long and

61 Inscription on the stone in Syria, in Hughes, 'Australians and the fall', 36.

> complicated night movements in utmost secrecy were carried out with extraordinary precision. Beersheba was taken at the charge, the Light Horse galloping over Turkish trenches into the town.
>
> Later Jerusalem fell, and then Jericho, and in 1918 the onward march continued **to the grand finale when Chauvel had the supreme satisfaction of riding at the head of his men into the ancient and far-famed city of Damascus.**

In Chauvel, Lord Allenby possessed 'a cavalry leader of undoubted genius'.[62] The war diary of the 10th Australian Light Horse also described the elation of all ranks on being first into Damascus. In his detailed biography of Harry Chauvel, Alec Hill wrote: 'if it [Australians being first into Damascus] is a matter of no military importance, [it] was not without significance to the men who had begun the long march from the Canal two and a half years before'.[63]

The life of the Lighthorsemen

Much of the experience of the lighthorsemen in the Sinai and Palestine Campaign had been wearisome and monotonous with waterless sand and burning skies. Everyone was relieved when it was all over. They had knocked on the portals of Palestine in their ever-onward surge. Twice they had tried to gain a foothold into the Turks' strongly-fortified citadel of Gaza and twice been repulsed after penetrating it, only to leave 'the half-held

62 'Prominent Personalities. General Sir Harry Chauvel, GSMG, KCB', *Table Talk*, 10 April 1930, 13 (author not acknowledged).

63 AJ Hill, *Chauvel of the Light Horse : a biography of General Sir Harry Chauvel*, Melbourne University Press, 1978, 178.

prize'. Finally, the 6th Light Horse Regiment lay in a wadi near Gaza, awaiting the third and final attempt.

For eighteen months, the campaign had dragged on amongst the sands after the Turks' disastrous attempt to cross the Suez on pontoons. From that occasion, the 6th Light Horse and others had forced the enemy back, but oh, so slowly with the fiercest of battles and warfront encounters. The desert with its ever-changing sands was frequently a dreary battlefield for the lighthorsemen.

The desert – a hard taskmaster – offered little and demanded much. The lack of water for men and horses; the continuous glare and heat with numerous sandstorms that covered them with dust; and the endless sameness had a sharp psychological effect. The desert campaign had been mostly ruthless guerrilla warfare. Attempts to build trenches were mostly aborted, the sand would pour back in as soon as they were dug. The heavy sand had broken the vitality of the horses. A shortage of food soon developed for the animals – they nibbled at anything, their tails and manes. They nosed their droppings for undigested grains. Through this practice their, 'bellies became filled with sand'.

While desert had heaped hardship upon them, it still held a strange fascination for the troopers. Its sheer magnificence would have left vivid memories to all who survived. Sleeping in the open made them feel the closeness of nature; the stars at night appeared low in the heavens. Some of the more sensitive and religious felt like the Israelites of old, who must have passed through the same wilderness to approach the land of milk and honey.

Yet there were many mute graves that testified to the two failures at Gaza that made the Turks feel impregnable – but they were not, in the end.

The lighthorsemen always worked in sections of four and their rations were also issued in this manner. When in action on foot, one of the four troopers held the horses of the three. Thus they saw themselves as four brothers-in-arms and a very close bonding was formed. So they looked after each other for the duration.

Some sandhills were alive with desert dogs, pariahs akin to wolves. They came near the line at night, creating bedlam 'with their piercingly blood-curdling yells'. The troopers found themselves shooting them with their rifles in the light of the moon.

The lighthorsemen lived for the present. Death was always nearby. They saw so many of their comrades and close friends die. The war seemed never to end. Home seemed – and was – a long way away.

Rats burrowed over large sections of the desert hills like rabbits. To walk on or ride over them risked a broken leg. And scorpions gave them hell in some places. The rats were even a greater menace at night. They scampered across the bodies of sleeping troopers; they were difficult to keep out of tents and other shelters. And sometimes snakes were found inside blankets – deadly vipers.

In contrast to the heat in daytime, the cold at night penetrated the men's clothes and they used an extra pair of socks as gloves while riding, which mainly took place in the dark. Weariness was universal.[64] Nevertheless, one

64 Donald Black, *Red Dust*, Ch 1; originally published in 1931, adapted by Graeme Hoskens for *Digger*, no 70, March 2020, 24-31.

trooper wrote his final assessment:

> We learn to value our friends, to know what they mean to us. We each depend on the other, if one is weak we all fall. Friendships made this way are forged and tested in the white-hot heat of the great divide. We know more of each other than would ever be known under any other circumstances. We learn to love and appreciate our friendships accordingly.
>
> *Western Mail*, 2 February 1939, 9

Andrew Barton "Banjo" Paterson of *The Man from Snowy River* fame also captured something of the rapidly changing nature of the Desert War and of mateship in a piece of popular verse:

> In this war we're always moving, moving on,
> When we make a friend, another friend has gone.
>   Should a woman's kindly face
>   Make us welcome for a space
> Then it's boot and saddle, boys, we're moving on.
>
> "We're Always Moving"[65]

Paterson later claimed: 'there are five elements in Egypt: earth, air, flies, fire and water in the order of seniority'.[66]

The Banjo and the Remount Unit

> He [Field Marshal Allenby] came to inspect our horse depot – a great lonely figure of a man, riding silently in front of an obviously terrified staff. He seemed quite

---

65 Cited in Clement Semmler, *The Banjo of the Bush. The Life and Times of AB "Banjo" Paterson*, University of Queensland Press, St Lucia, 1974, 165.

66 AB Paterson, "Hell-Fire Jack" (General JR Royston), Walter Stone (ed.), *The Best of Banjo Paterson*, Summit Books, Dee Why, 1977, 448.

Portrait by George Lambert
(AWM ART02780)

glad to recognize a friend in me. For a Remount officer is like a Field-Marshal, he has no hope of promotion and no friends whatever in the army.[67]

So wrote "Banjo" Paterson on his first encounter with Field Marshal Allenby who had just arrived from France to take over supreme command of the Egyptian Expeditionary Force from Murray. Paterson captured the sadness of a solitary man with heavy responsibilities.

By this time, Paterson was a Remount Officer in Egypt, a famous Australian of the literary variety: a poet, a former practising solicitor, a journalist, war correspondent and would-be grazier. He was born in 1864 at Narrambla, the eldest of seven children of Andrew Bogle Paterson, a grazier who died on 1889, and his wife Rose Isabella. His father was a lowland Scot and his mother was native-born on a station near Orange. Thus Banjo was part of the landed gentry and enjoyed a bush boyhood on another property near Yass. As he grew up, he saw the horse in action at picnic races and polo matches as well as their work in droving sheep and cattle and driving coaches and carriage. He was aware of the accomplished horsemanship of men on the Murrumbidgee and in the Snowy Mountains. All of this experience generated his lifelong enthusiasm for horses and one of the

67 Banjo Paterson, 'Lord Allenby. A Retrospect', Stone (ed.), *The Best of*, 334.

main reasons for enlisting and becoming a Remount Officer in Egypt,[68] apart from the idea of adventure.

As a boy, he rode a pony to attend a bush school at Binalong and went to Sydney in 1875 to attend Sydney Grammar School where he soon became a prize-winning scholar. He was not a boarder, but lived in Gladesville with his grandmother Emily Barton. He failed, however, to gain a university scholarship and became an article clerk instead at sixteen and was admitted as a solicitor on 28 August 1886. For ten years, he practised in a well-regarded partnership. During that time, he was an all-round sportsman and a sophisticated socialite. His grandmother, a published poet, had a major influence on him living with her and travelling to school and work by ferry to Circular Quay. She engendered his interests in art, music and literature. From boyhood, Andrew had a passionate interest in writing and writers.

He had early writing success with popular bush ballads in the *Bulletin*, including the famous "Clancy of the Overflow", "The Man From Snowy River" and "Waltzing Matilda". He soon became well-known nationally and even overseas as the 'Bard of the Bush'. For hundreds of thousands of readers, Paterson, in opposition to his rival Henry Lawson, expounded the happier side of bush life; the leisurely life of the shearer and drover who saw 'the vision splendid of the sunlit plains extended' and, at night, 'the wondrous glory of the everlasting stars'. He eventually became a professional author and an Australian celebrity,

68 Clement Semmler, 'Paterson, Andrew Barton (1864-1941)', Geoffrey Serle (gen. ed.), *Australian Dictionary of Biography*, vol 11, Melbourne University Press, Carlton, 1988, 154-7.

even icon. *The Man from Snowy River and Other Verse* (1895) sold 7,000 copies in the first twelve months.[69]

"Banjo" was to serve in two wars: the South African or Boer War and the Great War.

His sense of sportsmanship was at the core of his growing respect for the Boers as fighting horsemen. When he returned from South Africa in late 1900 before the war's end, he began a series of highly popular, well-attended public lectures in eastern Australia, including Tasmania about the nature of the South African War. In his writings as the *Sydney Morning Herald* correspondent and his talks, he glorified the British Empire's role in South Africa. He expounded it in verse as well:

> His column [that of General French] was five thousand strong – all mounted men – and guns:
> There met, beneath the world-wide flag, the world-wide Empire's sons;
> They came to prove to all the earth that kinship conquers space,
> And those who fight the British Isles must fight the British race![70]

His personal ideology comes through clearly as an Empire man using cant terms like 'world-wide flag' (the Union Jack), 'world-wide Empire's sons', 'kinship conquers space' and 'the British race'. No doubt his many public talks carried such language of Empire sentiment. In his narrative verse, the Empire's heroic soldiers came from New Zealand's 'flax and fern', from 'cold Canadian snows', from 'Queensland

69 Stone, 'Introduction: Andrew Barton (Banjo) Paterson', *The Best of*, 11-22.
70 AB Paterson, "With French to Kimberley", *Rio Grande and other verses*, Cornstalk Publishing, Sydney, 1926, 7.

plains' and New South Wales: 'From every coast, from every clime, they met in proud array' and '... With rifle-fire and lancer charge their squadrons back we threw'.[71]

Paterson hankered after the excitement of being a war correspondent and an itinerant lecturer and, above all, being where the action was. He left the legal profession after ten years and began a series of journalistic excursions to visit exotic places, for example, China, Japan and the Philippines. London became his main target for a time.

A few months after the outbreak of the war, Paterson went to London to seek an appointment as a war correspondent with a national newspaper, but failed to gain one. Instead, he obtained a job as an ambulance driver at Lady Dudley's Australian Hospital in Wimereux, just north of Boulogne in France, with her volunteer bush nurses. He would collect patients at the railway station and conduct them to the hospital. He didn't stay there long, but returned to Australia with the hope of enlisting despite his age. He had heard that a company of horse experts was being formed to take charge of the horses of the Light Horse. Despite his age, he was able to enlist in the 1st AIF.[72]

Paterson was fifty years of age when he was off to London on the first convoy to get to the Front as a war correspondent, travelling privately with two battalions. He had a craving for a free life after his marriage to Alice Emily Walker of Tenterfield on 8 April 1903. (They had a daughter Grace in 1904 and a son Hugh in 1906).[73] But he quickly returned to Australia with the intention of enlisting.

71 Paterson, "With French to Kimberley", 8-9.
72 Stone, 'Introduction: Andrew Barton (Banjo) Paterson', 11-29.
73 Semmler, 'Paterson', *ADB*, 156.

Thus, on 24 September 1915, wrongly stating his age as 49 years and seven months, the middle-aged, but still athletic Paterson – a man of many parts – applied successfully for a commission in the Remount Unit serving in the Middle East. He was in fact fifty-one and seven months. He remained a correspondent with the *Sydney Morning Herald*, but was now embedded in the 1st AIF as a commissioned officer.

Paterson filled out the application on 24 September. He wrote of his experience as a dispatch rider in South Africa and as an ambulance driver in France. As a prominent member of Sydney society, he gave as his postal address the Australian Club and his home address in Cooper Street, Edgecliff. He declared himself as very fit. He believed he was able to bear the physical problems and strain the individual faced 'with the performance of military duty'. He portrayed himself as most eager to go.

He was commissioned as lieutenant (and soon captain) in the 1st AIF on 13 October 1915, joining the 6th Squadron in the second remount unit where his knowledge of horses would be put to good use.

Around a quarter of the Light Horse who had fought in Gallipoli had stayed behind in Egypt to look after the horses, including the rough-riders to break in the wilder outlaw horses that had been brought from Australia and elsewhere.

The 1st Australian Remount Unit was made up of riders from Victoria, South Australia, Western Australia and Tasmania. The Banjo's Unit – the 2nd – was formed from horsemen from New South Wales and Queensland. At fifty-one he was still an excellent skilful rider. He was good, confident officer material and was soon promoted to captain before he left Sydney. He sailed to Egypt on the Orient Steamship Company's *Orsova* that had been turned into a Transport A67. He arrived at the Suez Canal on 8 December. The Remount Unit set up camp at Zeilous. After Christmas, they moved to Maadi al Khabiri. There, they broke in the 'rough uncivilized horses' brought over by army buyers and prepared them with efficiency for the lighthorsemen in the desert. They were busy as they had 50,000 horses and 10,000 mules pass through the depot to 'civilize' sufficiently to bear a heavily-accoutred trooper on their backs and under fire and be fit enough for long rides across the harshest of country at night. The two Remount Units performed an essential task in war preparation. Without them, the Light Horse would cease to be.

Captain AB Paterson was given command on 21 October 1916. Major General Harry Chauvel was his old Sydney Grammar schoolmate and recommended his promotion to major, when they moved the remounts to a new Moascar base near Ismailia on the western bank of the Suez Canal. Paterson's roughriders displayed their skills consistently and drew large crowds of idle men on leave or in convalescence.

The work was hard, monotonous and full of danger from injury. Some men had been horse-breakers and show-buckjumpers; others were farmers from wheat or sheep properties. The Banjo never had to tell a man twice to get on a horse. He organised some shows for the troops left in Egypt and from the many hospitals recovering from wounds, injuries or sickness.

On General Allenby's arrival on 27 June 1917, he weeded out the non-performers from all ranks and radically reorganised the whole of the Egyptian Expeditionary Force. The Banjo had known Allenby as a major in the Boer War. When Allenby arrived, he had just received sad news that his only son Michael had been killed in France on the Front. His son had been a lieutenant who had been awarded the Military Cross for bravery in the face of the enemy. Paterson sensed that the grief had made the general even tougher: 'Where he had been granite before he was steel now'.[74]

Paterson reflected on the aftermath of the Desert War when it ended and the reception given to Allenby as supreme leader:

> Hospital cases were carried out on stretchers and wounded men limped out on the arms of orderlies to wait by the [railway] line till his [Allenby's] train went by. As soon as the train was sighted a roar of cheering broke out and was kept up till the train with its solitary figure on the car platform swept out of sight.[75]

None of Banjo's horses would see Australia again. Early in 1919, orders were issued that, because of Australia's strict quarantine laws which had been put in place, none of the thirty thousand Australian horses would return except one, Sandy, the horse of General William Bridges who had died from a sniper's bullet on Gallipoli. Some horses were bought by the British Army for the Indian cavalry, a few to Arabs who treated them cruelly, or so they say. More than a thousand were shot and buried in a mass grave. AB "Banjo" Paterson, who had to manage it, was sickened and shattered.[76] On

74 Paterson, 'Lord Allenby – A Retrospect', *The Best of*, 329-40; Grantlee Keiza, *Banjo*, ABC Books, Sydney, 2018, 1-2; 439-91.

75 Paterson, 'Lord Allenby – A Retrospect', 340.

76 Kieza, *Banjo*, 459.

April 1919, Paterson with his wife, who had come over in 1918 as a hospital assistant to work in the Cairo hospitals, left Egypt for Australia aboard the *Kildonan Castle*.[77]

After the War

Harry Chauvel continued to pursue a senior military career in Australia with his usual intensity. He had been rewarded with the highest of honours, including the Knight Grand Cross of the Order of St Michael and St George (GCMC) and Knight Commander of the Bath (KCB) and the Croix de Guerre. On his return home, he became Inspector General, Chief of the General Staff and First Member of the Military Board. He was a modest, quietly spoken man; his two sons followed him into the Australian cavalry and studied at Duntroon.[78]

He was a Senior Patron of Legacy and chairman of trustees of the Australian and Victorian War Memorials. He was active in the work of the Red Cross and the Young Men's Christian Association. The latter was a manifestation of the religious faith his life had been built on. He was recognised by the Church of England in 1930 by being made a lay canon of St Paul's Cathedral in Melbourne.

When Volunteer Defence Corps were set up in June 1940, Chauvel was back in uniform again at the age of seventy-five as chief of general staff. Sir Robert Menzies as Prime Minister turned to him for advice. In 1944, his usually robust health began to fail. He died in Melbourne on 4 March 1945.[79]

77 Semmler, *The Banjo of*, 175.
78 'Prominent Personalities', 13.
79 AJ Hill, 'Chauvel, Sir Henry George (1865-1945)', *ADB*, vol 7, 627.

Sir Harry Chauvel GCMG KCB

(fffaif@org.au)

9

Soldiers from the Surf

We shall rear a race of finer men [Surf Life Savers] than the Anzacs whom the whole world admired.

CD Paterson, *Daily Guardian*,
29 November 1923

And I have loved thee, Ocean! and my joy
Of youthful sports was on thy breast to be
Borne like thy bubbles, onward: from a boy
I wantoned with thy breakers …

Lord Byron (from "Childe Harold's Pilgrimage")

Many claim the love of surfing is a defining characteristic of the Australian way of life. Yet the beach in Australian culture only became important around the turn into the twentieth century with the rapid growth of swimming as a sport before World War I.

In a process of acclimatisation – learning to feel at home on the beach as a popular recreational activity – the amateur surf life-saving movement has played a crucial role as the need for rescue on the surfing beaches became obvious after several drownings up and down the Eastern seaboard, where a large majority of Australians lived in the 1910s.

Memorial sculpture on the headland at Freshwater Beach: Duke Kahanamoku, the great Olympic champion who introduced surfboard riding there in 1916 (photo John Ramsland)

The surf life-saving movement, in its early days before 1914, took on a particular form: volunteer military-style brigades (later called clubs) of trained men who appeared everywhere soon after a popular spot for surfing was identified. The style of the movement in terms of its volunteer nature was replicated the formation of the 1st AIF in 1914.

No one was forced by compulsion to join a surf life-saving brigade or the 1st AIF, but young men in local communities were mightily encouraged by older patrons and the media to do so. The life-saving movement emphasised discipline, marching in unison on the sand (in carnival competitions) and intense skills training to save lives as did the Australian Army in a different way – the latter was trained to kill the enemy while protecting the lives of its own men and the former was trained to save and protect lives of citizens from drowning at sea.

Both organisations trained its member in the use and value of first aid and in how to handle rescue emergencies swiftly, be they of different kinds and in different locations: the surfing beach and the military frontline. The members of both wore uniforms while on duty, but these were different, appropriate to the organisation's activities.

* * *

The biggest early impediment to surf bathing by the Australian urban population was the strict daylight ban of the sport enshrined in Section 77 of the *Police Offences Act* of 1901 in New South Wales. As well, in local government there were regulations that empowered council Inspectors of Public Nuisances to enact Section 77 and so strictly prohibit surf-bathing on Sydney's beaches between about 9am and 6pm, with the morning time generally later adjusted earlier to 8am.

Outside the set times, both men and women were allowed to swim, usually in segregated parts of the ocean beaches. Frequently in these segregation sections of beaches, they enjoyed the surf while naked, as the neck-to-knee costumes were too heavy and cumbersome for the swirling, rough waves of the surf.

Popular myth records that in October 1902, the legal impediment was overcome virtually single-handedly on Manly Ocean Beach by a local newspaper proprietor and activist William Gocher who owned the *North Sydney and Manly News* in what was really a publicity stunt of defiance.[1]

Between the 1880s and 1890s, increasing numbers of Sydneysiders during the summer heat were beginning to realise what they believed to be the health-giving nature of salt water: open sea water where in 'broken waves provided a tingling massage to the bodies of men [and women] sufficiently intrepid to stand waist deep [in the surf] bobbing up and down'.[2]

At Manly Ocean Beach, in the corner of South Steyne on the southern end, they bathed from early dawn till 7am when the restriction imposed by the Manly Council started. An assigned policeman was on guard to prevent people from entering to bathe in the evening before 6pm.

Among the early morning and after-work swimmers was the famous Tommy Tanna, a South Sea Islander who worked as a labourer in the Manly district. Tommy never bobbed up-and-down and was an expert in shooting the waves into the

1 Sean Bradley, *The Bondi Lifesaver. A History of An Australian Icon*, ABC Books, Sydney, 2007, 16.

2 Reg S Harris, *Heroes of the Surf. Fifty Years' History of Manly Life Saving Club*, Manly Life Saving Club, circa 1960, 4.

shore. He dived flat with the breaking waves. Other bathers started to imitate his actions.Young Freddie Williams was one of the first to master this skill and others soon followed. It was sometimes called 'cracking the waves' with head and shoulders out of the breaking wave in a diving position parallel with the sand below. Some became strong swimmers and moved out further to the larger breaking waves. Many other men and a few girls became able and the practice spread through the northern and southern ocean beaches of coastal Sydney, then further south to Wollongong and north to industrial Newcastle. Manly had become the undisputed centre for body surfing as a new sport by the turn into the twentieth century. Other beaches, like Bondi, quickly followed.

William Gocher's campaign against the restrictive hours lead to a crusade that eventually succeeded and ocean beaches were opened up to surfing during daytime hours. Less restrictive swimming costumes were designed to accompany the new sporting craze popular among Sydneysiders. But the numbers of people getting into difficulties in the heavy, sometimes dangerous surf further out from the shore also increased.There were also some drownings. So the surf life-saving movement was structurally born.

Thus surfing, before the Great War, had become a national pastime in eastern Australia where both climate and beaches offered irresistible inducement for the most glorious of sports. Nowhere in the world was surfing so universal, or so it was claimed. For eight months of the year, the accessible ocean beaches were thronged in the daylight hours with men, women and children of every age and social class – the surf was regarded by many as a democratic location.

The safety of bathing on the open ocean beaches was largely due to the establishment of life-saving clubs or brigades which relentlessly patrolled the shores. Each morning volunteer life-savers would pick out the safer parts of the beach for swimmers between flags and were rostered on guard patrols (with military-style patron captains) to rescue those who got carried out by undertow.

Due to the formation of surf clubs, the percentage of drowning accidents were minimised. The men recruited for the patrols were usually strong surf swimmers who had passed exacting tests before admitted to a patrol.Their work was voluntary and unpaid on Saturday afternoons (after the work day finished in New South Wales), Sundays and public holidays when beaches were most crowded.The life-savers patrolled specific beach sections set aside with flags to contain swimmers together:

> A wide, far-reaching arch of flawless blue ; the deeper azure of a quiescent ocean stretching out to the dim infinity of the sky-line ; long, slow breakers lifting at first, imperceptibly, then steadily mounting, curling over and rushing forward in rollicking avalanches of snowy foam to the curving shores of a sandy beach – and on those white, sloping shores, hundreds of lithe, brown-limbed, muscular Apollos, drilled and trained to the last word in physical perfection.[3]

Australian urban dwellers in Sydney, Wollongong and Newcastle almost simultaneously discovered surfing as an attractive and exacting form of recreation. Aside from the

3 'Sons of the Sea', *The Australia Handbook* (Hotel Australia, Sydney), vol 5, April 1930, 7.

vitality-giving attributes, 'there was a suggestion that ... urban Australians had something of the challenge of the frontier at their doorstep'.[4] In the summer of early 1907, the *Sydney Mail* romantically summed up surfing's life-giving forces:

> The joy of life and the pleasure of healthful living, the stress of combat with the curling breakers, and the sense of victorious struggle, the flashing sunlight, the bright gleam of white sands and foaming water, and the exultant feeling of physical energy actively exerted in the open air vibrate through ...[5]

Swimming in the surf carried with it real dangers. Waves could prove more powerful than their size suggested. A sandbank might collapse suddenly. A rip, undertow or strong current might develop unexpectedly and sweep surfers away, out further to sea. Any such event might panic the inexperienced surfer who would attempt to swim frantically to shore and get into great difficulties through exhaustion. Drowning would then become a strong possibility. The safety problem was well defined by the great surf lifesaving advocate Judge Adrian Curlewis:

> Any surfer knows now that unbroken water means deep water, and it was to these spots that the unwary ones were moving. There was no one to warn them that the water piling into the beach in the form of waves would find its way out to sea again by scouring out deep channels. It was into these channels that a few bathers, endowed with more than ordinary swimming

4 Grant Rodwell, ' "The Sense of Victorious Struggle": The Eugenic Dynamic in Australian Popular Surf-Culture, 1900–50', *Journal of Australian Studies* (JAS), vol 23, issue 62, 1999, 58.

5 'Summer at the Seaside', editorial *Sydney Mail* (*SM*), 16 January 1907.

ability, found themselves repeatedly plunging to rescue their unhappy brethren who were being swept far out into the Pacific Ocean.[6]

From such acts of bravery, there arose a need for some sort of formal structure. On popular surfing beaches both north and south of Sydney and outside its harbour in seaside suburbs, men banded together in the summer of 1907 to form what were at first called Surf Bathing Associations of New South Wales. Between 1907 and 1911, surf lifesaving became well established from Wollongong to Newcastle.The clubs became highly competitive with each other on a regular basis.

By 1907, there was an amateur club at the beaches of Bronte, Bondi, Manly (both North and South Steyne), Coogee, Cronulla, Tamarama, Maroubra, Freshwater and Newcastle.A surviving photograph of the early 1910s portrays a surf carnival at Newcastle Beach in which a large crowd of formally-dressed spectators are watching from the upper beach in a roped off area. A flat-roofed surf shed with more spectators on its verandah is prominent and has emblazoned on it in large letters 'NEWCASTLE SURF CLUB & LIFE SAVING BRIGADE'.[7]

Bronte was believed by historical authorities to be the first surf lifesaving club formed in 1903 under the title of Bronte Life Saving Brigade; others believe that Bondi was founded before it in the same year. Primary evidence favours Bronte. Not that it really matters who was first in the short space of weeks!

6 Adrian Curlewis, 'Sons of the Sun' in Frank Hurley, *Sydney. A Camera Study*, Angus & Robertson, Sydney, 1948, 40.

7 Newcastle Beach File, LHD 919.442, Newcastle Local Collection (NLC), Newcastle City Library.

The pioneering surf lifesaving clubs became united under what later became known as the Surf Life Saving Association of Australia. It had its origins at a meeting at the Sports Club in Hunter Street, Sydney on 8 October 1907. The president of the Manly Surfing Club Frank W. Donovan, a local solicitor, chaired the meeting and Lyster Ormsby, a founding member of the Bondi Club, was appointed Honorary Secretary. Through this meeting, the organisation, named initially the Surf Bathing Association of New South Wales, came into being. F.A. Thorpe of the Maroubra Club was elected first president. M.J. Moroney of Newcastle was one of the vice-presidents. Thorpe was followed as president in 1909 by J.S. Lord. Newcastle and Stockton Clubs joined the Association in 1911, while Merewether joined in the 1912–13 summer season.

The Surf-Bathing Commission was formed in 1911–12 under Lord as chair to deal with the questions of safety on surfing beaches, adequate dressing room accommodation and lifesaving facilities in the form of sheds to stow equipment and hold meetings to address the increasingly heavy demands of the public.

Lord was succeeded as president of the Association by C.D. Paterson of the North Steyne Club of Manly Ocean Beach in 1912. The title of the Association was changed to the New South Wales Surf Life Saving Association and, later, in view to developments beyond New South Wales, 'Australia' replaced 'New South Wales'.

The Association functioned as a strict controlling body of the clubs, especially in methods of rescue in the sea and provided advice and instruction in all beach control and surf lifesaving matters. The handbook published by the Association became recognised 'as the world's text-book on the subject'.

The methods and gear of the clubs were standardised by the Association; examinations in surf lifesaving proficiency were evolved; awards were provided for candidates in competitions. The Association adjudicated in differences between clubs and co-ordinated with municipal councils on the safety of ocean beaches. Meritorious awards in three grades were issued by the Association for outstanding life-threatening rescues in the surf.[8]

Prior to World War I, the Association had become a vital force on beaches, from Sydney to the Newcastle district and to the Wollongong beaches (and later to Victoria, Queensland, Western Australia and New Zealand).

The 1908 Surf Carnival

> Spectacular Water Carnivals are held... and attract thousands from all parts to witness the greatest surf experts compete in interesting and novel competitions.
>
> *Australian Country Life*, 15 December 1911

An elaborate surf carnival held on Saturday, 25 January 1908 — Anniversary Day — on Manly Ocean Beach set the pace for other clubs and provided a basic pattern and structure for similar programs to follow. Described on their *Souvenir Programme* as *Manly Surf Club 1st Grand Carnival*, it was an outstanding success, attracting 30,000 spectators who were treated to a preliminary procession down The Corso

8 'Surf Life Saving — History of the Movement', *Surf Life Saving Displays and Beach Sports* (program) in honour of the Duke and Duchess of York, Manly NSW, Saturday, 26 March 1927, 4; Barry Galton, *Gladiators of the Surf. The Australian Life Saving Championships — A History*, AH & AW Reed, Sydney, 1984, 12–15.

(the main street of Manly) to North Steyne and along the Ocean Beach to in front of the Manly dressing sheds, led by the Nautical School Ship *Sobraon* band. Before the band was Venus portrayed by an attractive woman in a shell 'borne by four stalwart brown-backed men' ('The Birth of Venus'). Then came costumed men as an octopus, a sea serpent, elephants, lions, horses, dragons, devils, parsons, pirates, soldiers, cowboys, mayors and aldermen, Chinese mandarins, kings and emperors, Aborigines 'and goodness knows what else besides'. Young women accompanied along the sides of the parade as vivacious flower girls. After the surf lifesavers changed out of their disguises, 'many spectacular events and competitions' took place for the rest of the afternoon.

The entertainment continued with a mock lifesaving display, followed by an exhibition of rescue and release drill by the Manly Surf Club. After this, the Sly Brothers (the first professional Manly life-guards) showed their prowess in handling the surf boat in the breakers. 'The Landing of Captain Cook' was then enacted. Other spectacular entertainments followed to please the crowd.

After that, the more serious interclub lifesaving contests began between three clubs — Bondi, Manly and North Steyne. Members from other surf clubs participated in certain events. There was a line and belt competition for a trophy, an interclub life boat race and a 'Scratch Swimming Race through the surf under the auspices of the NSW Swimming Association for another trophy'. Later, a second scratch race through the surf was held, but this time only open to the members of the three competing surf clubs. There was an interclub tug-of-war contest.

An exhibition of Rescue and Resuscitation was presented by Metropolitan Police under the auspices of the Royal Life Saving Society, a movement that was to become associated with surf lifesaving clubs like Cook's Hill, Newcastle, in its early stages. Other contests followed including a ladies wading race, a walking greasy pole competition and a 'Brown Man Contest'. There were exhibitions of 'Surf Shooting' (body surfing) and fancy and trick diving. The *Sobraon* band provided a selected program of lively music during the afternoon.

A report of the line and belt competition appeared in the *Sydney Morning Herald*:

> The inter-surf life-saving competition with line and belt proved an exciting event... at the word "go" one man in each team swam out to the buoy and waited there. When they were all in position they went off, and after having reached the supposed drowning men, started to swim in with them to other men who were bringing the lifeline and belt out. When a man with the line reached his other two club mates the ropes were hauled in, and the first team (i.e. Bondi 1, Manly 2, North Steyne 3) to get their men ashore won the event.

It was indeed a great success for the movement. The crowd was huge. Every steamer leaving Sydney for Manly was packed while nearly every resident of "the Village" (Manly) was there to watch. The displays were witnessed by several State Ministers.[9] A huge amount of positive propaganda was

9 'Manly Surf Club', *Sydney Morning Herald* (*SMH*), 20 January 1908; 'Surf Carnival at Manly', *SM*, 20 January 1908; 'The Call of the Surf. Carnival at Manly', *SMH*, 27 January 1908; *Souvenir Programme. Manly Surf Club 1st Grand Carnival, Saturday*, 25 January 1908.

achieved. Lifesaving was placed on the map. The 1908 Carnival provided a template for the many others that followed.

Cook's Hill First Carnival, January 1915

While in existence for three seasons, the Cook's Hill Club had never run a carnival, although they had been on the verge a couple of times. The Club had steadily grown and could boast of a large membership of efficient lifesavers. The majority were youthful and the Club had an effective and able team of office bearers led by David Hall Thompson. Their beach drills had become attractive to onlookers:

Cook's Hill Life Saving Surf Club marching team (*Sydney Mail*, 1926)

> "Gunner" (Garnet) Dart, "Noble" (David) Thompson and stalwart Jim Antcliffe [*sic*] are instructors who take a lot of equalling, and it is encouraging to such an able trio that the Cook's Hill boys show an appetite when these gentlemen are serving out information.[10]

The Club's rise in prominence gave them the necessary confidence to run their own carnival. They had an added advantage as the sports journalist of the *Newcastle Morning Herald* saw it; the beach front at Bar Beach was 'second to none in the State' in amenities for a good crowd of spectators with an elevated enclosed reserve. They had their own clubhouse, even though it was already too small for

10 Unidentified newspaper article.

their large membership. The key attraction was to be the Rundle Cup Competition that locals had been following closely for some three years. It was noted that Cook's Hill were placing two teams in the field and had 'a double-barrelled chance of victory'.[11]

On 26 January 1915 on Anniversary Day (later Australia Day), Cook's Hill organised and held a major surf carnival — the first to be held at Bar Beach.[12] An important historic moment for the Club!

A day before the Cook's Hill Carnival, the *Newcastle Morning Herald* (*NMH*) predicted that it would be 'thoroughly successful' as it had an 'attractive programme' including the Rundle Cup Competition and the first round of the Northern District Surf Bathing Association Pennant Championship. The new clubroom would be officially opened. On the viewing areas, there would be 'ample accommodation' and 'an uninterrupted view of proceedings'. Enclosures had been erected there as well as on part of the beach. A big crowd was expected.[13] On the great day, although the 'sun blazed with uncomfortable intensity', a crowd of several thousands turned up, demonstrating the huge popularity of such carnival sports that now rivalled cricket and football.

The district, interstate and international Rugby Union contests had been suspended for the duration of the war because of its engulfing nature. In the following summer, surfing carnivals followed suit as the ranks of lifesavers

11 'Surf Carnival. Next Months Event. Cook's Hill's First Attempt', *NMH*, nd.

12 'Cook's Hill Carnival — the first at Bar Beach', *NMH*, 27 January 1915.

13 'Cook's Hill Carnival', *NMH*, 26 January 1915.

disappeared overseas. Nevertheless, the Cook's Hill first carnival was to prove a grand historic occasion.

The Carnival was a triumph for the Club; they won the March Past and retained the prestigious Rundle Cup for the second time by winning the R&R Competition to the loud cheers of the home crowd. The Rundle Cup thus came into the permanent possession of Cook's Hill. Stockton had won it in the 1911–12 season, the first time it was offered in the Newcastle Carnival; Newcastle won it in the following season, but then Cook's Hill won it in the next and then for the second time in 1915 — two seasons in a row.

As the *Newcastle Morning Herald* put it, the 'club won proprietorship of the handsome trophy presented by R.T. Rundle of Hunter St' — Rundle, who attended the carnival, presented Captain Jim Antcliff with a memento in the form of a 'gold brick'. Cook's Hill members, while pleased with their nicely laid out clubhouse provided by the Council, were noticed by the newspaper journalist to comment quietly that they felt it was already too small.[14]

After the 1914–15 season, carnival competition was suspended for the duration of World War I in conformity with Rugby Union competition between clubs and at the interstate and international levels.

The Cook's Hill team that won the Rundle Cup were the Club's first major surfing champions: J. Antcliff (Captain), J. McDermott, J. King, W. Moore, J. Williamson, F. Roberts (who replaced C. Bevege) and F. Dodd. The team was coached by Garnet Dart who was awarded an inscribed gold

14 'Surf Sports. Cook's Hill Carnival. Home Team wins Rundle Cup', *NMH*, 27 January 1915.

medal by the Club. Antcliff, Dart, Roberts and Dodd were soon to enlist. A photograph shows the Rundle Cup team in a studio pose in their smart black Canadian swimming costumes with the blue, red and white cloth badge with the well-known buoy symbol on their left breasts. They are youthful, handsome, well-decked out and superbly conditioned.[15] This was one of the first photographs to be mounted and placed prominently in the clubroom.

★★★

The surf life-saving clubs founded prior to 1914 all contributed to the Great War, sending young men overseas by popular encouragement and propaganda. Ten young men from the small Austinmer Life Saving Surf Club south of Sydney in the Illawarra district went off to war as volunteers and nine came back; only two from Black Head SLS Club joined up; in contrast, Bondi SLS Club had a large membership from its crowded suburban district where 79 enlisted in the 1st AIF – six were killed in action. Bronte SLS Club contributed twenty men with two deaths (one member had even fought in the Boer War); Bulli Club produced six 1st AIF men and one was killed in action; Caves Beach Club south of Newcastle saw five joining up (with no deaths). Forty-nine men from Clovelly left for overseas and only one died-in-action ; in central-northern NSW at Coffs Harbour – then a small club – one man enlisted and returned. At Collaroy on the Northern Beaches of Sydney, 38 men went overseas and two did not return; another had

15 Chris Conrick, *The Northern District Surf Life Saver*, SLSAA Newcastle Branch, 1989, 19.

even fought in the Boer War before the club was founded.

At Coogee, a large contingent of 88 soldiers from the surf left for overseas – five died-in-action; at Cook's Hill Club in central Newcastle 25 successfully enlisted and nine were killed in action; Corrimal Club on the south beaches offered a large contingent of soldiers, 69 with three deaths; Freshwater just north of Manly sent 79 – no one died; Helensburgh-Stanwell Park Club raised 50 enlistments with six deaths overseas; Manly-South Steyne produced a huge number of recruits, 171 with 12 deaths; Maroubra, one of the southern beaches of Sydney, sent 16 men and lost 15 of them, only one returned. Merewether sent one and he survived as did Moruya; Newcastle SLS Club had 198 volunteers for overseas and four died; Newport sent 25 volunteers with three deaths; North Bondi had 62 recruits with six deaths; North Narrabeen produced 25 soldiers from the surf and none were killed; North Steyne, also on Manly Beach, produced 60 recruits and four died-in-action; North Wollongong had a strong World War I enlistment of 84 of which 80 returned home; Ocean Beach had 2 recruits in WWI and one in the Boer War, but no one was killed. Port Macquarie had one soldier who returned and Redhead had three who also returned; Stockton on the northern coastal arm of the Hunter River at Newcastle had 7 recruits who all returned and Tamarama had 5 with one death; Thirroul had 4 recruits who all returned; Wollongong City Surf Club had one who returned; Yamba on the north coast of NSW had 19 servicemen overseas with two deaths; Coolum Beach had one WWI serviceman who returned plus two from the Boer War.

In Queensland, Maroochydore had 12 servicemen with no deaths and Mooloolaba had three with no deaths; Tweed Heads and Coolangatta on the Queensland border had a good contingent of 39 recruits with two deaths.

In Victoria, there was Elwood with a strong number of recruits, 42 with two deaths and, at Lorne, a solitary one recruit who was able to return.[16]

Combining the numbers of Newcastle's clubs – Stockton, Newcastle, Merewether and Cook's Hill – the industrial city to the north of Sydney had 231 enlistments with 13 deaths. The northern and southern beaches of Sydney were also strong locations for recruitment. The northern beaches had 378 enlistments with 21 deaths; the southern beaches had 314 recruitments with 35 who did not return.

Thus from these locations in New South Wales alone, there was a total of 923 lifesavers recruited to the 1st AIF with 69 deaths. The lifesaving movement was dominantly urban in nature as far as World War I enlistments, in contrast with strong countryside recruitment with other categories of men.

* * *

The Memorial that was Unveiled Twice

A unique war memorial stood, until a few years ago, in a windswept corner of Newcastle's Empire Park close to Bar Beach. It has now been renovated and placed in a prominent position in a grassed park above the surfing pavilion at Bar Beach on a slope leading to the large car park. It dramatically faces out to sea, remembering a few 'lithe brown-limbed …

16 Stan Vesper (ed.), *Those who served. Surf Lifesavers at War*, Playright Publishing, Caringbah, 2015.

Apollos'. The names of the fallen on the simple granite obelisk make it a testament to lost youth, a collective memory of one heart-breaking aspect of the local lifesaving club's history.

Cook's Hill Life Saving and Surf Club was founded in 1911 before the Great War. In early 1918, it set up a memorial committee to consider a permanent form of remembrance for their fallen. By that time, the Club had received news that six had been killed on the Western Front. The committee decided on a memorial outdoors near the clubhouse at the end of Parkway Avenue with its stern line of Norfolk pines up its middle. The fact that the founding members came from Cook's Hill decided the club's title.

Clarence Bevege, the club's captain in 1917–18, moved a motion that such a memorial should consist of an obelisk inscribed with the names of the six men. Meldrum and Markey, local stonemasons, would manufacture it. The club founder, David Thompson, would seek Council permission to erect the monument above Bar Beach. An agreement was reached with the Newcastle Council and negotiations were completed with the stonemasons who agreed to a special low a price of £70.

After some disagreement about the wording, Thompson won the day with the elegant prose, 'In the memory of fallen comrades who died in the Great War 1914–1919', placed above the names of the soldiers from the surf. At the base was a concrete model of a buoy representing the Club's badge.

The memorial was unveiled on Saturday afternoon, 8 June 1918. The Mayor, Alderman Robert Kilgour – a patron of the Club – presided, David Watkins MHR of the Federal Government addressed the crowd followed by Mr Gardiner

MP of the NSW State Government. Club members spoke led by David Thompson, a stirring orator. Martial music preceded the unveiling by the Mayoress when trumpeter James King played "The Last Post". The band then played, ending with "God Save the King".

On the back of the memorial now facing the sea, a lone inscription reads:

ERECTED BY THE COOKS HILL
LIFE SAVING & SURF CLUB
8TH JUNE 1918
D. H. THOMPSON
HON. SEC.

The unveiling, however, was premature. When the event occurred, three other Club members had not yet been killed in action as the war rolled on into the second half of 1918. Their names had to be added on the side panel of the memorial.

At the second unveiling, Kilgour, the first life member of the Club, emphasised that they were assembled to express their gratitude and appreciation of the service rendered by the 'brave lads' inscribed on the memorial. David Watkins stated that 90% of the original Club members who were eligible had enlisted.

In his rhetorical manner, David Thompson had the last word in his annual report:

> That valued and ideal member Sergeant E.S. ("Oily") Curley and those gallant younger men Pt. W. Carratt and Trooper Caldwell are linked with such worthy men as Pt. A. Smith. Sgt. E. S. Malcolm, Pt. J. Antcliff, Corp. George Coleman, Corp. A. Dodd and Corp. Williamson

M.M. *To lives such as these death does not destroy, it merely catches, crystallises and makes permanent character, leaving a priceless bequest to Society.*

While the Great War was declared on 4 August 1914 and the Armistice was signed on 11 November 1918 and hostilities ceased, peace was not declared until 28 June 1919. This is why the Cook's Hill Memorial cited '1914 – 1919'. Gradually, the survivors returned home.

But when did it all begin?

In the 1914–15 season, Cook's Hill Club was one of the strongest clubs north of Sydney. They boasted an executive of eleven, 25 active members (that is, fully qualified with a Bronze Medallion from the Royal Life-Saving Society) and 20 members under training. In addition, there were 4 Associate or Honorary Members, a total of 60. By the end of that season, many enlisted; their superb level of physical training ironically made them highly suitable for war.

In 1911, Thompson laid down the Club's objectives: to study and practise the methods of life-saving ; to encourage first aid work; and to instruct and encourage swimming and the 'Natatorial Art'. Although there has been a revolution in lifesaving techniques, these objectives remain unchanged today.

In the early years of the Great War, the number of active members peaked at 67 before a second wave of young men reached enlistment age.

Cook's Hill soon began to do well competing in Sydney carnivals. By 1913–14, it was the most successful Northern club, defeating prominent Sydney clubs like Manly, Bondi and Cronulla. They held an iron grip on the

March Past, won many surf races and R & R competitions. Jim McDermott, who was awarded the Royal Shipwreck Society Medallion for bravery on two occasions, was their first great swimming champion.

On Anniversary Day 1915, they permanently won the Rundle Cup for R & R which was competed for over three seasons in the district. 'Big Jim' Antcliff – a giant of a man – was the team captain and the club captain, but he soon enlisted.

The Cook's Hill Boys joined the rush to enlist. In the 1915–16 swimming season, some were farewelled by the Club and given a shaving kit to take with them overseas.

★ ★ ★

But what happened to those who eventually appeared on the war memorial, which was unveiled on two occasions and now in its third location facing the sea?

Both **Private Alf Smith** and **Sergeant Ted Malcolm** fought in the grim Battle of Fromelles after surviving the Dardanelles campaign. British military authorities had chosen the site for the first major Australian offensive on the Western Front on a section just south of Armentières. A salient known as Sugarloaf was heavily fortified by the Germans with concrete blockhouses with machine guns in gun ports.

The ill-fated Allied attack took place at 6pm when there was still good light on 19 July 1916. Alf was cut down by machine-gun fire with many comrades on the charge forward. Each enemy machine gun on the salient became surrounded by a circle of death. The narrow Front allowed German artillery and machine guns to sweep the entire Allied advance. The men in khaki were cut down like cornstalks with a scythe, costing 1,917 Australian lives in a 27-hour period. Fromelles was Australia's worst one-day death toll in war. Alf and Ted underwent a terrible experience, before they were mortally wounded.

News of Malcolm's death eventually reached the press in faraway Newcastle. Described as a prominent and popular surf lifesaver, he had been promoted to sergeant. Some weeks before Fromelles, he had accompanied the famous Sergeant Albert Jacka, the first Australian VC at the 1914-18 War, on a successful sortie. They negotiated No Man's Land under fire and reached the enemy Listening Post where they gained highly useful information they were able to communicate to command headquarters.

In the Battle of Fromelles, Malcolm was first reported missing; later, death was confirmed. Private Milgate reported that he was with Ted when he was killed in the German trenches at Fleurbaux. Earlier, he had been wounded in fierce hand-to-hand fighting after taking out five German troopers. The other men tried to persuade him to go back, but he refused. He dug himself into a trench for the night. He then went missing, but his friend Milgate saw him hit and die heroically. Later, his body became lost in the chaos.

When Malcolm's death became known at home, a memorial service was held in St John's Church of England, Cook's Hill. The Cook's Hill Boys attended *en masse* to remember their well-regarded comrade.

Private James Antcliff was an iron-moulder at Goninan's. A giant of a man and a mighty surf swimmer, he was Club Captain on enlistment and one of the Club's founders in 1911. He lived with his widowed mother and eight siblings and was the family's breadwinner.

Private James ("Big Jim") Antcliff as Captain of CHSLSC, Newcastle, at Bar Beach 1916 before leaving for overseas (courtesy of Greg Antcliff)

Unlike Fromelles, the Battle of Messines Ridge was a well-planned significant victory. But Jim's 36th Battalion, Newcastle's Own, suffered major casualties – 430 men were killed. Jim was one. His carrying party, laden with ammunition, was the target of an exploding shell that killed or wounded all but two. Alfred Alderton, his close comrade who was present, takes up the story:

> Well, our section,... was just about to hop the parapet when a great explosive shell crashed ... burst right on top of us ... As soon as I regained my wits I turned around to see how Jim had fared, and to my horror and dismay I found poor Jim had passed to the great beyond.

Death was instantaneous. Held in high esteem by B Company, Jim was a favourite with everyone and considered one of the best soldiers in the Company.

The Club regretted that Big Jim's 'fine manly figure' would never again lead their March Past in carnivals. It seemed hardly creditable, so profound was their sense of loss.

Corporal George Coleman was an ironworker who lived in Cook's Hill. He enlisted in the 18th Battalion and fought in Gallipoli. He later found himself in the trenches at the Battle of Pozières. He also fought in the Second Battle of Bullecourt and was wounded, but recovered and returned to his battalion. He fought in the ferocious Battle of Menin Road and was killed while digging in a shell hole. George was remembered as broad and nuggetty and a good swimmer.

Corporal Arthur Dodd was a grocer in Cook's Hill shopping centre and an energetic founding member of Cook's Hill Surf Club. Like Jim Antcliff, he fought in the Battle of Messines Ridge. He was wounded twice on the same day. Later, he was killed on the third day of the Battle of Passchendaele on 12 October 1917. He was buried in a field west of the village of Passchendaele. At first, Arthur was declared missing in action. He had been in charge of a Lewis gun and was considered cool and brave in all situations. At war's end, neither his body nor his burial place was found, so he is commemorated on the Menin Gate in Ypres.

Acting Sergeant Vincent Wilkinson MM of the 34th Battalion was also killed in the 3rd Battle of Passchendaele close to Ypres on 14 October 1917, two days after Arthur Dodd. On that occassion, Lance Corporal Wilkinson was acting officer-in-charge as his superior had been seriously wounded. A shell exploded and shrapnel struck him down, one piece cut through his wrist and the other through his heart. He died instantly.

Sergeant Bloomfield wrote: 'He was a brave boy and was well liked by his comrades and officers'. Vince had been recommended for promotion twice and had won the Military Medal. Had he lived, he would have received a commission.

His Military Medal was won at Messines Ridge. The communication lines were broken and he volunteered to re-establish them. He had run over 800 yards under intense rifle fire and shelling. He succeeded with great bravery. His body was never found and he is commemorated on the Menin Gate.

Trooper William Caldwell was killed in the Jordan Valley on 14 July 1918 and was buried in the Jerusalem War Cemetery. He was the only Cook's Hill Boy not to die on the Western Front.

William had undergone training in England in the School of Signallers, like Vince Wilkinson. He was killed when he was attached as a signaller to the 2nd Light Horse. He was involved in a ferocious conflict against the Turkish and German forces at Mussalabeh. After the attack began, Caldwell was on duty at the telephone in the dugout when a shell hit the parapet, wounding him. He died three hours later.

Before the war, Bill was an apprentice fitter-and-turner to the government railways in Newcastle. He lived in Merewether.

Sergeant Edward Curley seems to be the first of the Cook's Hill Boys to enlist on 11 May 1915. He was the only married man amongst the Club members who failed to return. He landed in Gallipoli and later was evacuated to hospital on the island of Lemnos with enteritis. He rejoined his unit on 18 September. On Gallipoli, he was in the assault on Hill 971 and Hill 60. It was four months on bully-beef and biscuits, with poor conditions and an appalling shortage of water.

His battalion was evacuated and disembarked in Marseilles to join the horrendous Battle of Pozières. It is a miracle he survived; the location seemed to have been breathed upon 'by Stromboli or Vesuvius' with the heavy German bombardment.

"Ted" was wounded in action in August 1915 and evacuated to England, rejoining his unit in France in May 1917 in the First Battle of Bullecourt. Wounded again in September, he was taken to the United States Hospital in Rouen. As tough as ironbark, he rejoined his unit the following month.

After 21 days leave, he took part in the defence of Amiens in the Battle of Villers-Bretonneux during the German Spring Offensive of 1918.

Ted wrote to his sister expressing his pride of the Battle of Villers-Bretonneux: 'I think I am able to say that our boys have done something in this war by saving one of the finest towns in France'. This seems to be his last letter home.

His final engagement was a turning point for the Allies — the 3rd Battle of Morlancourt. Ted, a bridge builder by trade, after surviving for so long, was hit by machine-gun bullets in August 1918. He had been caught in the merciless criss-cross lattice of flying bullets. Ted remained conscious and spoke to his comrades calmly telling them that he was 'gone'. He realised nothing could save him even though the war's end was in view. He was severely wounded in the thighs and died bravely thirty minutes later surrounded by his comrades.

Private William Carratt was nineteen when he was killed. He had been working on Walsh Island in Newcastle Harbour as an apprentice gas worker-fitter when he joined up.

He was involved in a series of "Mop-Up Battles" after the Allied breakthrough at Le Hamel on 4 July 1918 under Major General John Monash. On the day of Carratt's death, Chuignes had been captured in the big final push. Unfortunately, there was a German bullet with his name on it. When Bill, who was a runner, stopped to assist a wounded man on the road between Villers-Bretonneux and Péronne, he was mortally wounded.

After the capture of Mont St Quentin, the victory drums

began to sound. The price for victory was, however, far too high and would continue to resound throughout the years to come — *après la guerre*.

The Cook's Hill Boys who appear on the club's war memorial fought in the Battle of the Dardanelles and on the Western Front in the Battles at Fromelles, Messines Ridge, Pozières, Bullecourt, Menin Road, Passchendaele, Villers-Bretonneux, Morlancourt, Hamel and Chuignes. And in the Jordan Valley at Mussalabeh — thirteen battles, an unlucky number.

CHSLS Club members 1915; about 29 eligible men enlisted; Pte Antcliff standing tall behind the surf reel. He was killed in the Battle of Messines Ridge

Stan Veale and the Attack on German New Guinea

In a remarkable coincidence, Stan Veale of the then small, but elite Elwood Surf Life Saving Club in Melbourne, was responsible for ordering the first shot to be fired by Australian troops in both the 1914-1918 and the 1939-1945 wars.

On Wednesday, 5 August 1914 at 9am Melbourne time, Australia declared war on Germany. Just before midday, the

German ship *Pfatz* sailed down Port Phillip Bay in Melbourne towards the Heads and the open sea when the news reached the *Alvina*, the Port's Examination ship, that war had been declared. As *Pfatz* approached the Heads, Stan Veale – a volunteer sailor on board the deck of the *Alvina*, ordered that the 'H' flag be hoisted, signalling 'Hostile'. In response to this signal, the gunnery of the fort at Port Nepean fired a shot across the bows of the German vessel. That became the first shot fired by Australia in the Great War. The *Pfatz* was then captured, the crew became prisoners-of-war and the ship was later used as a transport vessel in the war.

In the Second World War, Veale was the Naval Extended Defence Officer in charge of the Bass Strait approaches to Port Phillip Bay. At 1.50pm on 4 September 1939, he gave the signal for a shot to be fired across the bows of a ship which had failed to identify itself. It turned out to be the Australian freighter SS *Woniora*. So it was the first shot fired by Australia in the Second World War, beit a mistake.

Richard Stanley Veale was born in 1893 and attended the Albert Park suburban school in Melbourne. He joined the Albert Park Swimming Club which eventually became the Albert Park Life Saving Club. After the war, he joined the Elwood SLS Club (as the Albert Park Club has been terminated) and became a qualified lifesaver with a Bronze Medallion. Interest in the life-saving movement influenced Stan, as he was universally known. On 30 April 1909, he joined the Commonwealth Naval Forces as a cadet. It became the Royal Australian Navy in 1913. After the *Pfatz* incident, Stan was promoted to midshipman and then he volunteered to serve with the Australian Naval and Military Expeditionary

Force in German New Guinea (see Chapter 2).

The force's intention was to destroy the dangerous wireless stations in German New Guinea which was a vital communication link with the German light cruiser fleet present in the Pacific and even in the Indian Ocean. It was a jungle battle with the German defences – the first Australian battle of the Great War. Veale was placed in charge of a field gun firing at the enemy.

There were other surf lifesavers in the Expedition: Walter Smith from the Clovelly Club; John CL Holland, Nelson C Smith and Herman Stiefvater from the Manly Club (that is, the South Steyne Club).

After returning to Australia at the height of the war, Veale served in the Royal Navy in the Pacific, Chinese and the East Indian Stations of the British Empire. After WWI, he served in the Royal Australian Navy Reserve and the Royal Australian Naval Volunteer Reserve. Thus the value of volunteerism in the surf lifesaving movement stayed with him all his life.

In 1919 with the war over, Veale joined the Elwood SLSC. In it, he held a number of senior elected positions, including President. In 1935, he was elected as a life member and a life governor of the Victorian branch of the Royal Life Saving Association.

He served in the Royal Navy in the Second Word War based in Australia. In 1945, he was promoted to commander and appointed Director of Naval Recruiting. He received the Volunteer Reserved Decoration (VRD) twice. He was transferred to the retired officers list in 1952, thus ending 43 years' service with the Royal Australian Navy.

In 1979, the Queen appointed him as a Companion of

the Most Distinguished Order of St Michael and St George, recognising his service to the Royal Life Saving Society and the interests of ex-service personnel.[17]

Garnet Dart, Cook's Hill SLSC founder, 9th Ambulance Co, 1st AIF

Garnet Dart and his Welcome Home medal

During the 1914-15 swimming and surfing season at Bar Beach, Newcastle, the Cook's Hill Life Saving and Surf Club held a 'Smoke Concert' – for men only – to farewell three of their members who had volunteered to fight for King and Empire overseas in the Australian Imperial Force. It was one of a series of 'Smoke Concerts' during the surfing season to farewell their members who volunteered. Nine were never to return. They died in action on the Northern hemisphere battlefields of the Great War.

On this occasion, the three young men were Lindsay Pike, the club's Vice-Captain, Frederick Dodd, a member of the managing committee and Garnet 'Gunner' Dart,[18] the Club's Treasurer and Assistant Instructor. Frederick and Garnet had

17 Vesper, *Those who served*, 136.

18 'Gunner' was chosen as his nickname by the Club because of his military bearing, perhaps his distinctive parade-ground voice and his service in the Great War.

worked closely on the Club's committee whose minutes record that they frequently seconded each other's motions about practical matters to improve lifesaving organisation. Each of these departing soldiers was presented with a 'token of regard and good will' – a shaving outfit in a smart portable leather case – presented by the Chief Instructor, David Thompson as Club Secretary. David Hall Thompson was the original founder in 1911 and a devoted member of the Royal Lifesaving Society. It was noted in the minutes that the three recipients were 'much overcome' by the remarks and enthusiasm of those comrades present.

A forth recipient was absent: James 'Big Jim' Hartley Antcliff, the Club Captain and hero of surf rescues and competition events. He had had to leave for overseas earlier, preventing him from attending the presentation held in his honour with the other three. It is estimated that at least twenty-nine members of the relatively small club served overseas – nearly all of those who were eligible to join the 1st AIF.

Of the four young men honoured at the 'Smoko', three were to return after the war in 1919: Garnet Dart, Frederick Dodd and Lindsay Pike. Private James Antcliff of the 36th Battalion was tragically killed in action in the Battle of Messines Ridge in Flanders on 7 June 1917. He was buried in the Toronto Avenue Cemetery, Belgium. Also killed in action was Frederick Dodd's brother, Corporal Arthur Dodd, on 12 October 1916 in the Battle of Passchendaele. He is commemorated on the Menin Gate Memorial. But this particular story is about Garnet Dart who had a unique war experience.

Before Garnet left for overseas, the Surf Club presented

him with a small pure gold engraved medal for his tireless services to the Club as a coach for the three full foundation seasons: 1912-13, 1913-14 and 1914-15. This medal recognised Garnet as a leading foundational member of the Club. The only other gold medal to be awarded was to David Thompson at the same 'Smoko' of 22 July 1915.[19] Garnet had a significant role as the Club's pioneering Treasurer (1911 -12) and as an instructor and administrator in its early years.

When he returned from overseas in 1919, he received another small gold medallion – this one from the Newcastle West (NW) and Cooks Hill (CH)(suburbs) Returned Soldiers Welcome Home Committee as part of a crowded welcome at Newcastle Railway Station. It has a figure of a soldier holding a rifle on one side and, underneath, the caption: 'Welcome Home'. The other side is inscribed: 'G. Dart –Duty–Done for King & Country 1914-1918'. These two memories of important events must have been treasured by Garnet as they were left when he died and found among his effects by his son, Bruce. With the passing of time, however, Garnet's achievements have been forgotten.

Garnet Wilton Dart was born on 14 April 1893 in Newcastle in the County of Northumberland in New South Wales. When he signed his Attestation Papers to enlist for service overseas, he was twenty-two years and seven months. He had already served three years in the local militia training for war while working. He was employed as a clerk for the New South Wales Railways stationed in Newcastle. His father was James Dart, a Newcastle solicitor, of 41

19 'Annual Smoko Concert', 22 July 1915, Record Book 1911-1915, Cooks Hill SLS Archives, Newcastle.

Queen Street, Cooks Hill, in the old inner-city working-class industrial suburb. His mother was Sarah (née McLue). James and Sarah had nine children, four girls and five boys including Garnet. Garnet's father was one of the original patrons of Cooks Hill Life Saving and Surf Club. He took part at the first meeting of the Returned Soldiers Welcome Committee on 10 December 1918 and recommended that 'there should be some big function organised by the committee' to welcome the men back from the war. It was realised that they would be repatriated in small numbers.[20]

Garnet had convinced himself in 1915 that he could not kill another human being, even if he was an enemy German soldier. This decision influenced him to join the Australian Imperial Force's 9th Field Ambulance Company so that he could make a positive contribution to the war effort. He became the only known Cook's Hill lifesaver to join the AIF Field Ambulance and follow the lifesaving principles he had learnt in such an organisation.

On 2 December 1915 at Casula, Liverpool, he swore that he would 'well and truly' serve the 'sovereign Lord the King' in the Australian Imperial Force until the end of the War and a further period of four months thereafter, unless lawfully discharged before then – which he did 'faithfully' to the end. He pledged to resist His Majesty's enemies, which he did indirectly by protecting wounded Australian soldiers and risking his own life. Thus he 'faithfully' discharged his duties in the 9th Field Ambulance of the 3rd Division, AIF.

Garnet was a fit, compact, strongly built, muscular man of

---

20 'Soldiers' Welcome Committee', *Newcastle Morning Herald and Miners' Advocate*, 11 December 1818, 6.

5ft 5 inches in height. At his medical examination, he weighed at 142 pounds. He was described as having a dark or olive complexion, brown eyes and black hair and was a 'Methodist' by denomination. The medical officer approved of his appointment with the 9th Field Ambulance. Garnet appeared capable of doing the heavy lifting that would be required.

Arriving in Liverpool, Garnet was placed for a couple of days (2/12/15 to 5/12/15) in E Camp Depot at Casula and then spent three months training in the Field Hospital, Liverpool (6/12/15 to 7/3/16). Tent life with eight or so companions was a new experience.

Before long he was ready for overseas duties in the 9th Field Ambulance Unit which was attached to the 3rd Division AIF. There seemed no question that he should not be a vital part of a field ambulance.

Garnet Dart embarked from Sydney with the rest of the 9th Field Ambulance on the transport A8 *Argyllshire* which sailed on 11 May 1916. The 3rd Division were the last major unit to leave Australia. From then on replacements were sent in drafts.[21] Technically, Garnet was part of the regular infantry as a private. His registered number was 11945 determined on 2 February 1915. The army had the power to transfer him to any unit within the infantry.

He was revaccinated (No 3) on the left arm on 2 November 1915. When he returned to Australia after the war was over, he was demobilised on 8 August 1919 as still being fit without injury,[22] unlike many others.

21 Jeffrey Grey, *The Australian Army*, vol 1, Oxford University Press, 2001, 59.

22 Garnet Dart, Attestation Papers and War Record, National Archives of Australia.

During the Great War, Dart was to face dangerous frontline action on the Western Front where his job was to remove or transport the wounded, the dying and the dead from harm's way on the battlefields in No Man's Land and get them, by any means possible and as quickly as possible, to an Advanced Dressing Station, still close to the Front. This involved applying first aid – field dressings – to many seriously wounded men before transporting them on to a Field Hospital further back, but still within the sound of incessant gunfire.

Garnet's unit was entirely made up of male volunteers from New South Wales. It was formally raised at Liverpool during March 1916 when the disaster of Gallipoli had filtered back to faraway Australia. When the main contingent on the *Argyllshire* reached Southampton and England, they then completed further vigorous and exhausting training on the vast, windy and desolate Salisbury Plain. They were then moved to France and the Western Front on 23 November 1916.

They arrived in Steenwerck, Belgium Flanders, on the 27th. Their first task was to build and establish a tented Field Hospital to cater for the medical needs of the 3rd Australian Division. They also organised medical units in Pont de Nieppe to provide cleansing baths for Australian troops from the trenches in a former jute factory. The baths played a significant part in the rehabilitation and health of the weary Australian frontline troops.

The Company soon found themselves on the Ramparts of Ypres. Around them, the guns thudded, relentlessly. Then they moved down the Zonnebeke Road closer to the action where they were pooled with other units and equipped with a horse-drawn ambulance that was kept extremely busy during the 3rd Battle of Passchendaele.

The 9th worked mainly on the Ypres-Zonnebeke Road. They lived precariously under canvas with a constant undercurrent of fear of bombardment. The wounded were brought along the road on stretchers with two ambulance men or four, the handles slung on their shoulders in the all-pervasive mud, slipping and sliding and sometimes wading. When they reached the Advanced Dressing Station, the ambulance men frantically dressed the wounds of the frequently unconscious or delirious, so they could be moved on to the Field Hospital if they were able to survive long enough. Colonel AT White, the Chief Medical Officer of the 3rd Division, was awaiting the arrival of patients at the hospital with his colleagues and nurses.[23]

Sometimes, it took even more ambulance men to get the wounded on stretchers through the waist-deep treacherous mud. Other wounded were piggy-backed into the Advanced Dressing Station especially when they had frostbite or trench foot injuries. The work was so intense and difficult that some wounded had to be left outside on the ground on stretchers until they could be attended to. There were often queues along the roadside. Transporting the wounded was highly dangerous and, occasionally, ambulance troops received a bullet with their name on it and became part of the massive numbers of wounded or dead. Some of the walking wounded were able to find their own way to an Advanced Dressing Station and were met by the ambulance men, but those who were blinded or otherwise badly disabled had

---

23 Colonel Robert Likeman, *Australian Doctors on the Western Front*, Rosenberg, Dural, 2014, 27, 37, 107, 128, 308, 311.

to be escorted in – sometimes in a small convoy of slow-moving men endangered by machine guns and rifle fire.

The well-known symbol for an Advanced Dressing Station where ambulance men had to work tirelessly was a white cross on a black background in a circle. An Advanced Dressing Station with its distinctive sign was sometimes held in a cellar of a demolished or bombed out building below the ground level, often in a very confined space.[24]

The finest and most perceptive war artist Will Dyson was one of the few to depict in graphic terms what it was like to be in an Australian Ambulance unit. The two ambulance infantrymen in *Stretcher-Bearers near Martinpuich* are straining every muscle to carry a heavy wounded man on a stretcher through extremely rugged terrain with the smoke of gunfire around them (AWM No 16450). The strain and exhaustion on the faces of the two men is vividly captured.

The biggest problem that Garnet Dart and all members of the 9th Field Ambulance had to face was wound shock and haemorrhage. And yet the tenacity of life, as Garnet noticed, inherent in the human body was a constant source of amazement and even a major source of inspiration. People like Garnet were able to save many lives by their ready support and yet they received little reward and even less recognition in the annals of war. They were the forgotten heroes in the chaos of modern industrial warfare. A photograph, taken on 10 October 1917, was one of the few showing the 9th Ambulance on the Front at the height of the war in Flanders. Its caption poignantly reads 'Stretcher-bearers

24 Colonel AG Butler, *The Australian Army Medical Services in the War of 1914-1918*, vol II, Australian War Memorial, Canberra, 1940, 68-229, 959.

of the 9th Field Ambulance worn out on the Zonnebeke Railway Embankment'. It is possible that Garnet Dart could have been one of these men. In the midst of a wasted land, four ambulance men are stretched out in various positions sleeping soundly on the earth, their faces completely obscured by their protective helmets (AWM Official Photo No E941).

The 9th Field Ambulance set up a large Advanced Dressing Station for the wounded of the 3rd Australian Division (ANZAC) at White (Potyze) Chateau, but they had their headquarters in the former Ypres criminal prison on the ramparts. Later moving further south into France, they set up Advanced Dressing Stations for the Allied wounded near the Battle of Villers-Bretonneux where they tended many badly wounded and dying soldiers.[25]

The final action before the War's end for the 9th Ambulance was on the Hindenburg Line where they were kept particularly busy up until Armistice Day,[26] on the eleventh hour of the eleventh day of November 1918. The unlucky wounded on that day continued to be brought in from the battlefields.

Sometime later, the men of the 9th Field Ambulance were moved back to England to prepare for eventual repatriation to Australia and sometimes a troubled return to civilian life after seeing so much blood and gore, so much suffering of the wounded that they cared for in dangerous situations.

While in England, Garnet Dart, with some friends, seems to have been able to visit Newcastle-on-Tyne in the north while on leave, as a solitary postcard photograph held by his son Bruce attests.

25 Likeman, *Australian Doctors*, 307.
26 Likeman, *Australian Doctors*, 311.

The British Government awarded Garnet William Dart the 1914 Star, the British War Medal and the Victory Medal. On his arrival back in Newcastle, New South Wales, as already related, he was awarded a small Welcome Home medal.

At his final medical examination with the AIF on 8 August 1919, Garnet was required to write: 'I am not suffering from any disability due to or aggravated by War service. I am feeling fit and well'. On the same day, Garnet's statement was countersigned by the medical officer Captain Roy Tindale. He was then demobilised in Sydney.[27]

Return to Newcastle

On his return to civilian life, Garnet relished being once again heavily involved in the senior management of the Cook's Hill Life Saving and Surf Club as he had been in its foundation years before the war. By 1926 he was the Club's Instructor-in-chief – the Club's *Supremo* – and had become locally famous for his winning Cook's Hill March Past teams at surf carnivals. He continued to take the Club's motto "Excelsior" seriously. With these vigorous pioneers like Garnet, the Club went on to bigger and better things almost despite the Great War in which the vast majority of eligible members had fought on foreign battlefields. By the early 1920s reliant on Garnet's astute instruction, Cook's Hill became the most vital and successful

Always a major contributor to the lifesaving community, Garnet Wilton Dart received (as related) from the Cook's Hill Club at the 1915 annual Smoke Concert an engraved gold medal. The awards he was granted by the Royal Life

27 War Record.

Saving Society were the Elementary Certificate; Proficiency Certificate; Bronze Medallion; Teacher's Certificate and the Hon. Instructor's Certificate.[28] Thus he became one of the most qualified lifesavers in New South Wales. The Cook's Hill Club recognised his outstanding contribution by awarding him Life Membership.

For Garnet Dart, a vigorous community life had returned to him as before the war, but the haunting memories remained for many years. As the war artist Will Dyson described:

> They move with their stretchers like boats on a slowly tossing sea, rising and falling with the shell riven contours of what was yesterday no man's land, slipping, sliding, with heels worn raw by the downward suck of the Somme mud. [...] The fountains that sprout roaring at their feet fall back to earth in a lace-work of fragments – the smoke clears and they, momentarily obscured, are moving on as they were moving on before: a piece of mechanism guiltless of the weakness of weak flesh, one might say. But to say this is to rob them their heroism of its due – of the credit that goes to inclinations conquered and panic subdued down in the privacy of the soul. It is to make their heroism look like a thing they find easy [...] they are heroes because someone has got to be heroic.[29]

Apart from the Great War years, Garnet Wilton Dart served out his entire working career as a clerk on the New South Wales Government Railways rising to Timekeeper

28 *The Royal Life Saving Society Handbook* (founded 1891), London, nd, 14.

29 Ross McMullin, *Will Dyson. Cartoonist, etcher and Australia's finest war artist*, Angus & Robertson, Sydney, 1984, 182-3.

and Paymaster at Tyrrell House, Telford Street, Newcastle – after which he retired. On 9 July 1962 at the age of 69 years, he passed away, a Great War survivor. He had two sons, Ronald Garnet and Bruce, and a daughter, Norma Jean. On most days of his life, he swam to keep fit following the ideals of lifesaving. He was a well-respected and liked member of the Newcastle community during his lifetime. Like many others, he kept his 1914–1918 frontline wartime experiences to himself and rarely talked about them.

Sir Frank H McNamara of the Elwood SLS Club

A sudden roar, a mighty rushing sound,
a jolt or two, a smoothly sliding rise,
a tumbled blur of disappearing ground,
and then all sense of motion slowly dies.
Quiet and calm, and earth slips past below,
as underneath a bridge still waters flow.

Jeffrey Day, "On the Wings of the Morning"

Sir Frank McNamara VC as a young aviator in the Australian Flying Corps, 1st AIF, 1916. He was a member of the Elwood SLS Club (*Those who served*, 135)

Frank McNamara had a unique and distinguished long-term military career in both world wars, in the First AIF as part of the Australian Flying Corps, the Royal Australian Air Force (RAAF) and the Royal Air Force (RAF) in not an uncommon arrangement for long-term appointments. He was awarded the Victoria Cross and Knighted. He is the only surf lifesaver (Elwood Club) to be awarded a VC for gallantry – as far as is known – as well as being surf lifesaving's most distinguished aviator.

Despite the appallingly heavy casualty rate for pilots in the struggle for air supremacy during the Great War, the air battle retained some of the glamour which was rapidly lost on land, whether on the Palestine deserts of the Middle East or on the Western Front. In the air, the most important role was reconnaissance; the second role was shooting down enemy aircraft and also some primitive efforts at bombing. It was, nevertheless, a theatre for some good, clear heroics, according to many.[30]

Francis (Frank) Hubert McNamara was born in 1894 in the small impoverished Victorian town of Rushworth, near Bendigo, which had been founded in the 1850s goldrush and developed as a timber town and then a dairying district. His father William was a forester in the timber industry. He married Rosanna O'Meara in 1892 and Frank was their first child who was soon joined by five brothers and two sisters. The whole family attended Mass at the local Catholic Church.

As a boy, Frank was a carefree trickster and adventurer even in the church. He would get his young school friends to take up the front pew and call "Amen" before the priest completed the prayers. He and a team of ten-year-old boys got lost bushwalking. By the time they were found at midnight, the search party noticed Frank in charge of the group around a fire; they had even trapped a small rabbit for their evening meal.

---

30 John Percival, *For Valour. The Victoria Cross, Courage in action*, Thames Methuen, London, 1985, 77.

Despite many mischievous exploits, Frank was a gifted scholar who usually topped his year. He went on to win a scholarship to Stepparton Agricultural High where he excelled.

In 1910, his father was promoted in his company to deputy chief land valuer and the family moved to an imposing house in one of Melbourne's more affluent suburbs.[31] At this stage, Frank, a good athlete and swimmer, joined the Elwood SLS Club and was successful in achieving his Bronze Medallion from the Royal Life Saving Association.[32]

McNamara joined the senior cadets in the local militia – 46th Infantry Battalion Brighton Rifles – when compulsory military training was introduced by the Commonwealth of Australia on 1 July 1911.

He completed his education at Melbourne Continuation (High) School in 1910 and the following year he joined the state Victorian Education Department and became a junior or apprentice school teacher. In 1914, he successfully completed all the requirements for the two-year Trained Teachers Certificate with the Victorian Department and was a relief teacher at a number of state schools during the first half of 1915 as many other teachers enlisted in the 1st AIF, causing a teacher shortage.[33] After the war, he completed a Bachelor of Arts with First Class Honours part-time.

Frank had been at Melbourne Teachers Training College completing his teacher's certificate when the war broke out. He was promoted to lieutenant in the Brighton Rifles on

31 Staunton, *Victoria Cross*, 47-49; Robert Macklin, *Bravest. Australia's greatest war heroes and how they won their medals*, Allen & Unwin, Sydney, 2011, 84-93.

32 Vesper, *Those who served*, 135.

33 Staunton, *Victoria Cross*, 47.

1 July 1915 – already his powers of leadership were being recognised. Frank then applied to attend a course on 'military aeronautics' and was accepted at the Cook Point Central Flying School in August 1915. The School had been founded in 1912 and opened to train pilots in February 1914 before the war began as part of the Permanent Military Forces. Frank was totally captivated by the notion of flying.[34]

From Cook Point Flying School members of the Australian Flying Corps were sent to various theatres of war overseas – a half-flight to Mesopotamia and eventually four squadrons fought in the Middle East, as did McNamara, and on the Western Front between 1916 and 1918.[35]

On 18 September 1915, Frank made his first solo flight at the Flying School and his first forced landing three weeks later. While still pretty raw and inexperienced, but extremely enthusiastic, he and his No 1 Squadron embarked on the liner *Orsova* for the Middle East. When they arrived in Suez, they were immediately attached to the Royal Flying Corps station in Egypt and accommodated at Heliopolis for further training on older Avro 504A biplanes. Frank McNamara was among a group who were sent to England for more intensive training due to their lack of military experience.

They then returned to Heliopolis on 24 August and were somewhat dismayed that No 1 Squadron had only been allotted to fly the notorious BE2c, best known ironically to the German flyers as 'Fokker fodder'.

Frank had a brief illness, popularly known as 'pharaoh's revenge'. When he recovered, he flew on his first sortie in

34 Macklin, *Bravest*, 85.

35 Douglas Gillison, *Royal Australian Air Force 1939-1942*, Australian War Memorial, Canberra, 1960, 1.

October, carrying out reconnaissance over the Sinai of the Turkish Army. His aircraft was hit by ground fire, but he was unaware of it until he got back to base. He landed as the last of his oil ran out. His commanding officer was reported as having said: 'You must have the luck of a Chinaman', but indicated, nevertheless, that he was impressed.[36]

The next two months saw the British and Australian flyers moved closer to Palestine. The Ottoman Empire had established large forces in Gaza and its surrounds. By this time in December 1915, the Allies as a whole including the Anzacs had been forced from Gallipoli. The Anzacs were then sent mainly to the Western Front and more Turkish troops were thus freed up from Gallipoli for Palestine.

This threatened British power in Egypt which was nominally neutral, but housing large Allied forces including the Light Horse and squadrons of Australian Flying Corps. The British with the Australian Forces under them were able to defend the Suez Canal, but the growing Turkish army presented a huge threat.

Under newly-appointed General Edmund Allenby, who was an outstanding tactician, British hopes were revived and his battle plans made good use of aeroplanes. As the Allied troops moved into Turkish-held territory, No 1 Squadron moved up along the Sinai's coastal plain in close support.

At dawn on 9 January 1916, McNamara took off with Ross Smith as observer to provide aerial support for a major land attack.[37] They reported on enemy troop deployment which led to the success of the Australian Light Horse being

36 Macklin, *Bravest*, 86-87.

37 Ross Smith and his brother Keith would later become celebrated aviators for making the first flight from London to Australia in 1919.

able to encircle the Turkish defenders. Later in the day, Rafa was overrun and the way was cleared for a further advance towards Gaza and Beersheba, the terminal Turkish railway. Such air reconnaissance was proving an important asset to the field commanders and their supremo, General Allenby. Their work soon became central to the whole campaign and Allenby's ultimate success. But during the campaign, German anti-aircraft defence became increasingly effective.

After his dangerous sorties on several occasions, McNamara would find patterns of bullet holes all over his wings. Moving towards Gaza, Lieutenant Francis Hubert McNamara was one of a small group of flyers in No 1 Squadron piloting one of two Martisydes recently delivered by British authorities. These carried Howitzer shells in place of bombs. The shells were timed to explode 40 seconds after release.

McNamara was taking part in a raid on a railway junction at Ramleh with others when one of his shells caught in the release section and then exploded 9 metres below his aeroplane. Shrapnel burst upwards and hit the pilot in the legs and buttocks, inflicting some serious, but not life-threatening wounds. When he recovered his plane and himself, he turned immediately to go back to base. He was bleeding profusely from his buttocks and struggled to keep control of the plane.

As he turned for home, he saw a member of his squadron had come down in distress in enemy territory beside the Turkish railway line. The pilot in it had detonated a smoke bomb as a distress signal for others to help. McNamara observed some Turkish cavalry had spotted the downed plane and were starting to head towards it from some distance in the desert.

Despite being under heavy rifle fire from closer Turkish infantry defence, he put his aircraft into a steep dive through enemy fire and made for a level area near the railway line to land and assist his comrade. The downed pilot was Captain Douglas Rutherford, a Queenslander who had served in the Light Horse on Gallipoli before transferring to the Australian Flying Corps. It was only his second mission against hostile forces and he was inexperienced, but eager.

While standing orders were to set fire to your plane if downed in enemy territory, Rutherford did not have time to start before McNamara landed. When he noticed McNamara was not getting out of his plane, he ran towards the single-seated Martinsyde. When he got there, he asked if McNamara could help him re-start his BE2c which, at least, had a second seat for the passenger. McNamara realised, however, that there was no time as the Turkish cavalry were galloping towards them. He was not even sure he could climb out of his cockpit because of his wounds. So Rutherford climbed on the lower wing of the plane and sprawled across the cowling of the engine to grab a strut on the other side.

McNamara opened his throttle to full power, pumped the rudder and skidded around to face the wind to take off with Rutherford hanging on desperately. Unfortunately, Rutherford's weight – he was a heavily-built man – unbalanced the frail craft and McNamara was unable to work one leg properly. The plane veered dangerously and began heading for a gully at about 50km/h. McNamara struggled with the controls and throttled back, but it was too late. The Martinsyde skidded into a gully where rocks ripped the lower left wing and tore away the undercarriage.

Neither man was injured in this situation. Their wild ride had taken them close to Rutherford's aircraft which had lost a tyre in the forced landing. Otherwise, it did not seem too damaged. It also boasted a Lewis gun for self-defence. By now, the Turk cavalry were in rifle range and bullets began flying around the two Australians. Rutherford assisted McNamara out of his plane. No sooner than they were heading towards the BE2c, McNamara's own plane received a bullet that hit the remaining bomb which exploded. The men continued to stagger together toward the BE2c.

Two others of the Squadron in the clouds above started diving towards the cavalry, slowing them down by firing as they went, to assist the men's escape. This gave Rutherford and McNamara enough breathing space to reach the plane. Rutherford helped McNamara into the cockpit. He tried to use the Lewis gun against the oncoming Turkish horsemen, but his field of fire was restricted, so he drew his revolver to keep them at bay. Meanwhile, Rutherford took up position standing beside the heavy bladed propeller for protection, while firing a couple of rounds at the marauders. Then McNamara signalled him and Rutherford gave a mighty heave of the propeller. Remarkably, it fired immediately and McNamara coaxed the engine into a mighty roar. Rutherford scrambled onto the lower wing and hung on tight. McNamara set off to level ground with the broken wheel, followed closely by the Turkish cavalry wildly shouting and shooting. Bullets swished around the two intrepid Australians. Frank McNamara held his course, opened the throttle and eased the plane into the air, away from danger before the cavalry reached them.

It was, however, only the beginning of the ordeal McNamara faced; they had about 120kms to get back to their base. His natural adrenalin soon faded now that the urgent physical action was over. But he had to pilot the plane as he bled with the inevitable waves of pain that came. His legs were stiffening. Again and again, he felt on the verge of fainting and was forced to put his head out into the 'ice-cold slipstream' to clear his mind from shut-down.[38]

On the wing, Rutherford shouted encouragement while holding on tightly. The journey in the sky seemed endless, but McNamara hung on with great determination. His spirit of adventure and *joie de vivre* kept him going. He put the plane down safely even with its broken wheel and promptly passed out as he switched off the engine. He was carried off the aircraft with three unexploded shells underneath by the anxious ground crew. The plane was pockmarked all over with bullet holes.

Rutherford was relatively unharmed. McNamara was rushed by ambulance to a base hospital and the standard anti-tetanus injection. Unknown to the medical staff, he was violently allergic to the drug and collapsed towards near-death experience. The surgeon later reflected: 'He was absolutely blue and cold, no pulse at all'. The doctor started artificial respiration. After half an hour, it seemed he gave a tiny breath – Death did not claim him. He was given an adrenalin shot with a hypodermic needle. His mouth was gagged open and his tongue was wagged to and fro. About an hour later, the blue vanished from his face and he was breathing slowly; in two hours, he was almost recovered from the close call,

38 Macklin, *Bravest*, 88-91.

breathing quietly and even talking. Later in the night, he was eating a plate of chicken and drinking champagne.

In the meanwhile, Rutherford had returned to combat and was involved in a similar incident soon after. This time, he and his rescuers were captured by the Turks and made prisoners-of-war.

On 20 April, Frank McNamara was promoted to captain and appointed flight commander of No 4 Squadron based in London. He was required to return to Australia to receive medical treatment. Before he left London, it was gazetted on 8 June 1917 that he was to be awarded the Victoria Cross for the action over Gaza, Palestine on 20 March 1917.

In 1921, the Royal Australian Air Force (RAAF) was formed and Frank McNamara was quick to enlist.

He served from then on, right through to the end of the Second World War in both the RAAF and on exchange to the RAF. He retired with the rank of Air Vice Marshal and made Britain his home. He was made a Companion of the Order of the Bath in 1945. He died of a heart attack at the age of 67 and was buried in St Joseph's Priory Austin Wood in Gerrads Cross, Buckinghamshire. His VC medal is held at the RAF Museum in Hendon, London.[39]

McNamara was the first WWI Australian airman to receive the Victoria Cross and the sole Australian VC recipient of the Palestine campaign.[40] As far as can be ascertained, he was the only registered surf lifesaver to receive the same award.[41]

The life savers represent the very highest class. They are

39 Robert Hamilton, *Victoria Cross Heroes of World War I*, Atlantic Publishing, Hertfordshire, 2015, 197.

40 Staunton, *Victoria Cross*, 47.

41 Vesper, *Those who served*, 134.

Harrold Hardwick, Manly Surf champion who won a gold and two bronze medals at the 1912 Stockholm Olympic Games. He fought in the 1st AIF in the 1914-1918 War. (State Library of NSW)

the Samurais, the oligarchs, the elite. They strut the beaches with superiority that is insolent, yet, at the same time, tolerant of the shortcomings of the lesser breed – a gladiator caste, envied by all men, adored by all women.

Egbert Russell, 'Australia's Amphibians', *Lone Hand*, I January 1910

Cecil Healy: A Soldier of the Surf

The Battle of Mont St Quentin was where Lieutenant Cecil Patrick Healy had his first and last experience of frontline fighting. A German defence line on the crest of a hill had just been overrun. Healy's unit began to pass over the crest and descend towards the river, coming in view for a moment of the old town of Péronne below with 'its ramparts and battlemented towers', the three wooded hills behind it, 'the wide brow and scrubby pate' of Mont St Quentin to the north and the rolling hills to the south. At that moment, German batteries on the farther side of the river plastered the slopes with shell bursts as they moved down.

On the 2nd Australian Division's Front, the woods were still held by dangerous and well-placed German machine-gun nests. Rushing one of these nests, Captain Bice of the 27th Battalion was shot through the eye. Soon after, Lieutenant

Healy pointed out another nest. After being wounded, he charged, only to be cut down and killed by a rain of bullets.[42] Charles Bean described Healy as being a commercial traveller and journalist, but he was much more than that – not just a champion swimmer of Darlinghurst, but a famed internationally-known Olympian.

A letter, dated September 5, 1918 was sent to a friend by a comrade who was an eye-witness to Cecil Healy's tragic death. It provides more specific detail than Charles Bean:

> … he was struck by a machine-gun bullet in the neck, and while lying wounded a burst of machine-gun fire got him in the right breast. He died about an hour after he was hit (between 7 and 8 am) near Péronne on August 29, during the preliminary stages of our attack on that place. He made good right from the start, and all the men and officers who were near him talk of his coolness and gallantry. I knew he would do well, and it is a thousand pities that he didn't get an opportunity of going farther after starting off so brilliantly. It was his first 'stunt', and unfortunately his last, which, by the way, was rather a brilliant performance by our troops. Jim McManamey, Doc Wallach, and Cecil Healy, three prominent New South Wales sportsmen, died with the same battalion.[43]

Healy was one of Australia's first Olympic swimmers. He won a silver medal at the 1912 Stockholm Games under extraordinary circumstances. It is not only this, however, or his many well-publicised deeds in the still-water baths, or

42 CEW Bean, *Official History of Australia in the War of 1914-1918. The AIF in France 1918*, vol VI, Angus & Robertson, Sydney, 1942, 783.
43 Cited in *SMH*, 30 October 1918.

the fact that he perfected the 'Australian crawl' for long-distance races that warrants attention. He had played a significant role in the development of the skill of body surfing at Manly and other Sydney beaches.

His achievements at the Stockholm Games enhanced the amateur tradition of heroic sportsmanship that Australians have worked into the fabric of their national identity. The Sportsmen's Battalions in the 1st AIF were established during the Great War with the belief that competitive sport was a glorious preparation for war.[44]

Healy's commissioning as a second lieutenant in the 19th Sportsmen's Battalion and his subsequent death in the frontline in his initial action contributed to this great Anzac tradition. The nature of his life and death was taken up by the Sydney popular press and placed in the public domain. By his death, however, Healy was spared the disillusion that was to touch so many committed Australians, especially ex-servicemen, during the interwar years.

News of Healy's enlistment on 15 September 1915 was taken up by the press as another page of wartime propaganda. A lengthy article about his life and achievements quickly followed in a March 1916 edition of the *Lone Hand* and, after his death, was reprinted in a 1919 memoriam edition.

Born on 23 November 1882 in Darlinghurst as the third son of a prominent Sydney barrister, Patrick Joseph Healy, and his wife, Anne Louisa (née Gallot), Cecil was provided with a fair start in life. Educated in a private enterprise boys school in Bowral on the southern highlands, he made his first

44 Murray Phillips, 'Football, Class and War: the Rugby Codes in New South Wales, 1907-1918', in John Naurigh & Timothy JL Chandler (eds), *Making Men: Rugby and Masculine Identity*, Routledge, London, 1996.

appearance in the media as an amateur competitive swimmer in 1895, when he won a silver cup for a 66 yard handicap in Sydney's old Natatorium. He then joined the elite East Sydney Amateur Swimming Club and determinedly built on his initial success to the point that by 1905 he was Australasian 100 yards champion, 'equalling the then world's record of fifty-eight seconds'.[45] He was also NSW champion on several occasions in the 1900s.

According to the *Lone Hand* article, 1906 was a particularly good year for Healy:

> [He] represented Australia at the [unofficial] Olympic Games held in Athens in 1906, but was beaten by Daniels, the meteoric American sprinter, and De Halmay, of Hungary. He would probably have done better had he not made such a hurried departure, which left him only a short time to prepare. A few weeks afterwards he almost dead-heated Daniels in the 100 yards Championship of England, and vanquished De Malmay … in the same event, although the swim was in a short baths, necessitating two turns. In the same season he gained the 220 yards Championship of England, afterwards visiting Scotland and Ireland, where he won more swimming honours and established new records for those countries. He met similar success in Paris, winning the 100 metres International Scratch Race in record time for France, also winning a 200 metres race in two minutes thirty seconds, which, under the conditions of the race – turning on a rope

45 'Cecil Healy: Swimmer and Soldier', *Lone Hand*, 1 March 1916; reprinted in H Healy, *Cecil Healy: in Memoriam*, Sydney, nd (certainly 1919).

> – was described by Mr Wm Henry, the great English swimming authority, as being equal to the world's best time for the distance.[46]

That year, Healy went on to other great honours during an international tour in European baths, but, it was claimed, he 'went to too much trouble in teaching the crawl stroke to swimmers of other countries, where it was practically unknown', and thereby demonstrating an exceptional generosity in a competitive sport. Other swimmers had begun to catch up with him.

Healy returned to Australia committed to perfecting the crawl stroke for long distance events, 'hitherto only used [experimentally] for sprinting'. A successful test came with his 1911 race against the great Frank Beaurepaire, 'the world famous Victorian', over the three-quarter mile course at Sydney's Domain Baths. Here an Australian record crowd assembled excitedly to watch the event and barrack for their hero. Both champions, however, were upstaged by the 'almost unknown' William Longworth, but Healy still beat Beaurepaire for second place. The following year, an Olympic year, was to prove to be Healy's greatest triumph.[47]

At the 1912 Stockholm Olympics, as a member of the Australasian four-man swimming team, Healy won a gold medal for the 800 metres Teams Championship and won a silver medal in the 100 metres final event, being narrowly defeated by the great American champion Duke Kahanamoku of Hawaii:

46 'Cecil Healy: Swimmer and Soldier'.
47 'Cecil Healy: Swimmer and Soldier'.

> In the semi-final of the 100 metres, Kahanamoku and two other American representatives did not, through some misunderstanding, make their appearance on the starting board, and the semi-final was swum without them, and resulted in Healy and Longworth from Australia, and Ramme and Bretting, of Germany, qualifying for the final. The position was a difficult one for the officials, and the matter was referred to the International Jury to decide. Healy strongly urged the Australian representative to insist on the Americans be given an opportunity to compete in the final, insisting that it would be unsportsmanlike to bar their entry. Finally, mainly owing to the Australian's attitude, and in spite of the opposition of the Germans, the Americans were allowed to compete in a special semi-final, with the result that Kahanamoku and McGillivray qualified for the final, in which the Hawaiian swimmer finished first and Healy second.[48]

Following another tour of Europe, where Healy's brilliant finishes became legendary, and writing a journal article wherein he predicted that war would cancel the 1916 Olympics, Healy returned to Australia a heroic sporting legend. He went on to champion the great virtues of popular body surfing, along with assembling more achievements in the tidal baths. The war came and Healy enlisted. His life was viewed by the press as a paradigm of the amateur sporting hero that warrants analysis.

Healy was 'one of the small band who battled for the right to surf at any hour of the day, which was strenuously

48 'Cecil Healy: Swimmer and Soldier'.

opposed by the local authorities'. He was a founder and inaugural captain of the original Manly Surf Club in July 1907 and 'as an exponent of the art of shooting the breakers there have been few better seen around our beaches'.[49] He never lived in Manly, but travelled by ferry to get to the surf and spend daylight hours on the beach followed by his fans.

A complete record of Healy's achievements in competitive swimming before the Great War dramatically defines his international status in the sport that led to his fame in Australia that lasted well after his death on the battlefield in 1918:

> 100 yds Champion Australasia 1904-5, 1905-6, 1907-8, 1908-9, 1909-10. Ex 220 yds Champion England and Australia : 100 yds, 220 yds, ex 300 yds, 440 yds and 500 yds Champion New South Wales; 100 yds, 220 yds, 440 yds and 500 yds Champion Tasmania; 100 yds, 100 metres, 200 yds, Australasian record holder. Winner International Scratch races, England, Scotland, Ireland, Germany, Belgium and Holland.[50]

In his 1944 official history of Australians in the Olympic Games, Harry Gordon documents in some detail Healy's deeds of sportsmanship at the Stockholm Games. According to Gordon, 'Healy gave a demonstration of the immaculate sportsmanship which characterised his career. He in fact sacrificed the prospect of an individual gold medal to ensure that his own version of justice was served'.[51] Like

49 'Cecil Healy: Swimmer and Soldier'.

50 Cecil Healy, 'The 'Crawl' Stroke. Art of Relaxation as applied to it', in Reg L ("Snowy") Baker, *General Physical Culture*, George Robertson & Co, Sydney, 1911, 42.

51 Harry Gordon, *Australia and the Olympic Games*, University of Queensland Press, Brisbane, 1994, 86-87.

Mark Taylor's great knock of 394 not out against the Pakistani XI during the 1998 tour, equalling Bradman's world record, and his subsequent 'sporting declaration' whereby he denied himself a world record score, Healy's deeds at Stockholm have been a story that has been retold to an extent that it has become a part of the fabric of the Australian identity.[52] It is the stuff that is talked about perennially at sports dinners and school assemblies across Australia. This is the very essence of the mythology that makes up the great Anzac tradition. Certainly, no history of the Olympic Games would be written that did not refer to the event.[53]

Sir John Monash recognised this when he assessed the qualities of our Anzac heroes: independent judgement, personal dignity, manliness, practicality, adaptability and a readiness to learn:

> The democratic institutions under which he was reared, the advanced system of education by which he was trained – teaching him how to think for himself and to apply what he had learnt to practical ends – the instinct of sport and adventure which is his national heritage, his pride in his young country, and the opportunity which came to him by creating a great national tradition.[54]

Of course, it was not only ability in sport which counted, but also it was sportsmanship of the type publicly displayed

52 See for example, 'Olympian Sacrificed Gold for Honour', *Manly Daily*, 22 April 1998.

53 See for example, *Australia Goes to the Olympics, 1896-1980*, Sydney, nd, 30.

54 John Monash, *The Australian Victories in France in 1918*, London, 1920, 290-91.

by Healy which was eulogised as that essential Anzac type.

The eulogised democracy of the surf was not an abstract thing, but one that touched Healy's performance at the Stockholm Games and was learnt through team effort. In the 1916 *Lone Hand* article, it is argued that the Germans opposed Healy's gallantry and democratic ideals. Indeed, it became a part of the Anzac myth. It had its supreme expression in Healy's military actions which, it was extravagantly claimed, turned the tide against Germany in the herculean struggles of 1918. With the ink of the Armistice document hardly dry, the Hobart *Mercury* declared that nations such as Britain and Australia that practised competitive team sports, inculcating values of fair play and sportsmanship where personal initiative combined with organised movement, developed mighty armies. Contrast was made with the Germans whose love of sport was expressed in the mechanical, individualistic gymnastics, where sportsmanship was unimportant.[55] The claim was that Germans wanted to win at all costs.

Even by 1916, as expressed by the *Lone Hand* article on Healy, the mythology of sportsmanship was being deeply embedded into the Anzac tradition. Australians were told that:

> It was his never-say-die spirit and his overwhelming sense of duty which impelled him to enlist in the Expeditionary Forces. The camp life was frankly distasteful to him, enlisting meant throwing up prospects for which he had been waiting for years; but like many other Australians, he did not hesitate when

55 *Mercury* [Hobart], 17 July 1918.

> the time came. Weighing carefully every consideration, he accepted the call of duty.[56]

Of course, his death seventy-four days before the signing of the Armistice, along with more than 60,000 Australians who 'gave their all', was a tragedy, but not considered wasted. Rather, the Anzac myth of the Australian identity grew from strength to strength.

Through Healy's victories in the still-water baths and at two Olympic Games, he was well known internationally. In 1916, the *Lone Hand* reminded readers that Healy's journalistic article on how to execute the crawl stroke was even taken up by the Amateur Swimming Association of England. Over 20,000 copies of the article were sold. It was even reprinted after his death. It was also included in Reg ('Snowy') Baker's famous 1911 publication *General Physical Culture*.[57] When there was a post-war publication of the English edition, Healy's Stockholm exploit had been immortalised.[58] Then there was the Cecil Healy Memorial Shield established by the NSW Life Saving Association.

Up until the 1960s as competitive surfing reached its height, this important shield in which Healy's memory and deeds were immortalised as a soldier of the surf dominated interclub competition. It was famous. It was declared in 1956 that surfing was:

> … truly Australian in spirit. Its character savors [sic] of sun-drenched sand and a free and boisterous surf. In it we see democracy function as it was meant to. There

56 'Cecil Healy: Swimmer and Soldier'.

57 Baker, *General Physical Culture*, 42-49.

58 F Baxter, *The Amateur Swimming Association Book on Swimming and Swimming Strokes*, London, 1921, 7.

> are no barriers of creed, class, or color [*sic*]. All these are forgotten in the wonderful spirit of humanitarian mateship.[59]

The shield was 'one of the most popular early competitions' up until the 1960s and was won by the club that showed overall superiority in water events throughout the season. The Manly club presented the shield to the Surf Life Saving Association at the end of the war 'to perpetuate the memory of the club's former captain'.[60]

For wartime propaganda purposes, the Australian press took up the details of Healy's life and death. By this time, propaganda had reached a hitherto unthought of influence on Australian society. In English-speaking countries, Harold Lasswell was among a number of social scientists who studied the manner in which propaganda techniques were developed during the war. He attributed one reason for the increased interest in propaganda in the mid-war years to a 'new inquisitiveness' in Western society. A more direct explanation was that the 'credulous utopianism' of the mass of people on both sides, who had been fed daily smorgasbords of propaganda dealing with how post-war reconstruction, would inevitably lead to a more equitable society for all. On the side of the victors, optimism was high with victory in the 'war to end all wars'. This inflated optimism quickly gave way to cynicism and disenchantment. Society did not develop as promised. Many people, according to individual temperaments, remained

59 History of Bondi Surf Bathers' Life Saving Club, cited in Richard White, *Inventing Australia: Images and Identity, 1688-1980*, Allen & Unwin, Sydney, 1981, 132.

60 'The Healy Shield', *SMH*, 18 July 1919.

uneasy, puzzled or directly angered at the deception of the propaganda they had experienced.[61] In democratic societies where propaganda has to be intensely persuasive to drag a population into war, the persuasive influence is more lasting and the disenchantment and cynicism more intense. Jowett and O'Donnell have pointed out that the war itself had conditioned society to accept propaganda as an integral part of mass society.[62] Consequently, Healy's exploits in the surf and baths have gained a preeminent stature in Australian society that they may never have done had there not been a war and had he not died the way he did.

Healy always had a particularly warm relationship with the Fairfax newspaper empire. For example, when the *Sydney Mail* ran a lengthy photographic essay on 'sport in city and country', it featured Healy emerging from the Manly breakers.[63] This image was later replicated in base relief on the Healy Championship Shield. Not surprisingly, notice of his death in the *Sydney Morning Herald* described how 'all the men and officers who were near him talk of his coolness and gallantry. I knew he would do well, and it is a thousand pities that he didn't get an opportunity of going further after starting off so brilliantly'.[64] The media report of the Requiem Mass in his honour was subdued, indicating his status as a modest middle-class Catholic gentleman and

61 HD Lasswell, 'Propaganda', *Encyclopaedia of the Social Sciences*, vol 12, 1934, 521-7; Harold D Lasswell, *Propaganda Techniques in the World War*, Peter Smith, New York, 1927.

62 Garth S Jowett & Victoria O'Donnell, *Propaganda and Persuasion*, Sage, 1986, 132-3.

63 'Sport in City and Country', *SMH*, 26 October 1910.

64 'Late Cecil Healy', *SMH*, 30 October 1918.

sportsman of conservative values.[65] The notification of the publication of *Cecil Healy: In Memoriam*, however, gave the press an opportunity to give full vent to a eulogy of the man's contribution to the war and Australian society. Here the virtues of sportsmanship in general and Healy's sportsmanship in particular were given to the Australian public:

> Australia is particularly proud of her sportsmen, and especially of those who combine a kindly nature with unusual skill in their special branch of athletics. When the average man declares that a particular champion is 'a true sport' he infers that his idol is one, who, in the heat of contest, does not forget that he is a man, or that to win is but a secondary consideration to that of 'playing the game'.

Thus Cecil Healy joined that band of Australian sportsmen, who have not only made a major contribution to their own sport, but have made a major contribution to Australian culture in a defining moment in the 1914–1918 War.

> It is such a man as this that we envisage when we recall the late Lieutenant Cecil Healy … it is not surprising that, when the cause of freedom and justice was threatened, he should have yearned to participate in the greatest game of all. His death … was the crowning point of his career which all lovers of true sportsmanship cannot fail to admire.[66]

Healy met his death foolishly racing up the high ground well ahead of his platoon, looking for machine guns – wanting to be a hero. His fearlessness provided the enemy

---

65 'Late Lieut Cecil Healy', *SMH*, 24 September 1918.
66 'Late Cecil Healy', *SMH*, 2 January 1919.

with too good a target. He was the first buried at the edge of Sword Wood, accompanied by a couple of other reckless

Cecil Healy joint grave near Péronne. He was killed on 29 August 1918 during the offensive of Mont St Quentin (AWM E0 3362)

Australians, just west of the Somme Canal where it runs west of Péronne.[67]

Manly poet Bruce Beaver evoked the two Manly Memorials that contain many soldiers of the surf years later after the Second World War:

That broken column set beside the wharf
Reminds the villagers of World War One,
Truncated youth, decapitated life;
The clichés tinted red with martyrdom.
The Corso sports a large memorial,
A marble pillar with a globe on top,
For ceremonious displays with all
The rhetoric of beer, ribbons of crepe.

67 Healy, *Cecil Healy in Memoriam* 1918, 45.

The smaller monument has dignity
Though placed beside a pier that displays sharks
In an aquarium for all to see
How big feeds upon little; how war slakes
The old communal thirst for sacrifice
In universal terms, not once, but twice.[68]

Duke Kahanamoku, Freshwater Beach, 1916
(courtesy Judy White, Belltrees Collection)

68 "The Village" XIII, Bruce Beaver, *Poets and Others*, Brandl & Schlesinger, 1999, 59.

10

Armistice

Dreams abandoned, lives without purpose, women without husbands, families without family life, one long funeral for a generation and more after 1918.[1]

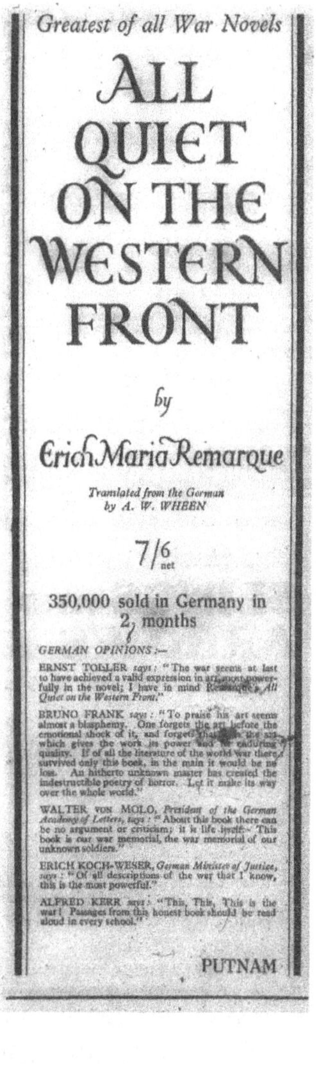

Erich Maria Remarque's famous novel translated by Lieut Arthur Wheen, an Australian WWI hero who enlisted from Sydney University. His translation of 1928 is still available today.

It has to be said persuasively that the Great War made Australia in a negative sense rather that a positive one, if we were to take into account the sum total of these issues and if we are seeking for the truth in Australian history.

Armistice on 11 November 1918 at 11am did not end it all – at all. Australia had lost over 63,000 men

1 Bill Gamage, cited in Ross McMullin, '"Heartstrings Aching for the Absent Boy": Years of Anguish – the Losses of War', *Victorian Historical Journal*, vol 86, no 1, 2015, 56.

dead and many more with wounds that were to pull their lives apart and tragically shorten them. Besides bereaved parents across the continent, there were all the bereaved wives, children, fiancées, girlfriends, brothers and sisters. There was a great deal of anguish in the country. It was but a microcosm of the war's massive devastation of European and, indeed, international life.

On 9 November 1918, Kaiser Wilhelm II – who famously said at the time: 'If my destiny is to be a tragic one, then let it come' – fled Germany on the Imperial train to a safe haven at Amerongen in the Netherlands after waiting at the Dutch-German border on the railway line for permission. He remained there in exile until his death in June 1941. Germany declared itself a republic and the Armistice was signed in a railway carriage by the German delegation at 5 minutes past five in the morning of the 11th, in the Forest of Compiègne near Paris – the headquarters of the *de facto* Allied Commander-in-Chief Marshal Ferdinand Foch. The armistice was to take practical effect from eleven o'clock that morning.

The German delegation consisted of middle-ranking politicians and comparatively junior military officers headed by Mathias Erzberger. Foch headed a purely Anglo-French delegation and there was absolutely no discussion of the American President's more moderate fourteen points. The Germans were forced reluctantly to accept 34 clauses that were to cripple Germany militarily and economically. There were extreme draconian demands of revenge. They also required the German troops to evacuate all occupied and disputed territories in 14 days, including Alsace Lorraine and, within 28 days, Allied troops would take over Germany west of the Rhine River and establish a bridgehead east of up to 20 miles (32 kms) to be occupied by an Allied Army. Huge quantities of weapons, 5,000 locomotives, 1,500 pieces of rolling stock, 10,000 trucks and all submarines and warships were to be given up. All monies taken from foreign banks were to be handed over; there were to be reparations and the British naval blockade was to remain in force. These clauses stunned the German delegation, but, after seeking higher approval, they were forced to sign the Armistice document, ending the war.[2]

By this time, the German Army's casualties officially totalled 100,000 soldiers, but the Central Powers as a whole lost about three and a half million lives. Both Ludendorff and von Hindenburg had resigned themselves to defeat. Von Hindenburg had become almost as strong an exponent of peace as he had been of prolonging the war. Ludendorff had advised against any further sacrifice of men. Thus peace negotiations were sought by the new German liberal Chancellor Prince, Max of Baden. But the Allies demanded unconditional surrender instead. It was clear that the Kaiser would have to go. He would, however, not go easily at first; he protested that he was a direct descendant of Frederick the Great. Such a person did not abdicate at any cost. Ultimately, a revolution in many cities that fell to workers councils in Germany decided the issue conclusively. A letter reached the Kaiser from Berlin: 'all troops deserted – everything completely out-of-hand'. It became clear that, without an army to fight the revolutionaries in the main cities, the Kaiser had to go.

---

2 Ian Westwell, *The Ultimate Illustrated History of World War I*, Hermes House, Leicestershire, 2011, 244-5.

Germany was the last Eagle to fall. The three European Empires all had symbolic Eagles on their official flags and emblems. Russia had been the first to go after a gigantic loss of men on the side of the Allies on the Eastern Front when Lenin and the Bolsheviks had eventually seized power in 1917 of the Imperialist Empire of the Tsar of All Russias and had signed a separate peace with Germany at Brest-Litork. Meanwhile, unrestricted German U-boat warfare and other factors had prompted the United States of America to join the Allies in the Great War.

After the death of Franz Josef of the Austria-Hungary Empire, his successor Karl had appealed to Germany to make peace with the Allies before it was too late, as his armies were beaten and his empire was disintegrating. The Kaiser and his generals, however, persisted and launched a major attack on the Allied line – the Spring Offensive of 1918. They nearly succeeded, but the British and the Americans engaged them in a fierce counter-offensive and the German Army suffered heavy casualties. The massive Allied counter-attack, which heavily involved the Australians and Canadians as spearheads, successfully used tanks in large numbers for the first time, causing the Kaiser to summon a council of war at his supreme headquarters in occupied Belgium ... But everything was to fall apart.

On 28 November having reached his haven in the Netherlands, Kaiser Wilhelm II wrote his formal abdication:

> I herewith renounce for all time claims to the throne of Prussia and to the German Imperial throne connected therewith. At the same time I release all officials of the German Empire and of Prussia, as well as all the officers

> and men of the navy and of the Prussian army, as well as the troops of the federated states of Germany, from the oath of fidelity which they tendered to me as their Emperor, King and Commander-in-Chief. I expect of them that until the re-establishment of order in the German Empire they shall render assistance to those in actual power in Germany, in protecting the German people from the threatening dangers of anarchy, famine and foreign rule. Proclaimed under our own hand and with the imperial seal attached
>
> Amerongen, 28th November 1918, (signed) Wilhelm.[3]

Thus the last Eagle had fallen. The Kaiser's abdication was complex and raised several historical complexities.

President Wilson's Fourteen Points, which would have led to a better peace in Europe, were substantially ignored by Britain and France in the Armistice. He had made several attempts to broker a peace deal culminating in his set of proposals put before the American Congress as early as 8 January 1918. The first five points covered general principles for a new world order, including the freedom of the seas, an end to secret war treaties and arms limitations. Points 6 to 13 addressed specific

Cartoon of Kaiser Wilhelm II, 'The Sands Run Out" (*Mr Punch's History of the Great War, 1919*, 263)

3 Cited, translated into English. in *Fall of Eagles*, BBC booklet accompanying the televised historical series, 1996, 30-31.

territorial issues such as the France-German dispute over Alsace and Lorraine. Point 14, most importantly, called for the establishment of an International body to settle disputes between member nations.[4]

It was a great pity that Wilson's ideas were ignored, apart from the eventual development of the League of Nations that was to have a rocky existence before the Second World War.

★ ★ ★

THE TOLL

Australian population: **4,870,000**
Enlistment: **416,809**
Serving Overseas: **331,781**
Serving On the Western Front: **295,000**
Serving at Gallipoli: **60,000**

Killed (All Services): **61,720**
Killed (AIF, 1914-18): **59,330**
Killed (Western Front): **45,0333**
Killed (Gallipoli): **8,000**

Casualties (AIF): **213,061**
Casualties (Western Front): **181,221**

Wounded (AIF): **153,731**
Wounded (Western Front): **136,188**
Wounded (Gallipoli): **25,600**

'The Toll', in Ken Inglis, 'The Fallen' (*Australian*, 11 November 1998)

Back to Australia's part in it all.

By Armistice, November 1918, there were approximately 185,000 Australian troops overseas: 95,000 in France and Belgium; 60,000 in England and 30,000 in Egypt, Palestine and Mesopotamia. One in every five Australians overseas paid the supreme sacrifice – either killed outright in action, or died of their wounds or from disease.[5]

A photo of massed Australian troops assembled and lined up in the main square of the French village of Vignacourt, on the moment of the announcement to them of Armistice, was unearthed above the ceiling inside the attic of an old cottage in the village. It shows the troops being read the conditions of the Armistice agreement. It is a moment in historic time captured

4 Westwell, *The Ultimate*, 244-5.
5 Juan Mahony, *The Digger's View. WWI in Colour*, self-published, New Lambton, 2014, vii, 246.

forever just prior to their throwing up their hats, cheering and shouting with glee.

Behind the troops leaning against a building's windowsill is Lieutenant Joe Maxwell VC chatting gaily with an attractive French woman who is looking at the scene from inside the large open window. The photo captures the typical Australian larrikin, Maxwell, a man of considerable charm for the young ladies. He had a genuine friendly and confident manner. Elsewhere in the crowd is Captain Percy Storkey, Sydney University's sole holder of a Victoria Cross. He can be easily identified. Storkey became Maxwell's best man at his marriage in Australia, soon after the war.

Maxwell later evocatively recounted the scene on that occasion in his popular memoir *Hell's Bells and Mademoiselles*, published in 1932 to much acclaim in Australia:

> Surging wildly into the square came the whole civil population dancing and singing. The bands blared the British, French, and American national anthems. The battalion 'clink' was opened. Restraint was flung to the winds. The villagers opened their cellars and wine flowed among the troops. We did not wait ... We dashed off to Paris.
>
> The city blazed with light and rocked with the sound of delirious rejoicing. Rockets flared; bands crashed; scores of thousands sang in unison; scores of thousands danced in the streets, on café tables, anywhere; scores of thousands of war-weary men grabbed bright-eyed mademoiselles in the endless whirl of gaiety that surged through the city from end to end.[6]

6 J Maxwell VC, MC, DCM, *Hell's Bells and Mademoiselles*, Angus & Robertson, Sydney, 1936, 236-7.

Despite the widespread gaiety, some veterans on November 11 found the world a lonely place in which it was hard to celebrate among the wild crowds of the city. A convalescing Australian soldier in London wrote about his memory of Armistice Day in verse:

The crowds are dancing in the streets below,
I hear their happy, dancing feet, I know
That Peace and Victory have come today.
But I – I cannot dance and sing as they,
For my soul is darkened with despair,
And close beside the hearth I've drawn your chair.
The Banners that bedeck my window-sill
    Fly out like phantoms in the gas-lamp's flicker,
Strange sounds and voices are about to-night
    And eerie shadows make the heart beat quicker.
What if your feet, your eager, running feet,
Were running up my stairs!
What if I suddenly turned my head,
And, in the doorway, you were standing there!
...
God, how the firelight flickers on the empty chair![7]

An extant photograph held by the Australian War Memorial (H0 3654) reveals an interesting facet about Australians, New Zealanders and South Africans on leave in Paris at the time of the Armistice. The woman in the centre is Ettie Rout, a New Zealand nurse working with Anzac soldiers. She met them at the Gare du Nord as they arrived on leave, providing them with a kit she called the "bluelight outfit"

7 MK Smythe, "Armistice Day", *Hermes*, vol xxv, no 3, December 1919, 220.

containing calomel ointment, prophylactics and other hygiene essentials.

She gave them the address of clean 'tolerated houses' (brothels) of which there were 500 checked weekly by doctors. Other addresses she supplied included her own where soldiers could obtain treatment, further supplies or financial assistance. Her mission was to prevent the spread of venereal disease.

Before dawn on 4 November 1918, Corporal Albert Davey, a miner from Ballarat, was hit by a German bomb, becoming the last of three Anzacs to die on a First World War battlefield before the guns finally fell silent. The two others were fellow sappers Arthur Johnson and Charles Barrett, both Western Australians. They were among a group of Australians about to construct a bridge for British tanks to cross the Sambre-Oise Canal. In the dark of the early hours, Albert Davey had been lying awake in a shallow trench in northern France, convinced that he was soon to die even though it was almost all quiet on the Western Front.

The previous day, he had been very depressed and had

pressured Captain Oliver Woodward to take care of his belongings and send them back to his wife Margaret, if he was to die in the assault ahead of him. Woodward complied as soon as he could, but Margaret was to receive them well after Armistice Day at their humble home in the large mining town of Ballarat, Victoria.

On the same day before Davey died, two Aces of the Australian Flying Corps were shot down by German fighters while escorting British bombers and protecting them over occupied Belgium. One was Captain Thomas "Rich" Baker, who had been credited officially with twelve combat victories or kills. The other was Lieutenant Jack Palliser of Ulverstone, Tasmania. He had brought down five German pilots in the preceding seven days.[8]

★ ★ ★

By November 11, 1918 at 11am, Australia had been at war for four years and three months; they had been battling, dying or surviving on the Western Front for almost 850 days. Elsewhere in Palestine, it was much the same.

On the final day of the last Australian deaths – 4 November that year – the German and Austrian governments had started, ironically, to sue for peace. On that day, they approached the American President Woodrow Wilson seeking Armistice on the basis of his Fourteen Points and follow-up public statements. They believed it was better to deal with the Americans rather than the more aggressive and vengeful French and British governments.

8 'Guns finally fall silent. Road to Remembrance. Australians on the Western Front', *Star*, Wednesday, 14 November 2018, 8.

The Germans had continued to fight in France and Belgium in the forlorn hope of establishing a defensive line that would give them more power to bargain for a better cease-fire for themselves. The fighting on other fronts continued as well. But in late October, the Austria-Hungary Armies and the Hapsburg monarchy both disintegrated and fell into social chaos.

When Kaiser Wilhelm II, the symbol of Prussian militarism, abdicated and Ludendorff and von Hindenburg relinquished their military powers, it was all over for the last Eagle, the great Hohenzollern monarchic dynasty of Prussia.

The Australian Prime Minister William Morris Hughes was on a speaking tour of the north of England doing his utmost to influence the Armistice agreement. But he went too far in his violently-worded public attacks on Woodrow Wilson's more enlightened ideas. Hughes was on the undiplomatic revenge trail against Wilson and his negotiations with the Central Powers. He was thus excluded from the key Allied discussions about Armistice. After all, the vast American Army in France had played a significant part in ending the war.

Lloyd George, the British Prime Minister, had started to view Hughes as a 'troublemaker and a demagogue', who was interfering with what was considered to be the delicate negotiations underway. In retaliation, Hughes attacked Lloyd George at the Imperial War Cabinet for not informing the Dominions, especially Australia, of British intention for peace talks; in this, Hughes was justified to some extent.[9]

After all of this, the French and British got their way about

9 Joan Beaumont, *Broken Nation. Australians in the Great War*, Allen & Unwin, Crows Nest, 2013, 503-12.

Marshal Ferdinand Foch (1851-1929), a French general who became supreme commander-in-chief of Allied forces on the Western Front from August 1918. He headed the Allies delegation to meet the German delegation for the Armistice agreement. He forced an unconditional surrender and refused any discussion of the American President's 14 points.

an unconditional surrender and the guns stopped firing. The German Army was withdrawn to the east bank of the Rhine River and rapidly demobbed; their submarines and other war vessels surrendered to the Allies. 370 British war ships, including HMAS *Australia*, *Melbourne* and *Sydney*, which were part of the Royal Navy, as well as French and US navy vessels, steamed in full battle array to meet the German High Seas Fleet in the North Sea to escort them to Scapa Flow in Scotland and there to be scuttled.[10]

Ten days after Armistice, the Australian Major-General Sir Charles Rosenthal,[11] had a ringside seat at the impressive formal surrender of the German fleet. It was a spectacular scene that he wrote about in his well-kept diary:

> This day is easily surely the greatest in the Navy History of the World, for the proud and boastful German Fleet has, under its own steam and manner by its own officers and men arrived in British Waters and has surrendered itself over to the British Navy

10 AW Jose, *The Official History of Australia in the War of 1914-1918, The Royal Australian Navy*, vol ix, Angus & Robertson, Sydney, 1928, 330-1.
11 KCM, CMG, DSO, VD.

> of glorious and stainless fame. Never was victory so complete and never humiliation so great.[12]

Born at Berrima NSW in 1875, Rosenthal was one of the most able, popular and successful commanders in the 1st AIF. He served in Egypt, on Gallipoli and on the Western Front, rising to the rank of Major General. A large man – universally known as "Rosie" by his men – was of great personal bravery; he emphasised the supreme importance of thorough training. After Gallipoli, he fought in the Battles of Fromelles, Stormy Trench, First Bullecourt and Lagnicourt as well as Second Bullecourt and Messines. He was wounded on four separate occasions. His brilliance as a tactician was dramatically illustrated by the magnificent storming of Mont St Quentin by his command of the 2nd Australian Division. He died at his home at Green Point, Gosford, at the age of 79.[13] He had been one of the first Brigade Commanders ashore at Gallipoli where he was twice wounded in a dance with death, but he survived to live a rich and productive life.

* * *

Sister Elsie Tranter, on 11 November 1918, had another heart-breaking day caring for deliriously ill Australian soldiers in an army hospital.

She wrote in her diary: 'France went almost mad with joy … singing and dancing in the streets … everyone kissing

12 Cited from Rosenthal's diary by Michael Caulfield, *The Unknown ANZACS*, Hachette, Sydney, 2013, 357.

13 "By Staff Officer", 'Celebrities of the AIF No 73. Major-General Sir Charles Rosenthal KCB, DSO, VD', *Reveille*, 1 September 1936; 'Vale! Sir Charles Rosenthal', *Reveille*, 1 June 1954, 12.

everyone they met'. But inside the hospital, she then wrote of a fair-haired young soldier nicknamed "sonny Jim": 'This poor little lad finished his battle towards the evening [on 11 November]. He was barely 18 years old and we were all so fond of him'.

On the day the war ended, about twenty Australian soldiers died of their wounds, or an illness in hospitals.

★ ★ ★

For Lieutenant George Mawby Ingram, a Bendigo carpenter, who had lost family members as well as many soldier comrades, the end of the hostilities was a bitter-sweet experience. He was the very last of 64 Australians who had won the Victoria Cross in the First World War. His brothers Ronald and Alex had both been killed on the Western Front in the stalemate of 1917. The Australians suffered dreadful casualties in the trench warfare of Pozières, Mouquet Farm and First Bullecourt.

George Ingram was born in Bendigo, Victoria, on 18 March 1889. He was educated at Lilydale state school. At fourteen, he had already joined the militia for military training attached to No 7 Company of the Australian Garrison Artillery. He attended a military exhibition in New Zealand in 1906 as a member of an Australian military contingent.

When he completed his apprenticeship as a carpenter, he moved to Caulfield and set up his own small business as a building contractor. He married Jane Francis Nichols according to a Congregational ceremony on 19 January 1910. They had no children and the marriage was unhappy. It dissolved after the war in 1926. Ingram was to marry twice more; his second wife died after the Second World War.

Ingram enlisted on 10 December 1914, at the height of the rush to enlist, in the 3rd Battalion, Australian Navy and Military Expeditionary Force and served in New Guinea as a corporal. He was discharged from the AN&MEF on 19 January 1916 and, on the same day, he enlisted in the 1st AIF, joining the 24th Battalion and arriving in France in January 1917. Only two months later, he was awarded the Military Medal. This was in March during the German withdrawal to the Hindenburg Line and won near Bapaume. The MM was awarded for great courage and initiative as a member of a bombing company. His accurate placement of bombs was particularly commented on favourably.

Soon after, he fell ill and was hospitalised in Britain until June when he was sufficiently ready to rejoin his unit. But in September, he was sent to hospital again. He rejoined his unit in France, however, on 10 October when he was promoted to company sergeant. Ingram was gazetted as second lieutenant on 20 June 1918, but three days later he was again in hospital and unable to resume duty until 12 July. He overcame his illnesses with some difficulty and was with his unit during the Allies offensives of 1918.

The capture of the village of Montbréhain east of Péronne was brilliant, but expensive in terms of the death toll. It was the last action fought by the Australians in the Great War. At Montbréhain, Lieutenant George Ingram became the 64th and last member of the 1st AIF to be awarded the Victoria Cross.

The previous day, the 24th Battalion had helped to capture the Beauvoir section where Joe Maxwell won his VC. They were expecting to rest, but were hurriedly organised to attack strongly-held German positions at Montbréhain, even though the war was drawing to a close. On 5 October 1918, they met with fierce resistance from deadly German machine guns as well as artillery. Nevertheless, they continued to move forward. Ingram in B Company had difficulty advancing because of sniper and machine-gun fire. In reaction, he led a platoon against one strong point under fire and succeeded, after a fierce fight, in capturing nine machine guns and killing 24 enemy.

When his company commander was wounded, Ingram organised and led a charge against an abandoned quarry that was heavily defended by forty machine guns and one hundred German soldiers. He, alone, rushed the first post and shot six of the enemy and captured a machine gun, perhaps to show his men how to do it. After that on the same day, he continuously displayed great dash and resourcefulness in capturing all the enemy posts in the quarry of Montbréhain inflicting many casualties and taking 62 prisoners.

On his final spectacular assault soon after, he captured at least 30 Germans trapped in a house cellar after shooting the machine gunner, who had been stationed in the cellar ventilator, with his revolver. The fierce fighting raged all day and it wasn't until 8pm that the objective was taken and completely consolidated.[14] 'Throughout the whole day, George Ingram Mawby showed the most inspiring example of courage and leadership and freely exposed himself regardless of the danger'.[15]

Ingram was decorated by King George V at Buckingham

14 Hamilton, *Victoria Cross Winners*, 358; Staunton, *Victoria Cross*, 195-6.

15 Ingram's citation in *London Gazette*, 6 January 1919.

Palace on 15 February 1919 and returned to Australia in April.[16]

★ ★ ★

The end of fighting, when it came, was abrupt with the signing of the Armistice on 11 November 1918. Bringing the Australian soldiers and nurses back to Australia loomed as a huge logistical problem – the numbers were scattered across three broad areas of Europe and the Middle East. There were 167,000 men still serving overseas let alone a solid number of Australian nurses. The quick end to the war had caught Australian authorities unprepared. Major-General Cyril Brudenell White had been brought over from France to establish the AIF Department of Demobilisation and Repatriation in London. Sensing the magnitude of the task ahead of getting them back in the first place to Australia before demobbing, he suggested that Lieutenant-General Sir John Monash, the highly successful commander of the Australian Corps, be given the task.

It was an inspired choice, but an exhausting one for Monash. With Australian Government support, Monash set out to do it as quickly as possible. Between December 1918 and September 1919, almost 200 voyages involving 137 ships, some of which made two or three trips, had taken place. Of course, there were problems and difficulties along the way, but Monash was a great problem-solver. During his time, 15,386 so-called English war brides and children (mostly two-year-olds or younger) were conveyed to Australia as well. 150,000 soldiers were brought home from Europe and Egypt. Some had decided to stay in England with their English brides.

16 Wigmore, *They Dared Mightily*, 70.

By October 1919, only 13,000 men remained in Europe mainly on guard duties. For Monash, it was a marvellous achievement, one that showed the great man at his very best.[17] The challenge now facing the men, who had been through the horrors of war, was to find employment and begin once more to take up the lives they had left behind.

We, who are left, how shall we look again
Happily on the sun, or feel the rain,
Without remembering how they who went
Ungrudgingly, and spent
Their all for us, love too, the sun and rain?

A bird among the rain-wet lilac sings —
But we, how shall we turn to little things
And listen to the birds and winds and streams
Made holy by their dreams ,
Nor feel the heart-break in the heart of things?

Wilfrid Wilson Gibson, "A Lament"

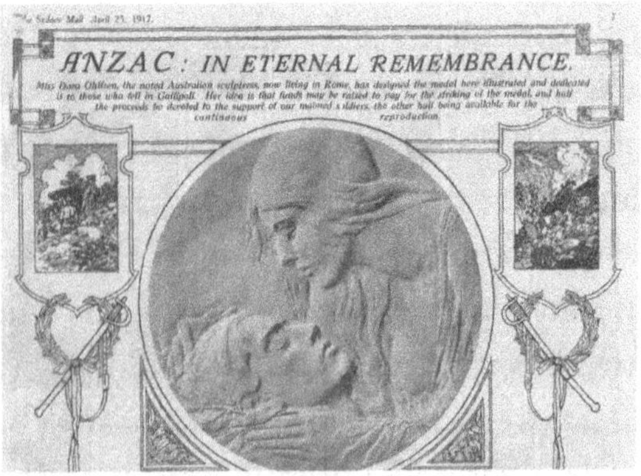

17 Robert Nichols, 'After the shooting stopped', *Wartime*, issue 45, April 2009, 26-7.

11

Remembrance of Things Past

On 1 December 1937, *Reveille*, the New South Wales magazine of the Returned Soldiers and Sailors League, was sad to report a tragic death. Their headlines carried a photographic portrait beside them which read: 'An Eminent Sculptor Dead [xxx] A Great War Veteran'.[1]

George Rayner Hoff, Kings Liverpool Regiment (BEF)

> It was George Rayner Hoff. … one of the foremost sculptors in Australia, died in Sydney on November 19 [1937] at the age of 42. His best known works in Sydney are the figures on the exterior of the Anzac Memorial [Hyde Park], and the central group of figures ["Sacrifice"] in the interior. This year he submitted the winning design for the memorial of King George V at Canberra.

Eminent historian Ken Inglis, in his book on war memorials in Australia, has accurately distilled the cultural significance of George Rayner Hoff's magnificent sculptures in three war memorials for the First AIF that have become

1 'Eminent Sculptor Dead +++ A Great War Veteran', *Reveille*, 1 December 1937, 5.

imbedded as icons in the Australian landscape and thus inform the modern collective memory of the terrible events of the Great War and its impact.[2]

Inglis places Hoff's successive commissioned contributions to the Dubbo (1925), Adelaide (1927-30) and Sydney (1931-4) War Memorials into the context of a vast range of small and large memorials across the Australian island continent – an estimated 3,000 to 4,000 are traced in terms of their origin and meaning. Art historian Deborah Edwards concentrates on Rayner Hoff's development of a distinctive Sydney vitalist school of Art Deco sculpture emanating from the School of Art at the East Sydney Technical School in Darlinghurst.[3] Deborah Beck, another art historian, concentrates on producing a definitive biography of the artist from his childhood influences onwards.[4]

Hoff had most certainly become 'the most successful public sculptor of his era by the early 1930s in Australia'.[5] His famous work *Sacrifice* must today be the most photographed of all sculptures in Australia by visiting tourists, professional photographers, amateurs as well as art book publishers. It is the most famous symbol of Vitalism in Art as it countered materialist, mechanistic and static views of reality in art and literature.

Sacrifice is animated by a sensuous, non-rational 'life energy', the *élan vital* of the French philosopher Henri

---

2 Ken Inglis, *Sacred Places. War Memorials in the Australian Landscape*, Miegunyah Press, Carlton, 1999.

3 Deborah Edwards, '*This vital flesh*'. *The Sculpture of Rayner Hoff and His School*, NSW Art Gallery, Sydney, 1999.

4 Deborah Beck, *Rayner Hoff. The Life of a Sculptor*, New South, Sydney, 2017.

5 Edwards, '*This vital flesh*', Introduction, 11.

Bergson that he defined as residing in the body. Bergson was influential to Hoff's ideas in his formative years as a sculptor while he was living and studying art in Nottingham in England's north. Inglis, Edwards and Beck agree that Hoff's group sculpture *Sacrifice* as the focal point of the Hyde Park Memorial is the greatest single achievement of his entire professional life as a public or civic sculptor and memorialist.

When Hoff was there, Nottingham had become an important intellectual centre for Vitalist influences on literary, artistic and political activity. Hoff's contemporary and author of *Sons and Lovers* and *Women in Love*, DH Lawrence, was also profoundly influenced by the movement. Another Nottingham intellectual Edward Carpenter promoted modern sexuality as the 'key to the creation of a new British society'.[6] Carpenter's ideas influenced both Rayner Hoff as an artist of great sensuality and DH Lawrence as a polemic writer of equal male-female sexual relationships in contemporary society.

The Isle of Man – situated in the Irish Sea equidistant from Ireland, Scotland and northern England – where Rayner Hoff was born, was a place with a sense of timelessness, as his biographer Deborah Beck was eager to point out. There were, she noticed, many stories of mythical creatures and fantastic characters inhabiting the island. Its strong Celtic traditions are hundreds of years old. Manx people are fierce about their political independence with Tynwald, the oldest continuously ruling body – it is claimed – in the world.

As an adult, Hoff drew extensively from such traditions in his

6 Edwards, '*This vital flesh*'.

art. His birthplace was deeply entrenched in his independent will and in his abiding interest in mythology and paganism.

In the Isle of Man's fertile and dramatic psychological landscape, Rayner spent his first eight years. All his siblings were born there before his parents moved to the north of England. Family members believe that the Hoff family had Dutch roots during the reign of Charles I as validated by their Dutch surname. Rayner's parents George and Elizabeth lived in St Helena's Cottage where George was employed as an industrial bricklayer and a sometime stonemason and where Rayner and his siblings were born.

Born on 27 November 1894, Rayner was named after his father, but was generally known by his middle name to avoid confusion in and outside family circles.[7] Rayner's father George was a stonemason as well as a woodcraftsman, who restored and repaired ornate woodwork in historical homes – a craft Rayner later participated with his father as well as stonemasonry. This was the earliest form of training Hoff was to receive in relevant skills for producing mature sculptures. George had a deep influence on his son's creativity.

When his family moved to northern England, Rayner, at the age of fifteen, enrolled in the Nottingham School of Arts where he studied architecture and allied subjects such as modelling, drawing, design and masonry decoration. He was awarded a silver medal for two of his architectural relief drawings in a national competition in his first term, thus showing his promise as an artist. The following year, he won a gold medal for a large relief. During his entire period of study at the School, he earned a living

7 Beck, *Rayner Hoff*, 1-18.

by working part-time as a professional modeller on many kinds of architectural works, especially in fibrous plaster.

When the First World War broke out, Rayner Hoff, in his fourth year at Art School and nearly twenty, enlisted in late 1915 as a volunteer and spent three and a half years in service in the British Expeditionary Force (BEF) in France. In that time, he spent twelve horrifying months in or near the frontline trenches.[8] What he observed was influential in a creative mind. The experience was indelibly etched and later revealed and manifested itself in his many war sculptures, most notably those on and in the Anzac Memorial in Hyde Park. The BEF, eventually recognising his talent and training, then employed him in the Topographical Survey Department, modelling three-dimensional maps from aerial photographs for staff instruction and planning until the end of the war. Such intense manufacturing activity in war zones later gave his sculptors a panoramic lively perspective combined with a highly productive work ethic.[9]

Rayner returned to the Nottingham School of Arts after the war for six months in 1919. He then took up studies in South Kensington London in the School of Sculpture, Royal College of Art. The head of sculpture was Professor Francis Derwent Wood. Realising Hoff's great talent and potential, he became his chief mentor. In reaction, Hoff became one of Wood's fervent devotees and a follower.

Derwent Wood RA was an outstanding British sculptor

8 'Eminent Sculptor Dead', 5.

9 John Ramsland & Christopher Mooney, 'Apollo must contemplate a world of which he has never dreamed', *ISAA Proceedings. The National Estate – Civic Heritage*, Independent Scholars Association of Australia, 2008, 174.

who designed many figures for public buildings in Glasgow where he was modelling master at the Glasgow School of Arts from 1897 to 1901. He was highly accomplished in the classical mode which powerfully influenced Rayner's own art.

In 1921, Hoff had gained from the Royal in South Kensington a Diploma in modelling, winning first prize for the graduating classes best work, together with the Royal College of Art's Travelling Scholarship for Sculpture.

Hoff had great success at the Royal College. In 1922, at the age of twenty-seven, he won the prestigious *Prix de Rome* which was heavily competed for by younger British sculptors. (Twenty years before him, it was awarded to François Sicard, designer and sculptor of the Archibald Fountain – also a war memorial at the other end of Sydney's Hyde Park, juxtaposing the Anzac Memorial with classical vitalist forms of Greek gods.) In England, the *Prix de Rome* was regarded as the blue ribbon distinction for any aspiring sculptor trying to achieve public recognition and fame. On it, Rayner went to Rome for further study, partly by observation and recording of the great classical masters and their works.[10]

Hoff was busy spending his time in Italy observing and drawing, rather than producing sculpture. He studied the great masters, like Donatello and Michel Angelo, to whom he swore a devoted allegiance that was to characterise his own artwork. Hoff steeped himself in Antiquity and Renaissance art.

While visiting Naples, Hoff received urgent word

10 'Eminent Sculptor'.

from his friend and mentor Derwent Wood that he had recommended him for the vacant position in Sydney of Public Instructor in Drawing and Sculpture at East Sydney Technical College in its School of Art, housed in the former convict-built sandstone Darlinghurst Gaol building. This was the first time the position had been offered in Sydney as the School of Art expanded its operation and its ambition.

Apparently, Wood had strong Australian connections. His wife Florence Schmidt was an expatriate Australian opera singer from Rockhampton in Queensland. The Australian painter George Lambert, the famous war artist, was a close friend of Wood. In sculpture as his last great work, Lambert created *Recumbent figure of a Soldier* or *Unknown Soldier* in the interior of St Mary's Catholic Cathedral (1928-30) beside Hyde Park, Sydney.

It is clear, Wood intended to shape Hoff's career along the same lines as his own, particularly in Glasgow where he was an instructor in a similar position. Apart from that, the Sydney position was a huge opportunity for Hoff who was short of money at the time and had been considering abandoning art for farming in Canada. Wood's advice persuaded Hoff to persist in his artistic endeavours by accepting the Sydney position when offered.[11] And he grabbed it with both hands.

Rayner departed immediately from Naples for London and a quick conference with his mentor Derwent Wood. Soon after in late 1923, he sailed for Australia and took up his position early the following year. He had married Annis Briggs, a fellow art student at Nottingham on 30 June 1920.

11 Ramsland & Mooney, 'Apollo must contemplate', 174-5.

They had two daughters, Sandra born in London in 1923 and Nereida who was born in Sydney in 1929.

It wasn't long before Rayner Hoff set Sydney sculpture and its circles on fire.

As Norman Carter, an artist and admirer of Hoff, put it:

> He came amongst us at a time when a sculptor of great talent was needed. As a community we were fortunate in obtaining the services of one who was capable of sensing the spirit of this particular period of our history, giving expression to it in various memorials.[12]

As an almost instantly-celebrated sculptor after his fan-faired arrival in Sydney, Rayner Hoff was soon to become more Australian than some Australians in his lifestyle and attitudes. He was an obsessed lover of the great outdoors, the surf, sand and summer, and a believer in the perfectible athletic body of contemporary Australians. He believed that he was part of a modern race of Australians which blended former nationalities, ethnic groups and gender considerations of equality between men and women. He soon became interested in the traditional culture and the perfectible bodies of Australian Aborigines in their natural state that was reflected in some of his finest sculptures created during his fourteen productive years in Australia, prior to his sudden death at the age of forty-two. It is noted that, among the carefully selected bodies used as his models, were sun-tanned surf lifesavers and outstanding swimmers and athletes. In an interview in 1931, he claimed extravagantly:

> I doubt if even the Ancient Greeks produced better

12 Norman Carter, 'Rayner Hoff – Sculptor', *Art in Australia*, 1 March 1938, 8.

> examples of physical beauty and grace. We [Australians] don't allow our bodies to become flaccid ... the call of the sun, surf, great open roads ... is all too strong for any to resist. Hence *we are active, virile and well and few nations show such an average of body perfection.*[13]

It is clear that he saw himself as part of the pronoun 'we'. He had quickly become an Australian, especially in his dominant outlook and this was reflected in his artworks, consciously and unconsciously. He surfed regularly at Bondi Beach and enjoyed the great outdoors, while being highly productive in a great variety of sculpture works.

In the 1924 Society of Artists Annual Exhibition in Sydney, Rayner Hoff exhibited an amazing twenty-three pieces of high quality sculpture. By 1926, he organised the first public exhibition of art by students of the East Sydney Technical College, Darlinghurst. As a teacher, he was a brilliant motivator and supporter of his devoted students. The exhibition was held in December to large crowds in the gallery of the State Department of Education's main sandstone head office in Bridge and Loftus Streets, Sydney.[14]

From then on until his death, Rayner Hoff maintained the status of being chosen by the people as a 'celebrity' artist who was frequently interviewed in the popular press. He was interviewed, when his opinion was sought, about such subjects as the Australian way of life, the perfectible body and the ideological purpose of art. Such press made him a well-known commentator to the man and woman in

---

13 'Our physique – Perfect says G Rayner Hoff', *Health and Physical Culture*, 1 December 1931, 38-39, cited in Beck, *Rayner Hoff*, 136 (Italics for emphasis by author).

14 Ken Scarlett, *Australian Sculptors*, Nelson, Melbourne, 1980, 260.

the street, at times controversial but always highly respected.

Memorials for the Military Dead

> Rays of amber on the doors were a metaphor for sunset; and the interior lighting and decorative detail, as in Dellit's Anzac Memorial in Hyde Park, drew the eyes and mind upward without the help of any devices taken from traditional Christianity.
>
> KS Inglis, 'Passing Away', *Australians*, Fairfax, Symes & Weldon Associates, Sydney, 1987

Rayner Hoff had reached the zenith of his prolific career and professional powers when he was chosen as the sculptor to work on C Bruce Dellit's masterpiece, the Anzac War Memorial building conceived in the Art Deco style. Bruce Dellit was a heavily-built 29-year-old architect who had pioneered Art Deco buildings in Sydney. Hoff was not Dellit's first choice as sculptor, but they soon became close friends and, after seeing Hoff's models, Dellit became convinced that he was the ideal choice.

Hoff had significant experience in contributing to war memorials in Australia. His first commission was for the Dubbo War Memorial in 1925, less than two years after his arrival in Australia. For the central-western NSW prosperous country town of Dubbo, he produced three bronze reliefs at eye level at the base of the large towering obelisk or tapered monolithic shaft of stone: *The Landing* depicting the crowded landing of gallant troops at Gallipoli in a lively portrayal of forward movement under gunfire; *The Light Horse* depicting, in action, the desert warfare and *18 Pounder in Action*, graphically depicting such an action with

Australian soldiers.[15] All three reliefs show exciting action and movement in war. In size, they are all approximately 12ft x 4ft.

The Dubbo Anzac Memorial, 1925,bas relief sculpture (photograph, Brian Yap)

In 1930-31, he followed up his completed memorial sculpture more spectacularly in the Adelaide War Memorial with huge figures 16ft high. Back in 1926, Hoff had originally been commissioned by the architects of the Adelaide Memorial,Walter Bagot and Louis Laybourne Smith, to create the reliefs and bronze statuary to be incorporated in their memorial. While Bagot had already done some preliminary sketches of the proposed statuary, Hoff's design got rid of a rather static heavy winged figure of one of the sketches changing it to a much lighter, more stylised winged spirit in the Art Deco style. It appeared to hover imposingly above the bronze group of contemporary symbolic figures below that he created.[16]

The central purpose of such types of war memorials in the Australian landscape is to make those who are absent – because of death – present again; those who already had a rendezvous with death in some desolate foreign place, 'in some scarred slope of battlefield' at 'some disputed barricade' between frontline enemies.[17] Hoff was determined to

15 Scarlett, *Australian Sculptors.*

16 Beck, *Rayner Hoff*, 154.

17 'Rendezvous with Death', Alan Seeger, killed in action, 1916.

capture the chaos and intense activity of modern warfare.

There was widespread commemoration of Australia's war dead both in capital cities, like Adelaide, and in the smallest villages in the vast countryside. Their graves were not available to the grieving. This was even more so as Australia's war dead were almost always buried in foreign countries. Such monuments like the Adelaide one, therefore, had to assume the role of the tomb or cemetery where, though set apart, the dead are felt to be present, hovering among the living in a place apart – in a psychological and symbolic sense. And yet the paradox of Australian war memorials is that, no matter how reverent they are, they can never really make the absent present in a real dramatic sense – except in some vague symbolic and solemn way. Such monuments create a larger, more vital presence even with that awful absence of bodies under the soil.[18]

The Spirit of Compassion, Rayner Hoff, National War Memorial, Adelaide, 1927

Working in his large sandstone-walled studio in the heart of Sydney together with his students, Hoff produced detailed designs for his Adelaide monumental sculptures.

18 Angus Trumble, 'Making the absent present. War memorials in the Australian landscape', *Art & Australia*, vol 37, no 2, 1999, 198-200.

In the same place, he modelled a one-quarter size clay maquette of the angels himself. Then his brother Tom, who had joined him as an assistant soon after he had arrived in Sydney, made moulds of the maquettes and caste them in plaster with the help of some of Hoff's more senior and gifted students. Eighteen packing cases were eventually sent to Adelaide by ship.

Hoff's plaster models were scaled up and carved in Angaston marble by a skilled team led by sculptor Albert Henschke in Adelaide. The carving of the huge angels took from 1927 to 1931 to complete. At 9.6 metres, the imposing Adelaide monument was considered the largest memorial built in the southern hemisphere.

Hoff designed and made the bronze figurative group *Youth* at the base of the monument in full scale looking up – three metres high – in his Darlinghurst studio. The group of three symbolised a male student in a modern suit, a young woman/girl dressed for the city and a farmer driving a plough, thus depicting typical contemporary South Australia. They were dressed in modern day clothes,[19] appropriate to their civilian calling in peace after the Great War had ended. They were handsome looking specimens of humankind, portraying perfectible bodies of a new race of men and women that modern Australia was creating.

So Hoff very carefully supervised the work mainly from afar – from Sydney, even sending carved fragments of hands and feet to his workmen in Adelaide, the stonemasons Julius Henschke and his brother Arthur.[20]

19 Beck, *Rayner Hoff*, 157.
20 Trumble, 'Making the absent', 200.

In the Adelaide monument, established in the North Terrace and unveiled to a huge crowd on Anzac Day 25 April 1931, Hoff had been informed by vitalist principles he shared with his close friend and versatile Australian, the prolific artist Norman Lindsay who was influential in the art world – that is, the equal and complementary male-female dualities with which he sought to break down the usual isolated solemn masculine warrior theme common in war memorial design with the absence of female figures.

On the obverse of Hoff's Adelaide memorial, a carved stylised angel of death hovers in a silent contemplation above *Youth* – the three smaller bronze figures on the base treated in a modern and naturalistic manner in contrast to the huge allegorical angel in marble above them. The bronze figures are overawed at the apparition of the giant sacrificial presence. The angel's power of life and death is partly conveyed through the phallic symbol of the sword which is held against a semi-naked body.

On the reverse side of the memorial is the carved *Spirit of Womanhood and the fallen soldier* bound together. In this allegorical depiction by Hoff, the giant female angel assumes control of the sword. The naked body of the dead soldier is nestled against her, head resting close to her naked breast while floating in thin air. Pure love and sexual love are blended in this image: mother and son and the two lovers. Separated from the power of the phallus in war, the soldier now finds erotic fulfilment and peace in death. Hoff's approach dismisses the more popular homo-erotism found in the Anzac legend, which is evident in Peter Weir's masterly war feature film *Gallipoli* (1981).[21]

The climax of Hoff's professional career, however, was reached in Sydney, rather than Adelaide or Dubbo, with the Hyde Park monument. Between 1930 and 1933, he worked feverishly on the numerous sculptures with the full support and encouragement of the Art Deco architect C Bruce Dellit. The massive external figures were in artificial stone, the reliefs in bronze and the internal figures in *Sacrifice* also in bronze. Marble was considered too expensive.

Rayner Hoff. Head in plaster by student Eileen McGrath, *Art in Australia*, no 46, October 1932

Hoff was assisted in a major way by his outstanding students at his sculpture school at East Sydney, in particular: Eileen McGrath, Otto Steen, John Moorfield and Barbara Tribe.[22]

Sacrifice was Hoff's masterpiece as described by Leigh Astbury in 1992. He argued that Hoff, a war veteran himself:

> … found psychological and artistic compensation in reconstructing the unblemished beauty of the intact male body. In *Sacrifice*, his major figure group inside the Anzac Memorial in Sydney's Hyde Park, Hoff alludes to the Spartan ideal of the soldier returning from war with his shield or on it.

21 Leigh Astbury, 'Death and Eroticism in the Anzac Legend', *Art and Australia*, vol 30, no 1, 1992, 72.

22 Scarlett, *Australian Sculptors*, 260.

> The suffering of women in war is acknowledged in three allegorical figures – mother, sister, lover-wife – which form the base column.

He saw the elision of the women's role made more ambiguous through their absorption into the bullet-shell or phallic shape of the base. The stylised Art Deco lines of the women's classical robes suggest 'the milling of a gun'. Their severity heightens the erotic suppleness of the flesh represented.[23]

The youthful body on the shield showed a bronze male head and neck inclined backwards towards the setting sun with the features of a modern Australian of about thirty-five years (with a modern parted haircut and a neatly clipped military moustache). A preliminary study of the face is on display in the Australian War Memorial, Canberra.

In 1932, art critic Howard Ashton claimed *Sacrifice* was the 'most beautiful and touching' work of sculpture that had ever been completed in Australia and a concept both simple and dignified.

Another critic in the same year described the work as:

> Borne aloft by women on whose shoulders the war placed the burden of sacrifice equally with the men is the outspread body of a soldier lying on a shield with the back of his head cupped in a woman's upraised hand. His arms fall back over a sword in an attitude suggesting crucifixion.[24]

---

23 Astbury, 'Death and Eroticism'.

24 Lionel G Wigmore, 'A Description of the Anzac Memorial Building, New South Wales', *Sculpture for the Anzac Memorial Building, Hyde Park, Sydney, N.S.W.*, Society of Artists' Exhibition, 1932, <https://trove.nla.gov.au/version/45828817>, p 8.

A second woman is carrying a healthy baby on her shoulders. It symbolises to Rayner Hoff as a vitalist the future generation that will overcome the tragedy of war. The third woman holds the warrior's feet in her hands.

The anniversary of the Gallipoli landing in 1916 was solemnly commemorated with several services in Sydney. A fund was commenced for the construction of a memorial in Sydney, given that the shocking numbers of Australian war dead were not brought home, but were hastily buried in foreign soil almost where their rendezvous with death had taken place.

In 1929, an open competition was held to design the memorial and won by local young architect C Bruce Dellit. His entry proposal included interior and external base relief sculptures and statues in marble, granite and brass. When Hoff was appointed as sculptor, the materials were changed to bronze and artificial stone

Dellit had designed the building in an international and functional Art Deco style with setbacks, buttresses and ziggurat-inspired stepped roof. It was completed in 1934, constructed of concrete, clad in grey-pink granite quarried at Bathurst in the central west of New South Wales. Hoff's twenty monumental figures of various types of military personnel of the Great War – including an army matron nurse, an air force officer, an infantryman and a Lewis gunner – were placed high on the exterior of the building. They were moulded and cast of artificial stone, in tone and colour harmony with the building's granite cladding, in Hoff's Darlinghurst studio. To the observer, the statues of a slightly darker colour appeared, nevertheless, to be hewn from the building itself and stand out as definite statements of aspects of war.

The interior of the building displayed Art Deco motifs with the central feature being Hoff's *Sacrifice*, a group sculpture seen from a rounded balustrade from above representing a fallen soldier stretched nakedly vulnerable and held aloft on his shield. It was the unblemished body of a tall slender young man almost a youth. Perhaps the figure symbolised for Hoff Australia's recruitment policy to select fit handsome young men. Here, he may have been making a subtle political comment.

Hoff's eastern side bronze relief panel depicted the Eastern campaign of the 1st AIF, from the Gallipoli landing to the campaign in Sinai and Palestine (10m x 1m), a complex sweep of moving history dealing completely with men's frontline activities, some dying, others struggling with their assigned jobs in difficult conditions, but all moving in the one direction.[25] Other bronze relief panels on other sides depicted separate theatres of war in World War I. These were detailed and equally evocative.

Eastern Campaign, Rayner Hoff. Part of bronze relief, Anzac Memorial, Hyde Park Sydney, *Art in Australia*

25 Peter Sheridan AM, *Sydney Art Deco*, Bakelite, Sydney, 2019, 336-9.

Hoff's expert team of well-trained student assistants on the Sydney monument were a closely-knit strongly associated group of sculptors and assistants who represented, perhaps, the sole instance in Australia of a coherent school of artistic production among sculptors in Australian history. They accepted without question Hoff's commands and demands. They created some of the most innovative, stylistically uniform and sexually adventurous sculpture seen in this country, all directed by Hoff's detailed masterplans.

Hoff and his students were particularly influenced by post-war reconstruction ideals in the context of themes of fecundity and the joy of erotic, virile youth – that is, the relationship between the creative and the procreative forces of life, as well as the function of art to express such heroic life forces in war that, sadly, frequently resulted in sudden death. They drew from the Assyrian, Egyptian, Aztec and Greek classical traditions and mythologies, but created clarity of line and definition of the body in action through stylised patterns of musculature based on live classical models with ideal Australian bodies. It was an arresting synthesis of what can be termed as Art Deco stylisation and decorative detailing with vital, almost over-realistic definition of musculature which gives the 'Hoff School' of sculptors their distinctive visual power, as found in the work of sculptors Eileen McGrath, Barbara Tribe, Marjorie Fletcher, Jean Broome-Norton, Guy Frank Lynch and Elizabeth Conlan.

Most went on to become well-known professional sculptors in Australia and overseas (for example, Barbara Tribe in England). Hoff and his remarkable student protégés became prominent with their iconic work on the Hyde Park memorial site at a time when Australia's colonial outpost image and position were decisively changing and transforming into the modern concept of the First World War, being widely viewed as the primary test of mature nationhood and its manhood, as was promoted by the official war historian Charles Bean and many politicians like Willian Morris Hughes. Australia was powerfully pursuing the idea of progress and a nationalist fervour, with 'optimistic concern to promote a successful independent Australia' – despite the contradictions of the Great Depression and widespread unemployment.

As Sydney University historian Stephen Garton has persuasively argued, war played a significant role in constructing particular masculine ideals in Australian culture:

> The Anzac legend of mateship, fortitude, larrikinism and anti-authoritarianism may have reflected an older bushman ideal but it translated it into something national and hence more readily available for a broad, popular and cross-class audience.

Such ideals undoubtedly reflected the 'fighting spirit' and extraordinary sacrifice; it also fostered an image of home as a 'feminised', domestic and perhaps mundane world. But masculine privileges in war could not hide the difficult problems of transition and adjustment into peace.[26]

Along with his friend Norman Lindsay, Rayner Hoff was working passionately to produce 'a new cultural renaissance in a society which they saw as intellectually isolated from

26 Stephen Garton, 'War and Masculinity in Twentieth Century Australia', in Clive Moore and Kay Saunders (eds), 'Australian Masculinities : men and their histories', *Journal of Australian Studies*, no 56, 1998, 94.

the chaos of war-torn Europe'.[27] The authors of *Sunrise over the Pacific* captured the meaning exactly of Hoff's greatest artistic work:

> Facilitated by the split-level architecture of the [Dellit's] building, *Sacrifice* presents two associated concepts of 'sacrifice' – one through a ground level view dominated by a column of three women and a [baby] child, and the other through a view from above, dominated by the lithe body of a young dead soldier. Radiating from the work, in bronze paving, are the flames of destruction. The soldier, who is both the Australian Anzac and a Spartan youth returning home dead on his shield, is carried literally by a caryatid – figures who represent the Australian mothers, sisters and wives-lovers who lost soldiers. Hence the soldier becomes simultaneously the brother, son and husband killed in war. The women represent the living – the soldier the dead. He signifies the past – they hold the future in the child one of them carries. Together the figures are meant to embody the abstract concept of sacrifice.[28]

The female figures seem welded together in a complex unity of the feminine, of 'home', of peace and the future. The classical allusion – the youth, the caryatid column and classical robes – project the work into a realm of timelessness, or of the past, present and future bound together in the one moment – almost a historical time-slip dramatisation full of emotional content.

---

27 Mark Ferson & Mary Nilsson (eds), *Art Deco in Australia. Sunrise over the Pacific*, Craftsman House, Sydney, 2001, 37.

28 Ferson & Nilsson, *Art Deco in Australia*, 44-45.

Major Controversy and a Rendezvous with death

> A wowser is an ineffably pious person who mistakes the world for a penitentiary and himself as a warder.
>
> CJ Dennis, *Backblock Ballads and Other Verses.*[29]

Rayner Hoff as celebrity was no stranger to controversy. *Sacrifice* was actually one of three sculpture groups of significance for his design of figures and his narrative to support Dellit's architectural creation. They were to be two other groups entitled *Crucifixion of Civilisation* (1914) and *Victory after Sacrifice* (1918). These were meant to supplement the dramatic moment in time depicted in *Sacrifice*, thus creating a much broader historical canvas of the period 1914 to 1918 on the warfront in allegorical form. Both of these works by Hoff and his students had been completed in one third plaster model form for display purposes in his East Sydney Technical College studio. They were to remain there apparently untouched until nearly the end of the 1930s. They were never moulded into bronze and realised on the memorial site. Nevertheless, both presented the female as an equal participant in the events of the war, even in death itself.[30]

Crucifixion of Civilisation as the initial moment was pyramidal in form and designed for a shelf near the eastern exterior wall beside the major external staircase at its top. This intended bronze group was to become the most controversial, especially among church leaders. Dominant was a beautiful naked and perfectly proportioned Art Deco figure of a young dead woman representing Peace and Civilisation. She

29 Cited in Amanda Langesen, 'Whither wowser', *Australian Book Review*, February 2020, 42.
30 Beck, *Rayner Hoff*, 224.

was hanging on Mars' sword of War, sometimes viewed by onlookers as a cross-like structure, with her head bowed and body hanging down in a crucifixion pose (without nails). The image is, nevertheless, clearly evocative of the image of Christ on the Cross. Behind her head were the classical symbols of war: the looming armour, shield and helmet of Mars the Roman God of War. At her feet lay several massacred bodies of soldiers mixed with the material chaotic wreckage of war.

Crucifixion of Civilisation

Victory after Sacrifice

Rayner Hoff, *Art in Australia*

Victory After Sacrifice, the second moment in time in a similar pyramidal form, is composed of a similarly naked young female, but very much alive and vital: breasts and head erect with arms upraised and the victor's laurel wreath in one hand, symbolic of a young progressive Australia as a new nation, standing in front of a figure of Britannia representing the Empire bearing a sheathed sword, emblematic of the cessation of the hostilities of the Great War. Below the feet of the naked woman representing victory is the wreckage of the dead in dying. The whole symbolised achieved victory to end all war.[31] *Sacrifice* was intended, thus, as the second stage inbetween or the second moment in the chronological order of Hoff's three creative ideas.

For Dellit and Hoff as close collaborators, the ideal of the spirit of sacrifice became the 'presiding deity' – in the Great War; institutional faiths had crumbled as they saw it and man alone stood firm. They were activated by the same humanistic motive: 'to stress the idea of sacrifice and embody a hatred of war by the representation of suffering'.[32]

As soon as Rayner's three models were put on public display in the gallery of the NSW Department of Education headquarters in Bridge & Loftus Streets and the *Sydney Morning Herald* published illustrations of them, the most Reverend Michael Sheehan, the Catholic Coadjutor-Bishop of Sydney, who at the time was in charge of the diocese, objected and condemned them outright. He angrily and publicly refused an invitation to attend the official ceremony of the laying of the foundation stone of the memorial. In this manner, he exposed the Church's objections. He took very strong and very public exception to the naked female on, what seemed to him, to be the symbol of the Christian cross as part of the suggestive symbolism of the *Crucifixion of Civilisation*. In this, he was wrong and had misinterpreted the meaning.

According to Sheehan, the two sculptural groups proposed by Hoff for the memorial were intended for Protestant observers and adherences in the secular community and were 'gravely offensive to those of the Catholic faith'. *Smith's*

31 Ramsland & Mooney, 'Apollo must contemplate', 182.
32 Trustees ANZAC Memorial Building.

Weekly used Sheehan's remarks as the basis for sensational front-page headlines:

Catholic Bombshell to Anzacs
ARCHBISHOP SHEEHAN
AND THE MEMORIAL DEDICATION
Courteous Refusal to Attend Either
'In Person or By Proxy'
Objection to Protestant Service and Crucifix Statuary

A crudely executed drawing by Virgil Reilly, the *Smith's Weekly* cartoonist, of the *Crucifixion of Civilisation* filled the front page – the naked breasts of the female figure were much enlarged to those actually on Hoff's model.[33]

Even the Institute of Architects were critical and Bruce Dellit wrote a hot reply stating he found them insulting to the Trustees of the memorial, to the sculptor and himself.[34] Dellit's loyalty to Hoff throughout the public crisis was extremely vigorous and absolute.

It was much more than a storm in a teacup. The Catholics' refusal to attend official ceremonies destroyed their ecumenical nature. Such ecumenical approach had previously been extremely common across the nation in such foundation ceremonies.

The Trustees of the Anzac memorial were disappointed and felt humiliated. Catholic had been set against Protestant in the city. Even the Master Builders Association wrote that 'the taking of a nude woman to symbolise civilisation crucified by warfare … is not acceptable to everyday life'. Such attacks multiplied, as well as a few defences in the

33 *Smith's Weekly*, 16 July 1932.
34 CB Dellit, Letter to the Editor, *Sydney Morning Herald*, 3 August 1932.

sensational news media. Hoff did receive some muted support from friends and artistic circles who claimed wowserism was on a rampage.

At that time, Dr Kelly, the Archbishop of Australia, returned from Europe. Immediately, he also roundly condemned Hoff's ideas in all the group bronze sculptures for the memorial. He argued that Christianity had to fight against 'animal passions'; the sign that the devil was 'in the streets'.[35]

Rayner Hoff's reply was quietly dignified. He felt broken unfairly on the wheel of public opinion. He claimed that the Anzac Memorial was 'designed in the spirit of reverence for those that made the sacrifice demanded by war'. Yet his purpose was to avoid glorifying war 'lest we forget its folly'. He much regretted the sectarian nature of the public conflict that had emerged in the city.

The church opposition by Catholic and most Protestant churches may have been unwittingly fuelled by Hoff's ongoing friendship with Norman Lindsay whose drawing *The Crucified Venus* had previously caused another huge controversy. Lindsay's images were, in fact, essentially a savage attack on all forms of Christianity. He depicted 'a generously endowed naked blond beauty nailed to a cross. A monk on a ladder is taking horrific delight in hammering the second nail into her left hand. Various figures are standing below the cross in Lindsay's artwork in eager and grotesque anticipation. There is an armed cavalier of the Cromwellian period, an ugly bishop with his mitre, a dour

35 'Fashion Crushes Woman's beauty. Dr Kelly Speaks', Sydney *Sun*, 29 September 1932.

Puritan in a huge black hat reading his Bible, 'a fanatical Rasputin, an excited Methodist preacher and so on'.[36] In his lively cartoonish illustrations, Lindsay depicts a savage indictment of the whole of Christianity. Hoff's work was nothing like this and had no such intention.

Linday's *Venus* had appeared as a plate in a book published in 1931.[37] It was the same time as the public unfolding of plans for the Hyde Park ANZAC Memorial. Essentially, a savage attack on Australian churches wowserism as Lindsay saw it. All clergy around his cross had ugly, grim, spiteful expressions, all appalled at the nakedness of the Venus figure on the cross. Clearly, the Catholic clergy recognised its unintended relationship and its purpose – in some error – with Hoff's heroic neo-classical and allegorical female figures depicting the fall and rise of civilisation. The artworks of Lindsay and those of Hoff had very little to do with one another in terms of their political purpose apart, superficially, from their pyramidal composition. It could be argued that Hoff suffered public humiliation by association.

By early 1933, the now nervous Trustees were claiming to Dellit and Hoff that they did not have enough money left to cast in bronze the two contested sculptural groups for the two open-air platforms of the building. Yet, as a compromise, they agreed to proceed with *Sacrifice*. Dellit, intensely loyal to Hoff, continued to seek support for his friend's treasured, but in effect rejected bronze artworks

36 '*The Crucified Venus*', Norman Lindsay's Pen Drawings', *Art in Australia*, Sydney,1931, unpaginated.

37 Plate 4, '*The Crucified Venus*', *Norman Lindsay's Pen Drawings* (unpaginated), Ure Smith, Sydney, 1931.

from a variety of influential people, but to no avail in the end. The cause was lost.

Finally, a humiliated and exasperated Hoff said he had no wish to force on the public anything that was distasteful, even to a section of the population. Nevertheless, he was backed by those prominent in the art world: Norman Lindsay, Norman Carter, Sydney Ure Smith and the Sydney University Professor of Architecture, Leslie Wilkinson – who were all vocal in their advocacy and support. Lindsay was, however, an unfortunate supporter to say the least.

Dellit saw the two rejected groups of sculptures as an integral part of his overall design and without them the memorial as a creation would remain incomplete. He deliberately left bare the granite shelves designed to hold the two works as a very public gesture and protest. And so it remains to this day.[38]

* * *

On Rayner Hoff's sudden and unexpected tragic death in 1937, C Bruce Dellit was moved to write:

> As an artist, Hoff had the qualities of greatness, his ability to portray the dramatic movement of life and the character of his subjects was ennobled by an amazing capacity to infuse into all his works a feeling of dominating power and strength; this capacity was the mirror of this man's soul.[39]

As with many veterans of the Great War, Hoff died

38 Ramsland & Mooney, 'Apollo must contemplate', 184-5.

39 C Bruce Dellitt [*sic*], 'Rayner Hoff. Power and Strength', *SMH*, 4 December 1937.

prematurely and at the height of his powers.[40]

To the ordinary person in the street, Rayner Hoff's artworks are vivid illustrations, extraordinarily descriptive in story-telling powers and full of interest and complexity of meaning. As historian Ken Inglis had put it, of all war memorial sculpture in Australia *Sacrifice* continues to be the most admired, 'a masterpiece of craftsmanship'. The classical allusion – youth and beauty, the caryatid column and the classical robes of the women – project the artwork 'into the realm of the timeless and universal'.[41] Yet the contemporary or Art Deco elements, like the devices of modern total warfare, pull the view back from the classical Spartan elements to the present in people's minds, or at least to now – the fairly recent past with relevance to the present time with ongoing dangers of war and chaos.

More broadly, Australia and New Zealand in a worldwide sense belong quantitatively to the most important regions for the development of Art Deco, especially in sculpture and architecture. In Sydney, Art Deco architecture and sculpture in the 1920s and 1930s willingly adopted a monumental favoured attitude. Characteristic of this is the Anzac Memorial, a modernistically simplified memorial, stylized into weighty

40 After surfing at Bondi on Sunday, 14 November, Hoff felt unwell and thought he had gastric influenza. His wife of 17 years, Annis Briggs, wanted to call a doctor but Hoff didn't want to worry him. He woke early the following Wednesday in great pain. An ambulance rushed him to Delaware, a local private hospital in Waverley. George Rayner Hoff died there on Friday, 19 November, two days after he was admitted. His death certificate stated the cause as haemorrhage/pancreatitis – revealed in the post-mortem . He had been in Australia for 14 years. Annis and Rayner had two children: Sandra, aged 15 and Nereida, aged 8 at the time of his death. Rayner was cremated at Rookwood Crematorium; Beck, *Rayner Hoff*, 235-40.

41 Inglis, 'Passing Away', 312.

proportion, completed in 1934 and erected in a present-day modernised Hyde Park as the centre of the city – designed by C Bruce Dellit, an admirer of Frank Lloyd Wright. The blockish sculptures high up on the exterior of the building dependent on a seemingly superficial formalistic Cubism, successfully blended into the architecture – executed by Rayner Hoff and his team.[42]

These monumental works rival Heitor da Silva Costa and Paul Landowski's *Christ the Redeemer*, an Art Deco stone sculpture of 1931 in Rio de Janiero on the mountain overlooking the harbour.

Some Art Deco and modernism historians find it unusual that, in Australia, Art Deco was considered appropriate for the design of memorials to honour the memory of so many thousands of Australian soldiers who died in World War I. Perhaps this is why Art Deco took such a hold in Australia (and New Zealand) to become a vital part of the collective consciousness during the late 1920s, when public competitions were being held for commissions to design and construct such monuments.

Art Deco was the style adopted by Australian architects of several major public memorials. Of the three or four most significant examples – the Melbourne Shrine of Remembrance (Hudson & Wardrop, 1933), the Sydney Anzac Memorial, Hyde Park (Dellit & Hoff, 1934) and the National War Memorial, Canberra (Emil Sodersteen, 1936) – it is Dellit's monumental edifice in Sydney that stands out internationally. It is now widely regarded as one of the

42 Norbert Wolf, *Art Deco*, Prestel, Munich, London, New York, 2013, 208-9.

masterworks of Australian Art Deco architecture.

Dellit had the vision that it was the architect's role to bring together history, technology and art, particularly in artistic collaboration with Rayner Hoff whose bronze sculpture *Sacrifice* came to form the centrepiece of the memorial, more so because of the public rejection of the other two bronze groups. The result was a structure that successfully merged modern forms which – in line with the historical sources of Art Deco – referred to the past, used new materials and art in a design that powerfully exploits its symbolic potential.

At the opposite end of Hyde Park stands another refined example of Art Deco, the Archibald Fountain, 1933 – the work of French sculptor François Sicard. It sets gently styled figures from classical mythology amid a geometric structure that is enlivened by sunray waterjets.[43]

The two Hyde Park memorials at either end, engendered by the First World War with the death of so many men-of-action, boldly declared the ideology of Vitalism in Art with the notion of healing at its centre. Both Hyde Park memorials were intended to heal the living and to remember the dead in the *style moderne* or Art Deco form in both its 'American streamlined and French luxe and lacquer visual styles, architectural masterpieces from the Sydney Harbour Bridge (1932) to the Anzac Memorial in Hyde Park (1934).[44] And, in between, the peaceful

43 Ghislaine Wood, *Art Deco 1910-1939*, National Gallery of Victoria, Melbourne, 2008, 244-5; see also Ramsland & Mooney, 'Apollo must contemplate', 165-91.

44 Daniel Thomas, 'Foreword' in Deborah Edwards & Denise Mimmocchi (eds), *Sydney Moderns. Art for a new world*, NSW Art Gallery, 2013, 13-16.

harmony of the Archibald Fountain (1932).

The location of the Anzac Memorial:

> … at the city's geographical heart was a metaphorical breathing point in Sydney's interwar program of modernisation – a solemn statement of the traumas that remained embedded in the public psyche and a foreshadow of the devastation of another encroaching world conflict.[45]

★ ★ ★

Under my window Time stood still,
  Looking backwards, all at a loss,
To a rubble mound on a blasted hill,
  A rubble mound and a wooden cross—
He was old and small and wistful seeming,
  Standing there in a city street,
But the torrent of life about him streaming
  Stayed where he stayed, till a heart scarce beat :
      The clock struck eleven—
      And the Dead Men laughed in Heaven
And Time stood under my window in defeat.

Then from the sky in columns bright
  Came they streaming in ranks of pride
As the bugle sang and years took flight;
  They had not changed since the hour they died!
They never age and with no misgiving
  Into the future they grandly press,
Each a captain of men still living,
  Leading us on by his selflessness.

45 Edwards & Mimmocchi (eds), *Sydney Moderns*, 79.

'Tis the last stroke of eleven—
All the regiments of Heaven
Droop their colors o'er the land they died to bless.

Henry Pryce, "The Ageless Army" (*Sun*, 11 November 1931)

Rayner Hoff captured the movement and poetry of Pryce's verse when he completed his memorial sculptures in 1934.

* * *

The post office on the Isle of Man has since remembered the memorial works of Rayner Hoff as well as the Anzacs who were born there.

John Joseph Corteen, a house painter by trade, emigrated from Castletown, the Isle of Man, shortly before volunteering for the 1st AIF. He departed on 4 September 1915 from Sydney with his battalion for Egypt constantly training aboard the troopship. He arrived on the Gallipoli peninsula and saw three months of intensely dangerous action against the Turkish Army until the 1st AIF evacuated in December. He was soon moved to the Western Front where he took part in many of the major battles until Armistice Day. Corteen suffered from an ear infections made worse by the noise of battle and spent time in hospital, but otherwise survived the war without further injury. In July 1919, he was discharged from the AIF, but chose to return to live on the Isle of Man in Castletown instead of travelling back to Australia.

Jon Gell of Pembroke House on Castletown Promenade migrated and joined the 4th Australian Infantry. He was killed in the Suvla Bay landing at Gallipoli between 6 and 8 August 1915. The exact date is unknown. He was 27 years of age.

Thomas Sayle Corlett migrated from Ballaugh to Western Australia in 1913 and took up farming before enlisting in the 3rd Australian Pioneer Battalion in February 1916. He arrived on the Western Front in November of the same year. He was killed in the Third Battle of Passchendaele by shell fire on 19 October 1917. He was 29.[46]

46 See John Ramsland, 'Rayner Hoff – sculpture for the 1st AIF and World War I', *Australiana*, vol 42, no 3, 2020, 33-41. Stamp series, courtesy of Isle of Man Post Office, design Louise Cornwall.

Selected Bibliography

Primary Sources

Research for this book has primarily drawn on archives of the Australian War Memorial (AWM), the National Library of Australia (NLA), the National Archives of Australia (NAA), the Mitchell Library collection of the NSW State Library, NSW State Records and several collections: Manning River Historical Society, Royal Australian Historical Society, Newcastle Library Local Studies.

Details of sources are cited fully in footnotes. Various contemporary film documentaries of WWI and related material are also detailed. Reference was made to various theses and manuscripts.

Secondary Sources

Astbury, Leigh. 'Death and Eroticism in the Anzac Legend', *Art in Australia*, vol 30, no 1, 1992, 67-73

Australians At War, The Illustrated History, The Five Mile Press, Scoresby, 2012

Barrie, Douglas M. 'The Australian Horse at War', in Elyne Mitchell (ed.), *Stories of Australian Horses*, Currey O'Neil, South Yarra, 1983, 99-103

Bean, CEW. *The Australian Imperial Force in France During the Main German Offensive of 1918*, vols v & vi, Angus & Robertson, Sydney, 1940 & 1942

Beaumont, Joan. *Broken Nation. Australia in the Great War*, Allen & Unwin, Crows Nest, 2013

---- & Alison Cadzow (eds). *Serving Our Country. Indigenous Australians, War, Defence and Citizenship*, NewSouth, Sydney, 2018

Bell, Kathrine. *The Australian Light Horse*, Murray David Publishing, Australian History Series, Davidson, 2009

Bennett, Scott. *Pozières. The Anzac Story*, Scribe, Melbourne, 2011

Black, Donald. *Red Dust*, Ch 1; published in 1931, adapted for *Digger*, no 70, March 2020, 24-31

Braga, Stuart. *Anzac Soldier, The Life of Sir Neville Howse Australia's First VC*, Hale & Iremonger, Sydney, 2000

Broadbent, Harvey. *Gallipoli the fatal shore*, Viking, Camberwell, 2005

Burness, Peter. 'The Victoria Cross in Australia', *Conflict*, issue 46, July 2009, 16

Burney, Allan (ed.). *Famous Fighters of World War I*, Key Publishing, Stamford, 2014

Butler, Colonel AG, DSO, VD, BA, MB, Ch B (Camb). *The Australian Army Medical Services in the War of 1914-1918*, vols I, II & III, AWM, Melbourne, 1938-1943

Cameron, David W. *Australians on the Western Front 1918*, vol 1, Viking, Melbourne, 2018

Caulfield, Michael. *The Unknown ANZACS*, Hachette, Sydney, 2013

Cecil Healy: in Memoriam, Sydney, nd (certainly 1919)

Cochrane, Peter. *The Western Front 1916-1918*, ABC Books, Sydney, 2004

Coulthart, Ross. *Charles Bean*, HarperCollins, Sydney, 2014

Coulthard-Clark, Chris. *The Encyclopaedia of Australia's Battles*, Allen and Unwin, Crows Nest, 1998

Cutlack, FM. *The Australians: Their Final Campaign, 1918*, Sampson Low, London, 1918

---- (ed.). *War Letters of General Monash*, Angus & Robertson, Sydney, 1934; Black Inc, Collingwood, 2015

Dearberg, Neil. 'Aussies on Horseback', *Military History Monthly*, issue 36, September 2013, 52-57

Dennis, Peter *et al* (eds). *The Oxford Companion to Australian Military History*, Oxford University Press, Melbourne, 1997

Denton, Kit. *For Queen and Commonwealth*, Time-Life Books, Australia, 1987

Doyle, Arthur Conan. *The British Campaign in Europe*, Geoffrey Blas,

London, 1929

Edwards, Deborah. 'Race, Death and Gender in the ANZAC MEMORIAL', *Art and Australia Quarterly*, vol 28, no 4, 1991, 476-81

Ellis, Alexander D. *The Story of the Fifth Australian Division*, Hodder & Stoughton, London, 1920

Fall of Eagles, BBC televised series and booklet, 1996

Faulkner, Neil. 'Assassination Sarajevo, 28 June 1914', *Military History Monthly*, issue 41, February 2014, 14-20

---- . 'Passchendaele', *Military History Monthly*, issue 83, 2017, 24-38

Faunce, Thomas. 'The Last Hours of the Red Baron', *Wartime*, issue 32, 2005, 20-21

Firkins, Peter. *The Australians in Nine Wars*, Rigby, Adelaide, 1971

Fischer, Tim. *Maestro John Monash*, Monash University Publishing, 2014

Franki, George & Clyde Slatyer. *Mad Harry, Harry Murray VC, CMG, DSO & Bar, DCM, C de G, Australia's Most Decorated Soldier*, Kangaroo Press, Pymble, 2001

Fussell, Paul. *The Great War and Modern Memory*, Folio Society, London, 2014

Gammage, Bill. *The Broken Years. Australian Soldiers in the Great War*, Melbourne University Press (*MUP*), Carlton, 2010

Garton, Stephen. 'War and Masculinity in Twentieth Century Australia', in Clive Moore and Kay Saunders (eds), 'Australian Masculinities : men and their histories', *Journal of Australian Studies*, no 56, 1998, 86-95

Gatfield, John with Richard Landels. *The RSL Book of World War I*, Harper Collins, Sydney, 2015

Gibbons, Floyd. *The Red Knight of Germany*, Cassell and Company, London, 1931

Gillison, Douglas. *Royal Australian Air Force 1939-1942*, Australian War Memorial, Canberra, 1960

Goddard, Chris. '"The earth holds not a braver gentleman". The life and death of John Hay', *Wartime*, no 2, April 1998, 20-23

Grant, Ian. *A Dictionary of Australian Military History*, Random House, Milsons Point, 1992

Grey, Jeffrey. *The Australian Army*, vol 1, Oxford University Press, 2001

Griffiths, Tony. *Douglas Grant : that Black Digger from the Scottish Mob*, Friends of Callan Park, Rozelle, 2019

Hall, Robert A. *Fighters from the Fringe*, Aboriginal Studies Press, Canberra, 1995

Hamilton, Robert. *Victoria Cross Heroes of World War I*, Atlantic Publishing, Hertfordshire, 2015

Hampton, Dan. *Lords of the Sky. Fighter Pilots and Air Combat from the Red Baron to the F-16*, William Morrow, 2014

Helmi, Nadine and Gerhardt Fischer. *The Enemy at Home. German Internees in World War I Australia*, UNSW Press, Sydney, 2011

Holden, Robert. *And the Band Played On*, Hardie Grant Books, Melbourne, 2014

Hughes, Matthew. 'Australians and the fall of Damascus, 1 October 1918', *Journal of the Australian War Memorial*, no 26, April 1995, 26-37

Idriess, Ion L. *The Desert Column*, 13th edition, Angus & Robertson, Sydney, 1944

Inglis, KS. *Sacred Places. War Memorials in the Australian Landscape*, Miegunyah Press, Carlton, 1999

Innes-Robbins, Simon. 'Allenby and the Battle of Arras', *Military History Matters*, issue 110, November 2019, 18-24

Jackomos, Alick and Derek Fowell, *Forgotten Heroes. Aborigines at War from the Somme to Vietnam*, Victoria Press, Melbourne, 1993

Jones, Ian. 'Beersheba: The light horse charge and the making of myths', *Journal of the Australian War Memorial*, Canberra, no 3, October 1983, 26-37

Journey's End, feature film, directed by Saul Dibb, 2018

Kelly, Michael. 'First to Fight', *Wartime*, issue 67, Winter 2014, 44-49

Kieza, Grantlee. *Monash. The Soldier who shaped Australia*, ABC

Books, Sydney, 2015

Laffin, John. *Digger. The Story of the Australian Soldier*, Cassell, London, 1959

Lasswell, Harold D. *Propaganda Techniques in the World War*, Peter Smith, New York, 1927

Likeman, Colonel Robert CSM. *From the Tropics to the Desert. German New Guinea, Egypt & Palestine, 1914-1918*, The Australian Doctors at War Series, vol 2, Slouch Hat Publications, Macrae, 2012

---- . *Australian Doctors on the Western Front*, Rosenberg, Dural, 2014

Likeman, Robert. *Australian Doctors on the Western Front*, vol 3, Rosenberg, Dural, 2014

Macdonald, Lyn (ed.). *Anthem for Doomed Youth. Poets of the Great War*, Folio, London, 2000

Macklin, Robert. *Bravest. Australia's greatest war heroes and how they won their medals*, Allen & Unwin, Sydney, 2008

McMullin, Ross. *Will Dyson. Cartoonist, etcher and Australia's finest war artist*, Angus & Robertson, Sydney, 1984

---- . '"Heartstrings Aching for the Absent Boy": Years of Anguish – the Losses of War', *Victorian Historical Journal*, vol 86, no 1, 2015, 41-59

Mahony, Juan. *From the Home Front to the Front Line. Images of the Great War*, self-published, 2001

---- (compiler). *The Digger's View – WWI in Colour*, self-published, New Lambton, 2014

Maitland, Major General Gordon. *Honours and Awards of the Army*, Playbill Military Publications, North Moore Park, Sydney, 2014

Manning, Frederic. *The Middle Parts of Fortune*, Text Publishing, Melbourne, 2000

Masefield, John. *Gallipoli*, New Holland Press, Sydney, 2011 (first published in 1916 by Rigby Ltd)

Maxwell, Joseph. *Hell's Bells and Mademoiselles*, Angus & Robertson, Sydney, 1936

Medal Yearbook 2018, Token Publishers, Exeter, 2018

Monash, John. *War Letters of General Monash*, Black Inc, Melbourne, 2015

---- , Sir John. *The Australian Victories in France, 1918*, Hutchinson, London, 1920

Monash. The Forgotten Hero, Film Victoria, Screen Australia, ABC TV, DVD, 2008

Moorehead, Alan. *Gallipoli*, Macmillan, Melbourne, 1975

Munro, Trevor. 'Private 6429 Albert William Bonser, 18th Battalion', *Digger*, no 40, September 2012, 34-6

Murray, Lieutenant-Colonel PL. *Official Records of the Australian Military Contingents to the War in South Africa*, Govt Printer, Melbourne, 1911

Murray, T. (Director) *The Skin of Others*, Feature film, Tarpaulin Productions, 2020

---- . (Producer) 'Douglas Grant and the skin of others', ABC Radio National, 2017

---- . (Producer) 'The skin of others: when Douglas Grant met Henry Lawson', Tarpaulin Productions, 2018

---- .& Hilary Howes. 'Douglas Grant and Rudolf Marcuse: Wartime encounters at the edge of Art', *History and Anthropology*, vol 30, 2019, 1-30

Newton, Dennis. 'Spectre of the Red Baron' (pts 1 & 2), *Journal of the Australian War Memorial*, nos 8 & 9, 1986, 46-53; 47-52

Nichols, Robert. 'After the shooting stopped', *Wartime*, issue 45, April 2009, 26-31

Norris, Sir Kingsley. *Annual Post-Graduate Oration. Major-General Sir Neville Howse VC*, reprinted from the Bulletin of the Post-Graduate Committee in Medicine, University of Sydney, vol 22, no 11, February 1967, 214-36

O'Meara, Peter and Scott Deverish. 'Sir Neville Howse (VC) Private John Simpson Kilpatrick and Private Martin O'Meara (VC) and their contribution to Australian military medicine', *Australian Journal of Paramedicine*, vol 8, issue 1, 3

Pedersen, PA. *Monash as Military Commander*, Melbourne University Press, Carlton, 1985

Pegram, Aaron. 'Under the Kaiser's Crescent Moon', *Wartime*, issue 76, Spring 2016, 32-37

Perry, Roland. *Monash. The Outsider who won a War*, Random House, North Sydney, 2007

Percival, John. *For Valour. The Victoria Cross: Courage in Action*, James Methuen, London, 1986

Petersen, Robert *War Service of Shore Old Boys during the First 50 Years*, Shore, North Sydney, 2006

Piggott, Michael. 'Stonewalling in German New Guinea', *Journal of the Australian War Memorial*, no 12, April 1988, 3

Ramsland, John. *Cook's Hill Life Saving & Surf Club. The First Hundred Years 1911-2011*, Brolga, Melbourne, 2011

----. *Venturing into No Man's Land. Joseph Maxwell VC World War I Hero*, Brolga, Melbourne, 2012

---- . 'Neville Howse: Surgeon and War Hero', in Maurie Garland (ed.), *At the Going Down of the Sun. A Manning Valley Remembrance*, vol 1: 1885-1918, Manning Valley Historical Society, 2014, 16-21

---- . *The Other Side of No Man's Land. Arthur Wheen World War I Hero*, Brolga, Melbourne, 2015

---- . 'Dedication of the Neville Howse VC Rest Area', *Digger*, no 51, June 2015, 38-42

---- , 'Clarence Smith Jeffries VC. War Hero, local hero, school hero', in John Beach *et al*, *To Climb the Hill. A People's History of Newcastle East Public School*, Newcastle East Public School, 2016, 64-67

---- . 'The measure of his genius. Two different approaches to a wartime general'. *Monash: The Soldier who shaped Australia* by Grantlee Kieza, ABC Books, 713p. & *Maestro John Monash Australia's Greatest Citizen General* by Tim Fischer, 33p., Monash University Publishing, *Australian Book Review*, no 378, January-February 2016, 58

---- . 'Australia's first Victoria Cross Winner. Sir Neville Howse, Rural and Military Doctor', 1863-1930, *Medal News*, vol 55, no 6, June/July 2017, 24-27

---- . 'The Road to Passchendaele', *Digger*, no 61, December 2017, 55-58

---- .'Commemorating James ("Big Jim") Hartley Antcliff No 2029, 36th Battalion AIF', *Digger*, no 61, December 2017, 20-25

----. *The Legacy of Douglas Grant. A Notable Aborigine in War and Peace*, Brolga, Melbourne, 2019

---- .'Rayner Hoff – sculpture for the 1st AIF and World War I', *Australiana*, vol 42, no 3, 2020, 33-41

---- & Christopher Mooney. Remembering Aboriginal Heroes. Struggle, Identity and the Media, Brolga, Melbourne, 2006

---- .'Apollo must contemplate a world of which he had never dreamed', Gretchen Poiner (ed.), The National Estate – Civic Heritage, Proceedings of 2008 Conference, Independent Scholars Association of Australia, Canberra, 165-91

Ray, Greg & Sylvia. *The Hunter Region in the Great War*, self-published, Newcastle, 2017

Reid, Richard. *Gallipoli 1915*, ABC Books, Sydney, 2002

Remarque, Erich Maria. *All Quiet on the Western Front*, trans from the German by AW Wheen, GP Putnam's Sons, London, 1929

Review of Geoffrey Serle. *John Monash: A Biography*, Melbourne University Press, Carlton, 1982, *Journal of the Australian War Memorial*, no 1, October 1982, 48

Scott, Ernest. *Australia During the War. Official History of Australia in the War of 1914-1918*, vol XI, Angus and Robertson, Sydney, 1936

Serle, Geoffrey. *John Monash. A Biography*, MUP, Carlton, 1982

Smithers, AJ. *Sir John Monash*, Angus & Robertson, Sydney, 1973

Starr, Alison Neville. *Neville Howse VC. Biography of an Authentic Australian*, self-published, Sydney, 1991

Staunton, Anthony. *Victoria Cross. Australia's Finest & the Battles they fought*, Hardie Grant Books, Prahran, 2006

Stevenson, David. *With Our Backs to the Wall. Victory and Defeat in 1918*, Allen Lane, Penguin, London, 2011

Stockings, Craig. 'Khaki in the classroom junior cadet training in

Australia 1911-31', *History of Education Review*, vol 37, pt 1, 2008, 16-33

---- & John Connor. *Before the Anzac Dawn*, NewSouth, Sydney, 2013

Sturgeon, Graeme. 'Public Sculpture: the pleasure and the pain', *Art and Australia Quarterly*, vol 25, no 2, 222-7

Summerville, Donald (ed.). *The Complete Illustrated History of World War I*, Centenary Special Edition, Media Factory, Sydney, 2014

Travers, Richard. *Diggers in France. Australian Soldiers on the Western Front*, ABC Books, Sydney, 2008

Tyquin, Michael B. *Neville Howse*, Oxford University Press, Melbourne, 1999

Vesper, Stan (ed.). *Those who served. Surf Lifesavers at War*, Playright Publishing, Caringbah, 2015

Visitor's Guide to the Battlefields, Somme Tourist Bureau Board

Wallace, RL. *The Australians at the Boer War*, Australian War Memorial, Canberra, 1976

Warner, Philip. *Passchendaele*, Wordsworth Editions, Hertfordshire, 1999

Wedd, Monty. *Australian Military Uniforms 1800-1982*, Kangaroo Press, Kenthurst, 1982

Westwell, Ian. *The Ultimate Illustrated History of World War I*, Hermes House, Leicestershire, 2009

White, John. 'The Unbelievable Truth: The "Red Baron" controversy 1918-1998', *Wartime*, no 2, April 1998, 18-19

Wigmore, Lionel with Bruce Harding. *They Dared Mightily*, 2nd edition revised by Jeff Williams, Australian War Memorial, Canberra, 1986

Wigmore, Lionel G. 'A Description of the Anzac Memorial Building, New South Wales', *Sculpture for the Anzac Memorial Building, Hyde Park, Sydney, N.S.W.*, Society of Artists' Exhibition, 1932

Wolff, Leon. *In Flanders Fields*, Longmans, Green & Co, London, 1960

General and Unpublished Sources

1000 Famous Australians, Rigby, Adelaide, 1978

Australia Through Time. 126 Years of Australia's History, Random House, Sydney, 1994

Australian Dictionary of Biography (*ADB*), Melbourne University Press, Carlton

Ayto, John & Ian Crofton. *Brewer's Britain & Ireland*, Weidenfeld & Nicolson, London, 2005

Baker, Reg L ("Snowy"). *General Physical Culture*, George Robertson & Co, Sydney, 1911

Barcan, Alan. 'The Classical Curriculum in Australian Schools', Fritz-Peter Hager *et al* (eds), *Aspects of Antiquity in the History of Education*, University of Hannover, 1992

---- . 'Latin and Greek in Australian Schools', *History of Education Review*, vol 22, no 1, 1993, 40-41

Baxter, F. *The Amateur Swimming Association Book on Swimming and Swimming Strokes*, London, 1921

Beach, John *et al. To Climb the Hill. A People's History of Newcastle East Public School*, Newcastle East Public School, 2016

Beaver, Bruce. *Poets and Others*, Brandl & Schlesinger, 1999

Beck, Deborah. *Rayner Hoff. The Life of a Sculptor*, NewSouth, Sydney, 2017

Bradley, Sean. *The Bondi Lifesaver. A History of An Australian Icon*, ABC Books, Sydney, 2007

Carter, Norman. 'Rayner Hoff – Sculptor', *Art in Australia*, 1 March 1938, 8

Chauvel, Elsa. *My Life with Charles Chauvel*, Shakespeare Head Press, Sydney, 1973

Clark, CMH. *A History of Australia*, vols V & VI, Melbourne University Press, Carlton, 1981 & 1987

Concise Dictionary of National Biography, The. vols I, II, III, Oxford University Press, Oxford, 1992

Cook's Hill SLS Archives, Record Book 1911-1915

Cunningham, Stuart. *Featuring Australia. The Cinema of Charles Chauvel,* Allen & Unwin, North Sydney, 1991

Digger, Magazine of the Families & Friends of the First AIF Inc; editor, Graeme Hosken

Edwards, Deborah. *'This vital flesh'. The Sculpture of Rayner Hoff and His School,* NSW Art Gallery, Sydney, 1999

---- & Denise Mimmocchi (eds). *Sydney Moderns. Art for a new world,* NSW Art Gallery, 2013

Ferson, Mark & Mary Nilsson (eds). *Art Deco in Australia. Sunrise over the Pacific,* Craftsman House, Fine Arts Publishing, 2001

Galton, Barry. *Gladiators of the Surf. The Australian Life Saving Championships — A History,* AH & AW Reed, Sydney, 1984

Gordon, Harry. *Australia and the Olympic Games,* University of Queensland Press, Brisbane, 1994

Harris, Reg S. *Heroes of the Surf. Fifty Years' History of Manly Life Saving Club,* Manly Life Saving Club (c.1960)

Hermes, Magazine of the University of Sydney, 1915-1919

Hurley, Frank. *Sydney. A Camera Study,* Angus & Robertson, Sydney, 1948

Jose, Arthur Wilberforce & Herbert James Carter (eds). *The Illustrated Australian Encyclopaedia,* Angus and Robertson, Sydney, 1925

Journal of the Royal Australian Historical Society (JRAHS)

Jowett, Garth S & Victoria O'Donnell. *Propaganda and Persuasion,* Beverley Hills, 1986

Luke, Sarah. *Callan Park. Hospital for the Insane,* Australian Scholarly, North Melbourne, 2018

Manning, Frederic. *Eidola,* John Murray, London, 1917

Mitchell, Elyne (ed.). *Stories of Australian Horses,* Currey O'Neil, South Yarra, 1983

Nauright, John & Timothy JL Chandler (eds). *Making Men: Rugby and Masculine Identity,* Routledge, London, 1996

New South Wales in 1881 published by govt authority, Thomas

Richards (ed.), 2nd issue, Sydney, 1882

Niall, Brenda. *Mannix*, Text Publishing, Melbourne, 2015

Norman Lindsay's Pen Drawings (unpaginated), Ure Smith, Sydney, 1931

Paterson, AB. *Rio Grande and other verses*, Cornstalk Publishing, Sydney, 1926

Pike, Andrew and Ross Cooper. *Australian Cinema 1900-1977*, Oxford University Press & The Australian Film Institute, Melbourne, 1980

Pollard, Jack. *Australian Rugby Union. The Game and the Players*, Angus & Robertson with the Australian Broadcasting Corporation, Sydney, 1984

Ramsland, John. *The Struggle Against Isolation. A History of the Manning River*, Library of Australian History, North Sydney, 1987

---- . 'Neville Howse VC, rural doctor and War Hero', unpublished talk, Hunter Postgraduate Medical Institute, 2 August 2014, Marina View Function Centre, Newcastle Harbour

Read, Herbert. *Collected Poems*, Faber and Faber, London, 1946

Record, The. Magazine of the Boys' High School, Sydney

Reveille. Official magazine of the Returned Sailors' and Soldiers' Imperial League of Australia (New South Wales Branch)

Royal Life Saving Society Handbook, The (founded 1891), London, nd

Scarlett, Ken. *Australian Sculptors*, Nelson, Melbourne, 1980

Semmler, Clement. *The Banjo of the Bush. The Life and Times of AB "Banjo" Paterson*, University of Queensland Press, St Lucia, 1974

Sheridan, Peter AM. *Sydney Art Deco*, Art Deco and Modernist Society of Australia, Sydney, 2019

Shirley, Graham & Brian Adams. *Australian Cinema. The First Eighty Years*, Angus & Robertson and Currency Press, Sydney, 1983

Souvenir Programme. Manly Surf Club 1st Grand Carnival, Saturday, 25 January 1908

Stone, Walter (ed.). *The Best of Banjo Paterson*, Summit Books, Dee Why, 1977

Supplement to The New South Wales Surf Bathing Association's Handbook, December 1914

Surf Life Saving Displays and Beach Sports (program), in honour of the Duke and Duchess of York, Manly NSW, Saturday, 26 March 1927

Sydney Morning Herald, 1914-1920

Throssell, Ric. *Wild Weeds and Windflowers. The Life and Letters of Katharine Susannah Prichard*, Angus & Robertson, Sydney, 1990

Tomsen, Stephen & Mike Donaldson (eds). *Male Trouble, Looking at Australian Masculinities*, Pluto Press, Melbourne, 2003

Ward, Russell. *The History of Australia. The Twentieth Century*, Harper & Row, New York, 1977

Wellington, Phillip. *100 Famous Australian* Lives, Ure Smith, Sydney, 1968

Wenham, Michael. '"My own darling laddie". In Search of George Wenham: an Aboriginal Anzac and the History of Denial', PhD (History), The University of Newcastle, 2015

---- . Unpublished address reviewing Ramsland's *The Legacy of Douglas Grant*, United Service Club, Newcastle, 3 October 2019

White, Richard. *Inventing Australia: Images and Identity, 1688-1980*, Allen & Unwin, Sydney, 1981

Wolf, Norbert. *Art Deco*, Prestel, Munich, London, New York, 2013

Wood, Ghislaine *et al* (eds). *Art Deco 1910-1939*, National Gallery of Victoria, 2008

INDEX

M

N

O

P

Q

R

Y

About the Author

John Ramsland OAM, FACE, was born in Manly in 1942 and grew up there. For forty-one years, he taught at all levels: NSW state high schools, 10 years; NSW Teachers Colleges for 5 years and 26 years at the University of Newcastle.

He is now Emeritus Professor of History at Newcastle. He is married to Dr Marie Ramsland and they have two adult sons, Mark and Paul.

John is the author or co-author of 26 books and at least 130 articles, chapters, reviews, conference papers and magazine and newspaper features. His co-authored *Remembering Aboriginal Heroes* (Brolga) has been recently re-released.

Brave and Bold (Brolga 2008) won the NSW Writers Centre Open Book (non-fiction) prize. John has won several other awards and commendations for his historical writings.

In 2006, he was awarded the Order of Australia for services through historical research into child poverty, the Indigenous experience and institutional life in colonial Australia and to education. In 2012, he was given the Lifetime Achievement Award, Wollotuka Institute of Aboriginal Studies.

His most recent book *The Legacy of Douglas Grant. A Notable Aborigine in War and Peace* (Brolga) has received universally favourable reviews.

- **Allan Stanistreet**, *Medal News*, vol 58, no 4, 2020, 44:
  Here we have an absorbing book by an Emeritus Professor

of History at the University of Newcastle, NSW, with eight other works on Australian [war] subjects. In it he explores the life and work of a distinguished Aborigine who was adopted by a white couple, given the name of Douglas Grand (their surname) and provided with a good education. An intelligent man of many talents … he enlisted into the AIF in World War I, being taken prisoner-of-war at the Battle of Bullecourt and subsequently proving an inspiring leader of his fellow prisoners. Douglas' adoptive parents were Scots emigrés and he was to become an accomplished bagpipe player, entertaining audiences throughout his life. Like so many of his fellow Aborigines he was to suffer from racism after the war – a situation not entirely eliminated to this day – but he retained his sense of humour and scholarly interests. Amongst other achievements, he was responsible for the design and erection of a striking war memorial to the ANZACs which still survives in Callan Park, Rozelle. Between the wars, he suffered from bouts of depression and had problems with alcohol but he continued to campaign on behalf of his fellow Aborigines until his death in 1951. It Is a jolly good read dealing with a rather neglected subject … Recommended.

• **Barbara Kelly**, *The Legacy of Douglas Grant.* A Notable Aborigine in War and Peace. A Historical Biography by John Ramsland, in *Newcastle Family History Journal*, June 2020, 19:

One hundred and one years ago, when Douglas Grant … returned to Sydney on 1st June 1919 after serving his country on the Western Front and as a prisoner-of-war in Germany, he discovered a far different place. Australia was in the grip of the Spanish flu epidemic with thousands of young and old dead by the end of 1919 – to be precise, 11,353 deaths, approximately half in New South Wales.

...

Members of the congregation in churches that remained opened, such as the Hunter Baillie Presbyterian Church in Annandale that Douglas Grant attended, were told to sit more than a yard apart in order to inhibit the contagion.

The quarantine camps that were erected in state borders for all travellers reminded Douglas Grant of the concentration camps he had seen in Germany during the war.

All ships from overseas, including troopships, were quarantined for weeks to the frustration of those who had been overseas for so long during the Great War.

...

John Ramsland writes with an historian's eye for detail in his latest book, *The Legacy of Douglas Grant*, a historical biography written in the creative nonfiction genre, which reconstructs the life of an Aboriginal boy, the only survivor of a cruel massacre in North Queensland.

Although famous in the media of the time, Douglas Grant finds not only the raging influenza epidemic on his return, but also rampant racism supported by Prime Minister, Billy Hughes' blatant racist-impregnated support of the White Australia Policy.

Douglas Grant was adopted by a kindly Scottish couple who sent him to Annandale Superior Public School where he excelled academically and won the school's prize for all-round achievement as a scholar. He wrote in a beautiful copperplate hand, played the bagpipes and spoke with the Scottish brogue of his adoptive family.

...

Douglas Grant loved to entertain by claiming that he was born in Scotland but explained, "when I was a small fair boy with red hair, I fell asleep in the hot Queensland sun for a couple of hours and when I woke I was as black as a black man like the harpooner character in *Moby Dick*. Even my hair turned black and I never became a white man again, not ever."

After leaving school he became an engineering draftsman in Balmain and, pre-war, a wool classer at Belltrees near Scone.

...

Douglas Grant fought for the rights of his fellow prisoners during the war, for ex-servicemen on his return from the war and for the workers during his time at the Lithgow arms factory.

Historian and accomplished writer of over twenty books, John Ramsland writes with a novelist's skill in this painstakingly researched biography.

On the cover of the biography the original 1918 black and white close-up photograph of Douglas Grant, wearing a Red Cross uniform while in a German concentration camp, has been convincingly coloured by Benjamin Thomas to highlight the face of a determined Aboriginal man with tear-filled brown eyes; the reader could be forgiven for thinking that the photograph has been taken from a recent film based on the book. (Yes, this true story has all the elements required to produce a wonderful Australian film.)

...

The Legacy of Douglas Grant commemorates a distinguished life and should be essential reading for all Australians.

RENDEZVOUS WITH DEATH

John Ramsland

ISBN: 9780909608996

			Qty
	RRP	AU$26.99	.....
Postage within Australia		AU$5.00	.....
		TOTAL*	$________

* All prices include GST

Name: ....

Address: ....

....

Phone: ....

Email: ....

Payment: [ ] Money Order [ ] Cheque [ ] MasterCard [ ] Visa

Cardholder's Name:..

Credit Card Number: ....

Signature:..

Expiry Date: ....

Allow 7 days for delivery.

Payment to: Marzocco Consultancy (ABN 14 067 257 390)
PO Box 452
Torquay Victoria 3228
Australia